Preface

THIS work is what it purports to be. For over thirty years I have been engaged in the active duties of a detective, and during that period I have acquired a comparatively thorough knowledge of the modes of operation adopted by the various classes of criminals who prey upon humanity. Being of the opinion that much loss and trouble might be prevented, if the entire community was enlightened upon these matters, I have prepared this work for the purpose of placing within the reach of every one, that information which is, or ought to be, a guarantee of security. In the hope that what I have written may be of service to my fellow beings in every walk of life, and that the experiences given, may convince the dishonestly inclined of the utter futility of the success of criminal actions, this volume is sent forth.

ALLAN PINKERTON.
CHICAGO, February, 1884.

THIRTY YEARS

YEARS

A DETECTIVE

Warwick, NY

Cover Art:
Cover photograph courtesy of the Library of Congress,
Antietam, Maryland, October 3, 1862.
(Library of Congress, Prints and Photographs Division.
Reproduction Number: LC-B8171-7929)
Gardner, Alexander, 1821-1882, photographer.

Designed by Jillian Harris
Art Direction by Bruce Hall

THIRTY YEARS
A DETECTIVE

ALLAN PINKERTON

Warwick, NY

Contents

Introduction

IN the preparation of the present work I have endeavored to carry into effect an idea I have entertained for several years. A purpose long considered, and the execution of which has occupied much of my time, has at length assumed definite shape and tangible form.

The knowledge which the general public acquires of the transactions of the criminal classes is, at the best, but meagre and unsatisfying. Fragmentary newspaper items—an abstract report of important trials, and, at times, costly personal experiences, have been the only means by which the reading public have been informed of the operations of a class of people whose numbers are enormous, and whose depredations are of daily occurrence. If the total amount of the dishonest appropriations of a single year could be ascertained, the sum would be appalling and almost incredible, and yet, as widespread as are the operations of the criminal, as universal his existence, and as fabulous the amount of which the public are annually plundered, the large majority of the sufferers to-day, are in ignorance of the manner in which their goods and valuables have disappeared. A bank, strong and seemingly impregnable, is entered between twilight and dawn. Vaults that were guaranteed to withstand any efforts that might be made against them, have in an incredibly short space of time, yielded to the skill of the burglar, and hundreds of thousands of dollars have been successfully carried away before suspicion is aroused, or an alarm sounded. Stores and dwellings have been broken into, under the very eyes of expert watchmen, and, despite every ingenious safeguard and protection, the midnight robbers have effected their escape with the property of their unconscious victims.

In broad daylight banks, moneyed institutions and financial firms have been defrauded of vast sums of money by the expert forger, the sneak thief, and the counterfeiter. Individuals of all classes have fallen victims to the horde of dishonest men and women who infest our communities —and yet the public are unaware of the means employed to effect their ruin, or the modes by which their disasters were accomplished.

This information I now propose to give, in the hope that by a wide-spread publication of the methods and plans of the criminal, I may be able to restrict his operations, impede his efforts, and prevent his disastrous successes.

Prompt and energetic detection has done much to prevent the spread of crime, and to limit the radius of criminal operations. A robbery of an Express Company by a professional thief is now no longer attempted; and by my efforts in the detection of the criminals who made these corporations their victims for many years, this result has principally been accomplished. It is true, the battle was a long, fierce and costly one, but in the end, the burglars and thieves were compelled to yield—the detectives were the conquerors, the robbers were sent to prison, and the result is that the Express Companies to-day enjoy an almost thorough immunity from depredation.

This is also the case with the larger banking institutions. A vigorous process of detection and an unrelenting administration of justice have awed the more ambitious of the criminal fraternity and secured enforced protection for the mammoth financial institutions of the country.

While this is true to a great and satisfying extent, it is also certain that the number of criminals of all grades has increased to wonderful proportions, and their modes of working and plans of operations have reached a degree of scientific perfection never before attained.

During my career as a detective, which has extended over a period of more than thirty-six years, I have been engaged in active association with crime and criminals of every grade and condition. From the most skillful operator to the mere tyro in dishonest practices, they have all come within the scope of my experience, and as a natural consequence, I have become familiar, not only with their manner of working, but with their various movements and associates.

During this extended period, crime in all its branches as well as the modes of detection, have made rapid strides, and both have developed into a science as complex and far-reaching as any that now engross the philosopher and the specialist. The detective himself has undergone a complete metamorphosis. The time was when a halo of romance was thrown around the disreputable "mouchard" of the Parisian Corps detective—when the "Bow street runner" of London and the "shadow" of the American police were the ideal detectives of the age in which they lived. All these have passed away, however, and to-day the American detective stands out in pure relief from all such associations. His calling has become a profession, and himself an intelligent, keen sighted and accomplished gentleman, relying upon his own high moral character, his superior intelligence and his indefatigable energy for the success which he has attained.

The reason and necessity for this advancement are evident. Crime itself has become more scientific, and its ranks are filled by men, who in honorable callings would have achieved both fame and fortune. Among the criminal classes to-day are to be found men of powerful minds, of strong will, and of educational advantages which, if correctly applied would have enabled them to make their mark in the professional and business circles of the community. Unfortunately, however, their great talents are prostituted to base uses. The greed of gain, the desire to possess themselves of the property of others, without the labor required for honest accumulation, have led them to adopt the nature of the vulture and to prey unscrupulously upon the community at large.

One of the great questions which presents itself for solution to the criminal is how to accomplish their objects, and yet succeed in shrouding themselves from detection. Success in crime, which is immediately followed by detection, would be, but an unprofitable and unsatisfactory experiment, and hence the best energies of the intelligent criminal are devoted to the achievement of success in such a manner as to baffle the detective, and secure immunity from punishment.

To prevent this, therefore, the detective must also be advanced. He must be possessed of a mind which is the equal, and, if possible, the superior of his antagonist. He must be endowed with a clear, honest and comprehensive understanding which will enable him to fathom the depths of criminal science, and a force of will and vigor of body necessary to overcome the nature and the dispositions of the men with whom he has to contend.

In addition to this he must appear the careless, ordinary individual, particularly to those upon whom he is to operate. Assimilating, as far as possible, with the individuals who are destined to feel the force of his authority, and by appearing to know but little, acquire all the information possible to gather from every conceivable source, and in the least curious or inquisitorial manner.

Possessed of an ability to adapt himself to every association in which he may find himself, and at the same time prolific in resources, he must be prepared at all times when emergencies arise which require quick conceptions and ready subterfuges. To-day, his associates may be of the lowest orders of humanity, and to-morrow he mingles with the best elements of the social community. He must at all times be upon his guard, ever ready to take advantage of the most-trifling circumstances, and yet, with an outward demeanor that dispels suspicion and invites the fullest confidence.

The profession of the detective is, at once, an honorable and highly useful one. For practical benefits few professions excel it. He is an officer of justice, and must himself be pure and above reproach. The public safety and the perfect fulfillment of his calling require this; and where the detective is found to possess these qualifications, success invariably attends his operations. The great essential is to prevent his identity from becoming known, even among his associates of respectable character, and when he fails to do this; when the nature of his calling is discovered and made known, his usefulness to the profession is at an end, and failure, certain and inevitable is the result.

Understanding all this, I have always instructed my men fully upon this point, and very rarely has it occurred that the operative has been discovered by any action of his own. Through every grade of criminal practice my men have penetrated and the results of their investigations have been fully and regularly reported to me.

I have thus been enabled to make the criminal and his works my especial study. I have endeavored to penetrate into the mysteries of his operations and to discover his methods of working. I have examined carefully into the most minute particulars, and have learned much that has been useful to me in prosecuting my profession as a detective. By this system of minute examination I have become familiar with the modes and practices of the men who have successfully broken into bank vaults that were considered impregnable; with the skillful handiwork of the forger and the counterfeiter, and with the numerous devices of the criminal in every branch of his vocation, and I have been enabled to keep pace even with their increasing knowledge and enlarged facilities.

The information which I have thus obtained I now propose to divulge to the public, believing that it is to their best interests that they should be made acquainted with the manifold schemes by which the expert criminal seeks to possess himself unlawfully of their valuables and money. The knowledge thus given may enable many to successfully guard themselves against the attacks of the burglar and the thief, and they will be benefited to the extent that security is attained.

It has frequently been a matter of surprise to me to note the almost universal ignorance which pervades the financial and commercial communities with reference to the workings of the men, who daily make them the victims of their wiles and misdirected skill, I have, therefore, felt it to be my duty to inform them as fully as I am able, of the plans by which the dishonest prey upon the thrifty and the fortunate. For the enlightenment of this class of people therefore, and in order to open their eyes to the many ingenious devices of the counterfeiter, the burglar, and the chameleon-hued thief, I have devoted myself to the preparation of recitals which follow.

Not alone to this class do I address myself, but to those whose business it is to detect crime, and to seek for the criminal in his place of hiding; for the detectives everywhere, and for the police authorities of the land, have I labored, and, I trust, not in vain.

The broad field of crime embraces so many varieties, and yet with the classifications so distinctly marked, that my labor has been considerably lessened in this particular, but in my endeavors to give nought but the facts, and those as exhaustive and comprehensive as possible, I have avoided, and I trust neglected, nothing that would contribute to its thoroughness both as to research and description.

I have followed the counterfeiter through all the ramifications of his truly scientific operations. From the time when, with a plenitude of State Banks, each with their own issue of notes, when the task of counterfeiting was comparatively an easy one—to the present day when the government stands forth in all the majesty of a note printer, and with every safeguard against successful imitation—every point in his manipulation of genuine paper and in his artistic substitutions have been explained with a fullness and truthfulness which, while they must be comprehensive, rely for confirmation upon the experiences of years.

Of burglary in its manifold forms, I have been equally explicit. In this connection I have given not only my own experience, but the statements, revelations and admissions of the criminals themselves. In many cases the materials have been furnished by men whom I have arrested, some of whom have reformed, and are now leading honest lives, and others who are to-day inmates of prisons. Evidence of this character must not be doubted, and the inner workings of the burglar's profession, as told by the experienced cracksmen themselves, must prove of interest to all.

It is, perhaps, a matter not to be exultant about, but, during my life as a detective, I have, for various reasons of a politic nature, become intimately acquainted with the men whom I was most anxious to apprehend, mingling with them in their ordinary walks, entirely unsuspected, until the time for action arrived and arrests were necessary. It has always been a matter of regret to me to contemplate the evil results of criminal practices, and in many instances I have interested myself in behalf of these men, and frequently, I am happy to state, with such success that, they have been won from their evil ways, and have afterwards lived an honorable life, and engaged in useful and remunerative pursuits.

Every branch of crime has been thoroughly treated; the modes and manners, the devices and expedients, the preparations and preliminaries, and finally, the nicety and skill with which the eventual operation is performed. It must not be imagined that the process by which a burglar enters your counting-house or store, or by which the counterfeiter and the forger succeed in inimitable imitations is simply the result of a few hours labor, for such is rarely, if ever, the case. Often days and weeks, and in many cases months, elapse before sufficient perfection is reached to warrant the attempted execution.

Of the many departments of crime, the most successful, and the branch which contains the largest number of practitioners, is that of pocket-picking, and so dexterous has the thief become, that active, wide-awake men have been robbed without being able to recall a single circumstance under which the deed might have been committed.

Men, experienced travelers, too, have retired to bed in elegant apartments in first-class hotels, and in the morning have been astounded at the fact that, notwithstanding their precautions with lock and key, with bolt and bar, the stealthy thief had entered their chambers, and while they peacefully slept had plundered them of their jewelry and their money.

To the operations of that fraternity who practice the "Confidence Game," I have given considerable attention, and their numerous expedients to fleece the unwary, are given in detail. This is one of the most dangerous classes which infest the community, and without a knowledge of their schemes, many astute business men have been successfully duped, and have lost considerable sums of money.

The shop-lifter, too; that bane of the merchant and the tradesman, receive their meed of attention, and their modes of proceeding are fully and comprehensively explained. The steamboat and sleeping-car thieves, those who prey so successfully upon the traveling public, and who in so many instances escape detection or even suspicion, have been treated by a master hand, and much of the material here used is from the pen of one of the most successful operators in this branch of crime, who is at the present time an inmate of an eastern prison.

The entire school of crime has been thoroughly searched, and the best and most reliable experiences only have been given. The work of "'prentice hands" has been deemed unworthy a place, and I have dealt solely with the adept, the skillful and the scientific.

As I have previously stated, the ignorance of those engaged in commercial and financial pursuits, has been one of the main impelling reasons for the preparation of this work, and I trust that by affording a knowledge of the modes of criminal working, I may be of service to my fellow men. "An ounce of prevention is worth a pound of cure," is an adage as truthful as it is ancient, and by pointing out the dangers that lie in the paths of the merchant, the banker and the private man of fortune, I may enable them to take such precautions as will render a successful attempt upon them an impossibility.

The Society Thief

AMONG all classes of people, it will be found that every one has a particular way of doing things, and that their every action is bound to bear some resemblance to each other, both in character and method; and this peculiarity applies with equal force to those who live dishonest lives, and who commit unlawful deeds. A knowledge of these peculiarities, which is only gained by long experience, is of great service to detectives in their efforts to bring criminals to justice. There are numerous ways, of course, in which a murder, a burglary or a theft may be committed, and a thorough detective will always carefully study every case that comes before him, in order to determine at the outset, exactly by what means and in what manner the deed itself was performed. Then, if the developments are such as to directly indicate the handiwork of the professional criminal, he will call to mind, among the number of criminals who have been brought to his knowledge, some one of the many, whose work in the past has shown any marked similarity to the case under investigation.

There are very few thieves indeed, who work in all fashions and in all places. The large majority of them make themselves familiar with a particular mode of working, and then carries on their operations among a certain class of people.

It is an unquestionable fact that there is a fine art in roguery as there is in the honest callings of the world, and men in this branch of labor, soon discover their peculiar fitness or adaptability for certain grades of work, just as in the trades and professions, individuals develop certain gifts which lead to prominence, fortune and success. A man may commence the career of a thief by simply stealing, but he soon discovers that there are certain places where he can steal more easily, and certain means by which his stealings can be conducted more safely. There are also localities where he can find more to steal than others, and where the property to be purloined can be carried away with fewer chances of detection.

As a matter of course the intelligent thief selects these in his future operations, and this leads to the creation of certain fancies about their work which cling to them for long periods of time. They grow to forming affections for certain places and certain people, and having a sort of pride in their operations, all these influences contribute to keep him in a certain well-defined routine, which is of vast importance to the detective and materially facilitates his investigations.

By this means certain well-defined classifications have come to be acknowledged and understood by all men engaged in the honorable profession of unearthing crime and bringing criminals to justice. So clearly are these classifications defined that it would be a comparatively easy matter to compile an extensive list of the crooked people who have either fallen into, or deliberately chosen and consistently followed their own peculiar lines of work.

It must not be supposed that the life of the detective is confined to the chase for daring murderers and desperate burglars; on the contrary, much of their time is devoted to the pursuit of other game—who if they do not excite as much general attention, are fully as dangerous and quite as difficult to entrap.

There is a class of criminals in active practice at the present time, who display exceeding ingenuity and artistic skill in other operations, and my labors in the present instance would be incomplete without devoting a short space to their description. They are very appropriately denominated "Society Thieves," and their presence is to be found through all the gradations of modern society, but owing to the reluctance of their victims to acquire publicity by a public prosecution, the general community learns but little of the movements of the society thief, and that little so incompletely and unsatisfactorily, that no adequate idea is gained of the extent and manner of their operations. Detectives are constantly hearing of them however, and so numerous and audacious has this class of criminals become, that the presence of a detective is as necessary at any social event of any importance, as the guests themselves. If the gathering is an unusually large one as many as half a dozen detectives are an absolute necessity.

The society thief is invariably a man or woman with more social standing than means to support it, and of late years they have been largely made up from the ranks of the needy but pretentious adventurers, whom English society has purged itself of, and who, having sought a refuge in America, are preying upon our wealthy and intellectual social circles.

The social gathering which offers the best opportunities for peculations is the wedding in high life, and the wedding thief, as a general thing, has matters entirely his own way. His first and greatest difficulty, however, is in gaining admission, but not unfrequently, strange as it may seem, he holds a position in society which enables him to enter by invitation. Sometimes he enters upon the pretext of being a newspaper reporter, and as society is very anxious to appear in the papers, he is cordially received—and sometimes he is obliged to sneak in. Once in, however, his course is easy, and he takes his choice of overcoats, hats, and other wearing apparel without the slightest opposition. He carefully inspects the numerous and costly presents, with a view of ascertaining which of the most valuable of the smaller articles will please him the best, and then, when unobserved, he slips them into his pocket or under his coat. At other times they merely watch for an opportunity to slip out of the crowd, upon some pretext or another, and then work at their ease in the deserted rooms in the other portions of the house. In some cases, whole houses have been thoroughly pillaged by them while dancing was in progress in the lower rooms.

These thieves steal only portable and valuable articles, and generally work alone, but frequently a husband and wife will engage in the business together, and in this way greater freedom and less liability to detection is the result. It is a matter of fact that not long since a very respectably dressed and exceedingly agreeable man and wife were detected in stealing some valuable trinkets presented to the little daughter of the host at a birthday party, and it was afterwards discovered that while the father and mother were engaged in this robbery, their son was dancing in the parlor with the young lady who was being plundered.

Among the numerous presents exhibited at a fashionable wedding in New York City lately, was a check from the father of the bride to the happy couple, for ten thousand dollars. During the reception which followed the ceremony, a daring thief abstracted the genuine check and substituted in its place a well-executed counterfeit and forgery. The thief received the money for the check at the bank on which it was drawn, and the forgery was not discovered until some days afterwards, when the young husband of the bride attempted to realize upon the bounty of his father-in-law. Every effort was made to discover this daring thief, but so long a time had elapsed that it was impossible to fasten suspicion upon anyone, and the search was at length abandoned.

The more public the wedding the better the opportunity of the thieves, and when the ceremony is solemnized in church, there is always a lavish display of costly jewelry which furnishes a rich harvest to the dexterous practitioner. Ladies and gentlemen don their best garments to honor such events, and, as a general rule, wear their most expensive articles of jewelry. The society thief is usually an excellent hand at picking a pocket, and a ready wielder of the "palm nippers," which are used to snip off jewels from the ears and persons of those who wear them. As a rule he is accompanied by an accomplice, to whom he passes whatever articles he secures, and should he be arrested, no criminating object is found upon his person, and it is difficult to make a case against him.

Strange and unnatural as it may seem, stealing at funerals occurs so frequently that it has come to be recognized by detectives as a distinct branch of the predatory profession, and is generally practiced by a male or female professional thief. These funeral thieves keep fully posted about the wealthy funerals that take place from time to time, and are generally present where any opportunity is presented to ply their vocation. They steal anything in the house of mourning, from mantel ornaments to jewelry, and generally without incurring much risk of detection. The publicity which is usually given to funerals, and the privileges which are extended to anyone who has ever known the deceased, to come and take a last look at him, render access to many houses easy, which would otherwise be closely barred against their intention. The funeral thief thus readily passes for an outside friend of the dead person, and is afforded the liberty of the house, which he never fails to utilize if there is anything to be stolen.

Perhaps the meanest sort of thief, who adopts any special line, is the one who robs children. This is called the "Kinchin lay," and is generally practiced by women, though there are many men, who are found following this despicable calling. Their process of operation consists simply in robbing children on their way to the stores to which they have been sent by their parents to make purchases—and it is to the credit of the American thieves that they are very rarely found guilty of following so mean a vocation. It was introduced into this country from England, but thanks to the vigilance of the officers, the thieves who practice the "Kinchin lay," are arrested so frequently, that it is fast growing into disfavor, and it is hoped, will soon cease altogether.

There is another class of thieves, mostly juveniles, who are known as theatre thieves. They perpetually haunt the doors of play-houses, and pickpockets indiscriminately amid the ingoing and the outgoing rush. Church thieves are also recognized as an independent branch of criminality, and there are others who make railway-depots the scene of their battles against society and honesty.

The street-car thief is another criminal who impresses himself frequently upon the public, but he is not so numerous as he used to be, for the conductors and spotters have learned to know and to guard against him.

As a general rule, those who engage in these forms of petty thieving alluded to, either go unpunished or escape with light penalties, owing to the fact that their victims are indisposed to incur the publicity of appearing as a witness in a police court trial, against them. The detectives, however, know a vast number of them and are fully acquainted with their peculiar methods of operating. When called upon in any particular case, they, as I have stated before, ascertain when and where the robbery occurred, and, as nearly as possible, the circumstances under which it was accomplished. This much obtained, it is the exception, when they are not able to get at once so far toward detecting the offenders as to suspect some particular person or persons of being the guilty one—and the result invariably justifies the original suspicion.

Thus it will be seen, that by carefully studying the peculiarities even of the small criminals, and from a thorough knowledge of their various classifications the detective is enabled, in a short time, to conduct important investigations to speedy and correct conclusions, which would be impossible with persons unskilled in all the minutiae of their profession.

The Pickpocket

IF we trace the career of the professional criminal to its incipiency, it will almost invariably be found that the first plunge into the vortex of crime has been that of pocket-picking. Among the alarming number of professional thieves of all grades in the country to-day, it would be difficult to find one who had not at the commencement of his dishonest experience, been engaged in picking the pockets of the innocent and the unsuspecting. It is equally true also that of all the departments of crime as now practiced, there is not one which contains a larger number of adept operators than that of pickpockets. In almost every crowded assembly they will assuredly be found. They follow the circuits of the racing season; they are hangers on about the traveling circus; and are to be found at the theatres, and in the church. At mass meetings, at merry makings and even at funerals, this pestilent thief obtrudes himself, and dismay and loss inevitably follow his appearance.

The grades of this class of criminals are exceedingly numerous, and range from the ragged urchin who steals a pocket-handkerchief to the expert professional who can with ease and safety remove a well filled wallet from the inside coat pocket of his hapless victim. The intermediate grades are well defined, and vary according to the skillfulness and daring of the thieves themselves. In this branch of crime women as well as men are active workers, and many of the female thieves are as successful as the men, in the ease and grace with which they relieve the unsuspecting of their valuables. There are some male thieves who confine their operations entirely to ladies, and there are others who could not be induced to rob a lady under any circumstances whatever. The female thieves operate indiscriminately, although they are more successful with ladies than with gentlemen. In the accepted language of the thief, those who operate on men are termed "Blokebuzzers," while those who make ladies their special victims receive the euphonious appellation of "Moll-buzzers."

A description of the means resorted to by the fraternity of pickpockets may prove both interesting and instructive, and as I have had a large experience with all classes of this community, I will endeavor to describe their operations for the benefit of suffering humanity.

In order to give due prominence even to questionable merit, I will begin by detailing the operations of the more ambitious of the male pickpockets, those who frequent the localities where the large banking institutions are situated, and endeavor to rob those who are entering or leaving the banks. For the accomplishment of success in work of this nature, four men usually travel together, who are generally called "a mob." The man who is to do the actual stealing is called the "tool," or "hook," and the others are known as "stalls."

After selecting their victim or "mark," who is engaged in drawing a large sum of money from the bank, one of the number will take up his position inside of the bank, where he can watch every movement of the man who is to be robbed. This is done in order to ascertain exactly where the money is placed, so that no delay may ensue in locating the desired "plunder." Having acquired the necessary information, the "stall" will inform his companions on the sidewalk in which pocket the money is secured, and they then proceed to business; as a general rule, a man who draws several packages of bills from a bank, will place them in his inside coat pocket, and in this instance we will assume that the person who has excited the cupidity of the thieves, has placed his money in the inside pocket on the right side of the coat. He emerges from the bank, reaches the sidewalk, and proceeds upon his way. The thieves follow him within easy distance, but will not make any attempt to accomplish their purpose unless they notice that he is about to enter a crowded thoroughfare, a car, a narrow street, or through a hallway into a building. If in a crowd or narrow street the thieves will, without any preliminary notice whatever, act as follows—two of the "stalls" will immediately manage to get in front of the man—and these men are called "front stalls"—this is done for the purpose of stopping him or blocking his way for a moment when the time arrives. The "tool" or "hook" will also get slightly ahead of the man, and when the moment for action arrives a slight cough will bring the two "front stalls" to a stand-still. This, of course, impedes the progress of the victim. Quick as a flash, and yet with an ease of motion that attracts no particular attention, the "tool" turns sideways, almost facing the man, but upon his right side. The "tool" usually carries a coat upon his arm for the purpose of covering his hand; with the concealed hand he will work under the man's coat, and taking the wallet or package by the top, will raise it straight up, until it is entirely clear of the pocket; then drawing it under his own coat, the robbery is complete. During this operation, which requires but a few seconds, the "stall" behind the man is pushing and shoving him repeatedly on the left side, as if with the intention of getting past him. The left side being furthest from where the money is concealed, answers two purposes: it not only serves to prevent the man from feeling or detecting the easy sliding motion of the wallet as it is being drawn out of his pocket on the other side, and it at the same time helps to turn the man more toward the "tool" or "hook," so that his work is rendered easier. While this operation is going on the two "front stalls" have not betrayed the slightest interest in the proceedings, and from all appearances are entirely ignorant of the fact that a man is being deliberately robbed behind them. They have not so much as turned their heads, and consequently do not know when the operation is completed, so that they may stand aside and let the victim pass. In order to overcome this, the pickpockets have adopted certain words or signals, which are thoroughly understood by the craft, and these signals are given by the "tool" or "hook." If he is rather slow about getting to the wallet or the money, and he notices that the front men are getting somewhat uneasy, he calls out "stick!" This means that in a few seconds he will be successful, and that they are to stay in their respective positions. After he has secured the wallet he will chirp like a bird, or will utter the word "lam!" This means to let the man go, and to get out of the way as soon as possible. This word is also used in case the money cannot be taken, and further attempts are useless.

It sometimes happens that it is somewhat difficult to get the wallet or package out of the pocket, and if any unusual force is used in withdrawing it, the man will feel it, and give an alarm. In cases of this kind, the "tool," when he has the wallet in his fingers and ready to be drawn out, will cry, "rouse!" At this signal all of the "stalls" give the man a general push at the same time, and during the confusion of the moment, the "tool" deftly pulls out the wallet and decamps.

While the detailing of this operation has taken some time, the operation itself is performed in a few seconds, and in almost every instance, without attracting the attention or exciting the suspicion of the individual who is so ruthlessly despoiled of his money.

As a general rule a merchant who goes himself, or sends his clerk to the bank to make a deposit, places the money and checks lengthwise in his bank book, which is generally shorter than the notes, and allows them to project beyond the edges of the book. The book is then placed in the inside pocket and so carried to the bank. A man is usually suspicious and careful when he is intrusted with a large sum of money and the thieves have therefore to be very careful in their manipulations. When a gentleman thus engaged, is subjected to a crowding or pushing from others, he naturally places his hand upon the book, which contains his money, in order to be assured of its safety. The thieves are perfectly aware of this, and when the opportunity offers they simply seize the ends of the bills which extend beyond the book, and by a quick and dexterous motion extract the money and leave the book remaining in the pocket. As a natural result, when the suspicious depositor by feeling upon the outside, finds his book safely bestowed within, he gives no thought to the fact that he has been robbed and does not discover his misfortune until he reaches the bank. This process is called by the thieves "weeding."

There are some people who imagine that it is an impossibility for a thief to rob them, and they are ever on the alert. These people place their bank book and money in the outside pocket of their sack-coat and by keeping their hand upon the book imagine that a robbery is impossible. The thieves, however, know better than this, and their mode of proceeding is as follows:

They patiently bide their time until the man reaches the door of the bank, which must be opened to admit him—one man will then step immediately in front of him, or a little to the left—and then stop right in front of the doorway pretending to look at a paper, or, to count some money which he has in his hands—the consequence is, that instead of pushing the man aside so he can use his left hand to open the door—the victim will, unthinkingly, reach out his right hand—which had hitherto guarded his pocket, and pull open the door—the "stall" immediately moves a trifle more to the front for a second, and then turns away—that second, however, is enough, for while the victim and his "stall" are thus engaged, the pickpocket has quietly taken out the money and decamped. This in thieves' vernacular is called a "tale trick," and bank messengers have frequently been robbed in this manner.

Should the money be carried in the pockets of the pantaloons, the methods are, of course, different. This style of robbery is much more difficult, and as a general thing is not so remunerative as stealing from men who are either going to or returning from the bank. The thieves who follow this branch of their calling are as a class more rude and rough in their appearance and nature, and their actions, while at work, are more abrupt and harsh.

This kind of robbery is generally practiced on the cars (called "rattlers") or in a crowd—and if upon the cars is performed on the platforms or in the doorways of these crowded vehicles.

It may be as well to state that among thieves certain terms are used to represent articles which otherwise have proper names. A pocket-book is called "leather"; a wallet "a pittman" or "pitt"; a pocket is called a "kick"; hands are termed "dukes"; a handkerchief a "wipe," and a hat is dubbed a "tile."

The thieves of this latter class will generally select for their victim (which they call a "mark") an elderly man, or one who appears to hail from the country. The first are usually more feeble and not supposed to be as sharp as a young man—while the countryman is supposed to carry more ready money about with him than a person belonging to the city.

The pickpockets board a street car and take their positions on the rear platform—always being careful to select a car which is already crowded. For the purpose of illustration we will assume that there is an individual on the platform, who looks as if he might have some money in his pocket-book. The first thing to be done is to ascertain in which pocket the money is carried, and to do this the thief lightly runs his hand across the front of both pockets of the "mark"—and this operation of feeling for a pocket-book is called "fanning." Should the pocket-book be found in the left pocket, the "tool" will say to his companions "left kick," and this will inform them all where the money is located. The "stalls" then surround the "mark," and the "tool" begins to work. With his hand covered with a coat over his arm, he inserts the two first fingers of his right hand, just beyond the first joint—into the victim's pocket, with the inside of the fingers against the pocket lining farthest from the body. First bending one finger and then the other, he draws the pocket up little by little, which is known as "reefing," until the pocket-book is drawn up within reach. The moment he is able to take hold of the pocket-book—called "tapping," he quietly calls out "Rouse!" the victim receives a rough push from the stalls—and out comes the pocket-book, which is at once passed to one of the stalls. This is done to guard against accidental discovery, for should the victim miss his money and accuse the "tool" of the theft, he will not find the book upon him, and that is generally sufficient to enable him to get off. The "stall" requires to be informed when the pocket-book is taken, and he waits for the "tool" to whisper "collar this!" or to chirp like a bird, when he knows that he is to receive the money, and that the robbery has been successfully ended.

In some cases, particularly among persons from the country, the travelers have heard remarkable stories about the picking of pockets, and have made up their minds that such a fate shall not befall them. To make sure of this they invariably travel about with their hands in their pockets and on top their purses. This careful and watchful traveler gets on a street car, and the pickpockets at once select him as their "mark." He is immediately pressed and hemmed in by the gang, and the hand that is not religiously guarding the treasure in his pocket is kept back by the shoulder of one of the stalls. A quiet command "tile him!" is given, and the countryman's hat is shoved forward from behind. The countryman not being able to use his other arm, pulls his hand out of his pocket and secures his hat. As soon as this is done, one of the "stalls" gets into position, and places his shoulder under the countryman's arm, thus preventing him for a moment from again placing his hand in his pocket. In a second the "tool" is at work, and in another moment the gentleman from the country finds plenty of room on the platform, for the thieves have left, and with them has disappeared his carefully guarded pocket-book.

When all the seats in a street car are occupied, a pickpocket will occasionally enter and take up a standing position in front of some gentleman who has his coat open. Hanging by one hand to the strap suspended from the roof of the car, and with a coat thrown over his other arm, he will attempt a robbery—swaying about with the motion of the car, he manages it so, that his coat will come directly under the chin of the seated passenger, and under cover of that, he will extract a pocket-book from the inside pocket of the man, who has no suspicion of what is going on. Diamond studs of great value have frequently been taken from the bosoms of unsuspecting passengers under the cover of a coat or newspaper, which the standing pickpocket manages to place under the chin of his victim, apparently caused by the motion of the car. If a diamond stud with a screw is to be taken, the thief after covering the stud with his coat or newspaper, will gently take hold of the screw with his thumb and forefinger, and draw the bosom of the shirt away from the body of the victim— the thumb nail is then inserted immediately back of the head of the screw and then with a firm twist or turn of the hand, the screw will come out. No matter how difficult this operation appears under ordinary circumstances, it will invariably yield to the application of the thumb under the setting of the stone. Should the diamond be set with a flat back instead of a screw, it is impossible to detach it from the bosom, and the thief will instantly desist from further efforts to remove it. A diamond pin is unfastened in the natural way and then raised up straight. A pin or screw stud is generally called a "prop," by the thieves.

Should the pickpockets attempt to work upon a railroad train, they generally select their victim in advance, by watching at the ticket office and noticing a prospective passenger who exhibits a large amount of money. Should no favorable opportunity occur to rob him while he is getting on the car, the thieves will wait until he is quietly seated, when one of their number will approach him, and in a voice or authority inquire:

"Where is your ticket for?"

The passenger, supposing his questioner to be a railroad official, will at once inform him, when the thief will reply:

"Then you must take the next car," indicating either the car in front or in the rear, at the same time picking up the traveler's valise, with a view of assisting him in effecting the change, and calling out:

"Come on, sir!"

The man follows obediently, and the mob is waiting for him on the platform. As soon as he appears he is at once jammed in, and robbed. Their previous knowledge of the location of his money renders their task an easy and rapid one, and the robbery is effected in a flash.

The stealing of watches is most extensively practiced, and an expert thief can perform this operation in a second. It does not matter where the man may be, or under what circumstances he maybe placed, so that he is standing still, or sitting down. The thief stands partly in front of his victim, and either under the cover of a coat or newspaper, or by placing his left hand under his victim's right arm, he seizes the chain and gently raises the watch up straight. When it is entirely out of the pocket, it rests in the palm of the hand, the ring of the watch between the first finger and the thumb. By pressing the thumb in one direction and the finger in an opposite manner, the ring is forced out of the watch, and then the chain is dropped easily, and the thief makes his escape.

Both watch and chain, however, are frequently taken, but this operation requires a few seconds more time. The bar or hook of the chain must first be taken out of the button-hole, and then taking the chain in his hand, the thief draws the watch up straight, out of the pocket, without attracting the least attention.

This operation is a very simple and safe one for the expert thief, but it is not a very profitable one, for the reason, that he seldom receives more than one-fourth of the value of the watch, from the dishonest pawnbroker who deals in stolen goods. The chain, if a gold one, is generally sold for its weight, and brings a uniform price.

In the slang of the professional, a watch is denominated a "super"—a chain is a "slang"—and the men who twist the rings or steal the watches are called "super twisters."

I will now refer to the operations of the pickpockets who operate upon ladies—who, as I have before stated, are called "Moll-buzzers."

As a rule the men who steal the pocket-books and purses of ladies, wear a sack-coat. In winter they operate through their overcoat pockets and in summer through the pockets of an ordinary sack-coat. In order to understand thoroughly what is meant by operating through the pockets, a few words of explanation are necessary. It must be borne in mind that the lining in the coat of a pickpocket is never sewed fast to the cloth at the bottom, underneath the pocket, this is always left open. The thief then rips open one side of the pocket at the top, and this enables him to thrust his hand right through, between the pocket and the cloth, to the bottom of the coat and out beneath. In the pocket proper he always carries a handkerchief, which is often of great service to him.

Thus much by way of preliminary, we will detail the further progress of the operation. The scene is an ordinary street car, and the seats are all occupied. The thief enters and at once takes up his position immediately in front of a lady, with one hand he grasps the strap hanging from the roof, and the other hand is seemingly thrust into his coat-pocket. I say seemingly, for really the hand of the thief is thrust through his coat, the end of which is resting carelessly on the pocket of the lady. With the hand which is pushed through his coat, the thief quietly pulls up the edge of the overskirt worn by the lady, little by little, so that he can reach the pocket. Having reached the pocket, the next move is to try the "reefing" process already mentioned, and then catching hold of the pocket-book, he draws it up into his own pocket and then steps away. Should the lady, by any chance, feel the motion of the man's fingers about her person, the thief quickly draws his hand up out of his pocket, and taking out his pocket-handkerchief, wipes his face with that very necessary article, in the most natural manner possible. This action, seemingly so matter-of-fact and easy, at once satisfies the lady that she must have been mistaken, and that the man before her could not have been attempting to pick her pocket, while he had his hand in his own.

This kind of work is also done on the platforms of the cars, while the lady is entering or leaving the car, only in such cases the "tool" has a "stall," who manages to place himself in the way of the lady, so as to keep her in proper position for the minute that is required to effect the robbery.

Sometimes the thief will seat himself beside the lady in the cars, and then he places his left side toward her. Taking out a newspaper, he will pretend to read, but he is merely spreading it upon his lap to cover the hand that is performing the work of dexterous theft.

A large number of ladies, having heard of these pickpockets, have become so suspicious that the moment a person, who has been sitting beside them, gets up to leave the car, they will at once feel on the outside of their dresses to discover if their pocket-books are safe. Thieves who are expert, know this full well, and so proficient have they become, that with two fingers they can open the pocket-book while it is safely within the pocket, and with the first finger bent like a hook, will clean out the contents, and leave the pocket-book apparently undisturbed; this operation is called "weeding a leather," and the dexterity and ease with which it is done, is simply astonishing.

Notwithstanding many statements to the contrary, an expert thief will rarely cut a dress or coat in order to obtain the money of his victim; this is not considered professional, and is universally condemned.

Many ladies carry their money in hand-bags and cabbés, which are now so fashionable, and this fact affords rare opportunities to the observant and sagacious thief. In order to be successful in this, they simply resort to the old method of covering the bag, so that it can be opened, the pocket-book taken out, and the bag reclosed.

This style of robbery occurs every day, and the favorite position for this work is in front of the large show windows of prominent dry goods firms, where the ladies congregate to study what is new, and to admire the beautiful and tempting displays.

Of the female pickpockets, they are generally of English nationality, with a slight sprinkling of Irish and American, but for the most part they are of the vulgar and abandoned class. They usually operate from under their shawl or cloak, and frequently with one of these garments thrown over their arm. They confine their operations principally to ladies, and work in a similar manner to the men. They are generally exceedingly clever manipulators, and, of course, have much better opportunities to ply their trade among their own sex, than men could possibly have.

The handkerchief thief, or "wipe lifter," is the lowest grade of pocket-picking—and is practiced only by boys or young beginners. It is generally the first step taken toward the attainment of dexterity and experience; and is the beginning of a career which inevitably leads to a prison.

I have thus attempted to give a general idea of the operations of the professional pickpocket, though I am aware that there are numerous other devices practiced, a description of which would only tire the reader. The modus operandi of the expert thief have only been given, and after the revelations here made, the public may take warning, and by being constantly on their guard will insure themselves from ever becoming the victims of the army of light-fingered gentry which infest every city of the civilized globe.

Store Robbers

THE men who rob stores, either by day or night, do not belong to any distinct class of criminals. Store-robbing may be resorted to by any man or body of men, whose experience in other criminal undertakings has given them that courage, foresight, and knowledge essential for such undertakings. None the less, however, their work must be performed as carefully and systematically as any other, in order to procure success and profitable remuneration.

The risks to be assumed, and the dangers to be overcome are also much greater than in any other branches of criminal practice. The stores that are usually considered as worth the effort of entering are generally located upon the principal business streets of the city, whose avenues are brilliantly lighted and patrolled by policemen whose presence is considered a synonym for safety.

A thorough knowledge of the approaches to the building, a careful watch upon all persons connected with the store, and a strict espionage upon the movements of the patrolmen, are the first requisites for successful work, and even when these have been put into operation, the main features of the robbery have not been attempted, and success is far from being assured.

Let me give some practical hints of the movements of these thieves, a study of which on the part of our merchants and business men may save them from serious and irreparable losses in the future. In my opinion, safety can be as successfully conserved by laying bare the movements and modes of operation of the thief, as by tracing him to his hiding place and securing his imprisonment after his offenses have been committed. Acting upon this opinion, I will describe the modus operandi of the store robbers, as far as they have become known to me, in the hope that these relations may be of service to those who are generally made their victims.

This class of robbers, if they thoroughly understand their business, always work in gangs of two, three, or four in number, in order that their operations may be quickly conducted, and that the movements of the police may be carefully watched while they are at work. The first thing to be done upon locating in a large town or city is to select the place upon which they design to work. Every care and precaution is taken in this particular, and when they finally decide upon a store to be robbed, they are fully posted with regard to everything that pertains to the business and personal habits of all connected with the establishment.

Their next move is to discover a house to let, and they prefer to secure one as close to the scene of their contemplated operations as possible. The most polite and suave of their number is usually selected as the spokesman and negotiator, who introduces himself to the owner of the premises as a stranger from a distance, who designs locating in the city, and intends to send for his wife and children when he has secured a home for their habitation. His story is straightforward and plausible; his appearance inspires confidence, and paying a month's rent in advance, he receives the key of the house, with the view of preparing it for the reception of his family.

At the expiration of a few days, this man again calls upon the landlord, and showing him a telegram which may be either genuine or bogus, purporting to have been sent by the wife of the burglar, and which contains the intelligence that she cannot come at present, owing to the serious illness of some of the children, which prevents their being moved at this time. This is done to allay any suspicions which the landlord might entertain should the house remain empty without explanation. The burglar then informs the landlord that he will keep the house for the month for which he has paid his rent, hoping by that time that his wife will be able to come, as agreed upon.

This explanation satisfies the landlord, who will not trouble himself further about his tenant. By this means the thieves have secured a safe store-room for a month's plunder, and the main part of the preliminary work is then considered accomplished.

Not more than one place is entered under any circumstances during a single night, and this rule is adhered to strenuously, however great may be the temptation.

Having located their object of attack, and being fully posted with regard to the means of reaching that object, no time is lost in getting to work. All robbers of this class prefer to effect an entrance from the rear, as it is considered far more safe than the front. A brace and bit and a couple of ordinary jimmies are all the tools needed for this purpose, and a door or window is speedily opened, and the passage into the store effected.

Failing to find a rear entrance, however, the thieves do not hesitate to enter by the front, although the danger and difficulty of such a proceeding is considerably increased. In the first place they attempt to fit a key to the front door from their own stock in trade, or the use of a skeleton. Should this prove a failure, they bend their efforts toward obtaining an impression from the genuine key in use by the owners of the premises. At first thought this would seem an exceedingly difficult operation; but the thieves rarely experience any trouble in effecting this object. They usually watch for the opening of the store in the morning, and as soon as the clerk enters the store two of the thieves follow him in. One of them states that he is in a great hurry to get some small article which is kept in the stock, and the clerk, to be accommodating, lays his keys down on the counter or desk, and proceeds to wait upon his customer. If they are laid upon the counter, the confederate obtains an impression of them in a moment, with the lump of wax which he carries in his pocket, handy for the purpose, and the question is settled at once. Sometimes, however, the clerk places his keys upon the desk in the office, and to get at them there, is not so easy a matter. The thief is prepared with an expedient, however, and the confederate politely asks permission to address a few letters, which he is anxious to mail as soon as possible. This innocent request is usually granted readily, and with his impression wax all ready, he accomplishes the work almost in the twinkling of an eye. The next move is to procure a blank key at a hardware store, and from the impression obtained; a perfect facsimile is made in a few hours. Having overcome this obstacle to their admittance, the thieves are now ready for work.

In effecting their entrance and removing their plunder from the store, the thieves are guided entirely by circumstances. Sometimes they commence early in the evening, sometimes at midnight, and at others it frequently occurs that they do not remove anything until the break of day.

If they are compelled to work the store from the front, thieves are exceedingly cautious in their every action. Awaiting a favorable opportunity, when the coast is clear, two of the gang will quickly and noiselessly enter, and at once lock the door upon the inside. Selecting their plunder from the most valuable stock in the store, they pack the goods carefully for removal, and then await developments from the outside. When they are ready to come out, they generally put a small piece of white paper under the front door, so as to inform the "crow"—as the outside watcher is called—that they have finished their work and are anxious to leave. This "crow" is constantly on the alert, and never approaches the door until he has located the policeman or watchman. If there is no danger of the speedy return of the patrolman the signal is given, the door is opened, and they prepare to remove their plunder.

If the goods can be taken away early in the evening, or at daylight in the morning, one of the gang engages an express-wagon, which, by paying a good price, he secures the privilege of driving himself. If, however, the goods cannot be taken until near midnight, a public hack is necessary for the purpose. One of the thieves "fixes" the driver and takes his place upon the box, and is thus prepared to act for the best interests of his "pals." As soon as the streets are deserted, the "crow" gives the signal, the hack is driven up to the front of the store, the goods are brought out and deposited therein, and in a twinkling they are all driving away from the spot. Very frequently, however, two or more loads of goods are taken away in a single night from the same store, and the hack returns with as much safety, as though the errand of its occupants was a perfectly safe and legitimate one.

Where the entrance is obtained from the rear, the thieves feel more safe, and although they may have longer work, they infinitely prefer that method of operation. Their point of attack is the back door, and they generally succeed without much difficulty in turning the lock, either with a skeleton-key, or with the nippers if the key has been left in the lock, which is usually the case. On most rear doors, however, they find that a bar has been placed across the opening, which holds the two doors tightly in position. This obstacle is easily overcome, and with their brace and bit they set to work. Some burglars use what is called the "extension bit," which is capable of boring a hole of from three to seven inches, and with this instrument a hole is bored through the door, large enough to admit the arm of a man. The burglar then thrusts his arm through the hole thus made, and the bar is lifted and removed without the least difficulty or delay. In case, however, that they have the ordinary tools, they use a one-inch bit, and bore a succession of holes close together, in this wise:

And thus, though somewhat longer in its operation, the same result is achieved.

There are other modes of entry into stores where it is found that there is a vacant story above, or chances for entrance through skylights—all of which are carefully noted by the party who makes the preliminary survey of the premises, and the burglars come prepared for such emergencies as they reasonably expect from his reports. With a vacant second or third story, an entrance may be effected by one of the thieves secreting himself during the day, or entering by means of the elevators and trapdoors—and these are by no means unusual occurrences.

The stores usually selected by these robbers are those which contain articles of value. Silks and laces are always eagerly sought for, and a first-class hardware store is no mean prey. The finer grades of cutlery and razors are articles that always bring good prices. A good hardware store is almost as good as a jewelry store and the risk from detection and inside watchmen not half so great, while the goods can be readily and safely disposed of.

The goods obtained by these robberies are at once removed to the rented house of the burglars, and no attempt is made to dispose of them for several days. When the first alarm however has subsided, one member of the gang takes a sample of each article and seeking out the receiver, or dealer in stolen goods, displays them, and inquires how much he will pay for the quantity they have on hand. By these means they invariably realize much better prices for their plunder than they would by bringing the goods in bulk, for they are thus enabled to bring the "fence" to terms, without affording him the opportunity of giving them away, and securing the goods for himself.

As the thief has taken the precaution to carry only samples of his wares, he is enabled to go from one receiver to another—and in a large city, there are a number of men, and women too, who deal exclusively and extensively in stolen goods—until he has received an offer that is satisfactory. Failing to do this in a day or two, the goods are then shipped to a distant city, where they can readily be sold for much better prices, as the danger of identification and recovery is far less.

The store robbers frequently practice a little sneak thieving on their journeys of preliminary examination, and jewelry stores are usually selected for their purpose, particularly if they discover that the nightly precautions are too great to permit of their being safely robbed after they have been closed for the day. Their manner of working in this connection is as follows—all jewelry stores, as a rule, are fitted up with tall show-cases, which are arranged against the wall, behind the cases on the counters. In these cases the silver-ware and larger articles are kept for display. The counters are generally short, arranged in rows with passage ways between them, and on these the cases containing watches and the smaller articles of jewelry are tastefully exhibited on small trays. The thieves enter the store and one of them, securing the attention of a clerk, walks deliberately behind the counter, and pointing to some article of silver-ware in the case against the wall, engages the clerk in bargaining for its sale; while thus engaged he stands between the counter and the clerk, who is obliged to turn his back to the counters in order to face his supposed customer.

While this is going on his attention is entirely diverted from the other thief, who seizes the first favorable opportunity to transfer some of the most valuable articles in the counter cases to his own pockets and to pass quietly out of the store unsuspected. In some cases, however, there are two lines of counters and cases on opposite sides of the store, and under such circumstances the clerk must be taken to a place at the upright cases directly opposite to the articles that are intended to be stolen. For this operation two men are required to work upon the clerk, while the third man does the stealing. One of the thieves does the talking with the unsuspicious clerk, while the second one, ostensibly reading a newspaper, completely conceals the actions of the third confederate while he is robbing the cases upon the counter.

There is another system of robbing wholesale houses, which in many instances has been remarkably successful. This is called the "note-racket," and is exceedingly simple. The thieves wait upon the outside until they learn that a certain member of the firm has gone out to lunch, or upon some business errand—which is easily ascertained by watching the premises—and then one of the thieves will enter the store and ask for the absent merchant. Of course he is answered that the gentleman inquired for is not in; whereupon the thief will express his deep regret and, as he has important business elsewhere, it is impossible for him to wait, but if he can procure a sheet of paper and an envelope, he will write a note and leave it. The desired articles are furnished him, and deliberately walking up to a desk, which he believes contains the money for daily use, he commences to write. His confederate now enters, and beckoning to the man nearest to the desk, engages him in conversation upon some matter pertaining to their business. The thief at the desk then quickly draws his skeleton keys from his pocket, unlocks the drawer, and with one deft motion cleans it out, then relocking the drawer, he comes toward the clerk, tearing up his note as he does so, and saying that he has reconsidered the matter and will call again in an hour or two. He then quietly walks out of the store and disappears, and his companion follows him as speedily as he can, without exciting suspicion. The dismay of the clerk when he finds that the gentlemanly inquirer has robbed his desk under his very nose can be better imagined than described.

The operations which I have here detailed have occurred quite frequently and in many cases the losers have been utterly at a loss to account for the mysterious disappearance of their cash.

In the latter case it will be seen that the utmost carefulness is necessary in dealing with all visitors who invade the office of a store, and that in no case should a stranger be allowed to come in close proximity with the desks where money or any valuables are kept. It is impossible to discriminate against visitors, for the most innocent appearing man is generally apt to be the thief, and hence a general rule of exclusion should be enforced.

In order to guard against the former class, those who come in the silence and darkness of midnight, many precautions are necessary and constant vigilance is required. It is essentially important that especial notice should be taken of any stranger who may call, no matter under what pretext the call is made, at the time the stores or the safes are being opened or closed. If the person who has the keys in his possession is addressed, and his attention requested, let him at once slip the keys into his pocket, instead of laying them down upon a counter or desk. Care must be taken that the thieves do not get even a good look at these keys, as a good look to some robbers is as serviceable as a wax impression.

Whoever is entrusted with the keys to the store or safe at night, should so guard them that they cannot be found while he is asleep—for in many instances the thieves have effected an entrance into the sleeping-rooms of trusted employees, and have either stolen the keys, or have taken wax impressions of them for future use, while their custodian was slumbering unconsciously upon his couch.

One of the best preventives against store robberies is to have a good light burning in the store all the evening, and the windows unobscured, so that all passers-by may have a full view of the entire interior; and in case employees sleep in the store, have the doors bolted at a point more than one foot above or below the lock.

As danger is always to be apprehended from the surroundings, the cellar or the floor above the store should never be rented to strangers of whose respectability you are not fully advised, and a constant watchfulness should be maintained for suspicious occupants of the buildings upon either side. Increased care is necessary whenever any of the adjoining buildings are unoccupied.

By a careful observance of these precautionary directions the dangers from robbery are materially lessened and perfect immunity may this be secured.

The "Boodle" Game

THIS is one of the most successful of the many schemes resorted to by confidence men to fleece their unwary but equally unscrupulous victims. It is safer than almost any other system of swindling, because it is practiced upon men, whose cupidity overcomes their judgment, and who in their desire to swindle others, become the dupes themselves. For this reason the "saw-dust swindler" invariably escapes punishment, as in order to arrest these men the victims are compelled to acknowledge their own dishonesty. As a natural consequence the swindled customers of these sharpers prefer to quietly submit to their losses rather than to advertise themselves in the doubtful light which would follow any attempt to punish the offenders.

To use the language of one of the most successful operators at this game, it is "the boss racket of the whole confidence business." It is, in fact, the best, the cleverest and the most remunerative of all the swindles in the profession, and a short description of the manner in which it is operated, will not be out of place in a volume of this character.

In the first place, it is necessary to prepare a circular, or an address, which will catch the eye and excite the greed of the victims, and for this purpose, the following is a fair sample of the first epistolary attack:

New York, 18--
Dear Sir:
No doubt you will think it strange how I obtained your name and address. It was as follows: My confidential agent, who passed through your town not long since, gave it to me. He said he thought you were a man who was in a position to handle my goods in safety, and I concluded to write to you; if I have made a mistake, do me no harm and let matters drop. My motto is, never harm a man who is willing to prove himself your friend. My business is not exactly legitimate, but the green articles I deal in are safe and profitable to handle. The sizes are ones, twos, fives, and tens. Do you understand? I cannot be plainer until I know you mean business, and if you conclude to answer this letter, I will send you full particulars and terms, and will endeavor to satisfy you on every point, so that if you are my friend, I will prove a true and lasting one to you, be the trade for one or one thousand dollars. Remember, I do not want money in advance, as I do not transact business in that way. I want simply to convince you that I am just as I tell you, a friend to a friend.

Yours in confidence,

****

This circular is neatly printed on good paper and may be dated from any city in which the swindlers are temporarily located. By traveling through the country and making minute inquiries about the inhabitants, they are enabled to discover the men to whom a circular of this kind would prove an attractive bait.

It is not often that they make a mistake, and hence their business is very profitable; and as I have said, comparatively safe. The name signed at the bottom of the circular is a fictitious one, and the address given is that of a saloon whose reputation is somewhat questionable. We will describe the operation of these men in narrative form, in order to more fully show the manner of its working.

Mr. Verdant Green, who is pretty smart at a horse trade, and is generally ready to dicker with anybody and for anything, receives one of these circulars, and the latent spark of dishonesty lurking within him, is fired in an instant. He realizes the necessity of caution, however, and he addresses the parties who have written to him, a cautious letter of inquiry. "What are the green articles which they mention?" "What uses are they intended for, and how does the opportunity present itself for making any money?" The reply to this is a direct invitation for Mr. Green to come on in person, and to see for himself what the possibilities for making a fortune are.

The result is that Mr. Verdant Green, attired in his best clothes, soon after makes his appearance in the city, and seeks out the particular saloon to which he has been directed.

He notices that the name over the doorway is not the same to which he was directed, and he looks again at the address and finds that he is to direct "in the care of Mr.

Sharp." This reassures him and entering the saloon he approaches the spruce looking bartender.

"Kin yer tell me whar I kin find Mr. Sharp?" The actions of the bartender upon this inquiry being made are an amusing study. He scratches his head, looks puzzled, and mutters, apparently to himself:

"Sharp!—Sharp—Mr. Sharp—No—er, I don't know any Sharp."

Then he calls out to some men who are playing cards in the back room:

"Heigh Jack! Did you happen fur to know any party named Sharp around yer?"

A grand chorus of "Nos," from the back room is the response, and Jack, who is one of the confederates, makes his appearance in the doorway, and critically examines the rural visitor. The examination being apparently satisfactory, Jack approaches the stranger, and in an oily tone, addresses him.

"Did you want to see Mr. Sharp? Well, he used to hang around here, but he's moved away—moved away—let me see—more'n two months ago, I reckon. B'lieve he's gone out o' town somewhere."

Mr. Verdant Green's face lengthens considerably at this announcement, and he sadly takes his departure, in a confused state of mind. He wonders where Mr. Sharp could have gone, and cannot understand how the letter he received only three days ago, could possibly direct him to a location from which the writer had moved away two months before.

While he is thus abstractedly reasoning out this strange complication, somebody comes softly up behind him and slaps him heartily on the back. Turning hastily around Mr. Green sees the glib-tongued, suave-mannered "steerer" who seizes him by the hand and says:

"Excuse me, sir, but—er—ain't you the gentleman as was lookin' fur Mr. Sharp?"

"Jes so, I am," replies Mr. Verdant Green, while his face brightens up perceptibly, "mebbe yer kin tell me whar ter find him?"

"Right you are!" exclaims the steerer. "If you want ter do business on the dead square, and no funny work, do you mind! I'm the one as can take you to Mr. Sharp. In fact Mr. Green, that's your name, I see, takin' the liberty to look over your shoulder at that ere letter—in fact, Mr. Green, old boy, I'm goin' right there now. Come along and let's take a drink."

Nothing loth, Mr. Green accompanies his new companion back to the saloon they had just left, and after draining their glasses, they start for the location of Mr. Sharp.

The quarters of Mr. Sharp are a small office with the blinds drawn down over the glass panes in the door, and a lot of fancy lithographs stuck up in the window. Over the door there is a small tin sign, with the very deceptive legend "Dramatic Agency," printed on it in white paint.

The steerer gives a peculiar knock at the door, which is opened cautiously a few inches, and an eye appears in the aperture. A voice calls out, "All right!" And then the door is opened and Mr. Green finds himself within the sanctuary of the saw-dust man, and is introduced to Mr. Sharp.

Mr. Sharp at once insinuates himself into the good opinion of Mr. Green, and being a jovial, good natured fellow, Mr. Sharp orders up a bottle of spirits and some good cigars. Having been introduced by the steerer with a quiet wink, Mr. Sharp is thus informed that the visitor is all right, and he begins business at once.

"Well Mr. Green, my friend here tells me you want some of our stock. Would you like to look at the green articles?"

Mr. Green signifies his willingness, and Sharp, without any further delay, dives down into his trousers pockets, and draws out a large roll of bills. They are of all denominations, from one dollar up to twenty, and are bright, fresh, crisp and clean.

It is perhaps unnecessary to state that these notes are genuine money, and have been obtained from the Sub-Treasury, only the day before, in exchange for old bills. As a matter of course their appearance is such as to deceive even the most expert judges, and no doubt would be entertained of their genuineness.

Mr. Green's eyes are distended to their utmost extent at this exhibition, and Mr. Sharp, spreading out some of the bills on the desk, says in a business-like, matter-of-fact way:

"There's some of the crooked stuff. Sell it to you for thirty cents on the dollar. Twenty-five down, and the other five after the stuff is delivered. We flatter ourselves that these goods are pretty well done. Just pick 'em up and see what you think of 'em."

Mr. Green picks them up, one after another, and examines them critically. He is perfectly astonished. Pulling out some bills from his own pocket, he places them beside the supposed counterfeits, and finds to his amazement, that the likeness is perfect in every particular and detail. At length, unable to control himself, he blurts out:

"Well, by Gosh! if this don't beat ennything I ever seed! By the great horn-spoon, they're es like es two peas."

"Well, rather," remarks Mr. Sharp, complacently; and then to urge the trade, he adds, with seductive persuasiveness. "You'll find we're the right sort to deal with, my friend. We don't take any advantage of our customers, never. If you have any doubt about the "chromos" being negotiable and all right anywhere on the Continent, why, we'll just go out and try them. Put 'em to a practical test, you know, and that'll settle it."

"Oh, 'tain't needful, I guess, stranger," returns Green, rather indecisively.

"Oh, yes, but we'd rather have the worth of our goods proved," says Mr. Sharp, determined to clinch his prospective sale. "So, if you please, we'll just step into the street, and go to any store you like, and buy something. If you don't get your change out of the 'chromos' without any fuss or foolin', why, the bargain's off, and you needn't have anything more to do with us."

This offer seems very fair and very inviting, and without further ado the party sally forth. A jewelry store is most naturally the objective of the rural stranger, as he desires to purchase something for his lady-love at home. Entering the store, and looking over the glittering display, a pair of earrings strikes the fancy of Mr. Verdant Green, and after critically examining them, Mr. Sharp inquires:

"Well, what do you say, Green, will these suit you?"

Mr. Green signifies his satisfaction, and thereupon Mr. Sharp takes out his roll of notes, and inquires of the store-keeper, in a careless tone:

"How much?"

"Five dollars," is the reply.

"Well, that's reasonable enough," answers Mr. Sharp.

"Just take it out of this."

Mr. Green now watches the jeweler with the keenest interest; but everything appears to be all right.

For the store-keeper, after glancing at the money a moment, places it in the drawer, and hands over the change without a question.

This settles the matter for Mr. Verdant Green, and when they at last reach the sidewalk, he gazes with a puzzled expression, first at the jewelry in his hand and then at the confidence man, who stands smilingly beside him. At length, in tones of profound mystification:

"W'all, I'll be gull darned, stranger, ef you don't beat the circus juggler all holler!"

It will be borne in mind that the money which Mr. Sharp has passed upon the jeweler was a genuine ten dollar government note, and hence, no difficulty or opposition was to be apprehended; but to the credulous Mr. Green, who believes the note to be counterfeit, the result seems simply wonderful. At this juncture, when the victim has been wound up to the proper pitch of unutterable astonishment, the confidence man says, suggestively:

"Well, now, you have come on to buy the chromos, you see how they work; how much do you want?"

In almost every case the victim will want from two to five hundred dollars worth of the stuff, and will so state, and after that the "saw-dust racket" is put into operation.

Sometimes the money is handed over in a roll, and in that case a roll of waste paper, with a few counterfeits on the outside, and then a genuine note for a wrapper is neatly put on, and when the victim has the roll safely stowed away in his pocket, the parties quietly drop him, and leave him to discover the deception at his leisure. Of course he is required to pay his own good money in advance of receiving the "green articles," and having received this, Mr. Sharp has no further use for Mr. Green.

At another time, when the amount purchased is large, the sharpers secure an old carpet bag, and stuffing it with green paper, they hand it to the poor victim to carry. Two of the gang accompany him on his way to the depot, and no opportunity is allowed him to gaze inside of the valise until he is on the train, and by that time the swindlers have fled safely away in the distance.

Sometimes the order given is quite large, and in that case the swindlers arrange it to send the goods by express, C. O. D. This meets with the approval of Mr. Green, and he unhesitatingly advances the twenty-five percent, with the understanding that the balance is to be paid when the goods are received. In this case it may be taken as a certainty that the box, which in due time is received by the expectant Mr. Green, contains nothing more valuable than a superior article of pure and simple saw-dust.

The feelings of the rustic would-be swindler may be imagined when he sees the interior of the box so carefully sent to him and realizes that he has paid his percentage, and the express charges also, for the proud privilege of writing himself down as one of the largest sized simpletons which this modern age produces.

It is needless to add that no exposure follows this disappointing and exasperating discovery, as Mr. Green would be compelled to divulge his own intended rascality before he could proceed against the mythical firm of B. Sharp & Co. In this manner the game is successfully worked, and the victims continue to add to the profits of the "Boodle Swindlers."

Hotel Thieves

PROBABLY no more prevalent or more popular branch of dishonesty exists at the present time than the robbery of hotels. From the first-class and aristocratic hostelries of the larger cities, to the well-kept and respectable inns and taverns of country villages and towns, the expert thieves select their victims, and their operations are, it is to be regretted, almost universally successful. Wherever travelers with money about their persons are to be found, there also will appear the professional thief ready to relieve them of the valuable possessions. Whenever any unusual excitement prevails in a particular locality which attracts a large number of visitors, the thief invariably follows, and, in most cases, reaps an abundant harvest. Fairs and horse-races, conventions and expositions, generally cause an influx of strangers to the city or town in which they are held, and the hotels are, in consequence, filled to overflowing. All of the visitors at times like these are amply supplied with ready money, and these gentry fall easy victims to the midnight robber who enters their sleeping rooms, and while the inmates are peacefully slumbering, rifle their pockets, and even search the beds whereon they are lying. These thieves do not, however, restrict their operations to the times of excitement and overcrowding of hotels, but upon ordinary occasions, when the public houses are occupied by the general class of the traveling public, their depredations are carried on with impunity, and with a degree of success that is absolutely startling. Almost daily the hotel-keepers of the larger cities are compelled to make restitution for losses which have occurred to their guests, who retired to their rooms in fancied security, and awoke in the morning to find themselves completely stripped of their money and every article of value of which they were possessed.

For several years past, the hotel proprietors all over the country have been made to suffer for the appalling number of robberies which have taken place in their respective establishments. Hundreds of these cases occur which are never made public, and which are never placed in the hands of the police or detectives for investigation, for the proprietors invariably prefer to arrange matters with their guests and to reimburse them for their losses, rather than give publicity to a robbery which would have the effect of injuring their reputation and frightening away their customers. Every possible precaution has been taken by the proprietors of these establishments, to prevent the depredations of these midnight marauders, but the evil has simply been abated not abolished. Private officers, watchmen and detectives have been placed on every floor assigned for sleeping rooms, and yet, despite their safeguards, robbers continue to gain access to the chambers, and unconscious guests are despoiled, almost under the very eyes of those who have been constituted the guardians of their safety.

All first-class hotels, in addition to the maintenance of a corps of wakeful and alert watchmen upon the outside of the chambers, have also placed safeguards within the rooms. Every door is provided with a double lock—that is, a lock which can only be locked from the inside of the room and cannot be reached from the outside, as the key-hole does not extend through the door. The ordinary lock upon the outside serves to admit the guest to the apartment assigned to him, and when once in, he locks his door from the inside with a lock that only operates upon the inner side of the door. These appliances form within themselves two distinct locks, one of which may be locked upon both sides, and the other only from the inside. Chain bolts, another ingenious contrivance, have also been put on many of the doors, and yet, with all these provisions against the entrance of the thief, the occupants of these rooms awake in the morning to find that they have been robbed during the night, and their doors show no evidence to the inexpert observer, of having been tampered with in any particular. To those unacquainted with the ingenious workings of the professional hotel thief this discovery is startling and inexplicable but to those who have studied the modes and operations of this class of criminals the manner in which an entrance has been effected, and the means used to accomplish their object, the solution is as plain as the sun at noon-day.

It is my purpose to fully explain the modus operandi of these expert thieves and to so fully inform the traveling public upon these matters, that if proper precautions are taken, and a rigid scrutiny of their doors and locks is made before retiring, an entry will be prevented and a successful robbery will be impossible.

Let us first consider the tools used by a first-class hotel thief, after which we will describe their uses and his manner of working with them. In the first place, it must be remembered, that this class of thieves is composed of exceedingly sharp and intelligent men, who are thoroughly alive to every circumstance whether of a favorable nature or otherwise. They are experienced in the use of tools and will handle a brace and bit with all the dexterity of the educated artisan. They are seldom caught napping, and are far better posted as to the whereabouts of the watchmen, than that worthy is of their proximity. From external appearances no one would think of suspecting the well-dressed, gentlemanly looking individual, who registers himself with a quiet and unassuming air, and whose tone and conversation bespeak both travel and education In the reading-room and at the dining table he is the dignified, yet affable gentleman of business, and his deportment is at all times unobtrusive and polite. He never dresses in the gaudy colors, or in the height of fashion, but his apparel is usually chosen with the utmost good taste, and a quiet style that stamps him as a gentleman of refined tastes.

His tools, which are generally of the finest quality of tempered steel, consist of a "bar-key," a set of six bits of various sizes, and arranged for either stem or tumbler locks; a small drill; a file; a "sectional stem"—or what is called the "widdy"; several pieces of wire, and a pair of nippers. These are all the articles, he needs, and frequently but a few of these are required, and their particular uses will be fully explained in their proper order. These implements do not occupy much room in the traveling satchel of the nomadic thief, and are frequently carried about his person. There is another article which might be mentioned, which, although forming no part of the tools, is of a very important nature, and that is a piece of white putty or pigment.

Armed with these instruments, and qualified by a long system of training, the hotel thief is now fully prepared to set out on his travels. His plan of operation is as follows: hotel thieves almost invariably travel in pairs, though their companionship is never manifested in public, and to all observers they are as distant and uncommunicative as the utmost strangers. They generally manage, however, to secure their rooms upon the same floor, and, if possible, without attracting undue attention, within close proximity of each other. Once established in their apartments, the work of active operation at once begins. The habits of the guests upon the floor they occupy are carefully studied, and they soon ascertain which of the chambers are unoccupied. These preparatory steps are always taken during the day. Having discovered the numbers of the vacant rooms, they make a thorough examination of the locks upon their own doors, as it is reasonably certain that every other door upon the same floor will be similarly secured. Having acquired this knowledge, they are ready to work. One of the men is set to see that the coast is clear, while the other quickly effects an entrance into one of the empty rooms. His tools are taken in with him. If there is only a single lock to contend with, the work is soon done—the "bar-key" with its appropriate bit opens the door readily from the outside, and no further arrangements are necessary for that room.

Where there is a bolt on the inside of the door, a hole is bored through the door from the inside immediately over the handle or knob, for the introduction of the "sectional stem," and then this hole is carefully puttied up and the small spot in the door is colored with a quick-drying material of the same color. Ascertaining that the corridor is empty, by a series of signals with his partner who is on the watch, the thief comes cautiously out, and covers up the hole on the outside in the same manner. In this way, provided they are not interrupted, all the vacant rooms on this floor are fixed, awaiting the influx of visitors in the evening.

Where the doors are fastened with double locks, the mode of "fixing" is different, and requires more time and labor. In the first place, entrance is obtained by the use of the invaluable "bar-key"—and then locking himself in the thief commences work upon the inside lock, the key of which is always in its place. This key is taken out of the lock, and a hole is drilled directly through the back plate of the lock and the door; this hole must be large enough to admit of the introduction of a fine pair of nippers for turning the key. The hole is then bored for the manipulation of the bolt, and then all is puttied up and painted over as before.

There is another mode of "fixing" the inside lock, which is frequently resorted to, but which is not so generally successful as the one above mentioned, and that is simply to bore a large gimlet hole through the lockplate and the door, and then to file a slot in the end of the key, like that in the head of a screw. By this means a large puttied hole on the outside of the door is avoided, and a small, sharp edged brad-awl inserted into the hole, will catch upon the slot in the end of the key, which can then be turned like a screw-driver and screw. Particular attention is always paid to the location of the bolts and locks and the position of the bed in the room, so that no delay may be caused by a difficulty in locating the sleeper immediately by the uncertain light which comes through the transom over the door, from the dimly burning gas in the halls.

These preparations being duly made, and from half a dozen to a score of rooms put in proper condition to be entered, the thieves patiently bide their time until evening. The registers are carefully watched in order to ascertain which of the rooms they have "fixed," are to be occupied, and an estimate is made, if it is possible to do so, of the individuals who have been assigned to them, with the view of selecting those from whom the richest harvest may be reaped.

The next precaution, and this is of paramount importance, is to carefully study the habits of the detectives or watchmen who perform their duties during the night. For this purpose the thieves are often compelled to delay their operations for two or three nights in order to become thoroughly familiarized with the movements of these guardians of the persons and property of the guests of the hotel.

Before detailing the manner in which robberies of this character are usually effected, we will describe the nature and the uses of the tools and implements, which form the stock in trade of an expert professional hotel thief.

The key and bits which these cracksmen use are of peculiar construction. They consist of a straight steel key-bar with bits which can be inserted at will, and they can be used either upon any ordinary stem lock or tumbler lock with perfect ease. The files, drills, awls, etc. are of the usual pattern, but are made of fine steel and highly tempered. The "sectional stem" is an instrument of great peculiarities and is a very useful tool in the hands of an expert workman. It is made of fine steel or iron and consists of two pieces of metal, one of which is about eight inches long, and the other about two inches, and is about as thick as a small brad-awl. These two pieces are joined together with a screw or rivet, which not being tight allows the foremost end to drop down when the joint has passed through the door. A piece of fine strong cord is fastened to the end of this stem, which on being pulled, draws the end down until it is at right angles with the piece to which it is attached, and by retaining the tension of the string, the instrument is kept in proper position for work. On the other end of this instrument is fastened a knob or ball, which enables the operator, by simply turning it, to work the point at the other end. This "sectional stem," is used for slipping the bolts on the inside of a door, and the manner of working it is as follows: the stem, both parts perfectly straight, is inserted into the hole drilled through the door over the bolt, the string is then pulled, which causes the end piece of the stem to drop down, thus forming an L, and then, when the handle of the bolt is touched, by simply turning the knob or handle, it is slipped as easily as though the operation was performed from the inside.

The "bar-key" is a very important instrument, and from the nature of its construction, in the hands of an expert manipulator, will open any ordinary door from the outside, without any previous preparation. It consists of the bar and handle of an ordinary key, with a slot in

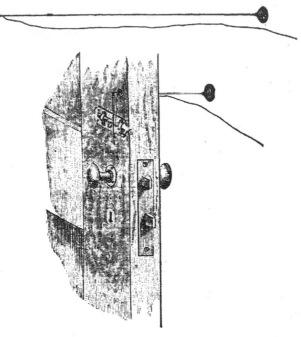

the end of it, into which may be inserted the bits, which are especially designed for the locks of the general hotel doors, and a screw which secures these bits in their places.

By the above arrangement, it will be seen that bits of different kinds and shapes may be inserted into the bar,

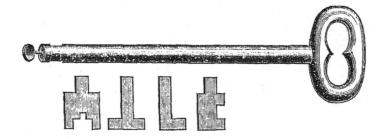

and the key of the rooms occupied by the thieves, will at once show them the nature of the bit which they will require in order to work upon the others. T and L bits are made in such variety that they will open any door not furnished with tumbler locks, and when tumbler locks are used, the necessary bits to open these doors can be readily procured or manufactured by the thief himself.

The "widdy" is a small piece of bent wire with a string attached, forming a sort of bow.

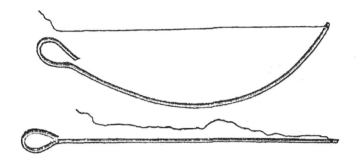

With this simple instrument running through a keyhole, if the bolt is below the lock; or a gimlet hole made for the purpose, if above the lock; a burglar can throw back any mortise, spring or sliding bolt now in use, no matter in what position it is, or how the knob may be placed. In addition to this, the "widdy" will operate the finest night-latch in existence, and for a variety of purposes it is one of the most useful of articles.

The pieces of bent wire are usually shaped as follows:

The first is used to throw back sliding-bolts, when the knob is *turned up*; the other is used when the knob is *turned down*. Four sizes of this wire are usually carried, so that if the first will not catch the bolt, the next is used, and so on. The advantage of this is, that the necessity of boring more than one gimlet hole in the door is thus avoided. The "widdy," however, will dispense with the use of these wires, as that instrument will perform its work anywhere. These wire instruments are usually made of umbrella wire, and can be readily fashioned into shape by a thief who understands his business, and the use of tools when made.

When everything is ready for the operation, and the guests are all sleeping soundly in their beds, the thieves begin their work. If the corridors are deserted, their labors are easy and their entrance into the chambers of the sleepers is easily effected, without risk and in a short space of time. If, however, there is a watchman on duty, a careful espionage is maintained upon his movements, and should he leave his post for a few minutes, sufficient time is given to the thieves in which to work. Five minutes is frequently all the time an expert thief occupies in "working" a single room. Armed with his "bar-key," his nippers and the "sectional stem," he sallies forth while his companion unobservedly maintains a close watch upon all the surroundings, and stands prepared to give prompt warning in case of danger.

If the sleeper to be operated upon has left the key in the outer lock, the nippers are used, and in a twinkling, that part of the difficulty is over, and the key is turned so quickly and noiselessly that no one would be aware of what was going on. If, however, there is an inner or double lock, and a bolt on the door, the putty from the drilled hole is quickly removed, the nippers are inserted, and in case the inside key has been prepared by filing, as I have mentioned before, the sharp awl is used, and fitting into the slot in the end of the key, turns it readily. Then the "sectional stem," the "widdy," or the bent wire is inserted through the hole over the bolt, the string is pulled, and with an easy turn of the wrist, the bolt is thrown back, and every obstacle to the entrance of the thief is removed.

Should the door, however, be fastened with the ordinary chain bolts, the manner of working them is as follows—the door is opened sufficiently to allow the burglar to put his arm on the inside and measure from the edge of the door to the edge of the plate. This, of course, is where no previous preparations have been made, but when the thief has properly "faked" the room, as he calls it— that is, "fixed" it for his entrance in the evening, the hole is already bored in its proper place. Through the hole thus made, a thin wire about the thickness of a silk thread is passed, and then, with the door opened, the wire is carried by the hand and passed through the eye of the "dog" on the inside. To the end of this wire a button is attached. The door is then closed and the wire is gently pulled, which draws the chain back to the opening in the end of the plate and it falls out. All impediments are now removed, and turning the knob softly, the door is opened and the thief noiselessly enters the room. The first thing to be done is to replace the plugs in the holes in the door. This is done in an instant, and then the thief, maintaining a stooping posture, springs for the clothing of the unsuspecting occupant. The reasons for adopting this stooping position or falling upon the knees is obvious, as every person in bed on being awakened suddenly, will naturally look up and not down. His movements are as rapid as the flash of the lightning, and as noiseless as the Indian on the trail. If he is successful in finding a good roll of money or a wallet he goes no further, but if only loose change is found, his next point of attack is the bed. Should the vest be missing, the thief knows that this garment has been placed under the pillow. Experience has taught him many things, and one glance at the arrangement of the bed sheet will tell him whether the sleeper has placed his valuables under the mattress or under his pillow. If the sheet is disturbed and is hanging down, near the center of the bed, he knows to a certainty that the mattress conceals what he desires, as the chambermaids invariably tuck the sheets in under the mattress; but if, on the contrary, the sheets are all snug and tucked under, he knows that his plunder is under the head of his victim. A few deft movements in either direction and the thief has secured the property, whether the same is placed under mattress or pillow. His exit is then made as stealthily as his entrance, and closing the door carefully behind him, he plugs up the door upon the outside.

In many cases, the thieves are sufficiently considerate to lock the door behind them, and their manner of proceeding is thus explained. After securing their booty the key is returned to the keyhole. Around the knob of the bolt, a silk thread is looped, and the ends brought through the crevice in the door to the outside. Pulling the thread, shoots the bolt back into its sheath, then one end of the thread is dropped and is drawn through the crevice and removed. The key is then caught from the outside by the nippers and on being turned leaves the door bolted and locked, as the victims left them before retiring.

Where there is but the ordinary lock and bolt, the entrance is frequently effected without disturbing or defacing the door in the least, the "widdy" is inserted through the keyhole and works the lock without any previous drilling, and thus the chances of detection are considerably reduced.

When the sleeper awakes in the morning, and to his dismay discovers that he has been robbed, his first movement is to examine the fastenings of his door. Finding nothing suspicious about them, he is perfectly dumbfounded and utterly at a loss to account for what has taken place, and even should he find that every-thing is unlocked, and the door undefaced, he naturally concludes, with a sinking heart, that he failed to take proper precautions before retiring, and reports so at the office. As this is a very common occurrence, the guest is solemnly cautioned to be more careful in the future, and by all means to deposit his valuables with the clerk before going to bed.

How a thief can extract articles from under a mattress or pillow without awaking a sleeper has been a continual mystery to most people. The mode of operation adopted by the thief is generally to bare the right arm to the shoulder, and then holding either mattress or pillow with the left hand, lifting it gently and with a steady motion, and then gently inserting the bare arm, pull forth whatever may be found concealed there.

The victims of hotel thieves are designated by the very delicate title of "patients," and the usual patient manner in which they submit to the operations of the skillful robber amply justifies the application of the term.

If a thief is disturbed or discovered he does not make any further attempt that evening, but quietly makes his escape to his room. Should he however, be successful, he rarely exceeds three rooms in one night, being generally content with what he has, and not caring to further increase the chances of his detection.

It sometimes happens, though I am glad to state, very rarely, that the persons who have been employed to guard the guests of a hotel from the visits of these nightly plunderers, are composed of pliable material, and the bestowal of a ten or twenty dollar bill upon one of these gentlemen will ensure his absence during the time the thief desires to work. It has not infrequently happened that thieves have remained unsuspected and in continued operation for a week in a single hotel, although that is generally the longest time in which thieves have confined their depredations to one place. In order to cover himself more completely for an extended period like this, the thief with brazen assurance will make a loud complaint at the office of having been robbed himself.

When entering a room, the thief is always dressed in soft woollen clothing, and wears woollen stockings upon his feet. The noise made by the rustling of a muslin or linen shirt, when everything is hushed and still, is often sufficiently loud or harsh to awaken people, particularly ladies, from a sound and comfortable slumber. Hence it is that the thief will invariably wear a woollen shirt when he attempts to purloin the valuables of his sleeping victims.

There is a certain class of hotel thieves who confine their operations to the time usually denominated the "sporting season." They follow the trotting horses and racers, and make the circuit of county fairs, base-ball games and such other exhibitions and entertainments calculated to draw large crowds. They generally arrive in a city or town two or three days in advance of the day on which these events occur, and then, by active work are enabled to find plenty of empty rooms to "doctor," before the tide of visitors sets in and the hotels are filled.

In a number of instances, the process of boring the doors has been obviated where there are transoms over the doors of the rooms to be operated upon, and sufficient time is not given to prepare the locks for the midnight visit. The instrument used in this case, is rather a unique contrivance, which anyone, whether a mechanic or not, can construct without difficulty. It consists of two pieces of thin, strong wood, one of which is about three feet long and the other about eight inches. One end of each of these two pieces are joined together with a screw, but are sufficiently loose to enable them to be turned around readily. On the end of the smaller piece there are nailed three small strips of wood, one at the end, and one on each side, which forms a sort of box, open at one end, as in the figure here shown.

In using this instrument, two men operate together. One of them places himself before the door, while the lightest one mounts upon his shoulders, and opening the transom fully, inserts his arm and hand, which contains the implement above described. He manipulates this instrument so that the boxed end of the stick will reach the handle of the key, which is then inclosed by the three raised sides of the stick. By pushing downward upon the long end of the stick, the box attachment is made to turn, and this, as a natural consequence, turns the key along with it, precisely after the manner of working a crank. The bolt is then shot back, with the aid of this stick, and in an incredibly short space of time, the door yields to their efforts, and the slumbering guest is at the mercy of the thieves. This plan has many advantages, as it leaves no traces of tampering with locks or keys, and the door is never defaced; but it has counterbalancing objections in requiring two men before the door, in the increased liability to detection and in the inability to work the locks as quickly as with the nippers, the awl, or the "sectional stem."

The operations of the hotel thief have thus been fully given, in the hope that the traveling public may take the warnings given, and guard against danger in the future. To the guest at the hotel, I would say, always examine the door of your room before retiring, and look carefully at the keys and the transoms. Never take a large amount of money or valuable jewelry to your rooms, but leave them with the clerk of the hotel, who will place them in the safe. This plan not only serves as a protection against the thieves, but compels the hotel proprietor to assume the responsibility of their safe keeping, and to make restitution in case of loss.

In this connection, and while laying bare the operations of the professional hotel thief, I may mention another specimen, which generally does not figure in court reports, and is seldom represented in the prisons of the country. I allude to the dapper, little traveling salesman, whose ideas of life are very high, and whose salary is correspondingly low. This latter fact, however, would never be suspected. He wears the latest and the most stylish clothing; from the crown of his lustrous tile, to the pointed toe of his irreproachable gaiters, he appears to be the well-to-do, *blazé* man about town. He carries samples of value, and his jewelry is generally of the first quality, while his limited supply of diamonds is all of the finest and purest. This young gentleman arrives in the city, he makes his sales to the trade, perhaps also makes some collections; and during the times not occupied with his business, which are many, he is having a glorious good time. A sojourn of a week will enable him to spend his moderate salary for three months. What then? Why, means must be devised to reimburse the depleted exchequer. But how? Ah, that is very easy. On the morning following some expensive orgie, the dashing young gentleman makes his appearance before the hotel proprietor in woeful plight. His eyes are wild, his dress disordered. What has occasioned this wonderful metamorphosis? The answer is soon given—the young man has been robbed! On the evening before, he retired to his room quite early. In the morning he awoke, only to find that his room had been entered; his clothing searched; his jewels and all his money, amounting to several hundred dollars, carried off by the reckless thieves. His story seems plausible. He is a gentleman. He represents a good house. What then? Why, the proprietor, to prevent the news of the robbery from being made public, and thereby injuring the reputation of the house, makes good the alleged loss, and pays to the poor victim a sufficient sum to reimburse him for all his losses. The young man departs downcast but grateful, and at the next city he extracts his jewelry from its hiding-place, and with a replenished pocket-book, he fully enjoys himself upon the proceeds of the robbery, which it is needless to add, he committed himself.

This young dandy is seldom discovered, seldom punished, but he is as much a professional criminal as the man whose actions and operations I have described in the fore part of this chapter.

Sneak Thieving

AMONG all the numerous branches, or departments of crime, there is not one so pernicious, and perhaps so uniformly successful, as that of sneak thieving. With noiseless, cat-like step the sneak will crawl to his prey, and without leaving a single trace of his presence, will escape unobserved, with large sums of money, under the very eyes of watchful and alert business men, whose duty it is to guard the treasures intrusted to their keeping. No trade or profession is exempt from the visits of these sneaking thieves, who penetrate through all the ramifications of both business and social life, and ply their vocations in the broad light of day. Unlike the burglar, the sneak thief does not await the coming of night, and under the cover of the darkness pursue his desperate calling. He needs not to be assured that his victims are sleeping to ensure his safety in his undertakings; his fields of operations are always among the active, the wakeful and the bustling. No dark lantern and ponderous "jimmy," no giant powder or diamond drill form the implements of the trade of the sneak thief; for the doors of wealth are always opened to him without force or violence, and the money and valuables which he takes, are placed within his easy reach.

The proselytes of this branch of crime range from the boy and girl in their teens, who rob unsuspecting merchants of small articles of merchandise, to the full-grown man who enters a bank during the bustle and activity of business and steals thousands of dollars.

In the larger and more ambitious operations of the sneak thief, success requires the association of three or four men, who thoroughly understand their business, and who by appearance and education are fully qualified for the delicate duties which devolve upon them. This association, as in the case of other combinations to defraud, is called a "mob," with their "stalls," and with the man who does the actual stealing, who is called the "sneak." The "stalls," for the most part, are men of fine appearance, who dress well, and are possessed of more than an ordinary amount of educational advantages. They are well posted in general business matters, and can converse intelligently upon the intricate questions connected with banks and banking. Never loud in their appearance or conversation, their entrance into a banking institution occasions no surprise or suspicion, and cashiers and clerks afford them desired information with as much consideration and politeness as they bestow upon their well-known and responsible depositors. The "sneak," however, need not be so well favored, although he frequently is as much of an apparent gentleman as his associates.

Before describing the movements of this class of criminals it may be as well to mention a few of the articles which are considered essential for successful operation. The most important thing is that the "sneak" shall be supplied with a pair of shoes or slippers that will make no noise—a creaking shoe being considered as a sure producer of detection—with little or no heel, and frequently with felt soles. The foot-coverings of the sneak thief are as noiseless as though he walked in his stockings. The low heel is a wise precaution, for almost every bank vault has an iron step or a bar on the floor against which the doors close and there would be great danger in striking against this if the heels were high. The slightest noise in the direction of the bank vault is certain to attract attention, and then detection is sure to follow. The "sneak" must also be provided with a large bag in which to conceal his booty; this is generally made of black flannel or muslin, and is furnished with a drawing string in the top, much after the fashion of the bags usually carried by lawyers. This bag is large enough to hold one or more tin boxes such as are usually found in the vaults of banks, and in which valuable papers, bonds, and money are kept. Sometimes the pockets in the coat worn by the "sneak," will extend around the entire inside lining, which makes the inner lining of the coat one immense pocket. This is used when the bag has been neglected, or where a sudden opportunity occurs to perpetrate a robbery, for which no previous preparations were made.

Skeleton keys of all patterns are carried by the sneak, so that if time allows he can readily open the tin boxes in the vaults, without the dangerous and troublesome task of removing the entire box, and at the same time delaying the period of discovery of the crime.

For the purpose of illustration we will select a bank in which, as is frequently the case, during business hours the vault doors are open and the strong boxes are unlocked. The vault, we will assume, is at the rear end of the banking-room, and the clerks, as they stand at their desks facing the customers, have their backs towards the vault. Should this be the case—and it frequently is so—there is generally a passage way or small gate at the end of the desks by which the clerks enter, and through which also the "sneak" can readily work his way. This is one of the most simple operations for the "sneak," and in which he is almost uniformly successful. One or two of the "stalls," will enter the bank, and in the most business-like manner possible engage the clerk in conversation upon some question of banking business. They either want some information about opening an account, or drawing a draft—and it is a very easy matter to prolong a conversation of this character sufficiently long to enable the " sneak" to crawl, on hands and knees, into the vault, and to hastily pick up all that he can conveniently carry away, and then to make his way again to the front of the bank. Of course this style of robbery is generally attempted in country banks, where there are but few clerks, and where the number of customers is small; but the number of such banks is far greater than the well guarded city banks with their army of clerks, and stalwart watchmen—and therefore are more generally selected by the watchful thieves.

It may be as well to state that of late years, it has become almost impossible to rob a well appointed and well guarded city bank. Every precaution has been taken, and every safeguard adopted which experience and sagacity can suggest, and every bank of any prominence has one or more strong limbed and alert policemen who are on duty about the interior during the entire time that the bank is open for business. The thieves, however, are as well posted on these particulars as the banks themselves, and therefore, they do not attempt the impossible task of robbing these institutions, but confine their operations to the more fruitful fields of country banks and those of the smaller cities.

Now, should the vault in the bank be so arranged —being placed at the end of the counter and at the side of the cashier—that any person entering it would be instantly discovered by the cashier, the "stall" then takes a prominent part in the transaction. Entering the bank, he addresses the cashier, and engages him in the calculation of the interest due upon a draft which he has in his possession, or consults him about the collection of some coupons, inducing him by degrees, to perform the necessary task of figuring up the possible results. The "stall" is meanwhile so placing himself that the back of the cashier will be turned toward the open door of the vault. With a natural desire to see what the cashier is doing, he will turn the paper in one direction or the other, so that that gentleman will be obliged to shift his position in order to accommodate his visitor. The ignorance of the visitor is quite surprising, and the questions asked are propounded in such an affable, insinuating manner, that the good-natured cashier, all unconscious of what is transpiring behind him, will exert himself to the utmost in order to fully enlighten his gentlemanly but decidedly ignorant visitor.

When the cashier has been sufficiently engaged, and has been turned around to the proper point of obliquity, the "sneak" will stealthily steal into the vault, and in a few minutes will emerge with all the available resources of the bank, concealed beneath his coat.

Not only is the vault a point of attack, but very often there are large amounts of notes piled up on tables or counters behind the railings which surround the cashier or clerk, and if these can be safely taken the labor of the "sneak" is made much more easy and more profitable than if he is required to enter the vault.

Now let us suppose that the bank is duly opened for business—the vault doors are open and the clerks are at their desks; that they would not be able to see anyone who entered or left the vault, and that the only way to get behind the counter is through the room of the president, which is in the rear of the building. Of course the president will of necessity perceive any person who comes into his room, whether to engage him in conver- sation or to pass through into the banking-room in front. To the uninitiated it would seem an impossible task to pass this watchful officer unseen, but to the professional sneak thieves it is very easy of accomplishment. Their plan of operations to effect their object is as follows—two of the "stalls" will enter the president's room for the purpose of consulting him upon some matters of financial import. If that officer is sitting in such a position as to control the entrance to his rooms, this is all the better for the success of the enterprise. One of the "stalls" advances to the desk of the president, and announces the nature of his business, while the other will quietly take a seat, and draw from his pocket a newspaper—and then opening it fully, will hold it, under the pretense of reading, in such a position as to entirely screen the view of the front door of the president's room. This will enable the "sneak" to enter the room; then the "stall" will quietly change his position so as to cover the doorway leading into the banking-room, and behind the counters. It will be noticed that the "sneak" is shielded by the newspaper from the moment it is opened, until it covers the door which leads to the vault. Once past the door, he quickly glides into the banking-room. If notes are handy he takes these, but if necessary he enters the vault and loads himself with all that is valuable within his reach. When he has completed his operation, the same manipulation of the newspaper is gone through, and again under its complete cover the "sneak" makes his escape. This whole operation does not occupy more than three or four minutes time, and this is generally the longest period that is required for successful work. Once the "sneak" has taken his departure, the interview with the president is quickly concluded, and the two "stalls," after politely thanking that officer for his kindness and courtesy, gracefully withdraw.

Another very frequent and successful method, where the above arrangement cannot be safely carried out, is for one of the "stalls" to procure a carriage, and driving up to the door of the bank, request the president to come out and transact some business with an invalid who cannot leave the vehicle. In such cases the name of the president or cashier is first obtained, and being addressed by his proper name when the request is preferred, the financial officer is entirely unsuspicious of danger, and emerges from the bank to await the orders of his invalid caller. Clerks and cashiers have also been called out in this way, during the dinner-hour, when they would be left alone in charge of the bank. Of course the "sneak" is on hand, and while the president or cashier is engaged in conversation on the sidewalk, he quietly enters and robs the bank. At other times the "stall" will approach a pigeon-hole of one of the desks in front and request to speak to the president, who is in his room in the rear, and that gentleman, being thus called suddenly, upon the impulse of the moment, will answer the summons and thus leave the way open for the hiding sneak.

Clerks whose positions are such as to prevent the entrance of the sneak to the vaults have very often been called by name to some pigeon-hole in the desk opposite to him, and there held long enough for the thief to accomplish his purpose. The manner in which the "stalls" acquire the names of the employees of a bank is at once simple and unique. They present themselves at one of the pigeon-holes at a distance from the clerk whom they desire to call, and pointing out the individual desired, inquire:

"What is the name of that young gentleman opposite? He looks very much like an old friend of mine."

The clerk thus questioned, without bestowing any thought upon the matter, will at once convey the desired information, upon which the "stall" acknowledges his error, and craving pardon for troubling him, withdraws at once. The information thus acquired is conveyed to another stall, and shortly afterward this confederate enters, and going directly up to the further pigeon-hole, calls the name of the clerk in a very decided tone of interest and acquaintance.

It is the first and governing principle of the "sneak," not to allow himself to be seen by anyone, for if any employee of the bank has noticed his presence, he will naturally feel uneasy and suspicious because he is aware of the fact that there is a strange man in such a part of the building, and his movements cannot be watched. To overcome this difficulty therefore the "sneak" enters the bank first and endeavors to get a good position where he will not be noticed—and then he will sit or stand apparently engaged in some intricate financial problem with paper and pencil. Sometimes he enters the president's room, which may be empty at the time—and if discovered before his confederates enter, he will excuse himself by saying that he is either waiting to see the president, or is expecting his mother or sister to come for the purpose of making a deposit of money, or to invest in some securities for which the bank is an agent. At other times he will enter the president's room with one of the "stalls," and then trust to the adroitness of his companion, in engaging the attention of the president, long enough for him to get into the vault quietly, get what is convenient to his hands, and return without his absence bring noticed.

At other times, particularly in a country bank, where there is but one man in charge of the bank at noon-time, and the position of this man is such that he can see any person who may enter, the two "stalls" will enter the bank, and while one of them is engaging the clerk by changing a large note, or in answering some question of a financial nature, the other will hold up a newspaper, and under the cover of this the "sneak" will make his entrance, and walking quietly as far as the counter, crouch down in a stooping position, and thus sneak towards his work, without his presence being known or even suspected.

The above modes of operation are among those most frequently used by the sneak thieves in robbing banks whose vaults, and the doors to their money departments are opened during the day. There are also many thieves who will gain access into vaults and behind doors, when what are known as "sneak" or "day doors" are placed on the vaults and kept locked during the day. The entrances to the interior of the bank—that is, that portion of the building-reserved for the clerks—are frequently supplied with doors which are always locked; and every clerk and messenger who passes through this doorway is required to unlock this door before he can be admitted. In such cases all the employees are provided with keys that will unlock this door, or there is a spring latch upon it which can be worked from either side. The "sneak," under such circumstances, will place himself near to this door and wait until some one comes, who unlocks the door to obtain an entrance. As a rule the locks on this door are spring locks, and as soon as the clerk has passed in he will shut the door violently behind him, which will insure its locking without further attention on his part. But the sneak thief is there, and as the door bangs to, he inserts a wallet or a wedge of wood between the frame and the door, and this prevents its locking. To enter through this door is the work of a moment, and with the "stalls" at work in front the rest of the story is soon told, and in a few moments he emerges again with his booty concealed about his person, and no one suspicious of his presence.

The "stalls" have numerous expedients to resort to, all of which answer admirably the purpose for which they are designed. Sometimes they will enter the bank and engage the teller or cashier in the purchase of a draft for a certain amount, then hand over the money, part of which is in small bills. Upon being counted, the amount will be found to be short three or four dollars and this will give occasion for an argument and a recount in order to discover the missing money, and while this is being done, the object is accomplished, and the robbery is effected. Again, at times a government bond is purchased, or gold is asked for paper money, or change will be requested for a large note by a man who has one of his hands in a bandage, who will request the cashier or clerk to place the money for him in the inside pocket of his coat and then to button the coat over the concealed money; all these things occupy time, and attract the attention of the bank officer— both of which are valuable to the "sneak" who is intent upon securing the funds of the bank, and in which he is generally successful.

Sometimes the thieves notice a pile of money on the counter of the receiving or paying teller and close to the pigeon-hole through which those officers transact their business. The teller is generally stationed directly behind this pigeon-hole, so that there is no chance for the thieves to get the money without being seen. The main object to be achieved therefore is to get the teller away from that pigeon-hole, if only for a moment. To call the teller outside to a carriage would simply cause him to lock the wicket at the pigeon-hole and thus spoil the chances of robbery completely; to call him away to any distance would also result in the same thing. Now enters the stall with his suavity and ingenuity. We will assume that the money is near the receiving-teller's window and that no one is near either the window of the paying or receiving-tellers. The "stall" will take from his pocket a genuine ten or twenty dollar United States note and, stepping to the window of the paying teller, address that official about as follows:

"I have just been over to the United States Treasury, and they told me that this note is a counterfeit—and it being such a good genuine-looking note, I thought I would just step in and let you and the receiving-teller take a good look at it." The paying teller takes the note, and surprised at the genuineness of its appearance, calls the receiving-teller over to examine it.

As the receiving-teller leaves his position, the "sneak," who has been preparing himself by purchasing a soap box at some neighboring grocery, now proceeds to perform his duty. The "sneak," who has wrapped the box in newspapers, has been standing at a desk outside, busily engaged in counting some money. No sooner, however, has the paying teller answered the call of his associate, than the "sneak" noiselessly carries the box to the counter, and setting it on the floor, leaps upon it and in a twinkling has taken all the money within his reach which he can readily grasp. Stepping down as quickly, he walks out of the door carrying his box along with him. He does this in order to leave nothing behind him which would give a clue to the officers, who would seek out the grocer who sold the box, and thus obtain a description of the individual who purchased it.

Sometimes the money is placed a short distance from the window, too far away to be reached by the hand, and in that case a cane and sometimes two joined together with a screw, with an iron hook at the end, is used. It is astonishing how successfully the thieves have worked an operation of this kind, and frequently hours have elapsed before the loss is discovered, and then it is too late to determine how the money disappeared or by whom it was taken.

The above recitals detail fully the operations of sneak thieves upon the vaults and money of banking institutions, and we will now consider their modes of operating upon individuals.

Gentlemen who transact business with banks, safe deposit companies and other financial institutions of the country are especial object of attack from the sneak thieves. The manner in which this fraternity operate upon a gentleman, who is either making a deposit or drawing a check at a bank, is at once simple and generally successful, and many sharp business men, who have deemed themselves proof against the advances of the wary thief, have been robbed of large sums of money by a process which would seem to be almost impracticable.

In the thieves' parlance this operation is termed a "turn trick," and consists in the clever act of turning a man away from his money, in order to enable the thief to make off with it.

To illustrate: a man receives a check for a certain sum of money, and for the purpose of receiving notes for the oblong piece of writing which represents the amount to which he is entitled, he goes to the bank, and presenting his check to the teller, requests the money. The obliging official counts out the required number of notes to satisfy the claim of the gentleman, and politely hands them over to the waiting claimant. It is but natural that the receiver of the money should recount it, in order to be assured that no mistake has been made, and that he has received all that he was entitled to. In all well regulated banks, desks are provided for this purpose, and the gentleman carries his money over to the desk and proceeds to verify the count of the bank officer. Of course the thieves have watched this transaction very carefully, and when the gentleman lays his money upon the desk, they are prepared for action. We will assume that the gentleman has received five thousand dollars in ten dollar bills, and that they are in packages of five hundred dollars each. Placing the money in front of him, he takes one of the packages in his hand and proceeds to count. This is the thieves' opportunity. The "sneak" immediately takes his position behind the man, and in such a manner that he will not be seen on either side, the "stall" then appears, and dropping a ten dollar bill upon the floor on the opposite side from where the money is lying, and about three feet in the rear of the man at the desk, politely touches the man upon the shoulder and inquires: "Is that money yours, sir?" and then walks away. The man will instinctively turn round, and seeing the note upon the floor, with no one near to claim it, and impressed with the fact that he must have dropped it, will stoop to pick it up. As he turns around, the sneak who has been carefully watching his movements steps toward the money, and as the gentleman stoops, he raises about three-fourths of the pile of money, and at once makes his way rapidly out of the bank. He does not take all of the money, for the reason that if the man was to notice the entire disappearance of his funds, he would immediately rush for the door and seize the first man going out. If, however, he finds part of his money remaining, he may not at first glance notice any diminution of it, or if he does, he will naturally desire to see how much is gone, and that second look has occupied time enough to permit the thief to gain the street, and he is out of sight in a second.

The dropping of a bill is not the only means resorted to by the "stall," to attract the attention of the man to be robbed. Sometimes he will have a check drawn upon another bank; he will then approach the individual who is counting his money, and holding out the check, will inquire in the blandest tones:

"Can you tell me where I will go to find this bank?"

The gentleman thus addressed will naturally turn to see upon what bank the check is drawn, and as he does so, the "stall" will step back a short distance, which will require the man to turn almost completely around in order to read the check, and while he is doing this, the "sneak" makes off with his money.

Another method is to suddenly accost a man who is counting money, with the inquiry as to which pigeon-hole he will have to call at, in order to obtain a draft, thus causing the man to turn around in order to point out the particular window at which the inquirer is to call. Some men, out of a pure desire to be of service to their fellows, have been known, on the impulse of the moment, to leave their money, and walk partly across the banking-room in order to point out the exact window to the doubtful inquirer. It is needless to add that this evidence of politeness is sadly repaid by the thieves and that upon his return, he finds, to his dismay that his money has entirely disappeared.

The next individuals who receive the attentions of the sneak thieves are the depositors at a bank, and in many cases they have been successful in robbing a man in full view of half a dozen waiting depositors without anyone perceiving the transaction. The manner in which this is done is generally as follows: A depositor on entering a bank will remove his bankbook from his pocket, and take his place in the line of waiting depositors. At a number of banking institutions the receiving-teller, after receiving each deposit makes an entry in his book kept for the purpose, and which is generally near his elbow, on the desk. And this entry is frequently made after he has returned the bank-book to the depositor whose money he has taken. As soon as a depositor receives his book from the teller, he withdraws from the window and makes way for the gentleman behind him, who immediately steps forward and places his book in the pigeon-hole, awaiting his turn to be attended to.

This is what the "sneak" has been waiting for, and should the teller pause before taking the book of the new-comer, to make some entry into his own book, he attempts a robbery. The "stall" drops a bill on the floor and calls the gentleman's attention to it, and as he stoops to pick it up, the "sneak" steps up and in a flash makes off with the book which is lying in the pigeon-hole, and with its entire contents. The depositor, turning back to where he left book and money, will naturally come to the conclusion that the receiving-teller has the book, and no exposure is made until the teller requests the book of the surprised depositor. This style of robbery when cleverly executed has caused many a quarrel between depositors and receiving-tellers—for as soon as the teller has finished his entry in his own book, he will reach up for that of the next depositor, and not seeing it, will request that gentleman to hand it to him. The depositor will insist upon having passed it over, and the teller upon not having received it, and the controversy waxes warm in consequence. Meanwhile the thieves have made good their escape, and are probably regaling themselves upon the proceeds of their dishonesty.

There have also been many instances where young men, having been sent to the bank for money, and having received it in notes, not in packages, have been "turned" by a bill on the floor, and the thief has stolen the larger portion of the money already counted; the young man returned to his counting, and remembering the amount at which he stopped, has kept right on from the uncounted pile before him, and, finding the total correct, placed the money in his pocket, and returned to his place of business.

When the employer, however, attempts to verify the account, he finds a very large shortage in the amount. The young man is positive that he counted the money correctly, and is certain that he could not have been robbed, as he kept his hand upon the money all the way from the bank. The young man, however, has forgotten the note he found upon the floor. The employer revolves the matter in his mind, becomes suspicious, and sometimes he has the young man arrested, hoping thereby to induce him to make a full confession, and restore the money of the stealing of which he is entirely innocent.

Another phase of sneak thieving is in the bank, when the gentleman who receives the money upon a check, requests the obliging teller to wrap the amount up in a parcel for him. The teller complies with the request, and makes the usual neat package wrapped in brown paper. The "sneak," who has been watching every movement, and is fully prepared for an emergency like this, draws from his pocket a piece of wrapping paper of exactly the same color, and with the aid of a few old newspapers, soon constructs a package precisely similar to the one handed by the teller to the gentleman at the window. Should this gentleman by any accident, or for any purpose, set this package down for a single moment, the watchful "stall" and "sneak" are upon him, and ere one can realize it, the victim has been successfully "turned," and the "sneak" has replaced the bundle of money by the package of newspapers, and decamped. The reason for the substitution of a similar package is quite plain; for should the man miss the package, and find it entirely gone, he would immediately cause the arrest of both the thieves before they could get away; but by the means of a "dummy" package, men have been known to carry the valueless bundles of waste paper for miles, and never discover their mistake until reaching their destination.

Safe Deposit Companies.

ANOTHER prolific source of profit to the sneak thieves, but rather more delicate and difficult of accomplishment than those recited above, is the robbery of individuals whose valuable securities are deposited in the vaults of those estimable and responsible institutions known as "Safe Deposit Companies." In all the large cities there exists one or more of these substantial edifices whose strong vaults are carefully guarded, and where the man of means may securely place his valuable papers and securities for a nominal sum. The value of these institutions to people of wealth cannot be over-estimated, and the security they afford is well worth the small sum which is annually charged for the use of their vaults. The vaults of these institutions are filled with innumerable compartments or small safes in which the individuals deposit their securities, and each depositor is furnished with a key which will unlock the particular safe which has been assigned to his use. One or more sturdy and reliable officers are constantly on duty in these vaults, and as the depositors make frequent visits to their strong boxes these athletic guardians soon become familiar with the faces of their customers. Every safeguard is thrown around the property entrusted to the keeping of these Safe Deposit Companies, and it would seem almost an impossibility for any dishonest person to obtain admission to their vaults, and far more incredible that they should succeed in their efforts of robbery.

Yet notwithstanding the many precautions that have been taken, the crafty thieves have not only obtained access to these vaults, but in several instances they have succeeded in robbing unsuspecting depositors in a manner, which was both simple and reckless in the extreme. It is therefore a warning to both the companies and their depositors that the following expose of the movements of the sneak thieves is made.

In all these large institutions a room furnished with a number of small individual desks is set apart for the use and accommodation of their patrons, and the depositor, after receiving his strong box from the vaults, can take his treasures to one of these desks and there cut off his coupons or extract such securities as he may need for immediate use.

In order to reach this room, a depositor must pass an officer who is stationed at the gate leading to this apartment, and who will not permit anyone to enter with whom he is unacquainted or with whose face he is unfamiliar. It would seem to be therefore a most difficult task for the thief or thieves to obtain an entrance into these apartments, and it would appear as an act of foolhardy daring for any dishonest person to make the attempt. Such admissions, however, have been gained, and, I regret to say, successful robberies have been perpetrated within the closely guarded walls of these very chambers.

Among the large number of depositors of these institutions, there are many whose visits to the vaults are not very frequent, and sometimes two, or perhaps three months may elapse between their visits; as a consequence of this the gate-keeper is sometimes unable to recall his face immediately, and deeming it impossible that anyone not fully entitled to enter, should present himself, he simply asks the applicant if he is a depositor, and being answered in a confident affirmative, he allows him to enter without further questioning. This is particularly apt to be the case if he has recently stopped a depositor, who was determined to satisfy him of his right to enter. The officer has a certain amount of pride in his ability to remember faces, and rather than confess his ignorance, will sometimes allow individuals to pass him without opposition. The "sneak" knows this, and sometimes will put himself in the way of the officer so as to be seen by him, but without attempting to enter, and apparently engaged in business with the company of another nature.

About the time, however, that coupons are becoming due, and the number of visitors is considerably increased, the "sneak," accompanied by a "stall," will present himself at the gate, and in a matter of fact manner will request admission. In his hand he carries a number of huge formidable looking envelopes of various colors, and he greets the gate-keeper with an affable nod and a smile of recognition, that at once disarms suspicion, and without the slightest difficulty he is admitted to the room reserved for the accommodation of depositors. The "sneak" and "stall," once inside of the room, proceed immediately to an unoccupied desk, and spreading their papers out, indulge in an earnest conversation, apparently upon some matters of business. Sometimes they will be engaged in looking over and assorting some papers. This is continued until they notice one of the regular depositors with his tin box open before him, perhaps engaged in cutting the coupons from some of the securities which the box contains. Carefully watching this gentleman, they will ascertain whether the securities he is handling are of a negotiable character—particularly if they are government bonds, which are great favorites with the thieving fraternity. Satisfying themselves upon this point they will approach him, the "stall" upon some ingenious pretext will then attract his attention or "turn" him away from his box, and while this is being done the sneak reaches over and quietly secures a package or two from the box and quickly starts for the door. If the victim has already examined the package taken, he may close his box and return it to the vault without noticing his loss. Should this be the case, his surprise when next he has occasion to use these bonds may be better imagined than described. On discovering his loss at this late day, it will be impossible for him to remember the trifling circumstance of a stranger asking him a question several months before, and the result is that he will fall back upon the bank, and will be ready to swear that his box has been robbed since he used it the last time, and he will be absolutely positive that the bonds were in the box when he last put it away. Safe Deposit Companies have been known to cover such losses, rather than suffer the publicity and injury that would follow an allegation that their vaults were unsafe or that boxes intrusted to their keeping had been tampered with by dishonest persons.

In some cases, in order to avoid danger and loss in this manner, the companies have arranged small private apartments in their buildings, where a depositor can be perfectly alone, and can lock himself in while engaged in handling his valuable property, or in detaching the coupons from his securities.

From the above it will be seen that the utmost care is necessary to be observed by a person who avails himself of the conveniences of a Safe Deposit Company—and by instantly suspecting anyone who approaches them while engaged with their strong boxes, losses may be prevented and a successful robbery completely frustrated.

In appearance the "sneak mob" resemble a party of respectable business men, and their manner of conducting themselves fully tends to confirm a belief in their respectability. They are always well-dressed, but plainly and neatly so, and they never wear loud or decided colors or a profusion of jewelry. Never, if they can avoid it, do they come together while they are engaged at work—and this is done in order that in case of any accident or the arrest of anyone of the party, no connection will be discovered between him and his companions, which would lead to their arrest as associates. While working in the banks they assume an air of business activity, and either carry in their hands, bundles of papers and envelopes, or a small number of notes which they are apparently engaged in counting. While engaged in conversation with any person upon whom they are operating, should they notice that the party is suspicious or afraid of them, they upon the presentation of the first opportunity bow to the first fine-looking business man who may be near to them. The gentleman thus addressed will naturally return the bow from the mere impulse of politeness, and the party who may be watching the thief will thus be thrown completely off his guard—thinking as a matter of course, that if he is on such well-defined speaking terms with Mr. Money-bags or Mr. Good-credit—he must, of necessity, be above suspicion himself.

As a rule, the members of a "sneak mob" room in first-class hotels, and always in separate apartments. They invariably travel first-class, though they never appear to be flush of money nor act in any manner that will attract undue attention.

The above covers the general operations of the sneak thief, and his companions or stalls. A business man in his communications with banks and bankers, should always be upon his guard, and ever alert to the advances of those well-dressed sneaks whose general appearance and genuine air of business men are well calculated to deceive even the most careful. Do not stop to pick up notes that may be found upon the floor of banking house, and never suffer your eyes to lose their vigilant watch upon the money, you may be engaged in counting. If these instructions are remembered and followed, the sneak thief will soon find his gains decreasing and his occupation gone.

To illustrate more particularly the practical modes of operation by this class of criminals, in another direction, I will relate the incidents of a daring and successful robbery, by sneak thieves, which took place in the city of New York during the month of January, 1878, an account of which may prove interesting.

Mr. James H. Bloodgood was a large and extensive dealer in stocks, bonds and real estate, and in addition to this, was intrusted with the charge and management of numerous estates of wealthy decedents. His office was in one of the most active and bustling business portions of the city, within easy distance of the various exchanges and banks, and in a building occupied by a number of prominent men and business firms engaged in monetary transactions on a large scale. The interior of his office was furnished in a luxurious and expensive manner, with walnut furniture, velvet carpets and a general tastefulness of arrangement that gave evidence of both wealth and refinement. Two large and handsome burglar-proof safes, of the most recent invention, occupied positions in this office and contained many articles of commercial value and financial worth.

On the day on which the robbery occurred, Mr. Bloodgood and his confidential clerk were both busily engaged at their respective duties. The elder gentleman had just returned from a visit to the Safe Deposit Company, and had withdrawn about sixty thousand dollars worth of state bonds for the purpose of removing the coupons and collecting the interest which was then due. While he was thus engaged in detaching these coupons, a stranger entered the office and requested permission to consult a directory of the city, in order to ascertain the address of a gentleman whom he was desirous of finding. Mr. Bloodgood politely handed him the book, and after an examination of a few minutes, the stranger expressed his thanks and withdrew.

Shortly after this episode, the clerk was dispatched upon some errand, and during his absence another strange visitor came into the office, and inquired the value of a piece of property, which had been advertised for sale by Mr. Bloodgood. While this man was engaging Mr. Bloodgood in conversation regarding the merits of the property in question, that gentleman noticed that another person had entered the office, whose movements appeared to be suspicious.

The state bonds were at that time lying exposed upon a desk in the front part of the room, and Mr. Bloodgood, imagining danger, gazed scrutinizingly at the new-comer, who, seeing that his movements were observed stood still; apparently unconscious of the suspicions he had awakened. After a prolonged conversation about the terms of the sale of the property, the two strangers left together, and Mr. Bloodgood, finding that they were companions, thought no more of the singular actions of his visitor. The clerk returned soon after this, and Mr. Bloodgood then left his office to procure his lunch without mentioning the matter to the young man.

Within a few minutes after the departure of Mr. Bloodgood, a gentleman, whom the clerk instantly recognized as the individual who had previously inquired for the directory, came in and informed the young man that there was a lame gentleman in a carriage in front of the building who was desirous of seeing Mr. Bloodgood. After questioning the man, and learning from him that the business of the crippled caller was urgent, and that he was in a hurry, the clerk stated that he would go down and attend to his wants. He turned to get his hat from where it was hanging upon the wall, and as he did so the man went out through the door and disappeared. The clerk closed and locked the door of the office after him, and descended to the street, where he found a pale-faced gentleman in a carriage, who appeared to recognize him, and called to him to approach the window of the vehicle in which he was seated. The stranger explained that he desired to make a purchase of another piece of property owned by Mr. Bloodgood, and as he appeared to be perfectly posted as to its location, size and marketable value, the clerk suspected nothing, and their colloquy was quite prolonged. Finally, the invalid, having concluded all the arrangements that were considered necessary at that time, requested the clerk to mention the matter fully to Mr. Bloodgood when he returned, and then, putting his head out of the window, he directed the coachman to drive on.

As the clerk returned to his office he met the man who had conveyed the message to him coming down the stairs, but, thinking nothing of this, he continued his ascent, and arrived at the door of the office. Here he was confronted with a scene of confusion which at once filled him with alarm. The door of the office had been forcibly broken; the doors of the safes, which were always unlocked during the day, were standing wide open, and their contents scattered promiscuously about the floor. Hastily entering the room he discovered, to his further dismay, that the sixty thousand dollars worth of bonds were missing, and that the safes had been rifled of their valuable contents. Instantly his suspicions fell upon the man whom he had met on the stairs, and the lame man who had called him to the carriage, and giving a loud alarm he rushed frantically down the stairs in the hope of overtaking them before they had succeeded in getting away. He was too late, however. The carriage was standing a few doors from the office, but the invalid and his accomplice had disappeared. The driver, on being questioned, stated that he knew nothing of the man, except that he had been engaged to drive him to this locality, and that he had left the carriage a few minutes before, stating that he would shortly return.

Disconsolately the clerk made his way back to the despoiled office, where he was soon rejoined by Mr. Bloodgood, who had returned from his lunch in blissful ignorance of what had transpired during his absence. A hurried examination was at once made, and the result proved that bonds and securities amounting to nearly two hundred fifty thousand dollars had been carried off by the daring thieves.

In a state of excitement bordering almost upon frenzy, Mr. Bloodgood rushed to my Agency, and hurriedly detailed the facts above related, and requested that the most active measures should be immediately taken to discover the thieves and, if possible, to rescue the stolen property.

Anxious that no time should be wasted in getting to work, Robert visited the office of Mr. Bloodgood, and made a careful examination of the place. From what could be discovered, and further information that was given, it was evident that the work had been performed by a gang of expert sneak thieves, who had laid their plans with a skill which bespoke the ingenious and daring professional.

Prior to this occurrence I had received information of the arrival of several professional thieves of this particular character, and as many of these men were known to me from previous experience, it was resolved to look them up at once. Operatives were immediately dispatched to the localities which this class of thieves usually frequented, and Mr. George A. Bangs and my son Robert, made every preparation for a vigorous prosecution of our search.

Both Mr. Bloodgood and his clerk were fortunately able to give accurate descriptions of the men who had entered the office, and the clerk distinctly remembered the features of the alleged lame man with whom he had conversed while the robbery was being perpetrated. The hackman was also found, and his description of the man he had conveyed to Mr. Bloodgood's office agreed perfectly with that already given, and from all accounts which could be gained, I felt reasonably sure of the identification of the two men, if I could succeed in reaching them. These descriptions, however, and the knowledge I had previously gained, of the arrival of a certain party of thieves, some of whom were known to me, were all the clues that I possessed on which to build a plan of detection, but I resolved to push the matter with the utmost boldness, and eventually unearth the scoundrels if it was possible to do so.

There is a peculiar feature about professional sneak thieves, which is perhaps not generally known. They, as I have already intimated, form themselves into organized bands or gangs, and as a general rule establish their resting headquarters in New York or some other large city. From this point they travel throughout the country, ever on the alert for opportunities for stealing where violence is not necessary in order to effect their objects. These bands or gangs seldom exceed five men in membership, who constitute one of their number as a leader, and by whose name they are generally known. The commands of this temporarily constituted leader must be implicitly obeyed when they are at work, but in all other respects a perfectly equal co-partnership exists between them, and the spoils are divided in a fair and equitable manner. A number of these gangs had been seen in New York immediately prior to this robbery, and the investigations of my men during the three days that followed this event, proved conclusively that one of them had mysteriously disappeared from the city. A comparison of their descriptions fully confirmed our previous suspicion, and speculation soon resolved itself into a certainty.

The band, who had thus disappeared, was known to be composed of four men, who had been connected together and had been engaged in thieving practices for a number of years, and some of whom had on more than one occasion suffered imprisonment. The names of these suspected men were Henry Miles, James Dougherty, William Shields and Joseph Bennett, but their numerous aliases were ingenious and often euphonious.

Having decided definitely that these parties were the guilty ones, plans were at once set on foot which were believed would prove the most efficacious, in leading to the acquirement of reliable information of their whereabouts, and ultimately to their capture.

Full publicity had been given to the fact of the robbery, and the financial circles of the country had been furnished with a list of the securities stolen, and duly warned against negotiating any of them, in case they should be offered for sale; and having thus taken means to stop any disposition being made of the bonds, and to apprehend anyone attempting to sell them, we commenced our search for the criminals. Our only preliminary course under the circumstances was to inaugurate a vigorous and diversified system of shadowing. Every person known to have been in communication with these suspected parties was placed under the watchful surveillance of my operatives—men in almost every conceivable garb, visited the haunts of the criminal classes which infest a great city, and all who were recognized as previous associates of the robbers were closely watched by expert detectives, whose movements excited no suspicion, but who followed them through all their daily and nightly wanderings.

There was one man who was known to have been formerly a member of this particular band, and it was supposed that he might still be in communication with them. This man was named Edward Marston, and he was naturally made a special object of espionage by my watchful men.

After a guarded but persistent inquiry it was learned that Edward Marston had ostensibly given up the criminal life he had led for so many years and was now living in retirement with his family, in some respectable section of the city, the exact location of which could not at first be discovered. After a time, however, he was met upon the street by one of my men, and being stealthily followed was seen to enter a neat brown-stone residence in upper New York—being a portion of the city occupied almost exclusively by people of unquestioned respectability. His dwelling-place being thus fortunately ascertained, a watch was placed upon the premises and every one seen to enter or leave the house was shadowed by persistent detectives.

In the meantime, I had not been idle in other directions. All the police authorities in the various cities in the country had been communicated with; the suspected parties had been fully described, and they were requested to acquaint me of the fact, should any of them make their appearance in these localities, but as yet nothing had been heard from them from any quarter. Their escape and disappearance appeared to be as complete as it had been rapid.

After shadowing the residence of Edward Marston for nearly two weeks, our efforts were rewarded by the appearance of an individual who was destined to prove of great value to us, in the pursuit in which we were now engaged. This individual was none other than the reputed wife of Joseph Bennett, one of the suspected thieves. She was a dashing and beautiful young woman, and it was alleged had frequently assisted her husband in his nefarious work. This woman received a great deal of attention in a very quiet way from my men, and not many days elapsed before their vigilance was rewarded. From her actions it was evident that she was contemplating a journey. On one of her shopping excursions, she purchased a trunk which was sent to her place of residence, and at various times she made other purchases which indicated that she was preparing to leave the city. At length, on one bright sunny morning in April, Mrs. Bennett left her home in a carriage, on the top of which safely reposed the trunk which had been noticed by the detectives; and at a short distance behind her followed a gentlemanly looking fellow, whose occupation would not have been suspected, but who designed traveling by the same train that carried the dashing beauty, if it was possible to do so.

The lady drove to the ticket office of one of the railways, and the detective approached as near as possible in order to learn her destination. He was able to hear her inquire for a ticket to Baltimore, and he immediately purchased a diminutive piece of card-board which entitled him to travel to the same city. Following the lady into the train, the detective seated himself in the coach behind the one occupied by Mrs. Bennett, through the windows of which he could plainly keep her in view, and at the same time escape being seen by her.

No event of any importance transpired until the city of Baltimore was reached, and here Mrs. Bennett was met at the depot, by a man who was apparently awaiting her arrival, and who appeared to be well acquainted with her. They talked earnestly together for a few minutes, and then, making arrangements for the transfer of the lady's baggage, they proceeded to the Washington depot, where a ticket was procured for Petersburg, Virginia, and the detective, following her example, found himself again a traveler in company with the wife of the suspected thief.

Without accident or delay the city of Petersburg was reached, and the detective had the satisfaction of seeing the lady safely deposited at Jarrett's Hotel, before making any attempt at domiciling himself. Having entirely escaped the notice of Mrs. Bennett, and having attracted no unusual attention to himself, the operative at length decided to secure quarters under the same roof with the lady, and thus be enabled to note more particularly whatever transpired.

The next day the wisdom of our pursuit was proven, for the lady was then joined by her husband, and the operative immediately telegraphed this important fact to my New York Agency. Upon receipt of this intelligence, Robert, in company with another operative, set out to join the parties at Petersburg. The papers necessary to effect the arrest of the parties were duly procured, and my son and his associate arrived at Petersburg fully authorized and determined to act decidedly in the matter, should occasion warrant it.

At the depot they were met by the operative, who conveyed the gratifying intelligence that Henry Miles and James Dougherty had also arrived, and were now the guests of the same hotel with Mr. and Mrs. Bennett. To avoid a premature recognition, Robert located himself in a portion of the city, some distance from the hotel, and arranged for prompt communication in case Mr. Shields, the remaining member of the band, should make his appearance, or if the others evinced any disposition to leave the city.

This question was fully and satisfactorily decided on the following morning, when William Shields, looking as rosy and innocent as a child, arrived in town and proceeded directly to the hotel, where he was assigned a room in close proximity to the others who had preceded him.

The time for decisive action had now arrived, and after dark that evening, Robert procured the services of two members of the city police, and repaired to the hotel, directing the men to approach the premises singly, in order to avoid creating any curiosity or alarm. It was nine o'clock when they reached their destination, and one of my operatives who had been constantly on the alert, informed Robert that the entire party were now in the room occupied by Bennett and his wife, and were evidently having a very pleasant time.

Noiselessly the men ascended the stairs, and on arriving at the door of the room, Robert knocked sharply for admittance. The men were arranged directly behind him, in order to follow him in at once. So assured did the occupants feel of their immunity from pursuit, that without delay or inquiry, Shields sprang to the door, and

quickly unlocking it, stood gazing in stupefied astonishment at the scene which met his view.

Directing one of the men to secure him, Robert
pushed forward and entered the room followed closely
by the others. The party were all assembled, and from
appearances, had been engaged in a friendly game of
cards—while a decanter of liquor and several glasses
were arranged upon another small table in the room.

Bennett uttered an oath and sprang to his feet, as
if with the intention of offering some resistance to the
unwelcome intruders; but a glance at his two companions,
who had already been secured, warned him that any
attempt of that kind, would be as unavailing as it might
be dangerous. The officers before him were fearless and
determined, and finding how fruitless his efforts would be,
he quietly submitted and allowed himself to be secured.

The advent of the officers was a complete surprise to
the baffled thieves, for until their unexpected entrance, they
had no suspicion that their hiding-place was known, or, in
fact, that they had been connected with the robbery at all.

All their baggage was at once secured, and the entire
party were marched to the jail to await an investigation.
Robert and the Chief of Police then made an examination
of the effects of the prisoners, and their search was soon
rewarded with the most gratifying success. In the bottom
of the trunk, which Mrs. Bennett had brought with her, was
found a large tin box securely locked, and on forcing the lid,
the officers were delighted to find every identical security
that had been taken from Mr. Bloodgood's office. Not a
single bond was missing, and the recovery was a matter of
sincere congratulation to the men who had thus run the
thieves to earth. Nor was this all, for after removing the bonds

and papers of Mr. Bloodgood, they found another package neatly inclosed in an oil-skin wrapper, and marked in rough characters, with the words: "This is another lot of stuff." Upon opening this package, the detectives discovered the evidences of another large robbery, for its contents consisted of fifty-one thousand dollars in United States bonds.

Of course no further evidence was required of the guilt of the prisoners, and on the following day, they were conveyed to New York City where they were duly committed to await their trial.

Inquiries in regard to the United States bonds, so unexpectedly discovered, led to the revelation that the National Bank of Courtland, New York, had been robbed in the month of July preceding the theft of Mr. Bloodgood's securities, and a list of the stolen bonds corresponded fully with those found in the strong box at Petersburg. They were immediately returned to the bank officers, who were profusely grateful for their recovery, all hopes of which had long ago been abandoned.

The trial of the thieves took place in due time, and after a full hearing, the parties were convicted and sentenced to long terms of imprisonment. That prison discipline will be at all beneficial to them, I have grave doubts, and I shall not be surprised if at some time in the future, I am called upon to pursue them for similar crimes, and I sincerely hope with similar results.

Mr. Bloodgood's gratitude was unbounded, and his joy at the recovery of his lost securities was unrestrained, and I am of the firm opinion that never again in his business career, will he be indiscreet enough to allow valuable papers to be exposed in his office so recklessly as to tempt the cupidity of inquiring strangers.

Palace Car Thieves

TIME and again, and at intervals too frequent for the public safety, come the reports of robberies committed upon the various railways throughout the country, and in every instance they have been perpetrated upon the famous palace cars, which are now so extensively patronized by that portion of the public who are able to afford the luxury of their superior appointments. In my own experience, I have had a number of such cases reported to me, and in my perusal of the journals of the day, I have found the records of many more. For the benefit, therefore, of those who have occasion to make long journeys, and, perhaps, carry large sums of money about their persons, I will detail the methods of the expert thieves, whose operations have heretofore been only too successful, and whose detection at the time has seemed to be a matter of impossibility.

The thief who commits these acts of robbery is generally accompanied by his wife, or a female companion, although during their journey no one would suspect an intimacy, or even an acquaintance between them, so studiously do they avoid each other.

Their mode of proceeding is about as follows. In every case the thief and his companion endeavor to secure the forward sleeper, or the one immediately behind the passenger coaches, and they never engage a berth at the ticket office in advance. The reasons for this are obvious. In the first place, they would thus incur the risk of being assigned to the rear coach; but what is of more importance, there would be the imminent possibility of their being separated, and it is utterly essential to the proper working of their scheme, that both the man and the woman should be assigned to the same car.

The first consideration is for the female companion of the thief to inquire of the conductor whether she can secure the state-room for herself, or failing in that, an entire section is the last resort. Should she be successful in this, she informs her companion of the fact by a prearranged signal, and he then secures a berth for himself in the same car. Thus far successful, but little remains to be done until the passengers have retired. In the meantime, however, the lady being alone, and, as is generally the case, young and attractive looking, becomes the object of considerable solicitude and politeness from the conductor, who, like all of his sex, has a tender feeling for unprotected beauty. To this gentleman, however, she is but distantly polite, and a few slight evidences of her contempt for him are sufficient to convince him that his attentions in that quarter are distasteful, and he therefore leaves her alone.

To the colored porter of the car, however, she is graciousness itself, and he, being but human, soon succumbs to the sweet smiles that are so lavishly bestowed upon him by the pretty and unprotected woman, who seems to rely so implicitly upon him.

While the lady is thus deporting herself with the conductor and the porter, the male thief has not been idle. He has made a careful estimate of his fellow-passengers, and has satisfied himself as to which of them are the most profitable objects of attack.

As the night advances, the passengers become fatigued, and soon the porter is busily engaged in making up the berths for the night. During this operation the thief neglects no opportunity to carefully observe, if possible, the movements of those around him, in preparing themselves for slumber. He, however, retires with the others, and soon all is perfect quietness, broken only by the labored breathing of the sleeping passengers.

The time is now fast approaching for active work, and the female prepares to play her part with becoming tact. The conductor has already retired, and only the porter is awake, engaged in one of the manifold duties of his position. In a few moments he hears his name gently called, and he knows that the voice is that of his interesting and gracious lady-passenger. Leaving his work he hastens to her, when the lady, slipping a generous fee into his hand, complains of a sudden and distressing headache—and requests him to bring a cooling glass of water; when he returns with the desired beverage, she invites him into the room, and in a piteous tone of suffering, requests him to moisten her handkerchief with the water, and press it to her aching temples. Only too willing to be of service, the gentle-hearted porter complies with her entreaties, and for twenty minutes or half an hour, he is engaged in his kindly ministrations. This is the opportunity for which the thief has been watching, and the moment that the porter steps into the section occupied by the lady, he commences his operations. As he steps from his berth it would be impossible to recognize the smoothly shaven, and ministerial looking individual who had retired a short time before. In his stead there emerges from the flowing curtains a man wearing a large and bushy beard, which entirely conceals the lower part of his face, and with a large slouch hat, which gives him a brigandish appearance very diffcrent from the meekness of his previous deportment. He is fully dressed, and upon his feet are a pair of cloth slippers. His right coat-sleeve is rolled up as far as it can be done, and thus prepared, he springs for the couch of his first victim.

As a general thing he finds the pocket-book or roll of money under the pillow, and in that case his success is of easy accomplishment, a few deft movements and the property of the unconscious owner has changed hands completely and effectually. Many travelers, however, retire to their berths, without removing their clothes, but if they are sound sleepers they can be robbed as easily and successfully as a person who disrobes—provided they are not lying on the side on which they carry their funds. A few seconds will serve to enable a thief to ascertain the location of the valuables of a sleeper, and if they are unattainable, he does not waste any time upon that victim but immediately seeks another.

Should, however, a person who is being robbed, awaken, and the thief has calculated fully upon such a misfortune, his actions are as methodical as if no danger was to be apprehended. Affording the aroused sleeper an opportunity for a full view of his disguised face, the thief at once springs for the front platform. Here he quickly throws off his whiskers and slouch hat, and enters the passenger coach ahead in his natural state, with smooth face and a fine silk traveling cap, which he has worn under the slouch hat all the time. Proceeding to the smoking car, he coolly lights his cigar, and while he is enjoying the fragrant weed the alarm is being sounded. The porter and the aroused sleeper are both hurriedly questioned by the startled conductor.

"Did you obtain a fair look at him?" is almost the invariable question.

"Yes, and I would know him among a thousand," is the almost equally invariable reply.

They both agree upon their description of the black whiskered robber, and a journey is at once made through the forward cars, for the purpose of identifying the bold marauder. While this search is going on, the thief, throwing away his cigar, leaves the smoking car and goes back to bed, passing the searching party on his way, and without a suspicion of his identity being entertained for a moment.

When the thief and his companion purchase their tickets for the trip, they usually do so with the view of leaving the train at some large town or city, about, daylight on the following morning. Preserving their appearance of being utter strangers to each other, they proceed to different hotels, and when night again arrives they are once more upon the road, prepared to operate as circumstances shall provide.

The mode described above is about the general plan adopted by the expert thief for the robbery of the passengers on the sleeping cars, although occasionally a man will be found who operates entirely alone, and without any assistance whatever. This individual generally watches the ticket offices closely and should he notice a well-filled wallet in the hands of some prospective passenger, who is likely to prove a good mark, he immediately engages passage on the same train and in the same car with him. When all have retired for the night, the thief carefully watches the actions of the porter, while he is engaged in brushing the shoes of the passengers, and if a favorable opportunity occurs, his work is accomplished in a flash, and the other passengers are left entirely unmolested. Should the porter be too watchful while at work, the thief will patiently wait until the sable guardian is caught "cat-napping," and then his object is quickly accomplished. The thief who operates alone, observes the same precautions with regard to disguises as detailed above, and his mode of proceeding is similar in case of the awakening of his victim.

Sometimes, however, the sleeping cars are made to bear the burdens of the wrongs of others, and robberies which never occurred are alleged to have taken place while the poor victim was asleep. A few years ago a case of this nature was reported to me, in which the amount involved was quite considerable. From the statements made to me at the time, it appeared that a young and highly respected gentleman, was the victim of the car thieves to the extent of nearly fifteen thousand dollars. This young gentleman had been engaged for a long time with a prominent jewelry house in New York, and his especial branch of business was the sale of diamonds and other precious stones to the trade throughout the Western country. In the pursuit of his vocation he frequently carried with him valuable gems, which aggregated in value many thousands of dollars. Careful and responsible to a remarkable degree, he enjoyed the fullest confidence of his employers, and no accident or misfortune ever befell him until the event which I am about to relate. Mr. Potter, for that was the young gentleman's name, had been upon one extended and very successful trip to the west, and having finished up his business, in an entirely satisfactory manner, was returning to New York, with the balance of his valuable samples, which were worth fully fifteen thousand dollars. The journey had been made in safety and without accidents until on the morning just before his arrival in New York, and upon the New York Central Railroad. Mr. Potter had arisen after a refreshing night's slumber, and made his toilet, when on reaching under his pillow for his vest, in which he carried his valuable stock—he was horrified to find that this article of his wearing-apparel was missing. He had placed it there before retiring and now it was not to be found. The thief, whoever he was, had made thorough work of his robbery this time, and had not only carried off the valuable booty, but the clothing as well. Mr. Potter's consternation and agony were unmistakable, and after a hurried but thorough search of the train, which it is needless to say was unsuccessful, the young man hastened to the establishment of his employers and in tearful tones, related the story of his great misfortune.

Prompt measures were at once resolved upon, and Mr. Potter was immediately conducted to my Agency by the two gentlemen. Here he again related his experience, and the recital in no wise differed from his previous relation. By request he made his statement in writing, and although fearfully agitated, he was enabled to declare on paper the occurrences exactly as they had been detailed before. Mr. Potter's employers were questioned, and they both united in expressing the utmost confidence in the young man, and were very urgent in their request for a thorough and vigorous investigation into the matter at as early a day as possible.

Before evening every employee and passenger on the sleeping car which carried young Mr. Potter to New York, had been interviewed, and their statements obtained in writing, and ere Mr. Bangs closed his eyes in slumber that evening, he had evolved a plan of detection, which he was fully prepared to put into operation on the following morning. The result is soon detailed. Within a week it was demonstrated beyond doubt or question that the irreproachable and highly respected Mr. Potter had gambled away his valuable stock, in a single evening, in one of the prominent western towns, which he had been required to visit. Piece after piece, and stone after stone, had been staked at the gaming table and lost, and when morning dawned, he was a ruined man and a thief. Instead of acknowledging his crime, his mind was active in inventing expedients to escape the penalty of his dishonesty, and the story of the sleeping car robbery was the result. It was not successful, however, and on being confronted with the evidences of his guilt, the miserable man broke down and confessed everything. In less than a fortnight most of these stolen valuables had been returned to their owners, and the dishonest young salesman was suing for mercy at the hands of the trusting gentlemen whose confidence he had so meanly abused, and upon whose credulity he had so wantonly imposed.

The above is only one of many cases in which the guilty have attempted to screen themselves from the consequences of their crimes by charging others with the deeds they themselves have committed, and it is but the truth to say that in almost every case detection has followed, and the really guilty have been brought to punishment.

It is not the less true, however, that expert thieves find in the numerous and handsomely appointed palace cars, a bountiful field for their work, and the traveler under all circumstances must needs be very careful in the disposition of his valuables and money when he retires. Should a thief be discovered in the act, be assured that the smooth-faced man, who has only been in the smoking car, knows more about it than he cares to tell, and if there is an interesting invalid lady on the train, experience will certainly prove her complicity in the crime.

In case of a robbery being discovered, therefore, in the morning, watch the passengers who leave the train early, and see if a gentleman whose clerical appearance would disarm suspicion, and a well-dressed lady, who has claimed the kindly ministrations of the porter during the night, are not among the number. If so, rest assured that this delectable couple know more about your missing valuables than any other living human being. The conductors and porters of the palace cars are, as a rule, I am glad to say, honest and above suspicion, and the thieves must be looked for elsewhere.

If the traveler, therefore, will take due precautions before retiring, or failing in that, will, if a sufferer, follow the directions I have given above, robberies will become few indeed, and the perpetrators can be readily detected, and promptly punished.

Steamboat Operators

THE traveling public of all kinds and classes seem to have been selected by the thief as fair victims, and every mode of travel is associated with more or less danger, from the presence of these dishonest experts. Upon the high seas, in the railway carriage, and upon the palatial boats that ply the waters of our large navigable rivers, the thief is invariably found, and his operations are untiring. Many unsuspicious voyagers have been made the victims of this lawless fraternity, and upon discovering their losses, are unable to recall a single individual, upon whom their suspicions would fall, with any reasonable degree of certainty. Men, also experienced travelers, who have taken every legitimate precaution against robbery, have been victimized as readily and successfully as their more unsophisticated neighbors, and have been equally at a loss to identify the thief, or to point out the individual who might be suspected of the crime.

The numerous vessels that ply upon the waters of the Mississippi River, have perhaps afforded a more bountiful harvest to the thieves than any others, and for that reason have been more generally selected by the experts. Voyagers are numerous, and in the main they are disposed to carry large sums about their persons, consequently the thief usually finds a passage upon one of these boats a fruitful source of profit.

It seems almost incredible, the degree of immunity from detection which these pilferers enjoy, yet it rarely happens that one of them is apprehended, and then, it is principally because his countenance has become familiar to the officers, and his previous presence on the boat has generally been followed by losses to the other passengers.

The steamboat-thief usually travels and operates alone, as from the nature of his business, he requires no assistance, and the presence of a partner might only lead to suspicion. He is generally a person of good address and apparently a well-to-do gentleman who may be traveling either for business or pleasure. He is polite in his deportment, suave in his manners, and from his appearance and actions would never be supposed to be the villain he really is. As most of these boats are provided with watchmen, the first difficulty experienced by the thief is to secure either the absence or the obliquity of these officials. As is generally the case, however, he finds but little difficulty in accomplishing his purpose in this direction. The men usually employed in such positions are as a class, of exceedingly extravagant habits, and their pay is entirely inadequate to enable them to gratify their expensive taste and to maintain their luxurious notions of living. As a consequence of this, the thief usually finds that a wise bestowal of a twenty or fifty dollar bill is often productive of wonderful results.

It must be noted, however, that there are many honorable exceptions to this rule, and that a majority of the officers, are men of the most sterling honor and unimpeachable integrity, whose silence or temporary absence could not be purchased at any price, or under any circumstances. It is unfortunate however, that there are numerous exceptions to this rule.

Prior to commencing his work, the thief has several important preliminaries to arrange, before he can rely upon successful operations. One of these—the "fixing" of the watchmen—I have mentioned. He must also observe the passengers carefully, in order to ascertain who among the number, will most certainly prove the most remunerative "marks" or objects of attack. He is enabled to do this very easily and very satisfactorily on the average boat.

Stationing himself within close proximity to the clerk's office, he can safely watch every passenger who purchases a ticket or secures a stateroom. From the personal appearance, and from the display which the purchaser makes of his money, added to the long experience of the thief, he is thus enabled to discover not only the individual to be robbed with advantage, but also the number of the state-room he is to occupy. The keys to these rooms are usually hung upon an ornamental rack, arranged for the purpose, and in full view of the observant passenger. By these means the victim is both "marked" and located.

As the locks to these state-rooms are mere pretenses, in fact, which simply ensure privacy and not safety, the thief requires but a single instrument to assist him in his work. This instrument is a pair of the indispensable nippers—and it frequently happens that the use of this implement is unnecessary. Most of the passengers have a deep-seated dread of fire, while on ship-board, and many of them leave their doors unlocked, so that in case of an alarm, no impediment will prevent them from reaching the deck at the earliest possible moment.

Having determined which of the passengers he will operate upon, the thief occupies his time in polite conversation or in reading until the time for retiring arrives. The most experienced and expert operators generally commence their work at about one o'clock in the morning. He removes all his superfluous articles of clothing, retaining only a woolen undershirt and his pantaloons. The reasons for this are two-fold—in the first place he is enabled to move about readily and without making the slightest noise, and in the second place, if any of the officers or waiters should observe him coming out of a state-room, they would naturally imagine that he was in search of the water-closet, and pay no attention to him, and he invariably seeks that locality, if he attracts the notice of officials. It will be remembered that these state-rooms have two doors, one of which opens into the cabin or saloon, and the other upon the outside into the passage-way which extends around the railing or gunwale of the boat. If the thief is working upon the same side of the boat on which his own state-room is situated, he always enters and leaves from the outside door and never under any circumstances from the inside or cabin. The labor of the steamboat thief is much lightened from the fact that passengers have but one place to hide their money, and that is under their pillows. They cannot put it under their mattress as in hotel-apartments, for the reason that the berths are furnished with but a single mattress which rests upon springs. This the thief regards as an evidence of great consideration and kindness on the part of the boat company, and his gratitude is so great that he never attempts to rob any of the officers.

Obtaining an entrance into a state-room through the open door, or by the aid of his nippers, he at once places upon his face a crape mask which entirely conceals his features, without interfering in the least with the clearness of his vision. A hurried examination is made of the clothing, and then if nothing is found, he carefully and swiftly inserts his bare arm under the pillow, and silently draws forth the coveted wallet. A first-class thief of this branch of the profession will never take jewelry under any circumstances. Securing the wallet he makes his way on the outside to his own state-room, and then applies what is known as the "weeding" process. "Weeding" consists in extracting all the large bills from the wallet, and substituting small ones—with which he is always supplied— so that the bulk will be about the same as it was before. Hastily returning to the victim's state-room, he replaces the wallet, and then seeks for other prey—all of which are treated in a similar manner until prudence calls a halt. The advantage of this "weeding" operation is, that passengers usually carry sufficient small change in their pockets to defray the expenses incidental to their trips, and finding their wallet or pocket-book apparently in the same condition as they left it—their loss is seldom discovered until they leave the boat, and then, as a matter of course, the thief has vanished to parts unknown, and the poor victim is utterly unable to account for the strange metamorphosis which has taken place in his money.

Should the loss, however, be discovered before the landing of the boat, and an alarm sounded, the thief himself is among the loudest to proclaim his own loss, and to demand restitution from the officers or the immediate apprehension of the unscrupulous appropriator of his money.

The reason for putting on the crape mask, *after* the thief enters the state-room of his victim, is that in case he finds the occupant awake, he immediately steps back, and begging the gentleman's pardon, says that he was just returning from the water-closet, and has made a mistake in the room. If this excuse is received in good part by the disturbed passenger, all is well and he continues in his work—never, however, troubling that party again during the night. If, on the contrary, the wakeful voyager is suspicious, the thief stops his labors at once, immediately retires to bed, and he will leave the boat at the first landing that is made. It will be seen therefore that the excuse of mistaking the room for his own would prove a very absurd one, if the person making it, presented himself with a crape mask upon his face.

The rapidity and expertness of these thieves are remarkable, and frequently but a few seconds are required to relieve a sleeper of his money pouch, and in a half hour's active work, a thief can rob a dozen rooms and effect all the changes and returns that are necessary to secure him from suspicion or detection. It is a matter of fact, however, that none but the most expert professionals adopt this line of operation. Many cases have been reported to me in which the despoiled traveler did not discover his loss until he had reached his destination, and frequently his home—and consequently, but little publicity was given to the robbery. This, it is needless to say, is much to the advantage of both the successful thief and the corrupt watchman, for in case of immediate discovery an investigation would be made, the result of which would be disastrous to the individual whose duty it was to be on the alert, and to preserve the safety of the sleeping voyagers.

There are, however, a few river thieves who may be regarded as second-rate operators, and these individuals will rob a passenger of everything in sight; money, jewelry, papers, and anything that purports to be of value; but never attempt to take anything from under the pillows of their victims from their lack of sufficient nerve, and the necessary amount of experience.

Should a first-class thief discover one of this latter character on a boat, and he is quick to do so, he at once approaches him, and firmly cautions him against carrying on his depredations while on the trip, and then, with a burst of generosity, will bestow upon him a sum of money, and promise more when the trip is over, and the work is done. This caution is always accepted, and by this means he prevents the mistakes of an inexpert operator, whose detection would be compromising to himself, and secures the privilege of monopolizing all the fat wallets which may be within the range of his operations.

In order, therefore, to be secure from the depredations of these marauders, I would warn all passengers upon the river boats, to carefully secure their money and valuables about their persons, and to lock their doors carefully when retiring. In these days of depravity and wickedness it is dangerous to trust to any ideas of assured safety, and the necessity for caution in making traveling acquaintances is always imminent. The smoothest tongue, and the fairest face may belong to the most desperate criminal, and an intimacy is sure to result in disaster.

I remember a case which occurred some years ago, when gambling was much practiced upon these boats, and when large sums of money were frequently won and lost upon a single night. Upon the occasion I refer to, there were three noted gamblers upon the boat, and during the evening these men succeeded in each winning a considerable amount of money from their unsuspecting fellow passengers. On the boat was a middle-aged clergyman, whose smoothly-shaven face and sanctimonious air proclaimed him to be one of the most orthodox of religious teachers. In quiet but decided tones he condemned the practice of gambling, and with solemn words of warning he endeavored to induce his companions to desist from indulging in the vices and hazards of play, all to no avail, however. The fascination was too great to be overcome, and with a sad face the holy man withdrew from the cabin, and sought communion with his thoughts on deck. When midnight arrived, however, and the games were closed, many of the passengers, whose whitened faces and glassy eyes betokened loss and remorse, were inclined to wish that they had listened to the admonitions of the warning clergyman. In the morning there was a loud alarm, and a hue and cry that rivaled bedlam with its confusion. The winning gamblers were wild and furious; oaths and imprecations broke from their lips in an incessant torrent, and dire vengeance was threatened upon some one whose actions had caused this strange uproar.

Inquiry developed the fact that during the night the state-rooms of the successful gamblers had been entered.

They had drank deeply, and therefore slept soundly, and when they awoke in the morning, they discovered to their dismay that their enormous winnings of the night before, together with their own money, had disappeared. An investigation followed, and then it transpired that the solemn faced clergyman had left the boat just about daylight, and had left behind him in his state-room the following epistle:

"To the children of the Evil One—Beware of the vices of gambling; for if you earn the wages of sin, the Christian minister will levy the toll of the devil.

ELDER SHORTSNIFFLE."

This, no doubt, fully explained the cause of the disappearance of the money, and the departure of the robber. The clerical looking monitor had decamped with nearly fourteen thousand dollars, and, so far as I know, was never apprehended.

House Breaking

AMONG the numerous branches of criminal practice in existence at the present day, there is one that seems destined never to die out or to fall into disuse, as long as humanity abide in habitations. From the very first inception of crime, this particular class, viz: the house burglars and midnight robbers, have existed, and their operations reach all classes of the community. Anyone, be they of high or low degree, who may unfortunately possess anything worth stealing, is liable to the unexpected and unwelcome visits of the housebreaker and the burglar. Locks and chains, bolts and bars, alike are of no avail in preventing the entrance of these midnight robbers. When darkness and silence are brooding over the city—when happy families have composed themselves for the peaceful slumbers which a day of toil has earned, the cracksman sallies forth, and while a world is wrapt in dreams, he noiselessly pursues his ignoble calling. Silently he plunders his unconscious victims, and then stealing away he leaves to the light and sunshine of another day the discovery of his visit and the losses which have followed his intrusion.

Dickens has immortalized a Bill Sykes and a Toby Crackitt, and through his wonderful genius we have learned much of the social life of this class of criminals, and it is a lamentable fact that these two characters are not isolated instances or mere creatures of the imagination. Every city is swarming with a horde of these reckless men who live by plundering their unfortunate neighbors in the darkness of the night.

Sleeping or carousing during the day, when honest men are toiling for the rewards of their labor, and the sustenance of life—these desperate prowlers crawl from their lairs when the midnight bells are tolling, and like the wolves of the forest seek their prey.

To prevent the depredations of these thieves seems to be almost impossible, and incessant vigilance and prompt punishments when detected have proven to be the only safeguards against their successful operations. While therefore, I am unable to prescribe the infallible ounce of prevention, I may at least suggest the homely pound of cure, and by acquainting the public with the mode of operation of these criminals, I may serve to promote the detection of the offenders by showing how their depredations are committed.

Romance and tradition have for a long period of time, accredited the cracksmen with being the most expert in their profession, but the experiences of late years have dispelled this delusion, and English and American detectives alike, have conceded that for perfect and ingenious work the American house-breaker is far more expert and daring than his transatlantic competitor. This distinction is by no means an honorable one, but that it is justly deserved, the records and detective experiences of both countries abundantly prove.

The English burglar spends more time in watching and locating the policemen and watchmen upon the outside of the premises he designs to enter, and in getting his numerous and superfluous tools ready for manipulation, than the American would require to effect an entrance and rob an entire house. The English thief, like his more honest compatriot, is slow, methodical, and above all, a devotee to rule and precision. The American, on the contrary, only considers the quickest practical way of securing his object and adopts it at once. The Briton invariably travels with his gang of three and often four members, while the Yankee in any case never requires and will not accept the services of more than a single partner. The case has yet to be recorded where an English cracksman ever attempted a midnight robbery alone and unassisted, but the instances are numerous where an American burglar has repeatedly effected hazardous operations without aid or help from anyone. These, of course, are cases in which the most expert or the most reckless have distinguished themselves, but as a general rule the American house-breakers travel in couples and their work is usually quickly, cleverly and thoroughly executed.

Of late years, through the vigilance of the police and detective authorities, the residents of large and populous cities have rarely been troubled by these unwelcome visitors, but those of the larger towns and villages are perpetual sufferers from their unexpected incursions. American burglars of the advanced type of the present day, have been known to deliberately plan a complete tour of burglaries, and their track could be legibly traced from New York to Chicago, and the more ambitious and thriving villages of the far West. It must not be imagined that these are mere random selections, or the result of ignorant guess work. On the contrary, every house that has been entered along the route has been carefully examined in advance, and the preliminaries arranged with a nice regard for successful and fruitful results.

The usual plan of these knights of darkness, who decide to work their way through the country, is to delegate one of their number to travel in advance, and by stopping a day or two in each place, and making ingenious inquiries from the keepers of saloons, hotel clerks and others, gain a complete knowledge of the wealth and habits of the most prominent residents of the localities in which he may rest. Obtaining this necessary information, this advance agent awaits the arrival of his partners, and when they appear upon the scene he points out to them the most available objects of attack, acquaints them with the details he has acquired, and then leaves the town himself, upon the next train. The reason for this is that should the mysterious appearance and questions of this man lead to his being suspected, should he be hunted down in the event of a pursuit, he can readily prove that at the time the robbery was committed, he was far distant from the scene, and quietly enjoying himself at a hotel in an entirely different locality. Under these circumstances it would be impossible to connect him with the crime, and his innocence is clearly established.

Another consideration of importance to the thieves is to select a town where a railroad train will pass through during the early hours of the morning, as this enables them to get safely away, frequently before the robbery is discovered, and certainly before suspicion attaches to them. As they are not burdened with any amount of superfluous tools or baggage, and never carry away any stolen articles but money, bonds or valuable jewelry, their appearance would not be noticeable and their baggage would be light.

If the burglars are about to attempt operations upon a place, about which they have received no definite information, and are in ignorance of the general character and wealth of their victims, they usually select some first-class block, and if there is an empty house in the vicinity, they will enter this, and then from the rear of this building operate upon their chosen mark from the back entrance. If, however, the houses are all occupied, which is generally the case, they will endeavor to secure a furnished room or board and lodging in some part of the block in question, and if they succeed in this, they make it a rule never to attempt to rob any of the inmates of the house in which they may be domiciled, no matter how great the temptation, for this would at once lay them open to suspicion.

The tools which are used by an expert American house-breaker are very few, and consist of a very light and ingeniously constructed folding ladder, about thirteen feet long, which can be folded up to the length of two feet, and readily packed in an ordinary trunk or valise, two small jimmies, a pair of nippers, a small gimlet, a set of small bureau picks, a jointed key, a thin glaze knife, some common matches and a few yards of strong twine. Thus equipped, he is prepared to plunder an entire town, if sufficient time is afforded him.

If the burglars have secured lodgings in the block, they generally commence operations as early as possible after the inmates have retired to rest. The man who is to enter the building dresses himself in soft woolen clothes, they making little or no noise in the apartment of the sleepers upon whom he intends to work. It has been demonstrated that in the stillness of midnight or the early hours of the morning, the rustling noise made by a starched white shirt has frequently aroused the sleeper, particularly if a female, from a sound slumber, and has often led to detection. On entering the house the burglar immediately discards his shoes and operates in his stocking feet.

After thus preparing themselves, the thief to whom has been delegated the performance of the outside work, quietly leaves his room, and sneaking down stairs opens the back door. Ascertaining that the coast is clear, he gives the signal to his companion, who, taking his folding ladder and other tools with him also descends to the yard of the premises they occupy.

Preferring to work as far away from their own quarters as possible, they scale several intervening fences or light walls, until they reach the desired house, and then commence their work upon the back door. If this door is not bolted an entrance is effected in a moment, but if it is thus secured, they have recourse to the window—and if that can be readily opened with the glaze knife, they gain admittance to the house as quickly as they could do had they used their nippers upon the lock of the door.

If the window, however, is tight or swollen, and the glaze knife cannot be used, and if the wind is favorable, they noiselessly raise their folding ladder to the sill of the window upon the next floor. This occupies but a few minutes, and as these windows are seldom fastened, many of them not being supplied with any fastenings whatever, they speedily effect an entrance. As soon as they have entered the building in this manner, the thief makes his way down stairs and quietly unfastens the front parlor window and shutters. This is done in order to deceive the inmates of the house and the police authorities, for when an examination takes place, they invariably arrive at the conclusion that the robbers must have gained an entrance from the front—never for a moment suspecting any of their neighbors, as the back door and rear part of the house is always found intact.

His next move is to unbolt the back door, and if the fences can be scaled easily or there is an alleyway in the rear of the house, he folds up his ladder and sends it back to their lodgings by the outside worker. As soon as the outside man has returned the ladder safely to his quarters, he hurries back, and is then stationed at the front door on the inside. Drawing the bolts, he stands with the key in his hand ready for an alarm. Should this be given by the inside thief while he is at work up stairs, his companion instantly unlocks the front door and throws it open, and then quickly and noiselessly springs for the back door. Opening this door, and stepping into the yard he inserts his nippers over the key from the outside, and when his disturbed partner appears and passes out, he closes the door gently and locks it from the outside with the nippers. They then sneak away and return to bed as quietly and easily as though nothing unusual had occurred.

If a policeman is attracted by the alarm and makes an investigation, on finding the front door open he naturally infers that the burglars have escaped by that means of exit, and in this view he is sustained by the inmates of the house who have found the back doors and windows securely locked and fastened.

After a thief has entered a house and commenced to work, the first and most important question is to discover where the valuables are kept. As the front sleeping-room upon the second floor is usually occupied by the head of the family, this is generally the first point of attack. If the door is simply locked, the nippers are brought into play and the key is turned as softly as though operated upon the other side, and the door is opened. Sometimes the door is fastened with a bolt and then the "jointed key" is used. This instrument is shaped and formed as follows:

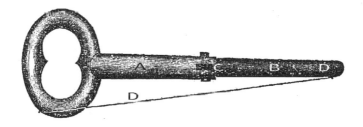

A represents the stock—B the inside lever—C the joint—and D is a wire attached to the end of the lever to draw it down when inside the door.

Obtaining the location of the bolt a hole is bored through the door, sufficiently large to admit the key. The joint then having passed through the door, the wire is drawn and the lever is thus brought to a right angle with the stock of the key, and directly against the handle of the bolt. A "simple twist of the wrist" is all that is necessary and the bolt is shot back.

Some people, however, have this door fastened with a bolt and chain, a staple being fastened in the door post to hold the end of the chain and the other end of the chain being placed in a slide, which is fastened upon the inside of the door. This chain admits the door being opened a certain distance, but not sufficiently wide to permit a man to enter. The burglar's methods of overcoming this obstacle, are simple and invariably successful. He simply opens the door wide enough for him to obtain the location of the bolt, and then boring a small gimlet hole over the spot—a strong thin wire is inserted through the hole and attached to the knob of the slide. The door is then closed and a gentle pull upon the wire draws the chain from the slide and it drops down, thus allowing free and uninterrupted entrance to the ingenious burglar.

Once in the room the clothing of the gentleman of the house is carefully searched. Bureau drawers are noiselessly opened by the aid of lockpicks, and pillows are carefully examined for hidden valuables. Thus from one room to another, the thief makes his tour of the inviting portions of the house, and when he has finished his investigations, he joins his "pal" at the front door.

They then take their departure by the back door, which they carefully lock behind them, and should time permit they will make an attempt upon another house in the same locality.

Sometimes in working on houses that are surrounded by soft and yielding ground, in which the shoes they wear would make an impression which might lead to detection, they wear extraordinarily large shoes, and after getting a short distance from the spot, throw them into a neighboring well. As a general thing, should the footmarks be noticed, suspicion falls upon some Negro, as a white man would scarcely wear such mammoth foot covers as those whose impressions are left in the ground.

The devices resorted to by the house-breaker are both numerous and ingenious and vary from the ideas given above, as the necessity of the emergency requires. Sometimes their entrance is effected through the scuttle in the roof, which they are enabled to reach by securing an unoccupied house in the vicinity, and then by crawling over the roofs of the intervening houses, reach their points of attack without attracting the attention of any out upon the street. In these cases, as in all others, measures are at once taken to provide a means of escape, and before operations are commenced, the front door and other points of egress are carefully prepared for their departure. In case of detection while at work, the thief will never retire through the roof, but will endeavor to mislead both the police and the inmates of the house, by opening the front door and escaping at the rear.

Back windows are frequently pried open with the aid of the strong and ingeniously constructed "jimmy," and in some cases the burglar obtains admission to a house in the daytime and conceals himself in some unoccupied room until the family have retired, when he issues from his place of hiding and ransacks the premises. Dishonest servant-girls too, have proven of valuable assistance to these thieves, and through their efforts, burglars have gained an entrance into premises which otherwise would have resisted their most persistent efforts. It has frequently been developed that these girls have been the wives, mistresses and relatives of the thieves, and that they have engaged service for no other purpose than to further the efforts of the men with whom they were associated, to plunder the families who have employed them.

Of course there are innumerable other methods adopted by this fraternity of dishonest men and women, and their processes vary according to the skill and ability of the parties engaging in the work. From boys in their teens to men whose hairs are whitened with age, the ranks of the house-breakers are filled, and their efforts against the public safety are unceasing.

I have thus described the general mode of working of the expert house-breaker of the present day, although much of their success depends upon the quick and noiseless movements of the thief himself, which are impossible of description and must be left to the imagination of the reader. To be able to pick a lock, to open a bureau drawer and rifle its contents, to search beneath the pillow of a sleeping victim, are all points of the profession upon which I cannot dilate intelligently, but that these men are constantly plying their vocations is fully proven by the records of our daily journals.

To house-keepers, therefore, I say, do not neglect the proper safe-guards before retiring for the night, and in case of detecting robbers in your house, do not search for your thief from the front door because you find it open, or upon the street; but rather seek the rear of your premises, and the chances are largely in favor of finding the disturbers of your sleep and the plunderers of your home, engaged in the attempt of scaling your fence and escaping by that means to their convenient hiding-place in the immediate vicinity.

Confidence and Blackmail

OF all the criminals of which I have attempted to write, the most insidious and pernicious are the confidence man or woman and the blackmailer. The confidence operator of which I shall speak first, is one of those insinuating personages who approach unsuspicious people in their daily walks, and sometimes at their places of business, and who by artfully identifying themselves with their personal affairs and business arrangements endeavor to so win their confidence that they may impose upon their credulity to their own dishonest profit.

The confidence game is generally practiced in large cities, and upon verdant looking strangers, whose manners and attire evince the easy-going and susceptible victim, though occasionally he will be found traveling through the country, and imposing upon the honest and industrious farmers and country store-keepers. One of the latest dodges of the confidence man has been recently brought to light, in which it was found that several wealthy farmers had been defrauded by the wiles of this fraudulent practitioner. The operator, in this instance, was a fine looking and clerical appearing old gentleman, who traveled through several counties in Illinois, and who pretended to be engaged in buying sheep from the breeders in that section of the country. In addition to this occupation, the venerable old swindler announced himself as a warm advocate of certain needful reforms of a public nature, in which all good citizens ought to be interested. He carried with him a number of petitions addressed to the legislature of the state, requesting them, among other things, to reduce taxation, and the salaries of public officers, and one to tax church property the same as other real estate. As may be imagined, he obtained numerous signatures to such important documents, and, in many instances, he succeeded in deftly transforming the simple petition, which the public-spirited farmer had duly signed, into a promissory note for a moderate sum of money, on which the signature of the farmer could not be disputed, from any doubt of its genuineness. These notes would then be transferred to innocent purchasers, whose knowledge of the makers of the notes was such that they willingly received their promises to pay, and loaned their money without a moment's hesitation. By this little scheme the daring swindler realized several thousand dollars before his operations were detected and by that time the smooth-tongued confidence man had disappeared effectually from the neighborhood and all search for him proved fruitless.

A Social Leper.

CRIME, I regret to say, is not entirely confined to the male portion of humanity. It is true that a woman does not often make a successful burglar or bank-robber. She is scarcely, if ever, discovered in attempts at forgery or garroting, but there are many other phases of criminality in which she figures prominently, and with as much effrontery as a man. I am reluctant to confess it, but her fair fingers have more than once been bathed in blood, and even when not an active participant in murder, how many times has she appeared if not as a conspiring abettor, at least as the primary and impelling cause. A visit to our prisons will convince the most doubtful, of the truth of this statement, and there will be found numbers of the so-called "fair sex" who have lived long lives of sin and shame.

Her favorite occupation, when criminally inclined, seems to be that of the sneak thief, the pickpocket, the confidence woman, and the blackmailer—the last being one of the most pernicious of criminal practices, and it will be found that, like the criminal man, the criminal woman preys upon humanity with all the rapacity of the vulture.

One of this latter class lately came under my observation, and her experiences I will relate here. For genuine romantic deviltry, and unscrupulousness, her equal is very rare, and yet she pursued her way so quietly, that few, except those immediately concerned in her movements, were aware even of her existence. Helen Graham was the name she assumed, and she was truly a beautiful woman. Her eyes, which were large and of the color of the hazel, beamed with a bright softness that won the hearts of those around her. Her fair face was crowned with a wealth of hair, and her cheeks flushed with the ruddy hue of health and beauty. Her voice was low and musically sweet and plaintive, while her language and address were full of that refinement which only education can give. Her slight but graceful figure, was draped with a quiet taste that was at once becoming and attractive, and in fact, to all outward appearances Helen Graham was a lovely woman, who might have gathered around her hosts of friends and admirers, and shone in the most brilliant circles of refined society.

And yet despite all these advantages and attractions, this beautiful woman, at the time I write of her, was arraigned as a criminal, and was compelled to answer for a crime which she had committed. Her eyes were filled with tears, and in a sobbing voice she entered her plea of "not guilty." As she sank back into her seat, and buried her face in her handkerchief, she was the object of universal sympathy. She was accused of assaulting a prominent and respectable citizen of New York, in a manner which might have resulted in serious consequence. She had thrown into his face a package of cayenne pepper, and when arrested for this offense, had openly accused the assaulted man of insulting her by making indecent proposals to her. As may be imagined a charge of this character urged against a gentleman whose high honor and respectability had been above reproach, had the effect of injuring him to a great degree, not only in his business, but among his social acquaintances. Friends were estranged from him, and he was regarded with disfavor by many who had heretofore courted his friendship and admired his sterling qualities. His only defensive course, therefore, was to cause the arrest of his fair assailant, the maintenance of his own character required it, and the preservation of his good name rendered it a necessity.

Howard Ingalls was the name of the gentleman who thus appeared as the accuser of the beautiful prisoner, who had excited the admiration and the sympathy of those who had gathered to hear the particulars of her trial. As this gentleman arose to give his testimony, it was noticed that his face wore a careworn look, which bespoke the great mental suffering which the vile charges of this woman had occasioned him.

In a frank, honest manner, Mr. Ingalls related his story. The young lady had called upon him at his office and had asked him for a situation, at the same time relating a pitiful story of her necessities. Something in her manner, however, led him to doubt the truthfulness of her relations, and he offered her no encouragement. A short time after this visit, two strange men called upon him, and impudently accusing him of assaulting the lady, demanded a written apology and the sum of five hundred dollars. These proposals were indignantly refused, and the intruders were ordered away. A few days succeeding this event, a boy entered Mr. Ingalls's office and informed him that a lady desired to speak with him upon the sidewalk. Following the boy to the street, the gentleman found himself confronted by Helen Graham, accompanied by two men who were entire strangers to him. One of these men handed her a package of red pepper, which without a word, she deliberately threw in his face, occasioning him severe pain and temporarily blinding him. He had immediately caused her arrest, when she openly accused him of attempts upon her virtue, which she had indignantly resisted.

While Mr. Ingalls was relating his story, the fair prisoner was visibly affected, her face flushed and the tears welled up in her eyes, which a moment ago, were flashing with indignation. All of this was not lost upon the spectators who imagined that these emotions were the outgrowth of outraged honor and womanly feeling.

After the testimony of Mr. Ingalls had been duly given, the judge requested the prisoner to take the stand, addressing her, to the surprise of all, by the name of Mary Freeland. As she heard this name, the fair girl started nervously and placing her trembling hands upon the railing in front of her, slowly rose to her feet. She gazed appealingly around, as if beseeching some one to assist her in reaching the witness box, and her counsel with an air of sincere concern, offered her his arm, on which she leaned heavily, and slowly approached the stand.

With great precision, and in a sweet low voice, she narrated her account of the assault, and the circumstances which, she alleged, had led to the commission of the act. No one to have looked upon that fair face, and those truthful speaking eyes, would have doubted for a moment the correctness of her story, or would have refused their sympathy for the unfortunate lady who appeared so tearful and so distressed.

Utterly ignoring the evidence of Mr. Ingalls, to which she had just listened, she told her version of the story. She testified, that she had seen an advertisement in a morning paper, signed "artist," and being in need of employment, she had answered it, receiving in reply a note signed "H. Ingalls," requesting an interview at his place of business, the locality of which was given.

Agreeably to this request, she had called at the designated place, and while there she was grossly insulted by the plaintiff, who had made improper proposals to her, and had attempted to compel her to submit to his vile purposes. Resisting him with all her strength, she struck him in the face, and escaped into the street. Burning with anger and seeking to revenge this insult, she had thrown the pepper into the eyes of the man who had attempted to outrage her honor.

During this recital Mr. Ingalls betrayed marked symptoms of nervousness and mental excitement, which to those around him, appeared to be evidences of his guilt, and frowning looks from all quarters were directed towards him. Circumstances seemed to be decidedly against him, and the sweet-faced girl, apparently so pure and so friendless, had won the sympathy, and imposed upon the credulity of those about her.

It seemed to them but natural that, resenting the outrage which had been attempted upon her, she would have been justified in punishing her insulter in any manner that suggested itself to her mind. Matters looked very dark for Mr. Ingalls, and as he attempted to approach nearer to the witness, in order to hear more distinctly her low and faltering tones, he was rudely repulsed by a brawny policeman who had been completely won over to the cause of the lovely defendant. Indeed at the close of her direct testimony, it seemed that instead of convicting the girl of a crime, Mr. Ingalls might be compelled to exchange places with her, and might be required to make financial reparation for the indignities he had put upon her.

But the defendant had bided his time—he had not been idle during the period which had elapsed between the arrest of the girl and the day of her trial. Trusty detectives had been engaged in searching for her antecedents, and their efforts had not been fruitless. Sustained by the consciousness of his own innocence, and determined to defend his own reputation, Mr. Ingalls had urged the officers to the completion of their task, and the results were now about to be made manifest.

As the last words fell from the lips of the weeping defendant, Mr. Ingalls boldly pushed past the interposing policeman, and advancing to the judge's seat, drew from his pocket a roll of manuscript, and handing it to one of the magistrates, politely requested his perusal of the contents.

The magistrate received the document and glanced carelessly at it, but as he read he appeared to grow more interested, and with a hurried whisper to his judicial brother, he finished his reading and passed it to him. These movements were not entirely lost upon the fair defendant, and a strange frightened expression came into her eyes as she fixed them intently upon the judge. Having concluded his reading, that official raised his eyes from the paper, and with a sternness of manner very different from his previous considerate treatment of her, he began as rigid an examination as has ever been witnessed in special sessions. Under the trying ordeal the guilty woman cowered in her shame—the mask was torn from the fair face, and she stood revealed as a beautiful fiend, whose seductive wiles had been the ruin of many who had been led by the witching spell of her charms into the abyss of moral destruction.

The document was an extraordinary one indeed, and it was no wonder that Mary Freeland, with her numerous aliases, quailed and trembled beneath the searching questions of the magistrate. Her true history was now laid bare, Helen Graham, it was shown, was of English parentage, and was now, despite her youthful appearance, past thirty years of age. Being the daughter of poor parents, she was compelled to labor for a livelihood, but disliking the drudgery of her life, and preferring her own pleasures, she ran away from home at an early age, and making her way to London, engaged herself as a barmaid in one of the largest tippling houses of that city.

Being possessed of great beauty, and with a captivating manner, she received a great deal of attention from the gentlemen who frequented the place, and among the number was a well-to-do wine merchant, who conceived such a regard for the girl, that he induced her to leave her place of employment, and accept his bounty. Eagerly accepting this glittering offer, the bewitching little barmaid was soon established in palatial apartments and speedily began to ape the manners and tastes of a woman of fashion.

From this intimacy a child was born, which is still living under the care of his reputed father. Becoming tired at last of the attentions of her middle-aged lover, she formed the acquaintance of a young and handsome fellow who was engaged as a messenger for a prominent London bank. Their intimacy was carried on without detection for some time, but at length, fearing the jealousy of the wine merchant, the fair Helen robbed him of a check for two thousand pounds which Henry Rothby, the bank messenger, succeeded in having honored, and the guilty couple fled to Great Yarmouth, where they lived as man and wife for two years, during which time another child was born which, however, lived but a few months.

Henry Rothby and his mistress sailed away from the shores of old England and arrived, in February 1879, at Montreal in Canada. In that city, they engaged board with the family of a respectable gentleman who was living with his wife and five children, in comfort and contentment. Very soon, however, the spell of the siren was cast over this happy home, and one morning the weeping wife awakened to the fact that her husband had eloped with the beautiful and demure Mrs. Rothby, whom she had received into her household with all the friendliness and affection of a sister.

The guilty pair made their way to Cleveland, Ohio, where they lived together a few months, when Helen, becoming tired of her new lover, left him one evening and went to live again with Henry Rothby, who had been in communication with her, and who was now residing at Patchogue on Long Island. Here they remained until September, when they departed in company. Rothby finally left his mistress in New York City, and returned to England. Helen, however, preferred to remain in the United States, and after the departure of her lover she engaged herself in the service of a prominent banker of New York. She did not remain in this position but a few days, as attempting her seductive wiles upon her employer, who was a man of honor; her immodest advances were met with a prompt discharge and a speedy ejection from the home she had attempted to disgrace.

Thus thrown upon her own resources, she formed the acquaintance of several men of doubtful character, and a few days after her discharge from the banker's family, two rough-looking individuals called upon that gentleman, and in a threatening manner demanded a large sum of money from him, accusing him of having acted in an improper manner with his recently discharged domestic, and threatening exposure in case of refusal. Their proposition was met by the angry banker in such a vigorous manner that the two visitors were forcibly ejected from the premises, and landed very unceremoniously upon the sidewalk.

Nothing further was heard of this matter, and the fair but frail Helen disappeared entirely for a time. In the early part of 1880, however, a pale but beautiful young girl, applied for a situation at the residence of a wealthy broker at Mont Clair, N. J. She related a pitiful story of needs and sufferings. How she had left her home in England to escape the commands of her parents, who insisted upon her marriage with a man who was distasteful to her. How the vessel in which she took passage, had been wrecked, and she had lost everything and was now in abject want.

Her story, told so simply and with such an ingenuous air of truthfulness, excited the sympathy of the lady to whom she applied, who immediately gave her employment and a home. Here she remained but a short time when she disappeared very mysteriously under circumstances that rather tended to impeach her integrity. From this time she appeared to have led a reckless and abandoned life, having as many husbands as there were months in the year, and carrying on a system of blackmailing that seemed to be quite profitable, and effectually evaded detection. At several places where she had lived with the various men who were introduced as her husband, she had been requested to leave on account of her vile and unladylike behavior. She was a sort of moral free-booter, no grade of society being too high and no degradation too low, for the operation of her hellish designs. Affecting a modesty and a virtue that were unimpeachable, she would be admitted into select social circles, and soon she would commit some act of glaring immorality which would bring upon her the loathing and contempt of her associates. Discovered in this, she would disappear temporarily, until again brought to the surface by some new revelation of wickedness and debauchery with which she was intimately connected. Her entire history was shown to be one of crime and immoral practices, and unable to refute the terrible accusations, the stricken woman acknowledged her guilt and sued for mercy. The trial was soon completed, and this designing and unprincipled woman was sentenced to a term of imprisonment, during which it was hoped some lessons of improvement would be inculcated.

With a sobbing cry, the young woman received the edict of the court, and then turning to a young man who had hitherto escaped attention, she raised her hands appealingly to him, but with a look of loathing he turned from her, and she was conducted away.

The vindication of Howard Ingalls was complete, and friends who had doubted his story before, and who had avoided him, now pressed forward to congratulate him upon the happy termination of his aggravating trial.

There is a sequel to this story, however, which is worthy of relation. After the policeman had conducted the prisoner to her cell, the young man to whom she had appealed requested to speak to the judge, who was busily engaged in gathering up his papers. The magistrate inclined his head to listen and the young man related his story. He was the son of wealthy parents who resided in a western city, where he was also engaged in business. Some time previous to this occurrence, while on a business visit to New York he had met the fair Helen Graham, who came to him with a sorrowful story of want and distress. He had been first attracted by the pensive beauty of the girl, and had provided for her wants. A growing intimacy had ripened into love, and entirely unconscious of the charges against her, he had offered her his hand in marriage, and they had been united only the day before the arrest.

The revelations of the trial had been a dreadful awakening to him, and now realizing the position in which he was placed he sought the aid of the justice to release him from the bonds which bound him to the guilty woman who had just been condemned to suffer for her sins. In due time the necessary papers were procured, the marriage was declared null and void, and Henry Gadsby returned to his western home a wiser man and, it is to be hoped, a happier one.

The Confidence Man About Town.

THE ways of the confidence man and woman, and the ingenious tricks they resort to, are as numerous as the planets, and frequently, as brilliant, and in the space I have allotted to this particular phase of criminal practice, I can only expect to give a few of the many incidents that have come under my notice. To attempt a full description would require a volume as extensive as the present one, and the reading, though entertaining, might prove tiresome from its very length. I will, however, give a few illustrations, in order to show the workings of this class of ingenious criminals, and to afford the reader a somewhat comprehensive idea of their operations.

Of course, the most common, and, strange to say, one of the most successful schemes, is that of watching either at railroad depots or hotels, for the genial and unsuspecting farmer or country merchant, whose well filled purse and general air of rusticity warrants a belief in his innocence and gullibility. The first move, therefore, is for one of the confidence men to approach the stranger, and with a frank and hearty salutation, to claim an acquaintance.

"Why, Mr. Harris, how do you do—and when did you leave Pumptown?" ejaculates the confidence man, as he grasps the hand of the astonished stranger.

"You must be mistaken, sir," he replies, "my name is not Harris, and I don't live in Pumptown."

"Well, I declare, sir. I beg your pardon, but you are the exact image of my friend, Squire Harris, and I thought I could not be mistaken. I am sorry to have spoken to you as I did, and I beg you to excuse me."

A further conversation ensues, in which the stranger and his victim adjourn to the bar, and over their drinks the victim informs his new found friend that his name is Mr. John Bell, and that he lives in Wellsville, and has come up to town for the first time in five years. After many protestations of good will and amiability the couple separate, and the stranger sees no more of the smooth-spoken gentleman who addressed him as Mr. Harris. During the course of the day, however, Mr. Bell strolls out through the crowded thoroughfares of the city, and while he is carelessly looking around him, he is approached by another man, whose manners are quite agreeable, and whose genial face is beaming with smiles.

"How do you do, Mr. Bell? I am glad to see you. What brings you to town?"

Of course Mr. Bell does not at first recognize his new friend, and upon asking for the desired information, the stranger tells him that his name is Marshall, and that he keeps a store at Waterstown, a few miles distant from Wellsville, and has met Mr. Bell several times in his native town. A few deft inquiries about people and localities which completely impose on Mr. Bell, and in a few minutes afterwards, the two men are laughing and talking like old friends.

This is the entering wedge, and after that any scheme that may be devised is put into operation. Sometimes Mr. Marshall has bought a lot of goods, and the firm from whom he has made purchases requires more cash than he has with him, and Mr. Bell is appealed to, to help his friend out until they return home. Sometimes Mr. Marshall has shipped a lot of goods to Chicago, but, not having cash enough to pay the freight, is very indignant, and exceedingly annoyed because the railroad company decline to accept his check in payment. Mr. Bell is then appealed to to cash a check for his neighbor, who offers his individual paper as a guarantee of his credibility. In other cases, the unsuspecting Mr. Bell may be lured into a gambling saloon, and under the excitement of the moment, may be tempted to venture his money on the uncertain chances of the game, which, it is needless to say, invariably results in loss and ruin to the rustic victim, and in some extreme instances Mr. Bell may be led to some secluded spot, drugged and robbed, and when his consciousness returns, he is unable to tell where and how he came to his present position.

These are a few of the many means put into practice by the ordinary confidence man, and I regret to say they are generally successful.

The Biters Bitten.

"BANCO," as it is now called "bunko," is another form of the confidence swindle, and first made its appearance at New Orleans in 1869. This game consists in "roping in" or inducing an unsuspicious victim, with plenty of money, and then fleecing him of all his ready cash and as much more as can be obtained from him. A little reminiscence that occurred a few years ago may not be out of place here as showing that sometimes "The best laid plans of mice and men gang aft aglee."

A party of sharp and notorious gamblers and bunko men were seated in a handsomely furnished saloon where games of chance were the order of the day, when one of their number rushed into the room exclaiming:

"Boys, I have just had an introduction to the richest planter in the Red River country. His name is Col. Oliver, and I understand he has sold his cotton and deposited the proceeds, about fifteen thousand dollars, with a banker here. Now get ready for a big game, and I will land him here in an hour or two. He does not carry any ready money, but his paper is as good as gold."

The game that was intended to be played upon the stranger was a lottery scheme, which was to be termed the Royal Havana Lottery, with drawings now going on. At ten o'clock that evening, the "steerer" made his appearance, accompanied by a large swarthy planter, who was finely dressed, and who wore in his shirt bosom a diamond stud of large proportions.

After going through the usual preliminary inquiries, the "steerer" produced his ticket for the lottery which had drawn eighty dollars, and the gold was duly counted out to him, when he immediately purchased two more tickets for the present drawing. Col. Oliver received one of these tickets from the steerer, and after being instructed in the manner of playing, he entered fully into the spirit of the game, which unfortunately went steadily against him until he had lost nearly eight thousand dollars. The Colonel took his losses good naturedly, however, saying that he had taken the chances and might have won. He however requested the gamblers to hold his drafts until morning so that he could get the money for them from his broker, as he did not wish that gentleman to think he would gamble so heavily. This promise was readily given, and the gamblers treated their victim to a bounteous and luxurious supper, in which the finest brands of champagne and the most delicately flavored cigars furnished a fitting conclusion. After this the party separated and Col. Oliver returned to his hotel. Meeting some friends then he entered the wine room, and while there, his former friends, the gamblers, who, flushed with success, were having a glorious time, also entered the room.

Saluting his new found friend as Col. Oliver, the leader of the gamblers invited the party to join him in a bottle of wine. While they were drinking, one of the gentlemen approached the gambler, and in a loud voice exclaimed;

"Major, I think you have made a slight mistake about Col. Oliver."

"How can that be?" inquired the gambler.

"Why," replied the other, "instead of being Col. Oliver, he is no other person than Detective William Pinkerton from Chicago."

This was enough, and without another word the discomfited gamblers handed the drafts, which were utterly worthless, back to William, and slowly and quietly drifted out of the hotel. Their little confidence game did not work that time, and ever afterwards they were more careful how they entertained rich planters from the Red River country.

The Verdant Scotchman.

THERE was another case in which the intended victim was a robust and wealthy Scotchman who was traveling in America for pleasure, and who temporarily stopped at one of the prominent Chicago hotels. This gentleman's name was James Templeton, and he came from Glasgow. While sauntering about the office of the hotel one evening, Mr. Templeton was approached by a dapper little fellow, in a Scotch tweed suit, with a dainty umbrella under his arm and a single glass in his eye. This young man approached the elderly gentleman, and politely introduced himself as Master Robert Campbell of Glasgow, a son of Campbell, one of the famous shipbuilders of that city. The old gentleman was exceedingly glad to meet with a fellow countryman, and they were soon chatting pleasantly together. A walk was soon proposed and shortly afterwards our two Scotch friends found themselves in a large saloon, where no less an individual than "Canada Bill," an old time swindler, was engaged in throwing the "monte" cards for an audience, all of whom were perfectly acquainted with his little game, and were in fact "cappers" for him. "Canada Bill" was losing money very rapidly when the strangers entered, and Mr. Templeton, after watching the game for awhile turned to the pretended Mr. Campbell, and expressed his opinion that the poor, old blind man was being deliberately robbed. Young Campbell, however, paid no attention to this, and a few minutes afterwards he commenced to play himself. He soon lost a small sum of money and induced his elderly companion to wager a small amount which was soon pocketed by "Canada Bill." Campbell then wanted to play for more money, and Bill said he would bet one thousand dollars, and nothing less that no one could pick up the "Jack." In the midst of the parley which ensued, Mr. Templeton unceremoniously seized young Mr. Campbell by the collar of his coat, and the seat of his trousers, and deliberately carried him out into the street. After carefully depositing the youth upon the sidewalk, he said, "Campbell, my boy, I say, I've saved you from being robbed and murdered. You were in a den of thieves. What would your poor ould father say if he saw you gambling with sharpers? But, Campbell," and here his voice dropped, "the poor, old, blind man was not sic a dum fool as he looked to be."

The honesty and the indignation of the old Scotchman were too much, and the pretended Master Campbell, who was no other than a regular "steerer" for "Canada Bill," and who had dressed himself as a Scotchman for the sole purpose of fleecing his warm hearted friend Mr. Templeton, was compelled to swallow his disappointment and look for other game.

A Confidence Man, Confidenced.

THE following incident which is perfectly true in all its details, will show how even the most astute confidence men are sometimes over-reached and in the end find themselves the victims of their own smartness.

During the month of August, 1883, an ordinary looking man, respectably arrayed, and wearing a broad brimmed hat and gold bowed spectacles arrived in New York City, and registered himself at a fashionable hotel in Broadway, as B. Ashley, of Abilene, Kansas. The stranger had just arrived in town by the Western express from Chicago, on the Erie road. His garments had been procured from a ready-made clothing store in Abilene, which gave him rather a rustic appearance, while his face and hands were brownly tanned from exposure. He walked with that peculiar parenthetical gait which indicates a long time spent in the saddle, and his bearing in other respects indicated the wild western borderman. Mr. Ashley soon developed other tendencies of the prairie type; he insisted upon going out for exercise every morning shortly after day-break on horseback, and upon these occasions he employed his own rawhide bridle, and his well-worn Mexican saddle, which formed part of his luggage. His accent was a peculiar blending of English and western types of speech; his eyes were weak, and he frequently consulted an eminent oculist in New York, preparatory, as he stated, to placing himself under the care of a prominent London specialist, after he had concluded his affairs in New York, and arrived upon the other side of the Atlantic.

Mr. Ashley appeared to have very little occupation beyond horseback riding at unearthly hours in the morning; visiting his medical adviser in the afternoon, and lounging about the immense and richly ornamental rotunda of the hotel in the evening. He was bountifully supplied with cash and he expended it with considerable liberality. He smoked a great deal, but drank little, because his physician had absolutely forbidden him to do so, on account of its effect upon his patient's eyes.

Many people about the hotel drank at Mr. Ashley's expense, but he himself seldom indulged in more harmful beverages than lemonade or some well-known medicinal spring water.

One day Mr. Ashley strolled through the lobby of the hotel in the company of a young man, whose face is well-known to the regular promenaders of Broadway. This young man is always faultlessly dressed and smooth shaven. He has prominent features, and peculiarly thin and compressed lips; he lives handsomely, and always has plenty of money. With this new-found companion Mr. Ashley, the weak-eyed child of the guileless west, occupied a seat in the bar-room for some time. Upon this occasion Mr. Ashley departed from his usual custom, and assisted in the absorption of a liberal quantity of champagne. After a time thus spent, the Broadway friend arose and took his departure, and Mr. Ashley sauntered again through the office of the hotel. As he did so, one of the clerks motioned for him to approach the desk.

"Mr. Ashley, how long has it been since you were in New York before?" inquired the clerk.

"Nearly eight years," answered that gentleman. "Never was here afore and never since until now."

"Do you know the person who has just left you?"

"Yes, met him two nights ago at the Madison Square. I couldn't buy a seat and he offered me one of his. Said his friend hadn't come, and he would be glad to accommodate a stranger. So we sat together. Seems to be a nice sort of a chap, don't he?"

"I have no doubt of that," responded the clerk, with a slight air of superior knowledge, not unblended with sarcasm. "That young man—in fact, that nice sort of a chap, is 'Hungry Joe,' one of the most celebrated confidence operators in America."

"You don't say," drawled the western man slowly, and with some little indication of astonishment. "Well, I'm darned."

He went thoughtfully away. That night the young man with the thin lips and the handsome clothes called for Mr. Ashley after dinner, and as they came through the office, the occidental innocent pulled out a large pocketbook filled to repletion with money, and taking about five hundred dollars from its recesses he deposited the wallet, with the balance of its contents, in the hotel safe. His companion watched this proceeding with a pensive face, but a gleaming eye, and then the two went out together. Mr. Ashley returned just in time to take his morning ride on horseback, and then retired to bed, where he remained until four o'clock in the afternoon. That evening he drew two hundred dollars from his wallet, and left the hotel.

"You are fully warned," observed the clerk, as he handed over the amount, "and it is your own fault if you lose any money to 'Hungry Joe.'"

"Correct," responded Mr. Ashley, stuffing the bills into his pocket.

His next appearance in the hotel was shortly after midnight, and this time he put three hundred dollars away in his wallet, with the declaration that "New York sharps might be pretty stiff on bunko, but they were a little behind the time on draw poker. In my country," he added, "two deuces and a bowie knife will open a Jack pot every time."

Mr. Ashley passed several days after this, in quiet and seclusion, and a full week rolled past before he drifted out again with his companion of the compressed lips. The next day he drew a round one thousand dollars from the safe, and seemed very much annoyed when the clerk smiled a broad and knowing smile.

"No game ever fazed me," said Mr. Ashley, doggedly, "and a man who can hold up his end with cowboys isn't going to be bested by any broadcloth brigade that was ever hatched."

There was a lull of eight or ten days, and then Mr. Ashley drew another thousand dollars, and a couple of days after that he drew eight hundred fifty dollars more. That afternoon he went for a drive with his gentlemanly companion. His face was clouded with sadness all the morning, but it was noticed that he appeared somewhat brighter on his return from the drive. That evening "Hungry Joe," and two of his well-known Broadway companions spent several hours in earnest conversation with Mr. Ashley. That gentleman's weak eyes made it necessary for him to wear his broad hat well down over his forehead, and when the three young men went away, the merest shadow of a smile played about the corners of the mouth of the western man. From the table at which they had sat, the three young fellows went direct to a telegraph office, where they sent the following dispatch:

"POSTMASTER, ABILENE, KANSAS:

"Do you know Benjamin Ashley, cattle raiser? Telegraph full particulars, my expense." R. DICKSON, Brower House, New York.

The reply to this communication was evidently satisfactory in all respects, and within two days Mr. Ashley received in his rooms at the hotel, a visit from the three confidence operators and a lawyer, who is more or less celebrated in the metropolis. After an hour or more had elapsed, the chief porter of the hotel was called into the room, and requested to sign his name as a witness to the signature of Mr. Ashley. This was done; the porter receiving five dollars for his trouble, and a sum of money was counted out and paid to Mr. Ashley by the young man with the thin lips.

That night the western cattle raiser deposited fourteen thousand dollars cool cash in the safe of the hotel.

Two days afterwards he took passage on a Guion steamer for Liverpool, having explained to the hotel clerk that he had sold a half interest in his Kansas cattle ranch to his friends, and that "Hungry Joe," as he was called, was going to retire from city life.

Mr. Ashley was accompanied to the pier by his enthusiastic New York acquaintances, who toasted him in the finest champagne, and adorned his stateroom with many delicacies, including a rich basket of flowers, in which the word "farewell" was artistically arranged, and altogether the departure of the cattle raiser, was accompanied by every mark of tender regard and esteem.

About twelve days had elapsed since the departure of Mr. Ashley, when a tall man arrived at the same hotel, in a carriage that was loaded down with trunks, steamer chairs and other appliances of ocean travel. Walking into the office he signed his name in large English characters: "Benjamin Ashley, Esq., London." The clerk looked up hurriedly, as if to apologize for not recognizing his guest, then looked surprised, muttered a hasty word or two, and assigned the stranger to a room all in a confused and preoccupied manner.

There was apparently another Benjamin Ashley. This man was tall and slender, well-dressed and pale. But he spoke with a slightly Americanized accent, not unlike that of the other Benjamin Ashley. The clerk was sorely puzzled, and that evening he took especial care to have the stranger's full name and address inserted among the list of prominent arrivals in all the daily papers.

The clerk went on duty early next day, and as he fully expected, one of his first callers was the thin lipped "Hungry Joe," who asked to have his name sent up to Mr. Ashley's room. Word was returned that Mr. Ashley would see the gentleman in the drawing room, and thither the clerk followed the confidence man. "Hungry Joe" was sitting in a large arm chair, when the tall man from London entered the apartment, and not recognizing his old friend, paid no attention to the new-comer. The Englishman, however, seeing no one else excepting the clerk, advanced courteously and said.

"Did you wish to see me? I am Mr. Ashley."

"Eh!" said "Hungry Joe," with a start, "you're not Mr. Benjamin Ashley?"

"Precisely."

"Not of Kansas?"

"Yes sir, of Abilene, Kansas. How can I serve you?"

The thin lips of the expert confidence man were white by this time, and they were more firmly compressed than ever. He regarded the tall Englishman in a dazed manner for a few minutes, and then he asked,

"Do you own a large cattle ranch twenty-five miles south of Abilene?"

"I believe I do. Why do you ask?"

"Been to Europe to have your eyes doctored?"

"Yes, sir," answered Mr. Ashley, with some surprise, "I have been abroad for four months. But my young friend, these questions are rather odd. Please explain yourself."

"Odd," echoed the Broadway man. "Well, I should think they were. If you are Benjamin Ashley, and you do own that ranch, the cleverest man in the country has given me a pretty bad deal, that's all. Why, it ain't two weeks ago that me and two friends bought a half interest in that ranch, and by God, the man who sold us, stopped in this same hotel!"

Mr. Ashley seemed rather astonished, and after a full explanation had been made, the following particulars were learned. The supposed Benjamin Ashley had lost three thousand two hundred fifty dollars at cards to "Hungry Joe" and his companions. This man had represented himself as the owner of the Ashley ranch, and was on his way to Europe to be treated for his eyes. Mr. Ashley had desired to make certain expenditures while in Europe, but his losses at cards would prevent his doing so, unless he could dispose of an interest in his ranch. The men had then telegraphed to the postmaster who had replied, giving details of the property which was valued at about fifty thousand dollars, and further stated that Mr. Ashley had gone abroad for medical treatment. Thus far all was satisfactory; the pretended Mr. Ashley produced deeds to establish his ownership, and thinking they had a chance to get twenty-five thousand dollars worth of material for fourteen thousand dollars, the three sharpers had clubbed together and raised the necessary amount.

"Really," observed Mr. Ashley, when all the explanations had been fully made, "I am very sorry for you, but you have evidently been made a victim of. For my part, I shall have no difficulty in proving my identity, and as for your friend, the bogus Mr. Ashley, he is probably one of my cowboys named Harry Barnes, whose description tallies precisely with what you have told me of the man."

"Well, sir," burst in the defrauded confidence operator, "that cuss has gone off to Europe with my money, hang him! And what's worse, he went off full of my champagne, and smelling of my basket of flowers. He's a d—d swindler, that's what he is."

Swearing and complaints were of no avail, however, and "Hungry Joe," with all his skill and success was compelled to acknowledge that he had been completely duped by a western cowboy.

Purchasing Witnesses.

IT is scarcely possible to place a limit upon the acting of unscrupulous men and women when in desperate straits to obtain money. I know of a case in which a woman deliberately hired herself to furnish a rich married woman, who was desirous of obtaining a divorce from her husband, with such evidence as would be sufficient to warrant any court in Christendom in granting the application, notwithstanding the fact that the husband so far as known, had led an unblemished life. The gentleman was a wealthy real estate owner, and being older than his wife, the lady had grown tired of his company, and desired to wed a younger man, who had captivated her affections. She had attempted previously to obtain a divorce and alimony on the ground of adultery, but failing to produce testimony to support this allegation the case was summarily dismissed by the judge before whom the case was tried. Then it was that the wife endeavored to purchase the testimony, without which it would be impossible for her to carry out her designs. A so-called private detective was called in, and through his influence, the woman was secured who agreed to furnish the required evidence. Dressing herself in plain black clothing, and with mourning jewelry, this woman called upon the husband at his place of business, representing herself to be a wealthy widow who was desirous of disposing of some property. This led to a second visit and being a woman of prepossessing appearance she soon won the regard of the unsuspecting husband, who gave her the best advice as to the transaction she had sought his opinion upon. At length a plan was duly arranged, and at the proper moment the wife, accompanied by witnesses, burst into her husband's private office, to find the hired accomplice, with her arms around the neck of the astonished and unsuspicious man, who vainly tried to extricate himself from this damaging combination of circumstances. In this case the husband was entirely guiltless of wrong-doing, but the evidence was too strong—the divorce was granted with liberal alimony, and four months afterwards, the designing and degraded wife, who had paid one thousand dollars for this manufactured testimony, was married to this young man who had ingratiated himself into her favor. As a truthful evidence of the utter depravity of human nature, this incident is sufficiently suggestive, and it was with consid-erable elation that I afterwards learned that the second husband of this woman ran away from her in a short time, taking with him several thousand dollars which she had fraudulently obtained from the man whom she had so basely deceived in the first instance.

The Medical Charlatan and his Merchant Dupe.

ONE of the strangest and perhaps the most ingenious and protracted cases of blackmailing came under my notice a few years ago. The parties were an unscrupulous medical charlatan, a designing woman and a reputable merchant, who in a moment, of weakness succumbed to the wiles and seductive charms of the immoral temptress. Mr. Samuel Wilkins was a merchant of high standing in the commercial world, and mingled in the first circles of society in a western city. A middle-aged man of family, whose wife was interested in many acts of charity and benevolence, and whose children were reared amid the comforts and restraints of a well ordered home, Mr. Wilkins was a fine-looking gentleman, a good liver, a hearty, whole-souled companion, and thus far no breath of scandal had ever touched himself or his home.

Mr. Wilkins had frequent occasions to visit New York, in order to purchase goods for his large establishment, and to transact numerous other matters of business connected with the proper management of his large commercial interests. While in that city he invariably made his headquarters at one of the prominent hotels, where he soon became known to the regular guests of this high toned hostelry. On several occasions while stopping at this hotel, Mr. Wilkins had noticed a lady of prepossessing appearance, who seemed to be alone and unattended. After repeated accidental meetings in the corridors and dining room of the hotel, an acquaintance, polite and deferential at first, sprang up between them. This intercourse soon led to quiet social chats in the parlor, during which the demure maiden informed Mr. Wilkins that her name was Mary Curtis, and that her parents, who were in comfortable circumstances, resided in a distant part of the state, where she might also enjoy the comforts of a home, but preferring the bustle and gaiety of the city, she had come to New York, and was engaged as a music teacher by several of the aristocratic families of the metropolis. A mutual affection soon ripened between the western merchant and the fair music teacher, and during Mr. Wilkins's frequent visits to New York, he escorted the young lady to the theatre, opera and to little recherché suppers, which appeared to be exceedingly enjoyable to them both. Mr. Wilkins also made several presents to his new found friend, which gradually increased in value, until expensive articles of wearing apparel were accepted with the same delightful grace and freedom as a bouquet of flowers or a box at the opera.

The natural and inevitable result of such an intimacy was that the seductive and charming Mary Curtis after a time accepted the protection and bounty of her wealthy admirer, and notwithstanding her perfect knowledge that he was a married man of family, she left the hotel and occupied the apartments which were selected and arranged for her by her middle-aged but infatuated admirer.

Mary was supplied with a liberal allowance of money, and every wish expressed by her was gratified by the enraptured merchant, who seemed to have completely lost his senses over the ravishing beauty, who constituted the charm of his existence, while he was engaged away from home. Day by day the demands of his pretty mistress became more exacting, and during his absences from her, which were inevitably long, the mails were burdened with her letters, in which some new caprice would require an additional outlay on the part of her married admirer.

Mr. Wilkins finally became annoyed at these frequent demands for money, and resolved to break off an alliance which was both dangerous to his standing in the church and society, should it ever become known, and extremely costly in a financial sense. On the occasion, therefore, of his next visit to New York, he determined to communicate his resolution to the young woman; but when he arrived he learned from the trembling lips of the young lady that she was in that peculiar condition in which another life than her own was struggling for existence, and that she feared she was about to become a mother.

This information fell upon the surprised merchant as the death-knell of his intentions of separating from the girl, and his hopes of avoiding further expensive outlays in her behalf. With many blushes and copious floods of tears the frightened Mary recounted her fears and forebodings, and her piteous appeals to her protector were so genuine and heartrending, that Mr. Wilkins, instead of effecting a release from his present entanglements, only found himself more deeply and hopelessly involved.

Shortly after this he had occasion to make a sudden visit to New York on an imperative matter of business, and he arrived in the city without having given Mary any intimation of his coming. On repairing to the house unannounced, he was surprised to find, calmly seated in her apartments, a tall, handsome gentleman who appeared to be making himself perfectly at home, and who exhibited marked evidences of confusion at this unexpected meeting.

Mary was the most composed of the three, and without the slightest trace of excitement, introduced the stranger to Mr. Wilkins as Dr. Philip Bristow, a medical gentleman whom she had engaged to attend her in her approaching accouchement, and who had simply made a professional call upon her.

Dr. Philip Bristow was a man above six feet in height, with broad shoulders and a commanding figure. His hair was long and black, and was worn in graceful curls, and his long, flowing mustache was of the same color; his eyes were dark and piercing, and his complexion was clear, though dark. Altogether the doctor was a very handsome man, with a fine careless air of bravado about him, which impressed one with mingled feelings of admiration and suspicion.

The doctor expressed himself as highly gratified to meet the husband of his very interesting lady-patient, and after a few words of amiable courtesy, he took his leave. Although somewhat suspicious of this strange visitor, Mr. Wilkins forbore to make any remark concerning his presence, and Mary, fully assured, devoted herself to the entertainment of her unexpected friend with a grace and charm which could not fail to have its effect.

Thus matters continued until the time arrived, and Mary was duly delivered of a bright, healthy boy. The information of this interesting event was conveyed to Mr. Wilkins by the urbane doctor by letter, as Mr. Wilkins was compelled to remain in Chicago, during the progress of this important addition to his cares and anxieties in New York.

When Mr. Wilkins next visited Mary he was surprised to find her looking very rosy and healthy for a new mother, and though still confined to her bed, she evinced an animation of spirits scarcely in accord with her weakened condition. The baby was brought into the room, in the arms of its nurse, and to Mr. Wilkins's experienced eyes appeared to be a remarkably robust and well-grown youngster for the limited time he had been favored with existence.

He began to grow more suspicious and alarmed, and when the handsome doctor called in the course of the day, and presented a bill for three hundred fifty dollars for his services, his suspicions were confirmed, and his alarm increased. He, however, held his peace, and with many professions of thankfulness, he paid the doctor's claim, and made further arrangements for the care and welfare of the mother and her babe.

On his return home, however, Mr. Wilkins sought his legal adviser, an old and valued friend and companion, and he related to him without evasion or concealment the details of the whole affair. The attorney, who was also a man of the world, at once gave the opinion that this was one of the most decided, but delicately operated cases of blackmail that had come under his notice, and advised Mr. Wilkins to extricate himself as soon as possible from the toils of this designing woman and her unscrupulous physician, who in the opinion of the astute attorney, was nothing more or less than her paramour, and fellow conspirator.

Mr. Sanford, the attorney, being a warm friend of mine, applied to me for assistance, and as I was well acquainted with Mr. Wilkins, and fully coincided in the opinion that he had fallen into the hands of sharpers, I agreed to undertake the matter and to secure his release from further demands if possible.

I at once set about the performance of my task, and ere many days I was in a position to fully gain all the information I desired. The doctor was carefully watched, and he was found to be one of the most notorious of those scoundrelly physicians who make a specialty of treating diseases peculiar to women, and who was a noted and unscrupulous abortionist. The house of Mary Curtis was also well shadowed, and it was found that, notwithstanding the fact of her recent motherhood, she received almost daily visits from this disinterested doctor, who always remained all night when making his daily professional calls.

Satisfied of the undue intimacy existing between Dr. Philip Bristow and Mr. Wilkins's fair and lovely Mary, my next move was to ascertain full particulars about the child, and with the assistance of an intelligent female operative, who gained the confidence of the nurse of the frail Mary, I learned enough to convince me that the child which had been imposed upon Mr. Wilkins, as his offspring, had been procured from some foundling asylum, for the propose of deceiving that gentleman, and strengthening the hold of these blackmailers upon their victim, who fearing the consequences of an exposure of his relations with Mary Curtis would be willing to submit to any demands upon his purse in order to insure secrecy.

Nor was I wrong in my convictions, and at last I was armed with sufficient proofs of the fact that Dr. Bristow and

Mary Curtis had lived together as man and wife before she made the acquaintance of Mr. Wilkins, and I had learned enough of this pseudo-doctor to know that he had been connected with similar experiments in other cities. The fact of the baby having been taken from a foundling's home was also proven beyond doubt, and at last, having obtained all the information I desired, Mr. Wilkins was instructed to peremptorily refuse to pay any further demands which might be made upon him from that quarter. This he did emphatically and without any unnecessary waste of words, and his refusal was met by a threat from the doctor to bring suit against him, and to inform his wife and family of his connection with Mary Curtis.

At this state of affairs, I came to the rescue in person, and boldly entering the doctor's office, I demanded an interview with the debased quack. Our conversation was very short, and as may be imagined, directly to the point. I informed the weak-kneed braggart that I was in possession of the facts of his early history, and if he persisted in hounding Mr. Wilkins, he would find himself in prison for a graver charge than blackmail, and with a sure promise of conviction and punishment. The medical fraud soon discovered that his dance was over, and after signing a paper, in which he acknowledged the whole scheme to be one of fraud and deception, and promising to leave the city with his equally guilty mistress, I took my departure.

A few days after this, the doctor disappeared mysteriously and the apartments of Mary Curtis were vacated. The child was returned to the foundling's home, and Mr. Wilkins was relieved from any further demands from this unprincipled pair of blackmailers. The lesson was not lost upon him, and after a frank and manly explanation to his wife, he settled himself down to a life of simple and happy virtue and content.

Of Dr. Bristow and Mary Curtis, I have heard at frequent intervals, but they have kept out of my way too carefully to incur another visit from me, which if ever repeated, would be to fully carry out the threat I made to them on the occasion of my first call upon the charlatan doctor and the blackmailing abortionist.

A Pretty Law-breaker.

SOPHIE LEWIS was a beautiful girl when I first met her. Her hair was of raven blackness and curled gracefully around her broad low white forehead, beneath which her lustrous eyes gleamed with a soft brightness that was bewitching. Her bright red lips and pearly teeth gave an additional charm to a face that was unmistakably beautiful.

The manner of my first introduction to her occurred under circumstances at once peculiar and not very creditable to the lady. Several years ago many of the principal dry-goods merchants of the city of Chicago were largely victimized by a numerous coterie of shoplifters who for a long time effectually eluded their vigilance. Every day articles would disappear, and in the most unaccountable manner. Clerks and "floor-walkers" were watchful and vigilant, but in spite of their utmost endeavors the closing of the stores at night would reveal the fact that during the day articles had been stolen which were more or less valuable, and in a manner which entirely escaped detection. The continued success of these thieves alarmed the merchants, and at length finding no diminution in the operations of these light fingered individuals, my Agency was applied to by several of the most prominent of the mercantile community. I accordingly placed in each one of their stores watchful operatives in the capacities of clerks, salesmen and floor-walkers, who were instructed to be ever on the alert for the detection of these pestilent thieves.

In one of the largest of these establishments, that of Brown, Armstrong & Co., I placed my son William A. Pinkerton, feeling fully confident that under his surveillance any attempt at shop-lifting would be met by instant detection and prompt punishment. One day shortly after his appearance in the store, he noticed a handsomely dressed young lady who awakened an instinctive suspicion in his mind. Why, he could not tell, but as she swept past him in flowing robes, the idea flashed through his mind that this lady required watching, and he quietly and unobservedly kept her in view.

The object of this unaccountable suspicion was a tall, well-formed young lady of about twenty years of age. Her hair was black and waving, and her dark eyes were full of expression, and a vivacity that was captivating, while the rich color mantled her cheek giving to the otherwise pale face a sweetness that was bewitching. Her apparel was of the richest material and of the most fashionable design; sparkling diamonds were suspended from her small shell-like ears and glistened brightly upon her taper-fingers.

Certainly not one who would ordinarily be accused of shop-lifting, but William could not overcome the suspicions which impressed him so forcibly as his eyes rested upon her for the first time. A beautiful ingenuous face is not always a sure index of the purity and honor of the possessor, and very often in my experience it has only been the outward sham which covered a base and degraded heart.

This woman wore an article of apparel called a "dolman," a loose mantle with wide flowing sleeves, which was made of the finest quality of silk. As William followed her carelessly around the store, he noticed several times that as she would inquire the prices of the various articles displayed upon the counters, those wide sleeves would invariably cover a large amount of space which was filled with numerous articles of value openly exposed for sale. In her hand the lady carried a goodly sized and very handsome shopping reticule of unique design, and the watchful detective was confident that several times in her wanderings about the store he noticed a suspicious movement of this embroidered receptacle.

A closer scrutiny rendered the conviction certain, and as the lady, having concluded her visit, turned to leave the store, William stepped in front of her. Politely removing his hat he addressed her, "I am very sorry, madam, but I am afraid you will be required to accompany me."

The beautiful face paled before the searching eyes of the determined detective, and her lips attempted an angry reply.

"What do you mean, sir?" she inquired, in a faltering voice.

"Only this, madam," replied William. "I think you have stolen goods in that satchel, and a search is necessary to disprove the accusation."

The pallor had left her face now, and a bright scarlet tinged her cheeks; her eyes flashed an angry gaze at the man before her.

"How dare you speak so to me?" came in quick utterances from the scornful lips. "Stand aside at once and let me pass!"

The air of command and dignity was most perfectly assumed, and the innocent look of her eyes might have deceived many; but William had been too well skilled in matters of deceptive appearances to be disturbed in the least by the bewitching display of anger on the part of the lady before him. Still maintaining his placid demeanor, he said:

"Madam, you may take your choice, you will either accompany me, or I will call an officer at once and place you in custody; but this mysterious satchel of yours must be examined."

As he spoke he reached out his hand and took from the unresisting arm of the lady the reticule which she carried. Finding her efforts unavailing, the lady recovered her composure and signified her inclination to accompany my son.

"You will find that the best plan," said William, as he offered her his arm; "you will thus avoid the mortification of a public exposure."

Requesting one of the gentlemen who composed the firm to accompany them, the trio quietly left the store, and after a short walk arrived at my Agency, where the fair lady was conducted into a private office, and where she breathlessly awaited the result of the investigation.

As was expected, the reticule contained several articles that had undoubtedly been stolen from the store in which she was detected, and, although of comparatively trifling value, the fact of her guilt was plainly demonstrated to the wondering merchant who stood by.

No sooner had the stolen goods been discovered than the merchant's manner underwent a remarkable change. Assuming an appearance of anger he addressed the lady in the most abusive terms, and finally, to the utter amazement of my son, he concluded by demanding of the discomfited lady the sum of three hundred dollars in order to compromise the matter, and to save her the exposure of a public trial.

This novel and unexpected turn of affairs was a complete surprise to William, and so exasperated did he become at this attempt to blackmail an unfortunate woman by a man of supposed respectability and business reputation, that rising to his feet and pointing to the recovered articles, he said:

"Mr., there are the goods that have been recovered; take them and leave this office; we have nothing to do with transactions such as you propose!" and then walking to the door he threw it wide open, then turning to the lady—"Madam, we have nothing further to do with this matter, and you are at liberty to depart at once." Before the astonished merchant could recover himself sufficiently to utter a word the woman had disappeared, and William had entered an adjoining room, leaving the discomfited blackmailer to find his way out as best he could.

The beauty of this sinful woman piqued the curiosity of my son and he determined to learn her history, and not long afterwards he was successful in acquiring all the information he desired in relation to her career and antecedents. The young woman was found to be one Sophie Lewis, a daughter of one of the most noted thieves of the day. She had been reared in an atmosphere of crime from her infancy, and had been a thief almost from the cradle. Her beauty had been a safeguard to her, and very often when detected in petty pilferings, her beautiful pleading, tear-filled eyes had saved her from the punishment which would have certainly overtaken one less favored by nature.

This was her first appearance in Chicago, and consequently her first introduction to the detective, who, although being perfectly conversant with the history of the father, did not until now know of the existence of this beautiful but dishonest daughter.

Shortly after this the beautiful Jewess, for such she was proven to be, became acquainted with a noted bank burglar and desperado named Ned Little. Her handsome face attracted the admiration of this lawless man, and after a short but loving courtship they were married. By this union five children were born, and the mother endeavored to bring them up in an honorable manner. Every attention was paid to their education, and, they never knew the precarious calling of their father who practiced his profession with unremitting ardor, and who accumulated quite a large sum of money.

At last, Ned Little getting into difficulty, fled with his wife and family to Canada where he would be safe from the officers of the United States, and here he established himself in a fine villa and lived in magnificent style for a number of years. Tiring at length of the uneventful life he was leading, he left his Canadian home and began again the life of crime which he had led before. It would have been better for him if he had been contented to remain where he was, for, very soon after this, becoming identified with several thieving operations, he fell into the hands of the officers of the law and was arrested on Long Island upon a charge of bank-robbery. Upon being searched a package of ten thousand dollars was found upon his person, which was recognized as having been stolen some months previously from one Mike Murray, a New York sporting man, who identifying his property was rejoiced to have returned to him a sum of money, the recovery of which he had long since abandoned all hope. Little was placed upon trial for his offenses and being duly committed was sentenced to a long term of imprisonment.

Sophie Little, the wife of the imprisoned burglar, from this time began a course of living which soon resulted in her downfall. She had previously contracted the habit of opium-eating, and very soon after this became a slave to the pernicious drug and to the use of morphine.

Leaving her children to the care of friends and in educational institutions, this woman, who still retained many traces of her former beauty, became connected with several gangs of sneak thieves and traveled over the country in their company. Her part in these transactions was what is known as a "call out," and the duty which devolved upon her was as follows:

The bank to be operated upon would be selected, generally in some country town where but few clerks were employed and where, during certain hours in the day, the office would be frequently left to the care of a single official. At that time a party would drive up to the front of the building in a carriage and would request the clerk to step out to the sidewalk, as the lady was an invalid and could not leave the vehicle. The unsuspecting clerk would comply with the request, when he would be immediately engaged in a conversation upon matters of business by the party who had requested his presence, and while thus engrossed, the rest of the gang, or whoever had been deputed to do so, would sneak into the bank and take any package of money that could be easily reached and make their escape; after which the clerk would be dismissed by his entertaining invalid customer and the party would make off with their booty.

For some time she continued this mode of living, and during the two or three years that followed her husband's imprisonment she had been associated with most of the prominent gangs of sneak thieves in the country, with whom she managed to successfully escape detection and to maintain herself and her children.

She soon, however, became morally bad, and the next information that was received of her was to the effect that, abandoning her old profession, she had adopted the nefarious calling of a blackmailer, and had on more than one occasion been successful in fleecing gentlemen of standing and supposed respectability of various sums of money. The first case that came to my notice occurred in Cincinnati, Ohio, where by her beauty and captivating manners she had completely won the affections of a prominent merchant of that city. This man was married and the father of an interesting family, but so thoroughly had the wily adventuress wormed herself into his affections, that the man, forgetting the ties which bound him to his home, careless of the duties which he owed to society, yielded himself to an infatuation he seemed unable to control. The result of this intrigue was that the merchant was lured into a chamber in the Grand Hotel, where this tempting siren resided, and then having disrobed, the unprincipled woman secured his clothes and impudently demanded the sum of ten thousand dollars, or failing to recover this, she threatened to alarm the house, when he would be discovered and his reputation ruined.

Finding it impossible to escape the snare into which he had fallen, the deluded man compromised with this depraved woman by agreeing to give her a check for five thousand dollars, which she accepted, and receiving this she permitted him to depart a poorer and a wiser man. When the designing woman presented the check for payment she was exceedingly surprised to find that her dupe had anticipated her, that payment had been stopped, and she was promptly arrested.

This was a turn in the tide, very unexpected to the adventuress, and learning that the merchant had succeeded in obtaining damaging information of her previous history, she was very glad to accept the terms he offered her and to leave the city at once.

Again she was heard from in Boston, where she was more successful, and where a pious member of an orthodox church, whose voice was loudest in the taber-nacle, and whose virtue was believed to be impregnable, succumbed to the bewitching glances of the seductive temptress and was glad to escape a scene of exposure by paying her a goodly sum of money.

After this adventure she returned to the West and lived for a long time in Detroit, where she again took up the business of a shop-lifter; but being detected, was arrested in that city and held for trial. Several influential gentlemen, however, at this time, out of sympathy for the five children, which this woman still maintained, inter-ested themselves in her behalf, and under a promise of reform, she was allowed her liberty.

Reform was impossible with a woman of her temperament; her appetite for excitement and wickedness remained unabated, and she continued the use of the drugs which had originally led to her degrading practices. For a time, however, she disappeared from the notice of the public, and but little was heard from her, but at length she came to the surface again, and in a more disgusting light than ever before.

In the month of September, 1879, a rather prepossessing female, apparently on the friendly side of forty, made her appearance in the city of Jackson, Michigan, in the role of a wealthy widow who was desirous of investing in real estate in that vicinity. She took up her quarters at a prominent hotel in the city, where she registered herself under the name of Mrs. Kate Larungie, and represented herself as but recently from the South.

She soon made the acquaintance of a prominent real estate broker, who at that time was quite wealthy, but who has since, owing to a succession of reverses, become impoverished. One day while she was walking along the main street with this gentleman, a buggy containing a gentleman of about fifty years of age and his wife passed them, and salutations passed between the two gentlemen. The occupant of the carriage was a Mr. Alvin Patton, a man of considerable means, and who despite his years, was regarded as a rather gay old boy. The comely form of Mrs. Larungie, and her stylish appearance, at once attracted the attention of Mr. Patton, and he lost no time in inquiring from his friend the name of the lady who so much interested him. The information was accorded him, and also the fact that the lady was desirous of purchasing real estate. As Patton was an extensive owner of property, he invited the agent to bring the interesting widow to his house, which he did, and the acquaintance thus begun soon ripened into an intercourse scarcely in accord with the strictest ideas of morality.

Mr. Patton's wife shortly after this departed for the South for the benefit of her health, and solitude reigned in the large mansion. The gay husband grew lonesome, and pined for the distractions of female society, and on the second evening after the departure of the unsuspecting wife, the dashing southern widow was admitted, under the cover of darkness, into the lonely residence of the disconsolate Patton. From that time forth, the sacred precincts of a respectable home were transformed into a Saturnalian realm, with the dashing and depraved widow as priestess over the nocturnal orgies. Patton invited two friends of the same "buckish" tendencies, and over cards and wine the hours passed away upon the wings of pleasure. What transpired within the walls of that reputable home would scarcely be a revelation for ears polite. The spell of the enchantress was upon them, and it was afterward testified that, heated with wine, these men would remove the drapery from the form of the lascivious widow, and hold high carnival in the presence of her unveiled charms. The woman, though apparently entering with hearty zest into these disgusting scenes, was simply playing a part, and never for a moment lost sight of her object; but unfortunately for the success of her schemes, she was too precipitate in her demands. On the fifth morning after these events had commenced, the widow demanded a sum of money from the owner of the house, and he, being of a miserly disposition, declined to accede to her request.

This was the signal for a scene of violence as unexpected as it was disastrous. The irate widow, seizing a large conch shell that lay conveniently near, dashed it through an expensive mirror, shattering it into a hundred pieces, and her temper gaining fury from the first ebullition, she became unmanageable. Curtains, luxurious furniture, and articles of expensive ornamentation were soon strewn about the room in a state of dilapidation and confusion that was appalling. The feelings of the surprised Mr. Patton may well be imagined, and summoning up all his strength and fortitude, the lady found herself upon the sidewalk. An attorney was immediately sent for, and Kate accompanied him to his office, where she divulged to him her demand for money and the events that had followed. She engaged his services in a suit to be commenced against Patton, at the same time accusing him of attempting to take her life with a revolver.

On the following morning the unscrupulous woman again repaired to the Patton mansion, and grasping the bell-knob rang a summons loud and long. The owner of the premises was within, but remembering the experiences of the preceding day, he declined to respond and for fully half an hour the undismayed widow pulled at the unoffending bell, and rained its tintinnabulations into the old man's ears.

Of course this proceeding attracted a crowd and the sidewalk was soon filled with pedestrians who enjoyed the scene immensely. At length, finding her efforts at the bell unavailing she began to try the windows, and finding one unfastened she raised it quickly and sprang into the room, boldly confronting the frightened Patton, who cowered trembling into a corner. Without a word, she rushed into the bedroom, and hastily removing her outer clothing, jumped into the bed. This was too much for the cowardly man to endure, and he immediately dispatched a servant to the house of one of his friends to come to his assistance. This friend was one of the two who had participated in the festivities before matters assumed such a warlike attitude, and he hastened at once to relieve the anxiety of the poor victim who had besought his aid.

Arriving at the house, the woman protested that she had been there all night, and made an attempt to repeat her demolishing operations of the day before. This the new-comer would not permit, and being a man of stalwart proportions, and of considerable nerve, he informed the woman that he would brain her with his cane if she attempted any further efforts of that kind. Finding that he was in earnest she desisted, and a policeman was finally sent for, who conducted the discomfited woman to jail.

A trial followed, in which the disgusting details of their illicit meetings were brought to light, and now a shadow is resting upon the homes of these men, who, until the advent of this dangerous creature were regarded as respectable and high-toned; and the woman, who was none other than Sophie Little, instead of receiving the money she demanded, found herself an inmate of a prison.

How long she remained in jail is not known, but it is believed that her pardon was urged by the very men whom she had attempted to bleed, and she finally returned to Detroit, where she conducted herself more quietly than she had done for some time previously.

In January, 1881, she became the mother of a child, and, considering the fact that her husband had been in prison for several years, and is still in durance vile, the matter occasioned some comment. The woman, immediately after her recovery, began again a systematic course of attempted blackmail, and more than one prominent citizen of Detroit was threatened with exposure as the father of her child, unless he responded liberally to her demands for money. But by this time she had become too well-known to succeed in her demands, or to work any harm in case of refusal, and the "morphine maniac," as she was now generally called, found herself defeated at all points in her pernicious attempts to injure the reputations of respectable men.

At length, becoming exasperated at her lack of success, or acting under the influence of her favorite drug, she attempted to take the life of a respectable citizen of the latter named city. Mr. Harding is a quiet mannered, reputable gentleman, who has always been regarded with favor by every one with whom he was acquainted, and the attack upon him was a surprise to many.

The circumstances attending this occurrence appeared to be as follows: During the month of March Mr. Harding had arrived at his office in the morning, and was engaged in transacting some business with three gentlemen who had called for that purpose, when a lady, heavily veiled, entered, and asked to see Mr. Harding. That gentleman informed the lady that he would be disengaged presently, and requested her to take a seat, which she did. After the business which had occupied his attention had been satisfactorily disposed of, the three gentlemen withdrew, and Mr. Harding turned his attention to the lady, who still sat heavily veiled in his office.

As the door closed upon the retreating figures of the three men, the woman arose suddenly to her feet, and, throwing aside her veil, addressed him in a loud, excited voice:

"Henry Harding, are you prepared to make reparation for the wrong you have done me?"

"I do not know what you mean," said Mr. Harding, utterly surprised at the demand so suddenly made upon him.

"You know very well what I mean," answered the woman, glaring fiercely at him.

"Indeed, Madame, I do not," quickly replied Mr. Harding.

Without another word, the tigress drew from under her cloak a large revolver, and pointing it directly in his face, pulled the trigger. The gentleman was too quick, however, for the excited woman, and, throwing up her arm, the ball was lodged in the ceiling. Instantly she was disarmed, and a policeman was sent for, into whose custody she was remanded, and by him she was conducted away.

She had evidently made a very bad selection in her choice of a victim this time, and all the vile charges she urged against Mr. Harding were utterly disproved by reliable witnesses, and at last the unfortunate and wicked woman will be allowed the necessary time for reflection and reformation under the correctionary influences of a loss of liberty and strict prison discipline.

What her future career may be it is impossible to say, but for her children who will be dependent upon the attention of strangers, and whose parents are both inmates of prisons, a feeling of profound sympathy exists, which may eventually lead them into the right paths and conduce to lives of morality.

I have thus attempted to relate several of the general features of the operations of the confidence man, the bunko steerer and the blackmailer, and have selected those in which the least objectionable revelations were made. There are many cases in which the disclosures are too immoral for recital anywhere, and particularly in a work of this character. I trust, however, in these revelations that I have given an adequate idea of the extensive work of a class of people who may be said to live by their wits, and by the prostitution of talents which would have been more valuable if correctly employed. The existence of these people is at all times precarious. Successful to-day, but to-morrow defeated, impoverished and in the clutches of the law, they finally drift along the swift current of immorality until they reach a miserable end. Too low and too small for great criminals, they have been content with petty crimes and base practices, and in the end the prison or the river are the last resorts of those who, not having the courage to lead good and honorable lives, they slink out of existence by the cowardly methods of the drunkard and the suicide.

The Burglar

IN attempting a description of the methods which have from time to time been adopted by the burglar, I approach a wide field for investigation—a field so varied and comprehensive, that to perform my labor satisfactorily, involves a task not easy of accomplishment. It may be said that ever since man attempted to put safeguards around his possessions, from the time that the thrifty and the cautious took the first measures to secure their valuables from unlawful appropriation, the burglar has existed. At first it must be admitted the precautions taken to secure safety, were both primitive and meager, and the methods of the thief did not of necessity, evince any indications of either merit or ingenuity. They were intended simply to break down the weak barriers which existed between the wealth of their victims, and their own desires to appropriate the property of another, and were in the main, successful. Experience however, is a stern and unyielding preceptor, and after each successful robbery, the honest mind was taxed to produce a newer and a better means of defense than the last had been. Not mere ingenuity alone would now suffice, for the thief became as ingenious as the protector, and despite many curious, and apparently efficient efforts at security, the burglar invariably succeeded in his object, and safely despoiled those who had sought to prevent his depredations by ingenious devices.

Science and invention now came into play, strength and security were believed to be synonymous terms, and stone and iron and steel were fashioned into various unique designs to resist the operations of the daring and irrepressible thieves. Vaults and safes of numerous patterns and of infinite variety were manufactured, and used for the protection of valuable and perishable property, from the devastations of fire, as well as from the operations of the dishonestly inclined. It is a lamentable fact, however, which must be admitted, that the thief kept pace with the skillful manufacturer, and that no sooner was some novel invention brought into general use, than the cracksmen had succeeded in discovering its weakest point, and after a short well-directed effort, obtained an entrance, and robbery was once more successful. Ponderous and imposing safes that seemingly would defy the attempts of a legion of burglars were opened with the ease of inserting one's latch-key into one's own front door, and morning revealed the visit of the burglar, the broken safe, and the exasperating absence of the valuables it had contained.

Incited to renewed efforts by the continued success of these desperate marauders, and resolved to perfect something that would resist their assaults, the numerous manufacturers applied themselves anew to the task, and each year witnessed some new invention or improvement, destined only to yield in the end to the increased knowledge and superior implements of the thief. It seemed that the skill of the burglar was equal to all emergencies, and in many cases, entrances were effected through parts of these strong boxes, which the manufacturers had entirely overlooked in their eager desire to make doubly secure the natural approaches to their contents. Strong bolts were made that were set into weak fastenings, and heavy impenetrable doors were attached to the safes by hinges, which were utterly inadequate to resist the force that was brought to bear upon them.

It is impossible to trace the various and almost numberless improvements, which have been made in the manufacture of fire and burglar-proof safes and vaults. How from cast and wrought iron-plates we have advanced to the chilled-iron, the steel, the franklinite, and the crossed bars within the lining, until it was hoped that honesty had at last triumphed. But the hope was a delusive one, and after the expended labor and skill of years, we have heard the confession made that the best thing even now that modern manufacturers can successfully claim is, that they have at last perfected a safe that will resist the efforts of the most expert burglar sufficiently long to prevent them from effecting an entrance in a single night. The claim is not, therefore, that their safes and vaults are absolutely impregnable, but that their powers of resistance are so great, that it would be impossible to open them by any means until the coming of daylight, and the increasing chances of detection, would compel the thieves to abandon their task uncompleted.

It is idle to decry, or to affect a contempt for the skill of the expert burglar, for experience has demonstrated beyond question that he is possessed of more than ordinary mechanical knowledge, and that his energy and patience are phenomenal. Nor is there any reason why this should not be so. The burglar is trained to his vocation by the hardest discipline known to man. From his earliest and most primitive efforts, until he has mastered all the intricate and difficult points of his questionable profession there are ever present before him two startling alternatives. The somber walls of a prison and a long term of servitude, in case of failure, and in the event of success, the possession of fabulous amounts of money, with which to gratify his every wish and desire.

Is it not to be expected, when by the labor of a few hours, a thief may win for himself many thousands of dollars, that he will bend every effort and devote every faculty of his being, to the accomplishment of his purpose? Criminal history contains many episodes in which the daring thieves have successfully carried away in a single night, money and valuable securities which have aggregated to several hundreds of thousands of dollars, and when we consider the latent desire for the possession, of money, which is inherent in every disposition, and the comparative ease and safety with which trained burglars commit their depredations, it is not a matter of wonder, that long hours and sharpened intellects should be devoted to the task of seeking the easier, and the more effectual means of accomplishing an object, the result of which are fraught with so much pleasure or pain, and which are attended with unbounded enjoyment or long years of suffering and unavailing regret behind iron bars.

When we consider the desperate hazard of the burglar, we can readily understand how careful, and how thorough must be the work which he attempts to do, and how much study and skill have been applied to the tasks which he has set himself to perform.

I have found as many mechanical enthusiasts among the fraternity of burglars, as will be discovered amid the throng of legitimate workmen, and no inventor ever labored more assiduously to perfect a laudable object, than have these desperate men devoted themselves to the discovery of the means to controvert their efforts and to render their inventions valueless and of no avail. In many cases, I have known expert professional burglars, who have expended hundreds of dollars in the purchase of one of these perfected and patented safes, for no other purpose than the endeavor to circumvent its promised safety by a careful examination of its various parts, and of numberless experiments, while secure from interruption or discovery. So exceedingly proficient have many of them become in the art of safe-opening, that I have known of more than one instance where burglars have been taken from their prison cells to open safes and vaults whose owners have forgotten the complicated combinations, by which it was safely locked at a previous time. This, too, after experienced workmen in the honest walks of life had expended their energies and resources in the futile effort to open the safe, without demolishing the costly works which had rendered security thus possible. In every case the burglars succeeded in mastering the combination after the labor of an hour or two, and to the surprise of the incredulous spectators, the ponderous doors were thrown open without the slightest violence or injury to the safes.

When, therefore, dishonest men have attained to such mechanical excellence, it behooves every one who desires the safety of their valuable property to be doubly alert, and ever on their guard against the invasion of their premises by men who are as daring and unscrupulous, as they are skillful and ingenious. Of course the cases mentioned above are rare, but that they occur is beyond doubt, and every, succeeding year but adds to the increasing knowledge of the criminal, and makes absolute protection a matter almost impossible of attainment.

It must not be supposed that the robbery of a bank vault is in every instance but the work of a single night, in which the thieves locate their premises, effect their entrance, demolish the safe and carry off their booty, ere the sun comes peeping over the hills, for such is not and has never been the case.

Indeed, investigation has always shown that weeks, and frequently months, have elapsed between the conception of the plot, and the actual, robbery. Examinations after a robbery has been committed, reveal startling facts, and in almost every case traces will be found, which prove beyond question that the thieves were as thoroughly acquainted with every movement of the bank officials, and with every portion of the despoiled premises as the occupants themselves, and in many instances there are unmistakable indications of the actual presence of the burglars, before the attempt was made to begin the active labor of breaking into the vaults.

As my object is to seek to avert future disaster by timely warnings, I shall endeavor to detail the various movements of the burglars from the time the idea of robbery is first entertained until the crime is committed, and the booty has been carried off. An active service of more than thirty years among this class of criminals enables me to speak from actual experience, and I shall detail only such facts as that experience has brought to my knowledge. If I shall be instrumental in creating a more vigilant spirit among those who offer tempting induce-ments to the skillful burglar, and if my warnings shall result in either decreasing the number of such crimes committed, or in hastening the discovery and appre-hension of the criminals themselves, I shall feel amply repaid for the labor I have performed, and for the time I have devoted to this service.

In personal appearance and manner, the expert burglar offers no warning note to the suspicious banker or merchant, and he may converse for a long time with one of this class without for an instant suspecting his calling, or being aware that the courteous and affable gentleman who is addressing him is at that very moment engaged in a watchful scrutiny, or in laying the ground for a robbery, which may hot only impoverish the institution he repre-sents, but impair its financial credit for all time. Instead of the vulgar, low-browed and sinister looking thief, who figures so extensively in police courts and quarter sessions trials, we have to deal with the gentlemanly and intelligent, the scientific and calculating man of the world. Many of these men have married into eminently respectable families, and have maintained a status in society which forbade the harboring of the faintest suspicion against their honor, or the slightest doubt of their standing in the communities in which they resided.

One of the most noted of this fraternity was believed for years to be connected with the Secret Service of the

United States government, and this belief was entertained, not only by his social companions, but by the young and beautiful lady to whom he was married, and by all of her high-toned relatives. It was not until the vigilance of the detectives under my guidance had traced this gentlemanly burglar to his aristocratic haunts and surroundings, that the revelation was made of his true character, and the humiliation and disgrace which followed this discovery, involved several of the most eminent families in a metropolitan city. It must, therefore, be understood, that expert and professional bank robbers are a distinct and exclusive fraternity, and under no circumstances are to be classed with dishonest practitioners in the lower grades of crime. They stand unrivalled among their associates, and rarely, if ever, stoop to any robbery below that of a bank.

Their ruling ambition is to perform their work in the most skillful and perplexing manner possible, and next to securing a startling amount of money and valuables, their especial pride is in leaving behind them indisputable evidences of their dexterity and skill in the calling which they have adopted, and which they prosecute so profitably.

In the years that have passed, marked improvements have been made in the tools and implements of these cracksmen. They no longer burden themselves with the heavy, massive and unwieldy tools and appliances of former times, or those which even now are in use by the English burglar, but substitute for them small and ingenious, but powerful implements of their own design, and frequently of their own manufacture. Not the least important among these are the simple lamp and blow-pipe for destroying the temper of the metals upon which they operate, and which science has taught these gentry to dexterously use, to soften the hardened metals which heretofore had occasioned so much trouble, and necessitated such a vast amount of labor. The small and highly tempered drills, which silently but surely, gnaw their way into the very heart of a safe—and that wonderful invention, the diamond drill, which has been proven on several occasions to be more than a match for the hardest metals of modern manufacture. Then, too, there are the air-pump; the copper sledge-hammers and mallets with their coatings of leather, whose tremendous blows are scarcely heard; and the all-powerful "Jack-screw," which is capable of a pressure of tons. These and many other like improved and finished tools, of which I shall speak more definitely hereafter, comprise the implements of the burglar of the present day, and in practiced hands render powerful assistance in their nefarious operations.

That so many gigantic robberies should have occurred in the past, and in many instances, without the slightest clue to the perpetrators, evinces, to say the least, a decided lack of that caution which should characterize all careful custodians of the finances of others. In some cases, it was shown that the work of the burglars had been going on, night after night, for weeks; that during the dark hours, while the world was sleeping, the thieves were digging their way, step by step, to the hidden treasures; and while apparently secure from intrusion or interruption in an adjoining building, they removed heavy walls of masonry, and at last entered the vaults, and escaped with their plunder before anyone, even the watchmen upon the premises, were aware of their presence. It may seem incredible, but the instances are not few where this very state of affairs existed.

The devices and expedients of the burglars are almost inexhaustible, and in the pages which follow I will attempt to describe some of the most important of them. No particular mode of operation will answer for all cases, and the robbers evince a fertility of resource and a ready adaptiveness to circumstances, which, while they produce humiliation and loss, cannot fail to excite admiration from an artistic point of view.

We will now attempt to detail, as fully as is possible under the circumstances, the plans of operation of this most dangerous class of criminals—the

Bank Burglars.
Locating their "mark."

ONE of the first things which the burglars consider is the choice or location of their object of attack. Great care is necessary in such inspection, as from the correctness of these investigations; the sole hope of success depends. In this selection various important points are fully and deliberately discussed. The approaches to the bank building are carefully examined, and the peculiar construction and location of the vaults are thoroughly learned from frequent visits to the interior of the bank by men, who, while apparently engaged in transacting some trifling business, or asking some question of a financial nature, are covertly taking notes of everything connected with the general arrangement of matters inside. If the building is occupied by other tenants, this fact is noted, and a general knowledge of the habits and vocations of these people is soon obtained. Adjoining buildings also receive their share of thorough examination, and when the advance guard of the burglars have finished their observations they are as fully informed of everything connected with the bank, as are the officers themselves. Especial attention is paid to the question of how the bank is watched after nightfall; whether the watchers remain within the building, or patrol the outside; and also to discover at what time the watchmen are relieved, or leave the bank in the morning.

Approaches from the rear, at the sides, or through the roof, are also carefully noted, and when all these facts have been acquired, the burglars are prepared to decide the important question as to whether the attempt is practicable or had best be abandoned. Many times, after devoting weeks to these preliminary examinations, the thieves have come to the conclusion that the difficulties in the way of success are too great to be overcome, within a limited time and without detection, and have consequently decided to seek some easier and more accessible object of attack. A large number of our bankers are in entire ignorance of the fact, that their institutions have been carefully examined, and that plans to rob them had at one time, been seriously entertained.

Of late years the banks in the larger cities, have been studiously ignored, even by the most expert professionals, because of the extreme difficulty of effecting an entrance, and the increased chances of detection. But even in such cases, evidences have been obtained which sustain the belief that this avoidance was only determined upon after the premises had been thoroughly and systematically examined. Banks in the less populous cities and in the larger towns therefore receive the attention of these experienced cracksmen, and every care and precaution are necessary to guard against their approaches.

One of the methods resorted to by some of the more expert of this class of burglars, and where heavy robberies are contemplated, is to ascertain, by watching the residence of the cashier, and then to gain an entrance to his sleeping apartment by the measures resorted to by house-breakers or hotel thieves. By this means wax impressions of the keys to the bank building, the vault and the safe, have been obtained while the cashier slumbered on peacefully, and entirely unconscious of the presence of the burglar at his bedside. From these wax impressions exact duplicates are made, and the burglar is then ready for successful operation whenever the proper opportunity arrives to secure the greatest amount of plunder.

Where this plan has been found impracticable, the cashier's house has been invaded by a number of burglars in the still hour of the night, and the entire household have been bound and gagged almost before they were conscious of what was transpiring around them. The cashier was then compelled, upon threats to murder him in case of refusal, to deliver up the keys to the bank, and in some cases, to reveal the combination by which the vaults were opened. Leaving one or two of their number to guard the prisoners the rest of the gang would hasten to the bank, and in a short time, the robbery would be successfully accomplished, and the burglars would effect their escape, before an alarm could be sounded.

In committing these robberies, the burglars exhibit as much reckless daring as mechanical ingenuity; and their exploits, in many instances, rival the imaginations of the romancer and the novelist.

In making their preliminary examinations of the banks throughout the country, the burglars have a very simple, but effective way of ascertaining whether there is a night watchman inside of the bank, without subjecting themselves to the danger and risk of being noticed in watching the premises for this purpose. The device consists of putting a small wedge between the door and the casing of the outer door, in the evening after the bank is closed, and by observing whether this wedge remains in its place until the bank is opened for business in the morning. This proof is deemed conclusive, as on anyone opening the door, the wedge would fall to the ground, and thus show that some one had entered or left the building after it had been closed the night before.

Outside Workers.

HAVING properly located their "mark," or the bank which from examination promises the most satisfactory results, with the least comparative danger of detection, these prospectors of crime notify their companions, who then meet to discuss the means of carrying out their designs of robbery. These being fully decided upon, the active work is begun, and in order to set forth their manner of working I have selected several well-known cases in which the modes of these daring burglars are fully shown.

Utilizing a Safe Manufacturer.

A PROMINENT bank in Elmira, N.Y., was selected, upon one occasion, by a band of the most reckless and expert burglars, with which this country has ever been infested, and they resolved to enter the vault and carry off whatever property it contained.

The bank was located in the Opera House building and the apartments directly over the banking-room were occupied as the assembly rooms of the Young Men's Christian Association of the City, and one of these rooms was found to be located directly over the vault of the bank. Here then was the point of attack—but a careful examination of the premises disclosed the existence of an obstacle which had not been taken into consideration. This room was entered through an iron door, which was secured by a lock of peculiar construction and with the workings of which the burglars were entirely unacquainted. It would have been a comparatively easy task to destroy the lock and effect their entrance by force, but as their labor would occupy several nights, and they would be required to open this lock upon each visit, the breaking of the lock was not to be considered for a moment. Nothing daunted, however, the burglars discovered the residence of the secretary of the association, and one evening they broke into his house and without disturbing the sleeping occupants, searched his pockets, and other receptacles in the hope of finding the keys, and thus obtain a wax impression of them. This, however, failed signally, as the secretary, from habitual caution, had hidden his keys under the carpet in his room, and the burglars were unable to discover them. They accordingly quietly made their exit from the premises, and on the following morning the secretary was greatly surprised to notice unmistakable evidences of a burglarious entry into his room, and considerably more so to find that nothing had been carried away.

The burglars now hit upon the expedient of forming the acquaintance of some one engaged in the manufacture of vaults and safes, who would be fully posted on the subject of patent locks, and whom they could make use of for their purposes. By careful inquiries, they succeeded at length, in finding a man who was engaged in the business, and by devious and tempting ways they began their approaches. In the end their promises of reward proved too glittering for his virtue, and he finally consented to aid them. This much accomplished, the rest proved an easy matter. A note from the city in which the burglars were located was written to the firm with whom the man was engaged, making inquiries about their safes, and this man was sent to Elmira, to look after the interests of the firm in that city. Upon his arrival, he was met by several of the burglars, and their plans were soon completed. It was arranged that a small wad of paper should be inserted into the lock of the iron door during the night, so that it would be impossible to open it in the morning. This plan resulted, as it was expected it would. The safe-man had caused his presence in the town to be generally known, and, on the following day, as soon as it was discovered that the lock would not work, he was sought out and requested to examine it, and, if possible, to repair it. This was just what was desired, and while making a pretense of repairing the lock he obtained impressions of the key. These, in due time, he furnished to the burglars and the difficulty of approaching the vault of the bank was thus cleared away.

The active labor upon the vault was then begun. The burglars located themselves in the suburbs of the city, and every night the gang repaired to the Y.M.C.A. rooms, and taking up the flooring continued their work. Night after night they labored, carefully replacing the floor after each visit; ton after ton of stones were removed and carried up to the roof of the opera house in baskets. There were three or four feet of solid masonry to be dug through, some of the stones weighing fully a ton. Then a layer of railroad iron was to be overcome, and after that a plate of steel, an inch and a half in thickness.

After weeks of patient and untiring labor, the burglars succeeded in working their way without detection, through all these obstructions but the last plate of steel, and were contemplating with satisfaction the successful end of their labors. Just at this time, however, the president of the bank had occasion to go into the vault in the evening, and he noticed with surprise, a thin layer of white dust upon the floor. At once suspecting that something was wrong, he notified an officer, and an investigation was instituted. The alarm was sounded to the thieves and all succeeded in making their escape except one of their number, who was arrested at the door, just as he was coming out. This was one of the most fortunate frustrations of a robbery known, for had they succeeded in their laborious enterprise, they would have secured over two hundred thousand dollars in greenbacks, and six millions of dollars in bonds. As it was, weeks of labor and toil were wasted, and the robbery from which such rich results were anticipated was a failure, while the defeated and disheartened burglars left all their valuable tools behind them when they fled. As an illustration of the patient and untiring energy of these burglars, this incident is fully convincing.

Undismayed, and with a courage worthy of a better cause, this same band of burglars were soon at work upon a bank in a different part of the country. This time they selected Quincy, Illinois, as their point of attack, and the same mode of operation was resorted to. Obtaining access to a room in the bank building, and directly over the vault, they commenced their work. Every night they took up the flooring, and continued their attacks upon the top of the vault. After patiently working for several weeks they at last, reached the safes, and two of their number descended into the vault. Here an air-pump was applied, and powder was forced through the crevices of the doors of the smaller safes, which were exploded without danger or discovery, and the thieves carried away with them one hundred twenty thousand dollars in money, and over seven hundred thousand dollars in valuable securities.

A Singular Performance in an Opera House.

A ROBBERY was at one time attempted upon a leading bank in Covington, Ky., and which but for the excessive caution of the burglars, would have resulted in serious loss to the bank and the community. This bank, as in the case of the one at Elmira, was located in the Opera House Building, and by an examination, it was found that the vault was directly under the auditorium. The burglars fitted a key to the door of the building, so that they would gain uninterrupted access to it, and every night the orchestra seats were removed, the flooring taken up, and work was continued upon the masonry which constituted the top covering of the vault. This was safely and expeditiously taken off, and the descent was made into the vault. Here they charged the inner safes with powder and glycerin, and the explosion which followed was a terrific one. So great was the concussion that resulted from this, that the entire ceiling of the banking-room was torn off, and fell to the floor with a crash, filling the room with a dense shower of bricks, dust and mortar. The watchers, who had been stationed outside, becoming alarmed at the noise, at once, gave the signal for flight, and the men, fearful of their safety, beat a precipitate retreat. In those vaults and almost within their grasp, were four hundred thousand dollars in greenbacks, and a million and a half dollars in good marketable securities.

The chagrin and disappointment of the burglars may be imagined, when they ascertained that their alarm had been a needless one, and that the discovery of the attempted robbery did not occur until the bank was opened on the following morning.

It may seem strange and almost incredible that such things could take place in a city, guarded by night patrolmen, and where safeguards are in existence for the protection of persons and property, but that they have occurred is proven, and that they may occur again at any time in the future, is by no means impossible. It, therefore, behooves every one connected with an institution of this character, to maintain the strictest watchfulness, and to neglect no precaution which tends to conserve safety and protection.

Burglars and Dynamite.

PITTSBURGH, Pennsylvania, was the scene of a daring and successful robbery a few years ago. The bank was a one story brick building, with a tin roof, and failing to secure any base of operation from adjoining buildings, and there being no apartments above, it was resolved by the burglars to make an entry through the roof of the bank building itself. On the first night, the robbers ascended to the roof, from the rear of the building, the tin covering was carefully cut and taken up and the boards of the roof directly over the vault were removed. After finishing their labors for that night, the boards were replaced, the tin laid down, and the joints cemented with a heavy application of red putty. So carefully and completely was this done, that although a terrific storm of rain and sleet occurred on the next day, the roof showed no indications of leaking, and no suspicions were awakened in the minds of the bank officials.

The next evening, the tin and boards were again removed, and work was resumed upon the vault. A layer of bricks was removed, and then the roof was replaced as before. This work was carried on faithfully until the night of the burglary, which occurred about ten days after operations had been commenced. As usual, two men went into the vault, while the others were stationed outside to watch. Inside of the vault were three chilled-iron safes and a burglar-alarm of most approved pattern. It was necessary to resort to their old method of explosion, and in this narrow room, with only a man-hole opening in the top, these daring robbers inserted dynamite, with the aid of an air pump, into the crevices of the doors. One explosion after another followed, and at last they succeeded in opening one of the safes which contained only about five hundred dollars in currency and about sixty thousand dollars in bonds. No less than twelve explosions took place in this small vault, and during all this time, the men remained to face the danger. The last report was a terrific one, and again the watchers gave the alarm. A retreat was thus rendered necessary, and the two men staggered out of the place, deathly pale, their clothes saturated with water, their lungs filled with the noxious gases, and themselves scarcely able to speak or walk. The bonds which they carried away, were afterwards "compromised" back to the bank, but the amount which the thieves realized, was comparatively insignificant.

Brokers Who "Open a Bank."

IN the City of Baltimore, not many years ago, a bank located in the busiest portion of the town, was successfully entered and robbed by an adroit gang of burglars who devoted more than a month to the task of effecting an entrance into the vault. The lower floor of the building adjoining the bank was vacant, and for rent; and one day, a very gentlemanly looking business man applied to the agent of the premises, and expressed his desire to lease the unoccupied premises. He exhibited letters from prominent merchants to insure his responsibility, and on being informed of the rental exacted, made no objection to the figure mentioned. He was questioned as to the nature of the business which he designed to carry on, and he informed the agent, with a bland smile, that his partners and himself designed to transact a brokerage business, and might eventually "open a bank." The sarcasm of the latter intention was not apparent until the bank in the adjoining premises had been successfully "opened" and the burglars had escaped. The offices were duly furnished and arranged for business, and during the business hours of the day, one or two clerks could be seen behind the desks with ponderous account books open before them, and they busily engaged in making entries therein.

Numerous packages and boxes were received and delivered at this place, and every indication of legitimate business was apparent to the casual visitors and passers-by. In the back part of this office there was erected a glass partition which cut off the rear of the room, and divided it into two offices. In this back part the work upon the vaults of the bank was done. A large hole was cut through the wall of the building, directly opposite where the vaults were located, and, night after night, these burglars labored assiduously at their task. Every morning the bricks and mortar, which accumulated over night, was either packed in boxes and shipped away, or carried into the cellar, and piled up in regular order; and the hole in the wall was covered by a large hanging map of the United States, which served the double purpose of concealment and ornamentation. At length the bricks and stones were all removed, and nothing but the iron lining of the vault stood between the thieves and the object of their desires. On Saturday night work was begun upon this iron lining. It is a noticeable fact that the final work of all these bank robberies is generally performed between Saturday night and Monday morning, as the thieves thus have more than thirty-six hours for uninterrupted work. With their drills the burglars bored a succession of holes in a line about a foot and a half square, and before many hours they had succeeded in making an opening sufficiently large to admit of the entrance of a man into the vault. This much accomplished, the rest was easy, and although there was a watchman inside of the bank, the burglars succeeded in opening the inner safes, and numerous tin boxes belonging to special depositors, and making good their escape with over a quarter of a million of dollars in money and valuable securities which could be readily negotiated. This robbery was not suspected until on the following Monday morning, when the cashier on opening the vault, was surprised to find the daylight shining through from the hole in the wall, and the entire contents in utter confusion and disorder.

An examination quickly followed, and resulted in the discovery of the manner in which the entrance had been effected, and also in disclosing the fact that the gentlemanly neighbors had succeeded in their intentions of "opening a bank," and had disappeared entirely from the scene of action.

The Oyster Dealer.

A DECENT looking man, some years since, called upon the cashier of a large bank, in a seaport town, with a view of renting the cellar and basement underneath the bank, representing to him that he wished to open an oyster store; that he had some means to invest in the business, and thought he could make it pay if anybody could. He also stated that he intended to be particular about his customers—selling oysters by the quart only. After some further conversation, the cashier granted him the use of the cellar, and the place was fitted up and opened in due time as a first-class oyster store—the best only were kept, which were brought there in large quantities and quickly disposed of. Two men, strangers in the city, were employed and kept constantly at work opening the bi-valves. They were quiet, inoffensive, and industrious looking men, whose calloused hands betokened hard labor. Besides these an industrious lad, also a stranger, peddled, and delivered the oysters to customers and the business went on prosperously. The banker and cashier, of course, had no time to pay any special attention to their tenants, supposing everything to be right. The rent was regularly paid monthly, and that was all they expected. This state of affairs continued on for some seven months; the oysters being received and disposed of with great regularity, until one fine morning the banker woke up to learn that the bank had been entered—moneys, securities, and all were gone—a "clean job." The vault was "burglar proof," the safe "the very best," but our *honest* oyster-men had silently worked their way up into both, commencing below and going through the bottom of the vault. Indeed, they had it all their own way, and had taken their time, as well as the contents of the vault, which they reached without much trouble. The banker was, of course, horrified to learn that the vault and safe were not "*burglar proof.*"

The Dentist.

NOT long since the cashier of a bank in a large town, was called upon by a very respectable looking man representing himself as a dentist, in search of an office. Having noticed one over the bank, which he considered desirable for the purposes of his business, he proposed to rent the same, and the price being mutually satisfactory, the dentist took possession and fitted up the interior in a handsome manner. His business did not thrive so prosperously as he had imagined but he consoled himself with the remark, that "commencing business is always up-hill work, but patience will compel success in the end." He proved himself to be a first-class operator, however, and several of the bank clerks submitted themselves to his artistic manipulations to their entire satisfaction. During these operations, the dentist won their good opinions, and at the same time adroitly elicited some valuable information concerning the vaults of the bank. The dentist was occasionally visited by friends, who, by a singular coincidence, always came in the evening. These friends evinced a fondness for card-playing, and evidently played late, as the ever-watchful policeman had, on several occasions, observed them leaving the dentist's quarters at very early hours in the morning. No attention was paid to this, however, and the dentist struggled along for a considerable length of time. At last one May morning, about six months from the time the dentist started in business, the bank was opened as usual in the morning, but the door of the vault strenuously resisted all efforts to unlock it. An expert was immediately sent for, who soon demonstrated the weakness of the vault and safe.

The secret was out as well as the money and valuables which the vault contained. The ceiling of the vault was torn out, and the debris had been carefully carried away, by the dentist's card-playing companions. The respectable and struggling tooth extractor and his confederates had done their work successfully. Copper-headed mallets, chisels, blow-pipes, and drills had mastered the "invulnerable steel burglar-proof safe," a little powder had finished the work, and the immense treasures were reached and successfully carried away by the burglars, who had succeeded in pulling, not only the teeth—but the wool over the eyes of the unsuspecting bank people.

The Shoemaker.

A COUNTRY banker, having a room to rent over his bank, put up a notice to that effect, and before many days received a call from a shoemaker, who desired to ply his vocation in that particular locality. The banker being satisfied, the shoemaker obtained possession, fitted up the room as a work shop, engaged three journeymen and a boy, set them to work making shoes, and from the industrious appearance of the establishment, our worthy cobbler seemed to have plenty to do.

The bank below was solid and substantial, with a good reputation for soundness and security against burglars. The safe was a large one, in which the banker placed all his valuables, as well as all his confidence. The bank was guarded at night by one of the clerks, a relative of the banker, who slept therein.

Subsequent to the advent of the new tenant, this young clerk formed the acquaintance of a dashing, jolly young fellow—a new-comer in town, with plenty of money, who dressed in style, and in fact just the kind of a man "for a fellar to have a good time with." He made a great deal of the young clerk, took him out riding, treated him right royally, and soon won the young man's good will and confidence.

One Saturday evening, several months after the shoemaker's first appearance, the young clerk was invited out riding by his now bosom friend and companion. They drove out into the country a short distance, to spend the evening with a number of young ladies, of whom the clerk was very fond. Here they remained, and the time passed away so swiftly and agreeably that it was two o'clock

Sunday morning before they thought of going back. After their return, their horse was put up, and a "night-cap" indulged in, when the clerk invited his friend to sleep with him in the bank. As it was so late, or rather so early, of course the invitation was accepted, and both being tired out, slept apparently very sound, because the clerk subsequently remarked that "he heard no noise during the night." It was late in the morning when they got up; went out, took an "eye-opener," breakfasted together, and then separated for the day. As it was Sunday the bank was not opened for business and the clerk did not remain there during the day, and only returned late at night to retire, seeing then, nothing in appearance wrong with the safe.

On the following morning, however, the banker found a difficulty in opening the safe, and he sent for the village blacksmith and a locksmith, who, after working until four o'clock in the afternoon, succeeded in effecting an entrance, when lo and behold, the entire back of the safe was found ripped open and torn out. The stairway leading to the cobbler's room ran along and behind the safe, and a hole cut from the stairway (carefully concealed during the day), gave the thieves a fine opportunity for working the safe itself effectually, at the same time completely hiding their tools and implements, and ultimately gave them admittance to the cash. Strange to relate, no one ever thought of going up stairs and looking for the shoemaker, until long after the robbery was discovered, and then all traces of him had been obliterated. The young clerk is still puzzled to know why his genial, good-hearted friend should have disappeared at the same time as the cobbler and his company did.

The Barber.

A NEW bank in a Southern city, situated under a new hotel, owned by the banker, had adjoining it, a small building, which had been unoccupied for several months. The bank vault, which was adjacent to this building, was new, well built, and contained a large safe of the most approved construction, and warranted "burglar proof." The cashier was one day approached by quite a respectable looking person, who expressed a desire to rent the vacant building with a view to opening it as a first-class barber shop. He was informed that a barber shop had already been opened in the hotel, and the chance of success for another one so near, was small. The enterprising stranger, however, said he feared no opposition, that he had before this done a successful business under less favorable circumstances; that he intended keeping expenses down; would sleep in the shop, would employ only two or three assistants to commence with, and with a well fitted-up place, good barbers, and sufficient time to establish himself, he did not fear the result. Everything seeming satisfactory, the building was placed at the disposition of our *soidisant* barber, who lost no time in fitting it up regardless of cost. The opening was a grand success; plate mirrors reflected on all sides; luxurious chairs invited customers, and attentive barbers soon attracted a lively patronage. The rent was always promptly paid, and the banker congratulated himself upon having secured a good and harmless tenant. Bye and bye the boss barber induced two of his brothers to visit him. They were dashing, well-dressed young fellows, not remarkable for any family likeness, and evidently not barbers, but moved about town a great deal, transacting a little business at the Exchange now and then, and apparently undecided as to what business they would follow. They seemed well behaved young men, too—always at home early in the evening, and never known to be out late at night. Not a very long time after this, an old and very intimate friend of the barber's also came to town, and took board at a hotel nearly opposite the bank. He was a frequent visitor at the barber's, and being such a warm personal friend, was always invited into the back room, where he passed the greater part of his time.

All this time the Bank was supposed to be well guarded at night by two men, whose business it was to keep one another awake and frighten away burglars. The weather being very warm, these two men would occasionally sit at the open door of the bank, seeing no danger in that, as there was no other entrance. In a short time the barber's friend from across the way made the acquaintance of these men, and would occasionally go over and sit with them of an evening, chatting, joking, and making himself generally agreeable. These visits, in time, became more frequent, until finally the watchmen looked for him regularly. He would entertain them with racy anecdotes, comic songs, amusing stories, etc., always given in a very loud voice, and he was "such good company" that they invariably regretted his departure. Thus matters progressed for months, until, one Monday morning the barber's shop failed to open at the usual time. The watchmen at the bank wondered at this, and took another turn around the bank before the arrival of the clerks, but saw nothing else unusual. The cashier arrived at the customary hour, and proceeded to unlock the vault, when, of course, the same difficulty arose that has been mentioned before, and the same steps were taken to force it open. In short, "the bank was robbed." An examination disclosed the fact that the front of the vault was intact, but the part of it adjoining the barber's shop had been pierced, and the back part of the massive safe torn out. The work had been done so silently that the two watchmen had failed to hear anything, and the work had been completed by Saturday night so far that nothing but the lining of the safe (left by the thieves to throw off suspicion) remained to be removed.

This, of course, was only the work of a few minutes, and thus was perpetrated one of the heaviest bank robberies that ever occurred in the South. The thieves, with their large booty, had taken an early train on Saturday night, and by the time the robbery was discovered, on Monday morning, they were near New York, and beyond capture.

Inside Work.

THE various robberies which I have described were actual occurrences, in which the thieves operated in accordance with the movements I have detailed, and despite every imagined precaution, the banks awoke to the sudden and disheartening revelation that irretrievable loss and ruin were the results of the burglars visits.

The above cases are but a few of the many that have occurred, and I have given these but to show the general manner of working from the outside of the bank.

I will now proceed to detail their movements and operations, when approaches from the outside and from adjoining buildings are impossible, where their labors must necessarily be performed within the bank building proper, and also their operations upon the safes within the vaults. It is in these operations that the burglars display that mechanical skill and ingenuity which have rendered them so dangerous to the banking communities and to safe manufacturers generally, throughout the country.

From my own experience with some of the most noted of this profession, I am able to give such particulars of their modes of working, as will fully disclose many of their transactions which heretofore have seemed to be almost inexplicable. I will also endeavor to explain their various tools and implements and the manner in which they are used.

In gaining an entrance into a bank from the front numerous devices are resorted to, according to the necessities of the case, though in the majority of instances, the burglars prefer to work upon the vaults from the outside. Where, however, the bank is unprotected to a great extent, or the outside watchman can be overpowered, the entrance is made into the bank building from the entrance, and the attack is made upon the front part of the vaults and safes. Two instances which have occurred during my experience will serve to show their manner of overcoming any human obstacles to their success.

Burglars in the Role of Policemen.

IN one of the Eastern cities, there was located a bank which excited the cupidity of the burglars, and they resolved to attempt the robbery by as bold a manner as has ever been chronicled. One of their number, fully disguised as a policeman, called at the bank one afternoon, just before the bank was closed for the evening, and requested to see the cashier. On being presented to that officer, he informed him that the lieutenant of police of that district, had received positive information that an attempt would be made to rob the bank on that or the following evening, and that in order to frustrate this attempt, and capture the thieves, he desired the privilege of sending down four of his men, who would be placed inside of the bank building, to assist the regular bank watchmen. The cashier was greatly alarmed at the intelligence, and at once consulted with the president upon the important matter, and between them, they resolved to adopt the suggestion of the officer of police. It was then quickly arranged that the four men should enter the building singly, in order that no suspicion might be awakened, and that all of the men should be safely lodged within the bank before six o'clock. Particular stress was laid upon the necessity of keeping the matter entirely secret from every one connected with the bank, except the two officers who had been consulted, and the watchmen who were to receive the assistance so much desired. The cashier desired to remain within the building during the night in order that he might witness the capture of the burglars, and the policeman said he would submit this request to the lieutenant and return with his answer; after the lapse of an hour, he again made his appearance, and stated that upon reporting the wishes of the cashier to the lieutenant, that officer had considered the matter fully, but was strongly opposed to such a proceeding, and advised the president, cashier and clerks to go to their homes as usual, so that if anyone was watching on the outside, this fact would be duly noticed and the burglars would take no alarm. He assured the officers, that there was no danger of failure, as the police were ahead of the thieves, and were perfectly acquainted with their movements and intentions, and that as the bank was one of the heaviest in the country every precaution ought to be taken not only to save the bank from loss, but to secure these dangerous and desperate men, and bring them swiftly to justice. Recognizing the force of these arguments, the officers of the bank expressed their willingness to abide by the wise suggestions of the policeman, and requested that the four men be sent and disposed of as the lieutenant should deem best.

When the two watchmen made their appearance that evening, they were directed by the president, to admit the four policemen who would arrive, one at a time and to abide by their instructions. At the appointed time a policeman strolled carelessly along and found one of the watchmen at the door, and he was cordially received and admitted. This same procceding was repeated until the four knights of the locust were safely admitted to the bank, and all were quite elated at having escaped the notice of anyone upon the outside. These guardians of the law were a formidable looking body of men and were well-armed, each being equipped with a brace of massive revolvers. They acted with extreme caution, talked knowingly and evidently fully understanding their business.

The time was passed in pleasant conversation until about eight o'clock when one of the men remarked that he was thirsty, and would like to have a drop of beer, at the same time proposing to go and procure enough for the party, and inviting one of the watchmen to accompany him. The watchman cheerfully assented to this, and the door was carefully closed after them, one of the remaining officers stationing himself at the door to await their return and admit them. The other two policemen and the watchman then walked back towards the president's room, when suddenly the tallest and most powerful of the policemen seized the unsuspecting watchman from behind, while the other forced a gag into his mouth, and in a moment, he was bound hand and foot, and thrown upon the floor, while a blow from an iron jimmy soon reduced him to a state of insensibility. Removing him to an obscure corner the pseudo-officers returned to the front door to await the return of the other. As they entered, and the watchman was walking toward the rear part of the building he was dealt a stunning blow upon the head, and fell like a log at the feet of the men who thus were perfect masters of the situation

The burglars, for such they were, had now no opposition to fear from any one, and after admitting two of their confederates, who were anxiously waiting in an adjoining alleyway, with all their necessary tools and implements, they began to work in earnest. The entire gang were experts in the use of the peculiar tools of their criminal profession, and before many hours, with the aid of blow-pipes, drills, copper-mallets and jimmies, the immense safes were ripped open, their contents exposed, and moneys, bonds and securities were extracted to the value of nearly three millions of dollars. Hastily packing their valuable booty into the satchels which they had prepared for the purpose, the burglars left the bank, and their unconscious victims, and ere daylight dawned they were far upon their way from the scene of their burglarious operations.

It was not until the arrival of the cashier that the injured and manacled watchmen were released, and the robbery was discovered. The story was soon told however, and the bank officials with rueful faces, realized how utterly and ruinously they had been deceived. The whole plan and story was an ingenious fabrication, and the burglars were, as may be inferred, bogus policemen, who had procured their uniforms from a convenient tailor and who played their parts to perfection.

A Cashier as a Burglar's Assistant.

AN Eastern bank, located in a pleasant interior town, was honored a few years ago, by a visit from two celebrated and gentlemanly burglars, who drove into the town with a handsome carriage and two dashing horses. They stopped at the best hotel in the place, and remained in the locality several days, during which time they transacted some trifling business at the bank, changing some large bills and indulging in pleasant conversation with the cashier and clerks who regarded them as very agreeable persons indeed. This was not all that they did however, for during the evenings they quietly watched the cashier when he started from the bank, and following him cautiously they ascertained where he lived, and carefully studied the approaches to the house. They next followed the clerks to their respective habitations, and among other things, they learned that the bank was unoccupied at night. The town itself was not a large one, although several extensive manufactories were in operation there, and it was ascertained that the inhabitants were orderly and regular in their habits and usually retired at an early hour. It was also learned that the few saloons were closed at eleven o'clock, so that the town at midnight was as silent as the churchyard in its vicinity. In addition to this, the gratifying information was gained, that there were no policemen in the town at all, and that no opposition was to be met with from any of the authorities. All these facts were carefully and cautiously gleaned by the observant burglars, and after they had satisfied themselves upon all these important points, they took their departure, and drove away.

Not long after this visit however, on a dark and stormy night, the cashier was rudely awakened from his slumbers, and as he started up he was amazed to find himself surrounded by a number of men, all of whom were completely masked and disguised. The leader of the gang ordered him to dress, after which they bound and gagged him, threatening all the while to murder him if he made the slightest sound, and enforcing their threats by presenting their cocked revolvers at his head. His wife, who was in an adjoining room with a sick child, the servant girl, and two other inmates of the house were also visited by members of the gang and quietly secured. Returning to the cashier, a demand was made upon him for the keys of the bank and vaults. Refusing at first to comply, the muzzles of their pistols were placed against his head, and he reluctantly yielded to their commands, and the keys were surrendered. The leader, who addressed his men by number instead of by name, then directed two of the band to remain in the house to guard their prisoners, while the rest of the gang hurried out to pay their respects to the bank. A short time elapsed, when one of their number returned, and ordered the cashier to accompany them—bound and gagged as he was, he was compelled to walk to the bank, and on arriving there he was required to open the vaults and safes with his own trembling hands, after which he was sent back to the house under guard. The entire contents of the safes were soon transferred to the possession of these daring and desperate burglars, and every article of value was taken. They, then, after carefully locking the safes and the doors of the bank, returned to the house of the cashier, and replaced the keys in his pockets. Leaving the entire family terrified and firmly bound, and notifying them that if they attempted to go out or raise an alarm, they would be killed by some of their number on the outside, the party took their departure, and made good their escape before pursuit was begun in the morning.

These two cases illustrate a few of the methods by which the thieves gain an entrance into some of the banks, and thus succeed in their designs of robbery. In other cases false keys, which have been previously obtained form wax impressions, convenient windows and doors in the rear, form the avenues of entrance to these midnight plunderers.

Methods, Tools, and Implements of The Burglar.

IN all cases of robbery, it is necessary to have some one of their number conveniently and safely stationed on the outside, who is to give the alarm in case of danger. The usual method of arranging this very necessary matter is for the burglars to secure a room on the opposite side of the street, as near to the bank to be operated upon as possible, and this room is generally on the second or third floor, and in the front of the building. When the night arrives for active work, the confederate is stationed in this room, from the window of which he drops a fine strong cord. This cord is then taken by the robbers and carried across to the second story window of the bank, and then continued through to the point where the work upon the safe is to be done. After the burglars have entered the building, either by false keys or any prearranged mode, if the string is in the second story, a hole is bored through the floor and ceiling, and thus let down into the spot where the men are at work. One of the burglars then fastens the end of this string to his hand or arm, and the slightest pull from the other end is the signal of danger and the men then make their escape as best they can. This is the plan generally adopted by the burglars, and it has worked successfully in almost every instance.

In attempting to open a safe, there are several modes which may be adopted according to the necessities of the case—wedging, drilling, the use of the screw, or by blowing with powder. This latter plan, however, is but seldom used of late years by professional burglars, as the noise of the explosion is apt to be heard outside and thus give the party away. The most approved plan is to open the safe with the least noise, and to do this the door of the safe must be forced. This operation requires tools that are both strong and fine, and they must be manipulated by men who understand how to use them. One of the most ingenious and forcible of these contrivances I will attempt to describe at length. This instrument consists of a plate of steel ten inches long, eight inches wide, and about one-half an inch in thickness, in which are fastened two upright pieces of steel which are to act as the support for the upright brace.

This bed-plate is screwed securely to the floor in front of the door of the safe, by six large screws. The box in the center, as I have stated before, is the "slot" which is to receive the upright post or brace. This brace is of peculiar construction and is made entirely of steel. It is three feet six inches long, about four inches wide and an inch thick, with an extra piece of steel of the same thickness, and about four inches square fastened to the top. In the center of this brace there is an opening about an inch wide and nearly a foot long. The following diagram will afford a correct idea of this brace.

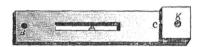

The foot of this upright is placed in the "slot" in the box in the base and then tightly bolted through, the center hole B fitting snugly in the box. In order, however, to make this more firm and to brace it for the pressure it is required to sustain, another smaller plate is screwed to the floor behind E and a strong brace is fitted into this and rests under the shoulder formed by the additional piece of steel upon the top C. When set up the brace with its various component parts presents the following appearance.

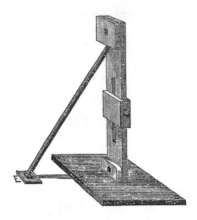

From these comparatively light materials, the burglars have now constructed a brace that is capable of resisting the pressure of tons. In the above cut it will be noticed that there is another attachment, which is a box-slide, also made of steel, the face of which is provided with a number of counter-sunk centers. This box is arranged so that it will slide up or down upon the upright brace at will and can be fastened to its place with a screw (E 2).

With this brace duly-placed in its position the burglar is now ready to commence work upon the door of the safe.

The next implement is the feed-screw drill, which resembles the following figure.

One end of this drill is placed against the sliding box upon the brace, and the other, which holds the drill, is adjusted to the spot where the hole is intended to be drilled into the door of the safe. H shows the feed-screw of the drill, which as the drill cuts into the iron at G, extends the length of the brace, and thus keeps the drill in its position. With this drill, it is claimed, that an inch hole can be bored through the best wrought iron safe door in ten minutes.

After this hole has been successfully bored, the upright is then unshipped from its first position, and instead of a brace it must now perform the duty of a lever. For this purpose a steel screw with a peculiar notch in the head of it, is used.

The upright is then placed horizontally across the front of the safe; the head of the screw is inserted into the hole bored into the door and wedged tightly in, the shoulder being on the inside of the door plate. The thread of the screw is then passed through the opening in the center of the upright, and is made secure with a nut upon the outside. This fastens the upright, or lever, as it has now become, tightly to the safe door. By this operation the double or shoulder end of the upright is brought into position near to the lock of the safe. In this end, it will be noticed, there is an inch hole K, with a screw thread worked into it; into this hole therefore a strong steel screw, an inch in diameter, with a strong square head is inserted, and this screw is then turned by means of a stout steel wrench.

The screw being placed so as to bear directly upon the side of the safe door, and the wrench being turned by two strong men, it is thus pressed against the door with terrific and unrelenting force, and something must inevitably give way inside, and this is generally one of the bolts.

Sometimes, however, the bolts hold too strongly, and though they may be loosened, the door will only be opened perhaps not more than half an inch. This affords an opportunity for the introduction of another powerful instrument in the hands of the burglar, namely, the "compound jimmy." This is an implement made of fine tempered steel, and in two sections, each section about two and one-half feet long, and generally of one and one-half to two inches thick, square, and tapering to an edge at the end.

With this instrument, supplemented by the combined strength of two muscular men, the door is soon forced open, and the property of the bank is at the mercy of the plunderers.

The operations detailed above are such as are used on safes and vaults with but a single door. If in a vault, this method simply overcomes the outer door, and the burglar will find that he has not yet reached the treasure, for that is contained generally in an iron chest inside of the vault. The tools which previously were so efficacious are now found to be too heavy for this new task, but the burglars are prepared for this emergency, and lose no time in renewing their work. A small number of steel wedges are now produced, and starting in one corner they proceed to drive them in, with muffled copper hammers, within a few inches of each other. Ten or twelve of these wedges are inserted in this manner, taking care to drive each of the upper ones as the lower one widens the breach, and loosens their power. When the wedges have produced an opening large enough to introduce the "compound jimmy," that instrument is inserted, and the doors yield to the pressure that is brought to bear upon them. There is no resisting this terrific force, and the contents of the safe are soon exposed.

There is another method which has been put into practice upon single door safes with a great deal of success, and which has frequently caused suspicion to rest upon some innocent young clerk in the employ of the bank. The operation is simple and only requires correct calculation.

All safes are supposed to have three bolts, one at the top, one at the bottom, and one at the center, but all are connected by one bar, and as a consequence, if one bolt is knocked out, the others share the same fate, and are rendered useless. The plan therefore is for the burglar to calculate the position of the center bolt and the point at which this bolt would come out upon the outside and then to drill a hole in the manner above described directly opposite this point. When the hole has been drilled through to the edge of the bolt, they insert a steel punch, and then with a good strong blow or two with a heavy hammer the bolts are completely demoralized. The safe is then opened, the money extracted, the safe closed, the hole in the side plugged up, and no one is able to tell without a thorough examination just how the work was done.

Several modes of blowing a safe with powder have been used, but the easiest and more general one is to drill a hole into the lock, and then force powder through this hole and explode it, which would result in the destruction of the lock and the removal of all obstacles.

In this process very frequently gun-cotton and nitro-glycerin have been used as the explosives, and an ingenious sort of syringe is used for this purpose.

Another method of "blowing" a safe with powder is to putty up all the crevices of the safe compactly except two points. At one of these points the air pump is applied, which exhausts the air within the safe and at the other point the powder is drawn in by the force of the suction, caused by the pumping out of the air at the other outlet. By this means the doors of safes have been forced literally from their hinges by the effects of the explosion.

It has also been a practice to draw the temper of hardened irons with the ordinary blow pipe, consisting of a spirit lamp and a tube, such as jewelers use.

This is quickly done, after which the safe may be drilled with a common steel drill.

Astute burglars make a practice of thoroughly acquainting themselves with all the particulars of the construction of safes, as well as of their locks, and many safes have been opened by drilling out all the riveting of the inner lining, and of the bolts and lock which fasten the same to the outer shell of the door, the position of these rivets being obtained by exact measurement from the outside.

Some safes are so constructed as to give no receptacle for powder or blasting material, excepting in certain apertures of the lock, but so well acquainted with their peculiar internal arrangements do the thieves become, that they are able by measurement from the outside, to know exactly where to place their drills.

The most obstinate safes have been made to yield to the ordinary jack-screw, which is applied in two ways, either by drilling a hole in the door, generally about three quarters of an inch in diameter, then with a screw tap, cutting a thread for a slightly tapering-screw, which by a lever is made to fit tightly into the hole. An attachment is then made with the screw and jack, the latter being supported by a rough frame, and held from the safe by timbers placed against the jambs, when the shell of the door is pulled out by main force, breaking the rivets.

The other method of using the jack-screw is to force the door inward, breaking it into pieces that are easily removed by the "jimmy."

When an abutment for the jack-screw cannot be obtained by placing timbers against a solid partition or other object, a brace is obtained by securing one end of a long timber to the floor, and blocking up the other end, so as to be in a position, central to the door of the safe. Against this and the door, the jack is placed.

A great many fire proof safes throughout the country have been opened simply by the pick and jimmy. With safes that are manufactured of ordinary plate iron, all that is necessary is, first with several well directed blows with a pick to make an aperture just sufficient to receive the sharp end of the jimmy in one corner of the panel, then with the jimmy the iron is ripped and torn out the whole length of the panel, thus exposing the filling—the latter is picked out in a few moments—the bent end of the jimmy is then inserted behind the bolt, and the same pried back by main force, breaking the wards in the lock. This operation has frequently been performed in from fifteen to twenty minutes.

Thieves have adopted a good many ingenious ways of picking locks, and some of them have attained a delicacy of feeling, by which they have been able to determine with fine instruments the exact distance it was necessary to raise each tumbler; but of later years many of the locks have been specially constructed with the view of foiling anything of this kind. Tumbler-locks requiring large keys have been opened by forcing around in them a blank steel key, breaking the wards and forcing back the bolt.

The combination of some locks, it is claimed, can be ascertained by filling each of the apertures, to receive the pivots, with wooden pins, excepting one, in which a small particle of fulminating powder is exploded. Then by withdrawing the pins the exact length of the wards is determined by the amount of discoloration on these pins. The combination of the dial lock can be found by placing under the back of the dials a small peculiarly manufactured ratchet, so that at every reverse motion of the knob, a small puncture is made on the plate upon which it moves, or upon a disc of paper especially secured to it for the purpose of receiving these impressions or punctures.

A celebrated burglar in getting at the contents of the vault and safes of a noted bank had two of these combination dial locks to open, and did all his work in one night.

In all cases of bank robberies, the final work is generally done between Saturday night and Sunday morning. The tools used by professional bank thieves are those commonly used by mechanics—excepting the jimmy, which for the heavier work is made in several sections to be screwed together when required for use— being then about the size of the ordinary crow bar.

"Nipped in the Bud."
A Would-Be Burglar Trapped.

AN "ounce of prevention" is very often "worth a pound of cure," it is said, and events frequently justify the assertion. The following narrative of an accidental discovery and its subsequent benefit to the banking community of a thriving city, fully proves the correctness of that theory, and also furnishes additional support to one of the maxims of my Agency that "The eye of the detective must never sleep."

During the latter part of the year 1876, my son, William A. Pinkerton, was engaged in Chicago upon an operation which required him to temporarily consort with a number of professional thieves and burglars, and in the course of which he made numerous acquaintances among that fraternity. One day while he was in company with several of these "Knights of the Jimmy," at a saloon which was noted as a resort for this class of people, a letter carrier entered with a letter in his hand, and addressing the proprietor, said:

"I have a letter here for 'Tip Carroll,' directed in your care."

It was well-known among the frequenters of the place that "Tip Carroll," who was a notorious confidence man and general thief, had some time previous had an altercation with the proprietor of the saloon, which had resulted in engendering an enmity between the two men which promised to be lasting.

As the carrier threw the letter down upon the bar, the saloon keeper uttered an oath to the effect that Mr. Carroll might depart to Plutonian spheres before he would attend to the delivery of the epistle to him.

He tore open the envelope, and was about to read the contents when William interposed, and good-naturedly remarked:

"Never mind, Tom; I'll see that Tip gets his letter."

"Take it, then," said Tom, "I don't intend to bother with the infernal thing," and he tossed the letter over to William, who placed it in his pocket.

William thought no more of the matter until evening, when on returning to the agency; he remembered the events of the morning and drew Mr. Carroll's letter from his pocket. As he did so, an irresistible curiosity to know the contents took possession of him. He very well knew the character and the associates of the man to whom the letter was addressed, and he felt reasonably sure that a perusal of the missive would be of advantage to him in a professional way. He felt convinced that the cause of justice would sanction such a proceeding, and the sequel fully proved that he was correct. At length, satisfying all mental scruples, he drew the letter from its inclosure and read as follows:

"DALLAS, TEXAS, Nov. 1, 1876.

"TIP CARROLL,

"DEAR SIR:—I wish you would send me your address so that a letter could reach you without any person seeing it. I have some important business with you.

"Address,

"BUSINESS,

"P. O. Box,

"Dallas, Texas."

Feeling confident that something of a "crooked" nature was implied by this communication, William laid the letter before me on the following morning, and requested my opinion and advice upon the matter. Very little consideration convinced me that the surmises of William were well grounded, and I resolved to ascertain further particulars about "Business," and the nature of the "business" which he had with Mr. Carroll. I, therefore, directed William to reply to the letter in a cramped disguised hand to purposely misspell his words, and to request "Business" to direct his response to Peter Carroll, to the number of one of my post-office boxes in the city.

This was done, the letter simply containing the name of Peter Carroll and the number of the P. O. Box to which the communication should be directed. In about ten days after this, a letter was received with the Dallas P. O. mark upon it and addressed to "Peter Carroll, P. O. Box, Chicago, Ill.," and a perusal of its contents fully justified the motive which had led to the opening of the first letter. This epistle read as follows:

"DALLAS, NOV. 12, 1876." FRIEND TIP:—Your note came to-day. Now pay attention to what I have to say, I have a chance to make fifty or a hundred thousand dollars, if you know one or two good cracksmen that understand their business perfect. I will give them a good show. It can be done without any trouble, but they must understand their business. They are banks. Write in haste.

"Yours in confidence,

"BUSINESS,

"Box 1663,

"Dallas, Texas."

I now began to distinguish the flavor of a very large mouse, and I resolved to follow the matter up to a satisfactory conclusion. I accordingly prepared a reply to "Business," which I thought, would answer the purpose, and induce this would-be burglar to disclose his identity. The next day the following letter was written and mailed.

"CHICAGO, Nov. 16, 1876." BUSINESS, "DEAR FRIEND:—Yure note just received. i can git the people you want to do yure buisness and do it well. They will be two of the best Gopher men in America. But now you must talk business. You kno I must kno you. Of corse you kant egspect me to go into anything of this kind without knoing who I am dealing with an all partickilars, rite me at once an let me kno, an I will give the matter attention an furnish good men. Rite what make the Gofes are, so they can tell what kind of tools to bring "Yours truly, "TIP."

This letter, as I fully expected, had the desired effect, and in due time the expected reply was received.

"DALLAS, Nov. 21, 1876.

"FRIEND TIP:—Your note came to hand to-day, and I was glad to get it. Now Tip, you ask me my name. I don't blame you in the least. Tip, those vaults are of common soft brick with dibold doors and insides; you can enter about nine o'clock and stay till five in the morning, and nobody to bother you if they don't make too much noise. There will be no trouble in the least if they are good at their business. Now Tip it is a long time since I seen you and you will be surprised when you see my name. But I hope and trust you won't reveal it, for here is the only easy chance you will ever have to make a fortune. All I want is for you to do just as I say; when you leave, come straight through, and when you come to Dallas, one of you register at the St. Charles, as W. J. Smith, St. Joe. Mo.; you, L. Evans, at Commercial Hotel; the other, C. Biddle, Baltimore, Mo., at Lamar Hotel. These are the hotels, and I will watch for those names, and don't go around until I see you, and if I don't see you the night you come, a postal will find me and I will take care of all. Tip, you must not delay, but attend to this at once; Tip, when you read my name you need not faint, for I guarantee it is all right, and if you will do as I say we will both be all right.

"My name is Tom Speider, you know me now; don't be alarmed everything is all right.

"1663, Dallas."

The true character of "Business" was now fully disclosed, and his name was at once recognized. Some fourteen years prior to this he had been engaged as a traveling pickpocket and confidence man, and had at one time been a member of the police force in Chicago.

At that time he operated with "Tip" Carroll, and was, therefore, personally acquainted with him.

I resolved to warn the bankers of Dallas against this man, and to make inquiries in reference to his present habits and occupation; I accordingly wrote to the president of the First National Bank of that city, giving him all the information that I had as yet received, and recommending him to inform all others engaged in the same business of the discovery I had made; I stated the matter fully to them, and advised a course of action which I thought would result in bringing the would-be burglar to justice. A few days after this I received a letter from Mr. Kerr, the president of the bank I had addressed, stating that after consultation with the various banks and bankers in the city, they had resolved to place the matter entirely in my hands, and that I should take such steps as would not only prevent the present scheme from succeeding, but that would result in placing Mr. Speider where he would not be likely to do any further mischief of the kind contemplated.

The letter also contained the information that Mr. Speider was advertising himself as a detective, and was engaged in watching several of the banks in the city of Dallas. From his position, therefore, he was fully qualified to carry out the scheme which he had suggested, and had his original communication not fallen into the hands of my son, he might have been successful in robbing the institutions which trusted him of a considerable amount of money.

As it was, however, I determined to outwit this pseudo-detective, who was a gross libel upon the profession, and to arrange such a plan as would bring him within the pale of the law and its punishing influences.

Knowing full well that Speider was acquainted with Tip Carroll, and that it would be impossible to personate that individual in consequence of such acquaintance, I prepared a letter which requested delay in consummating arrangements, and had it mailed from the city of New York, where it was alleged Carroll then was. The letter stated that Carroll would return in a short time, and as soon as he arrived in Chicago, he would arrange to carry out plans proposed to him. This was intended to pave the way for a suggestion which would enable others to take the part originally designed for Mr. Carroll, and in which I should have the opportunity of making the selection.

After allowing a sufficient time to elapse, another letter was prepared for Mr. Speider as follows:

"CHICAGO, Dec. 4, 1876." FREND TOM:—I got home Saterday and got youre postel. i saw my men yesterday and got em reddy to start, yesterday i got nocked down by a slay an run over an severely bruised, an my left elbo nocked out of joint, so i ain't fit to travel or do enything, but i will advance the money an send the men on to-day, they leave here to nite an will git there as as soon as this letter. they air from Buffalo, Arther Garrity will have a letter to you from me, he will stop at St. Charles hotel an will register name of W. J. Smith, St. Joe. Missorey. He is a man about 33 years of age, 5 ft. 9 ins., small thin face, brown mustash, dress ruff, dark overcoat, black slouch hat an stoop sholders, wen you mete him ask him how Buisness is in St. Joe. an he will say Business is about the same as it is here in Dallas, then he will reconise you an will introduce you to the pal who is Tom Emmett, an will register name C. Biddle, Baltimore, Md., at Lamar Hotel. Now Tom, i hav dun all i can fur you, an i leve you an the other men to say what amont of the swag i out to have, an i am only sorry i can't be present, i bot all the tickets and got the tools, so i out to stand in to sum extent. Garrity don't want to take the pullingjack i bout in New York, he says he can do the work without an i will see he has every-thing else, you will find him game, a good workman an a ded rite man. Now Tom for God sake be carefull, work shure. i will be anxious til i here from you.

"Ever yure frend,

"TIP."

Prior to dispatching this letter, I sent one of my opera-tives, Mr. Rogers, to Dallas, in order to arrange the plans necessary for the proper working of the operation I had perfected. Mr. Rogers arrived in Dallas in due time, and was met by Mr. Kerr, the president of the bank originally written to, and was conducted by that gentleman to the hotel where he was to lodge while he remained in the city.

Mr. Rogers found the banking men in a feverish-state of anxiety, which threatened materially to interfere with the success of our enterprise. They had all been informed of the matters thus far ascertained, and betrayed their interest in such a manner that Rogers was fearful they would betray our movements and thus frustrate the design we were desirous of accomplishing. It is always a difficult thing to manage an operation where those who are inter-ested are numerous, and where the proposed measures must be submitted to and discussed by many, and realizing this fact, Mr. Rogers endeavored to impress them with the necessity of the utmost caution. Finally, however, it was definitely arranged that the matter should be placed in the hands of two of their number who were to consult with Mr. Rogers, from time to time, and to whom all reports were to be made as the operation progressed. These matters having been fully arranged and everything being in readiness to commence operations. I got my two men ready in Chicago, and giving them full instructions and providing them with a full set of burglar's tools they started for the city of Dallas, to perform their parts as expert cracksmen.

One of them had been provided with a letter of introduction from the supposed "Tip," which read as follows, and which was to be shown to Mr. Speider after they met.

CHICAGO, Dec. 4, 1876. "FREND TOM:—The bearer of this, is my frend Arther Garrity, about who i rote you. He is a good frend of mine, an understands all about our buisness, talk to him just the same as you would to me, he is all strate. he wil interduce you to his frend, an tel you all about me. pleas du all you can fur him, with kind regards. i am yure frend, Tip.

The men arrived without accident at Dallas, and going to the hotels designated by Speider, they registered themselves as directed by him. In the evening, and before they had met Speider, they arranged an interview with Rogers, and obtained from him all the information that had been learned since his arrival, and also received his instructions as to their mode of proceedings.

On the following morning, as Arther Garrity (or as his name really was Woodford) was sitting in the reading room of the hotel where he had engaged quarters, he was accosted by a tall, stout, rather good looking man about forty years of age, who approached him familiarly, and extending his hand, said:

"How do you do, Mr. Garrity, how is business in St. Joe?"

Garrity arose, and taking the proffered hand of his questioner, replied with a smile and a wink, in the most approved style of the Gopher fraternity:

"Well, I guess business is about the same as it is here in Dallas."

During the time that he was awaiting the appearance of Speider, Garrity procured the services of a barber, and his hair was cut in the fashion so much affected by those who pass as sporting men, and as he tipped his hat over his eyes and greeted the newcomer, he fully portrayed the character he was personating.

The man who thus accosted him was Tom Speider, the writer of the letters, the detective-watchman, and would-be burglar, and after several inquiries in regard to the health of "Tip," and the accident which had suddenly befallen him, the two repaired to the bar of the hotel, where they cemented their acquaintance with a drink. After this they proceeded to the hotel where Emmett was stopping, and where they found him awaiting their arrival. Garrity introduced his companion to my operative, and the three men then strolled toward the outskirts of the city where they could converse with more freedom and without fear of being overheard. As they walked along, both men endeavored to impress upon Speider their ability for the work in hand, and so fully did they succeed, that before their return, the projector of the enterprise was quite enthusiastic in his praises, and perfectly sanguine of successful operation. He again wrote to his friend Tip, acquainting him with the fact of the arrival of the two men and of their intentions, and this letter was replied to by me to the entire satisfaction of the concoctor of the contemplated burglary.

The next day Speider took the two men to the locality of the bank which it was proposed to enter, in order that they might look over the ground and make their plans accordingly. The institution that was to be made the object of attack was the banking house of "Adams & Leanord," which was reported to carry daily balances of from fifty to one hundred thousand dollars, and whose building could be more readily entered than any of the others. Speider had charge of the watching of this bank, and hence the chances of detection would be considerably decreased. The two men carefully noted all the surroundings and freely debated upon their best course of action, and from the manner in which they discussed their plans, Speider was entirely satisfied that his friend "Tip" had made an excellent selection of men for the work, and his mind was already filled with visions of suddenly acquired wealth.

Meanwhile Rogers had consulted legal authority, and it was discovered that in order to fully sustain a charge of conspiracy, such as this would naturally be, there must be evidence of the complicity of more than one guilty party, and that in order to convict Speider of the charge he must be proven to have been connected with others than the detectives, in this attempted robbery of the bank. This information was communicated to Emmett late on the following evening, and they were directed to ascertain if there were not some other persons interested in this burglary than themselves and Speider. The next morning, therefore, by adroit questioning they discovered that the policeman who patrolled the beat in which the bank of "Adams & Leanord" was located was connected with the matter in some way, and that he was to manage matters so that the parties working inside should be duly warned of any approaching danger.

After dinner on that day Garrity and Emmett took Speider to their respective hotels where they secured the tools which had been brought for the purpose, and Speider after gazing at them admiringly, suggested that they be conveyed to his house where his wife would take good care of them and where they would be much safer than if they were left at the hotel, where the prying eyes of chambermaids and porters might discover their nature and thus spoil the whole operation. At this suggestion both men appeared to grow suspicious and gave vent to their doubts in such language that convinced Speider of their sincerity and which called from him such profuse expressions of fairness and square dealing, that the men were reluctantly convinced, and they finally wrapped the tools up carefully, which were carried to Speider's house and handed over to Mrs. Speider for safe keeping. Speider was finally led to speak of the policeman, and upon Garrity suggesting that he could not be trusted, the watchman declared that Duff, the policeman, dared not go back on them, as he had been implicated in several small burglaries prior to this which would send him to the penitentiary if he dared to do anything that would jeopardize the present undertaking. Garrity declined to be satisfied with this, however, and insisted upon seeing the policeman himself, so as to be thoroughly convinced that he was all right and would perform his share in the work without fail. Speider promised that the policeman should meet them that evening, when they could talk the matter over fully with him and that they would then be convinced that he could be depended upon to do all that was required of him.

This being satisfactorily arranged they agreed to wait until nightfall before taking any further steps in the matter, Garrity declaring that he wanted to be sure that everything was all right before he did anything further. That evening therefore the policeman was on hand and the four men discussed their plans fully. Duff was to get his partner away from the locality at an early hour in the evening, and was himself to patrol the streets in order to apprise those who would be working within of the approach of anyone who might hear the noises inside and give an alarm. It was further arranged that the following Sunday evening should be selected for the work and that everything should be in readiness for the operation at that time. It was also found necessary to procure a sledge-hammer in order to force the doors of the bank vault and Speider guaranteed to furnish this, which he did by stealing one from a blacksmith shop on the following evening and had it covered with sole leather by one of his boys in order to deaden the sound, and thus prevent detection.

From day to day Rogers had been advised of all that was transpiring and his information was duly forwarded to me and also laid before the members of the bankers committee, who had the matter in charge. The men spent their days in the various saloons and in a manner that avoided all suspicion of their true character and won for them the unqualified admiration of Speider.

Sunday afternoon arrived and everything was in readiness for the undertaking—a close examination had been made of the bank premises and the mode of effecting their entrance fully decided upon. As the time approached, Speider and Duff began to grow extremely nervous. Already they saw a fortune within their grasp, and had already devised plans of expending a considerable portion of it. The plan as arranged was that Duff should patrol the streets in the vicinity, while Speider was to remain on guard in front of the building. Garrity and Emmett were to enter the bank and perform the work and then the proceeds were to be divided in such proportion as had originally been agreed upon.

During the forenoon when it was arranged that Speider and Duff should be induced by my men to walk to another part of the city, Rogers accompanied by the sheriff and a Deputy United States Marshal, entered the bank building, in order to anticipate the arrival of the invaders. These men made themselves as comfortable as possible under the circumstances, and were fully prepared for the labor that they expected, would fall to their lot.

Late in the evening Garrity, Emmett, and Speider repaired to the residence of the latter, and received from Mrs. Speider the tools which had been left in her care. The dark lantern had been cleaned and filled, and was ready for use, and the sledge-hammer had been neatly covered with sole leather. Separating at the residence of Speider that gentleman took charge of the implements which he deposited in a safe place in close proximity to the bank while the others proceeded by a circuitous route, and reached the locality where they found Speider awaiting their arrival. Garrity, however, refused to proceed further until they were certain of the whereabouts of Duff, the policeman, and Speider started in search of him. In a few moments he returned with the blue-coated official, who explained that he had just been making arrangements to send his partner, who was weak and sickly, home, under promise of patrolling in his stead.

The two men were stationed outside, and then Garrity and Emmett, taking up their tools, made their way to the rear entrance of the bank, the door of which had been conveniently left unlocked by Rogers, who was waiting within. After waiting a few minutes under pretense of forcing an entrance, the door was swung open and the two men entered. Here they found the officers of the law and Rogers engaged in partaking of a midnight-lunch, and apparently taking things quite coolly. Seating themselves the new arrivals proceeded to pass the time away, occasionally striking the hammer against one of the tools, and flashing the rays of the dark lantern across the window in order to convince the watchers outside that they were busy. Thus they passed nearly three quarters of an hour and at the end of that time, thinking that Speider had become sufficiently impatient, and anxious, Garrity went out to see him. It was of the utmost importance that Speider should be captured inside the bank, and Garrity therefore informed him that they wanted additional help in order to open the door of the safe and requested his assistance.

By this time Speider was ripe for anything, and without a word of demurrer he started to follow Garrity into the bank. Garrity, however, cautioned him against this and told him to give a good look around before coming after him, and then he returned and informed the officers who stationed themselves in convenient positions for his arrest. In a few moments the door was slowly opened and the face of Speider appeared in the opening. Noiselessly he entered, and just as he had removed his shoes, and was about to advance towards the safe, Emmett flashed the lantern upon him and two officers grasped him by the shoulders. Two pistols were pointed at his head, and he realized at once that resistance was worse than useless. He gazed helplessly around and at length muttered:

"A put up job by God! and I am in for it!"

He was soon secured, and then Garrity and the Marshal started out after the policeman. Finding him in close proximity, a similar application of force and the like display of revolvers were sufficient to induce him to surrender.

A visit was then paid to the residence of Speider, and his family was arrested, Mrs. Speider being fully dressed and anxiously awaiting the return of her husband with the promised fortune, and the two boys lying in bed with their clothes on.

The entire party was marched to the station, and was duly bound over to await their trial, and the punishment they so richly merited was soon thereafter dealt out to them.

A feeling of relief pervaded the entire banking community of Dallas, when the success of our operatives became known, and all were united in praises of the efforts which had led to the discovery of the true character of a trusted watchman who was conspiring to defraud them.

Thus it was that the accidental receipt of the original letter of "Business," led to the unearthing of a contemplated crime, and effectually prevented the commission of a burglary, which under other circumstances, would have been successfully consummated.

The methods mentioned above are those which have been successfully operated by the burglars, who have infested the country from time to time during the past, and I have endeavored to show the daring and skill displayed by these reckless men, and the proficiency they have attained in their questionable calling. Nerved to his task by his fear of detection, and his desire to obtain the vast wealth of others without the labor of earning, and the delays of accumulation, the burglar brings to bear upon his undertakings, all the resources of his cunning and skill. Numerous expedients are resorted to and experimented with, until a plan is matured sufficiently to warrant operation with a sure prospect of success. Then comes the manufacturing of the tools and implements, which is easily accomplished, and the burglar is fully prepared for his work of plunder and destruction.

From the above it will be seen that too great care cannot be exercised by those who occupy responsible positions in the management of large financial institutions. The thief and the burglar are ever on the alert to discover the weak points in the bank buildings that come under their notice, and it behooves every one to see that no such weakness exists. Watchmen upon the inside and outside of the building, strict discipline among the clerical force, and a careful watchfulness, maintained upon all strangers who approach the bank, or are seen in the vicinity, will tend very much to secure the protection so much needed. "Eternal vigilance is the price of safety," and this fact is in no case more true and potent than in guarding banking institutions from the attacks and depredations of the daring and skillful burglars who exist in such large numbers throughout the country.

Forgers and Forging

FORGERY and counterfeiting are very closely allied to each other, the former being, in fact but another form of counterfeiting than those I have previously described, where the paper and coined moneys of nations and banking institutions are successfully imitated, and passed for their full value upon the ignorant and the unsuspecting. Forgery, in almost all of its phases, requires more skillful and delicate workmanship than ordinary counterfeiting, from the fact that the imitations thus produced must be so close and perfect, as frequently to deceive the very men whose signatures and forms are dishonestly copied. Banking house tellers are skilled in detecting the slightest variations from the genuine paper presented to them for payment, and they are quick to discover any defect in the signatures of their depositors with whose handwriting they have become familiar. To perfect, therefore, a forged check of some permanent business house or corporation, for a large amount of money, many things are required of the forger, which only those skilled in the art are capable of producing. In the first place, the style of paper on which the check is printed must be similar, then, as most depositors have their own specially printed checks, the imitation in the engraving of the various designs, must be simulated perfectly. Then comes the filling up of the body of the check, then the proper number, and last, though very far from least, the forging of the peculiar, and the well-known signatures of the drawers of the check. It must be remembered that it is not the casual and careless observer, who is to be deceived, as in the passage of counterfeit money, but the skilled and educated officer of the bank, who has been trained by years of experience, to a quickness of judgment and a sharpness of vision in such matters, which in many cases seem to be phenomenal. Not only must the forger be a finished penman, but he must possess a wide knowledge of the chemical qualities of the various inks which are used in the commercial world, in order procure perfect imitations of their colors and density; and he must be shrewd enough in a business sense, to obtain many trifling items of information, regarding the work he designs to perform, without which success would be utterly impossible.

It is, of course, necessary for the forger to obtain a genuine check, before he can accomplish his work of imitation, and this difficulty is generally overcome in a straightforward, business-like manner. If the check of a broker or a banker is desired, a small government bond is disposed of, and the forger requests a check for the amount, as he wishes to send it away by mail. No suspicion can possibly attach to a request of this simple character, and the check is given without hesitation. If a merchant has been selected as the victim, the forger has been known to make a small purchase and present a large note in payment, say a one hundred or a five hundred dollar note, and then to politely request that a check be given him for the balance due him, as he is afraid he may lose the money before reaching his home, which is outside of the city. This explanation is generally received in good faith, and the check is obtained. Various methods are adopted to meet the varying requirements, and in the incidents which I shall hereafter detail, their full working will be illustrated.

As may be imagined, only the most skillful men have been able to obtain any success in this particular branch of criminal practice, and hence the number of successful forgers have been comparatively small, although a sufficient number have existed to prove of severe embarrassment and serious loss to many careful and honest business men and sound financial corporations.

Hundreds of thousands of dollars of worthless bonds of corporations have been forged and counterfeited, and have been accepted as genuine by men who were considered excellent judges of such matters, and when detection occurred, it has frequently been found almost impossible to point out any material differences between the genuine and the imitation. Banks and savings institutions have loaned large sums of money upon these fraudulent imitations, and have carried them in fancied security for a long time, before their spurious character was discovered. When such things, therefore, are possible in this day of business intelligence, and advanced modes of commercial interchanges, it is evident that the individuals capable of producing such deceptions must be possessed of more than ordinary skill and genius.

In attempting to afford the reader a definite and somewhat comprehensive idea of the modes of operation of the forgers, I have selected several instances of successful work in that line, in order to more adequately illustrate this manner in which this work is done, believing this to be a better means of illustration than a mere technical description of their tools and implements, and their manner of using them.

Draft Raising.

DURING the year 1877 considerable consternation was caused among the banks of several of the Eastern cities, by the discovery of a number of raised drafts, which had passed unsuspected, through several banks, and had been paid without a doubt or question of their genuineness. The methods adopted by the men who had so successfully carried out this scheme, were exceedingly simple, but so complete was their work in its execution, that failure was almost an impossibility. Although several men were engaged in this fraudulent work, but two men were necessary for success at any given point, and hence they were not so liable to detection as if a number of confederates were engaged. It was the business of one of these men to enter a bank, and purchase a draft on New York City, for a certain amount of money, usually about fifteen hundred dollars, and a short time after this, another draft would be procured from the same bank for a small amount, seldom over ten dollars. These drafts procured, they were handed to the "raiser," or the man who was to alter the paper for their dishonest purposes. In a short time the small draft was raised to be a perfect duplicate of the large one, in every sense of the word, both as regards number, amount, place of presentation, &c. I have seen several of these altered drafts, and they were the most skillfully executed, of any articles of the kind which I had ever seen, and were in all respects well calculated to deceive. This work of alteration being fully completed, one of the men would then remove to another city, and forward the "raised" draft to New York by express for collection, or else would go to that city himself, and have it cashed through some respectable person. Immediately on receiving the money he would telegraph his companion in words previously agreed upon, informing him of the successful result of the first move. The other confederate, upon the receipt of this information, would then at once repair to the bank where the drafts had been procured, and presenting the genuine draft for the large amount of money, would request that the money be refunded, giving as an excuse for not using it, either that he could not be identified in the New York bank, and for that reason could not collect it, or that the business he had procured it for had not been consummated. The bank officials would at once recognize him as the person who had purchased the draft, and would unhesitatingly hand him back the money, which he had paid. Of course he would quickly disappear from that locality, never to be seen in it again— and the forgery would not be discovered until in the due course of ordinary business, the other draft for the same amount would be returned for payment. This mode of swindling had been done so successfully that more than a hundred thousand dollars were realized in an incredibly short space of time, and before any general well-grounded suspicion of foul play had been formed.

Being retained by several of the parties who had suffered severe losses in the manner above related, I soon succeeded in ferreting out the men who were concerned in these swindles, and they were eventually punished, besides which I recovered nearly thirty thousand dollars of the money they had so fraudulently obtained.

An Amateur Forger.

THE perpetration of successful forgeries have not been confined to those skilled in crime, or whose long experience in acts of dishonesty, have enabled them to deceive with impunity. There are instances on record where men whose previous lives have been stainless, whose honor was above reproach, have become by one act the successful forger, and the skillful criminal. In the year 1880, my attention was called to a matter which fully illustrates this proposition, and I will relate it here.

One afternoon, early in the month of July, and in the year I have just mentioned, a young lad sauntered leisurely through the park, which surrounds the municipal buildings in New York City. The lad was a bright, handsome fellow, in whose face was reflected the evidences of intelligence and honesty, but there was also a careworn, anxious look about him, as though he was in trouble. He finally threw himself down upon one of the benches, and drawing from his pocket a daily paper, began eagerly to scan the column of "wants." The shadow of disappointment deepened as he finished his perusal, wearily folded the paper, and placed it in his pocket. While he was engaged in reading, however, he had been carefully observed by a well-dressed man, who stood at some distance removed from him, and regarded him intently.

Apparently satisfied with his scrutiny, the man approached the bench where the boy was sitting, and took a seat by his side. His appearance attracted the attention of the boy, who noticed that one of the sleeves of his coat hung loosely by his side, the stranger having lost one of his arms.

The man addressed a few questions to the youth about various localities in the city, and finally inquired if he was engaged in any employment at present. To this, the youth replied that he was not employed and was very anxious to procure something to do.

"Can you write a good hand?" asked the stranger.

The boy replied that he could.

"Perhaps you are just the boy I am looking for then," said the man. "If you will come over to my hotel, and give me a sample of your handwriting, I can decide at once."

The lad jumped up with alacrity, and followed the man without hesitation. They proceeded directly to French's Hotel, and ascended to the upper-floor, where the stranger, unlocked one of the rooms and invited his youthful companion to enter. In the center of the room there was a table on which were scattered writing materials and directing the young man to take a seat, he requested him to write a sample of what he was able to do. The young man noticed that the paper which was handed to him contained the name of "Babcock & Co., Jacksonville, Florida," printed at the top of the sheet, and that it was an ordinary letter-sheet, used by business-houses in conducting their correspondence. The boy wrote for some time at the dictation of the stranger, who after examining it carefully, expressed himself well pleased with the result.

"I think your writing will answer very well," said he, after a pause. "I will not have any work for you to-day, but if you will call upon me to-morrow morning I will be able to give you something that will keep you busy."

The boy thanked the stranger for his kindness, and promising to report promptly on the following day, took his leave, the stranger at the same time placing in his hand, a bright silver dollar. Faithful to his promise, the boy called at the hotel on the next morning, and was shown into another room to which his prospective employer had removed since his first visit.

The stranger, whose name was afterward discovered to be James Babcock, greeted the boy very kindly upon his arrival, and placed a chair for him at a table near the window. After the boy had seated himself, Mr. Babcock handed him a piece of writing, to which the name of "A. J. Baldwin" was signed, and requested him to imitate the signature as nearly as possible. The boy made a number of copies of the name, endeavoring to follow closely the copy set before him, and at length Mr. Babcock expressed himself perfectly satisfied with the result he had achieved. He now placed a number of printed sheets before the boy, which he directed him to sign the name he had been practicing on, in a blank space which he indicated. The boy worked assiduously and successfully, filling in the signatures designated, and when he had completed his labors the stranger handed him two dollars, and stated that he had no further work for him just then, but would send for him if he desired his further services.

The boy, overjoyed at the large wages which he had received for comparatively such little work, hastened to his home, and acquainted his parents with the nature of his occupation, at the same time stating his belief that the papers which he had signed were bonds of some kind. The father of the young man at once became suspicious, and he resolved to communicate the facts to some one, who could make the proper inquiries, to discover the true nature of a transaction which smacked of apparent dishonesty, and in which his son had been made an innocent participator. He accordingly sought out a gentleman connected with a prominent newspaper, published in Brooklyn, N.Y., and the journalist, after cautioning his informant to keep the matter entirely secret, repaired at once to my Agency in New York City and gave the full particulars to my son, Robert A. Pinkerton. After listening attentively to the recital, Robert was convinced that some act of dishonesty was about to be attempted. The strange employment of the boy, and the character of the work he was engaged to do, fully justified this opinion, and he determined to sift the affair thoroughly, in order to assure himself of the correctness of his suspicions.

Careful and covert inquiries soon developed the fact that James Babcock was a member of the firm of Babcock & Co., who were largely engaged as dealers and packers of oranges and fruits in the city of Jacksonville, Florida. It was also ascertained that he had been in the city for some time, engaged in raising money on advances of sales, and other commercial paper, for the benefit of the firm he represented. A. J. Baldwin, the gentleman whose name had been imitated and signed to these documents, it was learned, was an ex-Mayor of Jacksonville.

After considering the matter fully, Robert wrote a communication to the Mayor of Jacksonville, Florida, asking for further information in regard to Babcock & Baldwin, and requesting if the matter was deemed of sufficient importance that an officer be sent on to investigate further into the affair.

The Mayor, on receipt of Robert's communication, at once called a meeting of his municipal advisers, and they, believing that some dishonest scheme was being consummated, dispatched the Chief of Police of that city, to New York with full power to take such measures as were deemed necessary under the circumstances. In due course of time that officer arrived in the city, and a visit was at once made to the residence of the boy who had performed the writing service for Mr. Babcock, and finding the young man at home, he related at length his experience with the one-armed gentleman.

Meanwhile, Mr. Babcock had been kept under strict surveillance, and he was still a guest at French's Hotel. On the following evening therefore, Robert, in company with the Jacksonville officer, and the boy, called at the hotel and inquired for Mr. Babcock. That gentleman was discovered standing in the bar-room, and was at once recognized as the individual they were in search of.

As the two approached him, he seemed to recognize the officer from his native city, and evinced the greatest confusion, when he found him in the company of the boy who had been used to facilitate his imitations of other men's signatures. Mr. Cooper, the Chief of Police, advanced directly to Mr. Babcock, and addressed him:

"Mr. Babcock, I understand that you have some Florida bonds in your possession, which we are very anxious to secure."

This was a bold stroke on the part of Mr. Cooper, but it was deemed best to waste no words with the gentleman whatever. It was suspected that the papers which Babcock was manipulating were bonds issued by the city of Jacksonville, because that city had been engaged recently in placing their bonds on the market, for the purpose of effecting several improvements in the condition of their water-works and streets. Hence it was deemed best to assume that these bonds were what Mr. Cooper designated them, and to accuse Babcock directly with the crime.

Mr. Babcock assumed an air of righteous indignation, on being thus accused, and replied:

"It is a lie, sir! I have nothing of the kind about me, and I do not know what you mean!"

"Very well, Mr. Babcock," quietly interposed Robert, "there is no use getting angry about it; we are authorized to search your apartments and then we will discover for ourselves whether you are speaking the truth or not."

At this threatened investigation, the bravado of Mr. Babcock suddenly deserted him, and his face paled perceptibly, a public exposure was not to his taste, and he broke down completely. After a momentary struggle he said:

"Come up stairs, gentlemen, and I will make a clean breast of the whole affair."

The party then ascended to the room occupied by Babcock, and after they had entered, he openly confessed to having a quantity of forged paper in his possession, but solemnly assured the officers that he had made no attempt to make any use of it.

An investigation of his trunks was then begun, which soon resulted in discovering the existence of forty-six thousand dollars in five hundred dollar bonds and forty thousand dollars in one thousand dollar bonds, of "The Sanitary Improvement Company of Jacksonville, Fla.," all purporting to be duly executed, and properly signed by the several officers of the company, and the city authorities, and to which was attached a well-counterfeited seal of the corporation.

The proofs of his dishonest intentions were too manifest to be denied, and Babcock, realizing that a full expose would inevitably follow this first discovery, at least concluded to make a free confession of his nefarious practices while in the city of New York.

It was developed, that Babcock was fully conversant with the fact of the issuing of these bonds, by "The Sanitary Improvement Company of Jacksonville," his native city, and was acquainted with all the gentlemen connected with that corporation. He was also fully informed, as to where and by whom the bonds were printed, and had laid his plans for forgery with a perfect knowledge of all the circumstances attending their issue. The bonds which were found in his possession, instead of being the work of clever counterfeiters, were found to have been actually printed from the original lithographic stones from which the genuine bonds had been printed, and by the same firm which had been engaged to do the work for the Jacksonville corporation. How this was accomplished can readily be explained. Babcock knew that these bonds were printed in New York City, and on his arrival in that city he had visited the printing establishment, armed with a forged order from J. Ramsey

Day, the Mayor of Jacksonville, ordering the firm to print an additional number of the bonds to the extent of one hundred fifty thousand dollars in denominations of five hundred and one thousand dollars. Of course no suspicions were entertained by the printers, and having but recently printed the bonds for the company, they were able to fill this second order at once, and Babcock received the bonds in a few days. The engraver who had made the seal was also imposed upon with the same plausible story, and he furnished to Babcock a perfect facsimile of the seal he had originally furnished to the Jacksonville authorities. Having been thus successful in obtaining the genuinely printed bonds and a perfect imitation of the seal, the only thing remaining to be done was to secure the signatures of the men who were connected with the issuing of these securities.

For this purpose Babcock had from time to time secured the services of a number of boys, in the same manner as that related by the boy through whom this exposure had been made. Each name had been signed and imitated by a different person, and by this means no similarity was manifested in the forgeries.

With this valise filled with these fraudulent securities, Babcock was about to set forth upon a journey to several western cities in order to raise money by negotiating them. He had made all his arrangements to leave upon the following day, and the officers had arrived just in time to frustrate his well-conceived plans.

Twenty-five thousand dollars of these bonds had already been disposed of, to reputable merchants in the city of New York, who had received them unsuspectingly as collateral security for goods and money which Babcock had obtained. To one firm he had given twenty-five hundred dollars, to another ninety-five hundred dollars, and to the third the amount of thirteen thousand dollars. These parties had no idea of the worthless character of the securities they had taken, and when informed of the fact were, as may be imagined, considerably surprised. Babcock, however, was compelled to make full restitution, which he did, not having, as yet, disposed of the money thus fraudulently obtained.

The counterfeiter and forger was duly arraigned for trial, and being eventually convicted was sentenced to an imprisonment which will no doubt have a salutary effect in preventing him from engaging in any further attempts to enrich himself at the expense of others.

This is a strange case, in which a successful forgery and a perfect counterfeit was accomplished by a man of good business reputation, with every prospect of winning a fortune by legitimate means—and with no knowledge of the forger's arts or intimacy with criminal men—and yet so successfully had he managed his fraudulent transactions that but for the revelations of the unsuspicious boy who had innocently served him, he would have been enabled to place upon the market a hundred fifty thousand dollars of spurious securities.

As it was, however, his scheme was detected, and instead of a successful issue of his fraudulent efforts, he found himself disgraced and humiliated and branded as a felon.

A Clever Forgery.
Reminiscences of Expert Forgers.

ANOTHER case that came under my experience, demonstrates fully the risks which large corporations are being continually exposed to by the intelligent criminal and the expert forger.

During the month of January, 1877, the commercial circles of Wall Street, New York City, were startled by the announcement of a heavy forgery, one of several that had been successfully operated within a very short time. The victims of this transaction were two prominent stock-brokers and the Union Trust Company of New York, with whom the New York Life Insurance Company had a large account. The forgery was most ingeniously contrived, and the perpetrators, whoever they were, displayed an almost incredible knowledge of the inner workings of the two institutions which they so successfully preyed upon.

The facts of the case, as far as could be learned, when the crime was first discovered, appeared to be as follows. The check, which was drawn for sixty-four thousand dollars, was dated on the second day of the month, although the discovery of its spurious character was not made until the eighteenth, a fact which operated to a serious extent against the speedy detection of the forgers.

On the day of its date the check, which purported to be drawn by the New York Life Insurance Company for sixty-four thousand dollars upon the Union Trust Company, was presented at the counter of the latter institution, for a certified endorsement of its worth and genuineness. It was printed upon one, or what appeared to be one, of the regular checks used by the insurance company, and bore the signature of the president and other officers of that institution. In all respects the dangerous little piece of paper appeared to be genuine, and the cashier of the bank to whom it was presented certified it without a moment's hesitation.

On the same day, a Mr. Horace Brown, a petty broker of Wall Street, accompanied by a gentlemanly appearing stranger, who gave his name as Joseph Elliott, called upon Mr. George L. Maxwell, whose office was in close proximity to the Stock Exchange of New York. Mr. Elliott presented a letter, which purported to be signed by Mr. Morris Franklin, the president of the New York Life Insurance Company, and which requested Mr. Maxwell to state upon what terms he would act as the broker in Wall Street for the company of which he was the president.

Mr. Elliott's address and bearing were those of a gentleman, and in the extended conversation which took place, displayed the knowledge of an experienced man of business.

The matter was fully discussed, and Mr. Maxwell requested time in which, to consider the question of commission, when Mr. Elliot took his leave. On the following day, the third of January, Mr. Elliott again appeared in the office of Maxwell, and displaying the certified check for sixty-four thousand dollars requested him to purchase fifty thousand dollars in gold on account of the New York Life Insurance Company.

Mr. Maxwell undertook the commission, and introducing Mr. Elliott to another gentleman in the office, it was finally arranged that the gold should be purchased at once, and the certified check was left with them for that purpose. On the 5th of January the entire transaction was consummated, the gold was purchased and delivered to Mr. Elliott, the check was duly deposited in the Mechanic's Bank, was honored, and, the business appearing to be fully and pleasantly settled, Mr. Elliott disappeared from the view of his brokers.

Nothing more was heard of the transaction until the 16th day of January, when the account of the New York Life Insurance Company with the Union Trust Company was audited, and the cashier was considerably surprised to find returned in his hand-book two checks of the same date and number although for different amounts. One of them being for one hundred fifty thousand dollars, and the other being the sixty-four thousand dollar check already alluded to.

The cashier had no recollection whatever of having drawn such a check and his investigations revealed the fact that it was not entered upon the stub of the checkbook. It looked wonderfully real, and the signatures of the officers seemed to be undoubtedly genuine, and he inquired of the president for information concerning its existence. That officer was astounded at the remarkable imitation of his signature, and the wonderful similarity which the check bore to the regular checks issued by the company, but he immediately pronounced it a forgery. An exposure at once followed, and measures were immediately adopted to discover the parties who had so successfully defrauded the bank. The loss was, however, reduced somewhat by a subsequent discovery that a gold check for ninety-five hundred dollars given by one of the brokers from whom Maxwell and his partner had made their purchases in filling their order for Mr. Elliott, had not yet been presented for payment, and certainly would not be, now that the original forgery had been discovered.

A general feeling of distrust was engendered in consequence of this discovery, and the brokers were placed under arrest. For a time, knowing and doubtful people shrugged their shoulders at various little matters which came to the surface at the commencement of this inquiry, and during this period of skepticism, the officers of the bank and other prominent individuals found themselves the object of censure and suspicion.

It has often seemed strange to me to notice the large number of wiseacres that are born of a sudden exposure of a great crime, or the commission of some action out of the ordinary routine, whether criminal or honorable. No sooner is the revelation made than suggestions the most ridiculous and farcical are made with solemn visage by self-conscious philosophers, who, until that time, had remained undiscovered, or at least unnoticed. I do not think I am making a rash assertion when I say that popular clamor, born of this attempt to appear wise, has scarcely ever been supported by subsequent events. In my experience, but a very small percentage of cases have been determined according to the prophecies of those, who were most eager to give advice, or to proffer their opinions. Be this as it may, however, the number of these "knowing ones" has not decreased, nor has their stock of knowledge been apparently augmented. This case was no exception to the rule, and had these governors of public opinion been consulted and obeyed, every business man upon the street who had been innocently connected with this transaction would have been condemned and excoriated. Fortunately for the good of society, however, there is a strong under-current of common sense which refuses to be guided by irresponsible clamor, and which awaits the determination of an issue before expressing an opinion upon its merits.

Mr. Brown stoutly attested his innocence of any knowledge of the forgery, or of any irregularity in the transaction so far as he was concerned. His statement was that a Mr. George W. Chadwick, whom he had known previously in a business way, called upon him one day for the purpose of having him dispose of some horse railroad bonds, which business he conducted to the satisfaction of Mr. Chadwick. A short time after this, he was again visited by that gentleman, who informed him that a large corporation which he did not name, was contemplating a change in some of their securities, and that he would introduce to him the agent of the corporation through whom the business was to be transacted. In a few days after this interview, Mr. Chadwick introduced Mr. Elliott to him, at which time also the introduction to Mr. Maxwell, before related, took place.

Notwithstanding these statements Mr. Brown and Mr. Maxwell were both held in bonds to answer any charge that might hereafter be made against them. These arrests had been made by the detectives connected with the Police Department of New York City, and it was not until after they had taken place that I was engaged in the matter at all. When the investigation had reached this stage, however, my Agency was employed, and I set about making such inquiries, as in my mind, would lead to satisfactory and convincing results.

Upon undertaking any investigation, no matter how trifling, my first effort is to get down to the foundation of the crime, and to ascertain, if possible, a motive for its commission. In this case, therefore, there must be a foundation; somebody must have forged this check before it was presented; somebody also must have been in a position to obtain one of the checks which were designed to be forged, and that somebody I determined it should be my first duty to discover.

Mr. George H. Bangs, my late General Superintendent, therefore paid a visit to the office of the New York Life Insurance Company, and requested an interview with Mr. Franklin, the president of that institution. After the case had been fully stated, and all the facts thus far obtained had been given, Mr. Bangs inquired of the president if the company were in the habit of retaining in their possession their cancelled checks after their return from the bank.

On being answered in the affirmative, Mr. Bangs requested permission to examine these cancelled checks, promising to explain his purposes afterwards. The request was complied with, and the numerous bundles of cancelled checks were produced.

It may be imagined that an institution of the magnitude of the New York Life Insurance Company necessarily draw a great many checks in the ordinary course of their business, and Mr. Bangs contemplated the portentous piles of narrow pieces of paper that were presented for his inspection, with serious misgivings. Undismayed, however, by the magnitude of the labor before him, and having learned from previous experience, how important is thoroughness in minute details to eventual success, he began the laborious task of examination. One by one the little pieces of paper, which were the tattered representatives of such vast wealth, were taken up and critically examined. The officers of the company looked on with faces in which speculation and wonderment was mingled, but finally, as the labor extended into hours, they left him alone to his task.

At last, after hundreds of these checks had passed through his hands, and under his close inspection, each one in turn being critically compared with the forged check, he gave a start of exultation and exclaimed joyously:

"I have it beyond a doubt!" So engrossed was he by his occupation, that he was unaware of the fact of his being alone, and that those whom he addressed had disappeared. Ringing a bell which lay near at hand, he requested the appearance of the officers of the company, and upon their arrival he placed the check he had found, in the hands of Mr. Franklin, saying:

"This, sir, without a doubt, is the check from which the forgery was made."

Mr. Franklin gazed at the paper in surprise; it was a check for one hundred fifty thousand dollars, and had been issued some weeks before the forgery.

"How can it be that this check could have been used by the forgers, and again find its way into the possession of the company?" asked Mr. Franklin, incredulously.

"It certainly has done so," answered Mr. Bangs, "and how I will explain hereafter—but—now let me show you how I am convinced of the fact which I assert."

"In the first place," he continued, "I take it for granted that checks for large amounts are rarely, if ever, folded by anyone who does your banking business, but are carried in a flat book or wallet for certification or payment."

"That is quite true," said Mr. Franklin.

"Very well. Now if you will observe this check, you will notice that it has not only been folded, but it has been soiled very much, as though it had been carried in the pocket. You will also observe that the cancellation stamp or knife has penetrated through this check, leaving several sharp angular corners. Now if you will observe, one of these corners extends over one of the folds and is perfectly flat." And he folded the check to demonstrate the fact. "What does this prove?" he asked. "Simply that the check was folded after it had been cancelled by the bank, and after it had been returned to you. The further fact is that this check was abstracted by some one connected with your company, and has been carefully replaced in its proper place in the package, after it had served the purpose of the forgers."

"Permit me to ask you one question," said the cashier of the company, now speaking for the first time; "admitting all that you have previously stated to be correct, what proof exists that the forged check was really made from this identical one?"

"I am prepared to explain that point, and a most important one it is, too," said Mr. Bangs, "and will do so fully."

Walking to the window of the room and taking the genuine and the forged check with him, he placed them both together, one upon the top of the other, against the glass, and requested the two gentlemen to come forward and examine them.

As they did so an exclamation of surprise broke from them both. The two signatures of the officers were not only exactly alike, but they were in precisely similar positions on the paper in both instances. Nor was this the only strange coincidence, but it was also apparent that in the genuine check, a roughness or imperfection, in the paper had caused the signature of the president to deviate from its proper line, and to show a slight irregularity in the formation of some of the letters. This irregularity had been faithfully followed in the forged check, although the paper in that document was perfectly smooth and free from blemish.

"You will see," said Mr. Bangs, still holding the two checks against the glass, "that there is undoubted evidence that one check has been traced from the other, and is not what is called a free hand forgery."

Both of the officers were convinced at once of the correctness of this assertion, and expressed themselves fully satisfied of the facts thus far adduced.

"Now," said Mr. Bangs, "our first duty is to find the clerk who abstracted this check."

To this task Mr. Bangs applied himself in a quiet and unsuspicious manner, and before the day had closed he was positive that he had selected the clerk upon whom to fasten suspicion. His first question was: "Who draws your checks, as a general rule?"

"They are invariably drawn by my special clerk," replied the cashier.

"Does he leave his check-book open upon his desk at any time?"

"Yes, sir; frequently."

"Who then has occasion to transact business with him, who might thus be able to see the book?"

"Well, there are three clerks who frequently have business with this man, and who would thus have ample opportunity to inspect the books."

"And by that means," said Mr. Bangs, "they would of course be able to know what numbers would be upon the checks at any particular time?"

"Yes, sir; undoubtedly," replied the cashier with a start, as a new revelation was opened to him.

These three clerks were therefore made the subject of a quiet scrutiny by Mr. Bangs, and after he had finished his examination he pointed out one of them as the man who had abstracted the check, and before he left the office he stated to Mr. Franklin in an emphatic manner:

"That young clerk, Charles W. Pontez, is the man who stole the check, and I will prove it so in time."

The astonishment of the two gentlemen at this statement was unbounded, but as they had placed the case in our hands, and had already received indubitable evidence that the forgers, whoever they were, had received assistance from some one in their employ, they signified their willingness to allow us to proceed in our own way.

The name of Charles W. Pontez was a familiar one to me, and his antecedents were readily recalled. Ten years before this time, he was a junior clerk in the office of the Union Transportation Company, and though a very young man gave promise of becoming an active and trustworthy accountant. The secretary of the company was Joseph W. Chapman, who has since figured in many daring schemes of robbery and forgery. At that time, however, he was a highly respectable man, moved in the best circles of the city, and was married to a very handsome and accomplished lady, the daughter of a prominent merchant. By a life of extravagance, he soon became involved in debt, and yielding at last, to the influence of evil associates he became connected with a gang of burglars and forgers of the genteel order. These men had their headquarters in a billiard saloon, located under Brooks Theater, and kept by a man who was known as Howard Adams, but whose real name was afterwards ascertained to be Carlo Justin Susscovitch, a Russian, and one who at various times had assumed other aliases to conceal his identity.

Even at that time Adams, or Susscovitch, was one of the sharpest and most accomplished forgers in the country, and it was through his influence, that Chapman, who frequented his saloon, was made acquainted with the members of the fraternity with whom he afterwards became associated. Among the number was Mark Shinburn, a noted burglar, who is now living in the luxurious enjoyment of his ill-gotten gains, and having purchased a German title of nobility, is now known as Baron Shindle. Shinburn, at that time, had succeeded in robbing the Lehigh Coal and Navigation Company at White Haven, in Pennsylvania, of a large amount of money and valuables, among which were certain negotiable securities. As Chapman was perfectly conversant with the banking and broking business, and possessed a reputable character, he was deemed an available party to dispose of these securities, and after a slight demur, he agreed to do so. Without the slightest difficulty, owing to his high standing in the community, he succeeded in disposing of several thousand dollars worth of these securities by depositing them as collateral for loans which he effected. It unfortunately happened that some of these White Haven bonds were widely advertised as stolen, and, much to the surprise and humiliation of Chapman, he was arrested as being concerned in that robbery.

Of course with his arrest Chapman's position of trust was vacated, and his character for honesty forever shaken. At his trial, however, his previous good name and business reputation were duly considered by the court, and upon his giving a plausible account of the manner in which the securities came into his possession, and surrendering all that he still held, he escaped the clutches of the law.

His social downfall was complete, however, and yielding to the temptations of the men who surrounded him, and being thrown upon his own resources, he entered with a number of others into a systematic scheme of forgery. Chapman, shortly after this, induced a poor young man named Joseph Randall, who was then under twenty years of age, and of unblemished reputation, to join with them. Randall was a valuable acquisition to this gang, having been engaged as a clerk in a prominent banking house, and was considered by his employers to be extraordinarily sharp and shrewd. To these parties Chapman also introduced his junior clerk, Charles W. Pontez, but although this young man was frequently seen in their company afterward, it was not known that he had ever engaged with them in any of their dishonest operations. The first attempt which these men, Chapman, Randall, Adams, Charles Becker and "old man" Hearing, as he was familiarly called, made, was in forging a check for a large amount upon one of the principal banks of the city of New York, and so skillfully was their work executed that they escaped detection and in fact suspicion.

After this, emboldened by their primary success, they pursued their vocation in Baltimore, Richmond, Memphis, Vicksburg, New Orleans, and several other cities in the South. Not with the same success, however, for at New Orleans they were discovered and pursued so closely, that they were obliged to flee the country, taking with them a large sum of money.

They went to Central America, where they speedily dissipated their funds, and then they resorted to other forgeries there. They were not successful, and were arrested, but they all managed to escape from the insecure jail in which they were confined. They then returned to the United States, but so changed in appearance that they were not recognized.

Chapman and Randall were suspected of robbing the Third National Bank of Baltimore, which occurred soon after this, and they fled to Europe, where they met Charles Becker and Howard Adams, who had been obliged to leave America to escape punishment. In London, Chapman and his wife rented a handsome house on the Neville road, which they furnished in a luxurious manner and entertained their friends sumptuously. The four men then started on a grand tour of forgery through the continent. In Turkey they attempted to forge the bonds issued by that government, but so hastily and clumsily that they were detected, and after a trial were sentenced to several years imprisonment. They were confined in the consular prison at Smyrna, and after a short imprisonment, Randall and Becker managed to escape, and by slow stages worked their way back again to London with a considerable sum of money.

Mrs. Chapman, hearing of the ingratitude of Randall and Becker, in leaving her husband in jail, wrote a letter to Charles W. Pontez, whom she had known for many years, and who still resided in New York. In this letter she requested Pontez to visit several friends of her husband, among the crooked fraternity, and solicit their aid in behalf of both her and her husband. Pontez performed the duty requested of him, but found that none of them were in a condition to render any assistance in effecting the liberation of her husband.

Meanwhile Adams, or Susscovitch, had made his way to London, and was a frequent visitor at the house of Mrs. Chapman. When he learned that no money was to be received from America, and knowing that Mrs. Chapman had some in her possession, he deliberately murdered the lady, and seizing her money and jewelry disappeared. This brutal and cowardly deed created great excitement in England, at the time, and among the effects of the unfortunate woman was found and published, this letter from Charles W. Pontez.

Susscovitch is now in jail in Ohio for forgery, and when his term expires, he will be sent back to England to answer for the murder of Mrs. Chapman, the discovery of his commission of that deed not having been made until he had been tried for the forgery in this country.

From these facts it will be seen that Charles W. Pontez, the correspondent of Mrs. Chapman, and the associate of the gang of forgers, and Charles W. Pontez, the clerk of the New York Life Insurance Company, were one and the same person. I was therefore inclined to believe that we were upon the track of the right parties.

From the clerk of the cashier of the insurance company, whose duty it was to draw the checks for the institution, it was learned recently Pontez had managed to have some business with him at the particular times when he would be engaged in filling up checks; that this had occurred frequently, and that he had conversed at these times longer than there was any business necessity for doing. No importance had been attached to this action at the time, but in the light of subsequent events, they were considered suggestive, and having learned thus much of the actions and previous associations of Charles W. Pontez, we were enabled to proceed with our investigation intelligently and with strong hopes of success.

The preliminary investigations of Horace Brown and George L. Maxwell were now concluded, and without reflecting upon their business honor they were placed under bonds to appear whenever required. This action quieted the public mind somewhat, and we were enabled to devote our attention to Mr. Charles W. Pontez. Every movement he made, when at all observable, was closely watched by trusty men, who followed him by day and by night without his knowledge. He was found to frequent drinking saloons, visit the theaters, to live in good style, but none of his associates seemed to be of a character to excite suspicion. At length, one evening an operative reported to my son, Robert Pinkerton, that Pontez had gone to the theater with a gentleman and lady, and that the face of the man appeared to be familiar to him, but he could not identify him with any degree of certainty. Eager to follow any clue that would lead to success, Robert at once repaired to the place of amusement designated, and closely scanned the entire audience, to discover the parties he was in search of. He soon singled out Pontez and his companions, and despite their changed appearances, he recognized them as Joseph Randall, the accomplice of Chapman, and his wife, a variety actress of great beauty and accomplishments, whom he had brought from Europe some time ago. This pointed strongly to the conclusion that the same gang who had so successfully defrauded the capitalists of almost every country in Europe, and section of the United States, were now at work.

Operatives were at once placed upon the track of Randall, when he left the theater. And when the play was over, the shadows followed silently after the trio. Charles W. Pontez had now been connected with a noted forger, many of whose deeds were known, and this forger the companion of the man whose wife had written to him asking his services in her behalf.

By a process slow and untiring, starting from this point the coils were slowly wound around these men. Night and day their steps were followed by silent, haunting figures; and yet, strange to say, from that night at the theater, Charles W. Pontez and Joseph Randall did not meet again. Knowing fully, however, the antecedents of Randall, and believing that in this forgery we had discovered unmistakable evidences of his handiwork, my vigilance never relaxed for a moment, and every movement he made was known as fully by me, as by himself.

This espionage was continued for two weeks unremittingly, and was at length rewarded. One night, during the latter part of the month of February, a cold, stormy night, when the sky was dull and heavy, and the white, feathery flakes of snow fell noiselessly to the earth; when the wind howled through the princely avenues of the great city, and the gaslights glimmered through the mists like rows of stars, the detective stood under the shelter of a doorway, and shiveringly watched the residence of Joseph Randall.

Soon that individual made his appearance, fully muffled up and protected from the storm, and making his way hastily to Broadway, he hailed a passing omnibus, and entered, followed at the next corner, by the detective who had run on in advance of the vehicle, in order not to excite suspicion. Reaching one of the streets in the lower part of the city that led to the ferries Randall left the coach and the detective followed suit.

When they arrived at the Courtlandt St. Ferry, the passengers were just emerging from the ferry house, having crossed from Jersey City, where the railroads deliver their passengers. Presently Randall darted forward, and grasped by the hand one of the arriving passengers, and as the stranger raised his face toward the light, the detective saw revealed to him the features of Charles Becker, another one of the noted quartette of forgers, whose history I have already given. The two men returned to the home of Randall, and after assuring himself that they were domiciled for the night, the detective took his departure and reported at the Agency.

Additional operatives were now detailed to watch the various parties, now under surveillance, and to note every movement they made. It soon became evident that some new movement was afloat. All of the parties made frequent visits to a house in Allen Street, in New York City, the names of the inmates of which could not be ascertained by the most diligent inquiries in the neighborhood; they were strangers and unknown. There could be no doubt, however, that this house was the general rendezvous of the forgers, and that it was at this place that their work was being done Events fully proved this, and one dark cloudy night about ten days after the arrival of Charles Becker, and after all of the parties had arrived at the house, an expressman drove up to the door with his wagon. Quickly afterwards three men appeared carrying a large bundle, which resembled bedding, and placed it carefully in the wagon. Just as they had accomplished this feat, three detectives advanced through the darkness, and laying their hands upon the men, demanded their surrender, at the same time directing the driver of the wagon to remain where he was.

This action had been so sudden, and evidently so unexpected, that for a moment, the three stood as if rooted to the spot and unable to stir, or to speak, and they were finally conducted away without opposition or resistance, the expressman following with his wagon.

A search of the house was made, and here they discovered undoubted evidence that the place had been occupied for the purposes of counterfeiting and forging. Lithographic stones, metallic dies, prints of bank notes, checks, and skeleton bonds of various corporations were found in profusion, including several spoiled proof-sheets of the forged check of the New York Life Insurance Company.

Becker and Randall were fully known to us, but the third man had not been recognized by the operatives who made the arrest. All doubts, however, were set at rest, when on being conveyed to the central station, the light revealed the ancient features of "old man" Hearing—the printer of the old gang, in which Chapman and Adams figured so prominently.

The contents of the wagon were next examined, and tightly packed between the bedding were found all the parts of a lithographic press, which no doubt were about to be removed to a more secure locality.

This furnished full proof of the guilt of these parties, and Charles W. Pontez was arrested on the following morning, very much to his surprise, and the quartette were duly held for an examination.

The trial of these men took place in due time and from the testimony adduced thereat, the whole plan of the forgery was detailed. Charles W. Pontez who, it was ascertained, had acted as groomsman for Joseph Randall, upon the occasion of his marriage, had stolen, as we suspected, the check from the vaults of the Insurance Company, where he was employed as a clerk, and had given the same to Randall. Randall then went to Becker—who was a son-in-law of "old man" Hearing—who engraved the imitations of the check, and Hearing did the printing. After this had been done, the tracing of the signatures and the filling up of the check was done by Randall, who also personated the Mr. Elliott, who managed the business of imposing upon the brokers and obtained the money.

During the progress of the trial, which was continued for several days, the prisoners were brought back and forth from the jail to the court room, by the officers of the court, and Randall, who was of a genial and jovial disposition, soon became quite intimate with the officer in whose charge he was placed, and as a consequence the vigilance of his custodian was considerably relaxed. One day, just as the court had adjourned for recess, this officer turned around to take care of his prisoner, when to his profound dismay, he discovered that he had disappeared. The alarm was given, but the most energetic efforts failed to discover his whereabouts, and he had successfully made his escape, literally walking out of court, under the very eyes of the officer whose duty it was to keep watch over him. Fortunately, for the cause of justice, he was recaptured by me—but had the previous espionage of Joseph Randall been less thorough, and had not every one with whom he had associated, been fully known, he might have obtained his liberty. As it was, so thoroughly had our work of shadowing been conducted in advance of the arrest of these parties, that by continuing that system of watching upon all of his associates, we were soon upon his track and he was again brought to bay.

The next time he appeared for trial, he did not escape, and the three principal forgers, Joseph Randall, Charles Becker, and "old man" Hearing, were duly convicted of their crime, and condemned to long years of imprisonment.

Charles W. Pontez was suffering with a severe illness when the trial of his companions took place, and the investigation in his case was postponed. He was never brought to trial as his malady soon developed serious symptoms, and he finally died in his prison cell, before the judgment of the court could be pronounced upon him.

The King of Forgers.

CHARLES I. BROCKWAY is another of the famous names in the calendar of criminal practices, and with whom I have had dealings on more than one occasion. This forger and counterfeiter is now about forty years of age, and exceedingly handsome in appearance. He was born and reared in the city of New York, and except when undergoing imprisonment, has made his home in that city. Soon after the war had closed, Brockway opened a faro bank in New York City, and was an extensive dealer in counterfeit money. From this he gradually became an adept in the forging and counterfeiting line and for nearly twenty years led the vicarious life of one, who outrages the laws and suffers its penalties.

On the occasion of his last arrest, I played a somewhat prominent part, and will relate that portion of his experience in this connection.

It will be remembered that in my sketch of Charles F. Ulrich, I stated that he was regarded as one of the best engravers who had been found willing to prostitute his talents to counterfeiting, which this country had produced. He was a man capable of imitating a complete Treasury note without any outside aid whatever, and this is something few mechanical engravers are able to effectually accomplish. The details of his career, his later arrest and his release during good behavior have already been related. Since that time Ulrich has resided at Trenton, N. J., and so far as known has confined himself to honest employment. In July, 1880, I received a communication from a member of a prominent law firm in Trenton, stating that Charles F. Ulrich was endeavoring to lead an honest life, but that he was being continually annoyed by numerous crooked people who from time to time sought his services. Among the most persistent of these was Charles I. Brockway. According to the letter I received, Brockway was hounding the reformed man to perform some counterfeiting work for him, and offering to pay him ten percent of all moneys obtained, in addition to a large remuneration for his labor in cash. The letter further stated that Ulrich was extremely desirous of ridding himself forever of these rascals, and the suggestion was made that some plan be devised by which Brockway, at least, might be captured and punished. A short time previous to the receipt of this letter, I had heard that Ulrich and Brockway were again working together, but when this later information was received, I at once became doubtful of the correctness of my previous impressions. With the view of ascertaining the truth in this matter, and in order to serve the community, which has always been my aim, I wrote a reply expressing my willingness to take the case in hand, provided Ulrich was really in earnest.

I demanded, however, that Ulrich should place himself entirely in my hands, in order that I might fully satisfy myself as to the genuineness of his desire to serve the interests of justice. Mr. Linden, the able superintendent of my Philadelphia office, was delegated by me to conduct this case, and the arrangements were left entirely to his own discretion and intelligence.

In compliance with a request made by Mr. Linden, Ulrich came to Philadelphia and exhibited two checks which he stated that Brockway had given him to counterfeit. One of these was on the old National Bank of Providence, and was regularly drawn by Henry E. Cranston to the order of C. L. Parker for one hundred nine dollars. The other was on the Fourth National Bank of the same city, and was for an exactly similar amount. This check was payable to E. L. Parker and was signed by Chase, Watson & Butts. The drawers of these checks were prominent business firms in Providence, and were known to be large depositors in the banks on which the checks were drawn. Charles Ulrich stated that Brockway was exceedingly anxious to have the counterfeits finished in three days. As this allowed but little time in which to perfect arrangements for a complete surprise and capture of the forger, Ulrich was directed to obtain a delay from Brockway on the plea of his inability to finish them properly in the prescribed time. To this Ulrich yielded a ready assent, and also promised to notify Mr. Linden whenever Brockway should call upon him. This delay afforded us full opportunity of communicating with the threatened Providence banks, and also of obtaining the full particulars, with regard to the obtaining of the two genuine checks which had been given Ulrich to imitate.

It was soon learned that these two checks had been procured from prominent stock-brokerage firms in Providence, as the proceeds of the sale to each of them of a one hundred dollar government four percent bond. The sellers in each case had asked for checks to be given them, on the plea that they desired to send them into the country. The banks were communicated with, and a reply was quickly received, stating their desire and determination to prosecute the intending forgers and requesting Mr. Linden to send an operative to Providence, who knew, and could identify the rascals. The Trenton attorneys were also informed of what had taken place, and taken fully into our confidence in the matter. It was suggested by these gentlemen, that the best plan would be to arrest Brockway when he called at Ulrich's residence, and receive the counterfeit checks, but as I knew that the mere engraving and printing of a check-blank which was not filled in or signed, was not an offense under the law, I resolved to give Brockway all the rope he desired, particularly as the trap into which he was about to fall was entirely of his own designing.

Ulrich was therefore instructed to so mark the counterfeit blanks that, while Brockway would not recognize any difference in them, the bank tellers, after being fully instructed, would be able to detect at a glance, any of them that might be presented for payment. This was accomplished by lengthening the lines in the border, where they met at the upper right-hand corner, so that instead of joining exactly, as in the originals, they projected to the slightest degree, and by altering the names of the original engravers at the bottom, from "Bugbee and Kelly" to "Rugbee and Kally." This change could only be detected upon a very close examination.

Brockway, all unsuspicious of the danger that was threatening him, called upon Ulrich at the time prescribed, and received a number of the printed blanks. The next day he called again and desired more, stating that he had spoiled all the others. These also were given to him. It was naturally supposed, therefore, that the following day, being Friday, was the day selected for the commission of the crime, and a trusty operative was therefore sent to Providence to look out for Brockway. The assistance of the Chief of Police of that city was invoked, and an intelligent detective was detailed to assist us in the enterprise. Two other local detectives were stationed, one in each bank, with instructions to arrest the "layer down" as the presenter of a forged check is called, as soon as he should appear, and to take him at once into a back room, in order not to give the alarm to any confederate who might be outside on the watch. My operative was then to be communicated with immediately, and he was to proceed at once to the bank and point out any of the Brockway gang whom he would be able to recognize in the vicinity. My operative, therefore, with his delegated assistant took up their positions in the post-office, which was directly opposite the old National Bank building, which it was supposed would be the first tried.

Since the commencement of his operations, Brockway has always worked upon a system which though perfectly familiar to the detectives, is one which is ingeniously calculated to baffle them in their attempts to fasten a crime upon him, so directly as to ensure a conviction.

It has been his custom to employ as an agent, a man whom he could trust, but one of such bad character and reputation that no jury would accept his uncorroborated testimony should he prove unfaithful. This man's duty was to impart his instructions to the rest of the gang, with whom Brockway himself never held any business communications whatever—and to see them carried out. One Charles Fera, otherwise known as the "Big Duke" has generally acted in this capacity for Brockway.

I scarcely expected that Brockway would himself go to Providence, and my plans were duly laid, to have him indicted there, after the arrest of his confederates, for sending forged papers into the state, secure a requisition for him, and then take him on for prosecution.

Another of Brockway's rules was to have duplicate forged checks prepared. The "layer down" was given one of them, which was simply indorsed on the back, to take in. The teller would naturally require identification. The "layer down" would then take the check and retire from the bank, destroying the document as he went. On the street he would be met by Brockway, who would hand him another check, similar in all respects to the one that had been presented, except that in addition to the endorsement of the drawer, it had also the words "all right"—or "O. K.," and the signature of the firm whose genuine check had been imitated.

The "layer down" would then return to the bank, and get the money without difficulty, the teller supposing the identification to have been freshly written. It would not have been at all "regular," to present the identified check first and Brockway was always too shrewd to take any such chances. Another rule of his was to have several "layers down." If one came out all right, another was sent in with a check, and if this succeeded, a third attempt was made. After this third attempt, however, he always stopped for the day. His watchers kept a lookout on the bank, and the broker's office until the next morning, and if no unusual commotion was observed, it was taken for granted that the victim's account was large enough to stand further depletion, and other checks previously prepared would be presented next day, and even the third day thereafter, if circumstances seemed to warrant the venture. The moment any sign of discovery was observed, however, the entire gang would incontinently flee the city.

In the selection of layers down, favorites were always sent in first, as the chances of detection were then the slightest; the last men were required to possess a large amount of nerve, as the amount drawn might overdraw the account of the party against whom the checks were drawn, and there would naturally be some searching questions to answer. Of course the amount of a firm's account in a bank was always a matter of guess work, and therefore involved great risk, although Brockway's rule was to select heavy concerns, leave a wide margin, and work up gradually.

But to return to our particular operation. Friday passed without sign. On Saturday, however, my operative, while at his post in the post-office, saw Brockway pass the old National Bank. As he reached a position in front of that building, he seemed to give a signal with his head to somebody who stood on the opposite side of the street.

Soon afterward he was joined by a young man, who held some conversation with him and after a short delay went into the bank. When they had disappeared it was ascertained that the young man desired to get a check certified, similar in all respects to one of the checks prepared by Charles Ulrich. Another young man had another check similar to the other one certified in the Fourth National Bank on the same afternoon. They then called upon Chase, Watson & Butts, and Henry E. Cranston, just before the close of business, and sold two more one hundred dollar four percent bonds, asking, as in the first instance, for checks "to send into the country." The object of this move, it will readily be perceived, was to get the last numbers of the checks issued by both the firms, upon which they intended to operate. This would give them all day Sunday to affix the numbers to the forged checks, and they would be ready to work without fear of detection from that source, as soon as the banks were opened on Monday morning. The object of having the checks certified, as above related, was to make them available for their face value anywhere in case anything disastrous occurred. The two original and genuine checks, from which the counterfeits had been imitated, reached the Providence banks on Saturday, in regular order from the Ninth National Bank of New York, having been deposited there by T. Winterbottom, a Spring St. undertaker.

All being in readiness, the officers awaited the assault they had every reason to expect would be made on Monday morning. Their anticipations were fully realized, for at ten o'clock on that morning, a man entered the Fourth National Bank of Providence and presented one of the forged checks. It was filled out for one thousand three hundred twenty-seven dollars. The detective who was on duty in the bank stepped up at the same moment and presented another check. The money was paid to the forger without hesitation, and he placed it in his pocket. The teller then gave the sign agreed upon, and the man was at once arrested. Word was quietly but quickly sent to my operative who was watching Brockway, waiting upon the outside of the bank, and almost before he was aware of the fact, that worthy found himself a prisoner. The first man arrested gave his name as Joseph Cook, but upon being confronted with my operative, he was at once recognized as Billy Ogle, a well-known confederate of Brockway's. Three hours passed by, and the patience of the detectives at the other bank was still unrewarded.

At one o'clock, however, a suspicious looking fellow sauntered in and presented the expected forged check. An attempt was made to arrest him, but he took to his heels, and was captured only after a long chase, in which the officers were obliged to use their revolvers upon the fleeing fugitive. This man was ultimately identified as George Howell, who was known to be in communication with Brockway, and who had left Chicago but a short time before.

It may be truthfully said that Brockway had been responsible for every forgery of consequence within the two years that preceded his arrest, and I have no hesitation in saying that his equal in that particular line of crime does not exist in the world. There never was but one check put forth by him that was stopped without previous warning. That was a forgery on the Fourth National Bank of New York, in which the signature and blank of Messrs. Fisk & Hatch, the famous New York bankers, were imitated to a remarkable degree of correctness. This firm, however, had a private mark upon their blanks, which the counterfeiters had overlooked, and the absence of this mark caused the cashier of the bank to hesitate a moment. The "layer down" at once took alarm at this and fled, but had he stood firm, he would undoubtedly have received the money.

Brockway is one of the most handsome men of the day. He is tall, well built, with a wealth of curling black hair, a full beard of raven blackness and a pair of piercing black eyes. Though an extravagant man in every respect, he is charged with no small vices, and was never intoxicated. At one time he kept a faro bank in partnership with the notorious Dan Noble, who was recently sentenced to twenty years imprisonment in England for the crime of forgery.

Brockway subsequently branched out as a counterfeiter, and being detected, served two terms in the New York State prison for that offense. His last incarceration was in Auburn, where he remained five years. During this term of his imprisonment, it was noticed that he seized every opportunity that was offered to him to practice with pen, ink and paper. He was released in 1878, and immediately set out on a career of wholesale forgery, through the West and South. In June, 1879, he and Bill Ogle, one of his pals, arrested at Providence were held on a charge of forgery on the First National Bank of Chicago, and a complete set of implements was found in his rooms. In this case he made a confession, in which he charged Samuel Felker, an ex-government detective, with having induced him to come to Chicago, promising him the full protection of the police, and even selecting the banks for him to work upon. This statement was corroborated by a subsequent confession made by Ogle, and so convinced were the authorities, that Felker was indicted, and Brockway was held in ten thousand dollars bail, as a witness against him. The case, however, has never been called to trial, on account of the lack of sufficient corroborative evidence—the main witnesses being both men of acknowledged bad character.

After his release, Brockway went to New York, and succeeded in perpetrating the following forgeries: Chemical National Bank, thirteen thousand; Second National Bank, seventeen hundred; Bank of the Republic, fourteen thousand; Chatham National Bank, seventeen hundred; Corn Exchange Bank, seven hundred; Phoenix National Bank, seventy-five hundred. There were undoubtedly other cases in which the banks sustained the loss and made no public announcement of it. The Chemical National Bank also did this, and I only learned of this forgery by accident. For the Phoenix Bank forgery, Brockway, James Williams, William Ogle, and Charles Fera were all arrested by me and held to trial in the city of New York. Williams turned state's-evidence, and Ogle, who was the first to be tried, was convicted and sentenced to five years imprisonment, but his case was afterward appealed. Fera and Brockway, however, managed to escape punishment on the old ground—the bad character of the witnesses against them, and the lack of corroborative evidence.

Brockway was, however, rearrested by my son, Robert Pinkerton, on a requisition from the governor of Illinois, at the instance of his bondsmen in the Felker case, and was sent to Chicago, but he soon succeeded in restoring their confidence in him, and, they again renewing his bail, he was released. He returned at once to New York and proceeded from thence to Baltimore, where he perpetrated successful forgeries on the Merchants and Third National Bank of that city, to the extent of ten thousand one hundred forty six dollars.

When the information of these forgeries was published, I felt confident, from the manner in which the work was done, that Brockway was at the bottom of them, and my son Robert meeting him a few days afterwards at Coney Island, openly taxed him with the crime.

Owing to some ill-feeling which grew out of the distribution of the Bank of the Republic job, a noted crook, Tommy Moore, shot Brockway in the back, and Moore was instantly shot and dangerously wounded by Billy Ogle. A dozen shots were fired and several were severely wounded, but the police made no arrests, and consequently no one was punished.

Brockway was brought to trial for this last attempt at Providence, and Charles Ulrich appeared as a witness against him. He also testified that Brockway had brought two other checks to him for counterfeiting, in which two prominent Philadelphia bankers were to be made the victims.

His career was thus brought to a summary end, and it is to be hoped that equal promptness and courage in detection and punishment will follow any further attempts of this audacious thief to plunder the unsuspecting public.

Corporations Floated By Forged Securities.
"Wild Cat" Insurance Companies.

ONE of the boldest, and for a time the most successful course, of swindling, by means of forged securities, was perpetrated in the city of Philadelphia a few years ago, and a record of that operation deserves a place in this connection. It is a story of swindling which was skillfully and successfully effected, was only discovered by accident, and even then the leader in the movement was able to adroitly explain away all seeming criminalities and thus for the time escape punishment. Finally, however, a second expose occurred and further concealment was impossible. The principal actor in this scheme was a young man by the name of George F. Holton, whose parents were wealthy, and whose position in society was of unquestioned respectability. He was a man of great natural abilities, and with a business capacity far above the average. In his youth he devoted himself to the study of medicine, during which time he gave great attention to the subject of toxicology, and acquired a wonderful knowledge of the effects of all poisonous materials upon the human system. His talents as a physician were never fully developed, however, and before taking his degree he relinquished his medical studies and entered into mercantile business. He first became engaged in the business of insurance in the city of Philadelphia, from which place he soon afterward removed to Chicago, where he established himself as an agent for several of the leading insurance companies of the East. Tiring of this vocation, he became a dealer in grain, but being unfortunate in this venture, he returned to Philadelphia, where he again entered the insurance business.

According to police authorities, the city of brotherly love was at that time the home of a number of "wild cat" companies, which, in the absence of a State Insurance Examiner, were enabled to successfully impose upon the community. George F. Holton was fully aware of the existence of these fraudulent institutions, and he had not been long in Philadelphia when he became identified with a corporation devoted to underwriting, whose anomalous title was that of "The Security." This corporation was organized by Holton, who also became its secretary and treasurer. This company, it is alleged, had no proper or solid monetary foundation, yet, so plausible, so smooth of speech and so insinuating in manner was Holton that he succeeded in inducing a number of respectable and reputable gentlemen in Philadelphia, to accept positions in the company, and to allow their names to appear as directors. By means of his extensive and thorough knowledge of the business, Holton soon placed the company in a good working condition, and organized agencies in all of the principal cities of the country. It appeared that there was another insurance company in existence of the same name as that adopted by Holton, which was a good, sound and responsible institution, and the confidence which this latter company enjoyed, induced many people to confide their business to the swindling concern, under the impression that the two companies were identical. The business of this new corporation prospered amazingly. The secretary was a thorough business man, well posted in insurance matters, and in a few months Holton had received about forty thousand dollars in premiums for risks which he had taken, and for the payment of which, in case of loss, the company owned no available assets.

The offices of the company were located on one of the principal business thoroughfares of the city, and were most tastefully and luxuriously furnished; dapper clerks were at the desks, and Holton, when he was seen, bore the absorbed manners of an anxious, hardworking and duty-loving man of business. More frequently, however, when not seen in the outer office, he was found in his private apartment in the rear, his feet perched easily on his desk, and a box of fragrant Havanas within his reach. Notwithstanding the weakness of its foundation, the insurance company prospered. The premiums were duly received, and when losses occurred to their patrons, they would sometimes be paid—provided some good purpose was to be served, but in many cases, the losses were contested upon some specious plea and the payment delayed.

A difficulty soon arose, to meet which some new and untried means had to be devised. The state had established an Insurance Department, and had appointed a gentleman, whose duty it was to examine into the condition and standing of the various insurance companies doing business in Pennsylvania, and also to require an exhibition of all of the available assets of these corporations.

This commissioner was an avowed enemy of the so called "wild cat" insurance companies, of which he had heard and seen so much, and he suspected that the Security was one of this delectable number. He accordingly notified Holton, that he would speedily examine the affairs of his company in order to discover its true financial condition. Instead of being overcome by this information, the inventive faculties of Holton were spurred on to heroic efforts, and he very soon devised a scheme, by which he could successfully deceive the watchful and suspecting commissioner. Aided by his thorough business knowledge, he caused a number of false and forged mortgages to be executed, upon valuable real estate in Philadelphia, and these papers were executed with a nicety, well calculated to impose upon anyone not having direct evidence of their spurious character. Then knowing full well that all reputable corporations have large investments in bonds, stocks, and other valuable securities, he resolved to present to the examining commissioner, further evidence of The "Security's" solvency, by showing them to be largely interested in United States and railroad bonds. For this purpose he managed to purchase for a small sum one hundred bonds of one thousand dollars each, which had been issued by one of the southern states during the war. Although these bonds had no real market value, he depended on the fact that the bonds which had been issued by the same state, since its reconstruction, had considerable value, to thus deceive the commissioner, and to make this dependence the more certain, the dates of the old bonds were changed, so as to pass for the more recent and valuable ones. Besides these he managed to secure from other bogus insurance men, and from dealers in stolen securities—some of whom are now in prison—a large number of stolen and forged United States bonds, of the registered series, the names on which had been duly altered to meet the emergency, and also some forged certificates of railroad stock. Thus fully armed for the examiner, Holton complacently awaited the appearance of that official. So reckless had Holton been in manufacturing his spurious mortgages that he had actually executed one for a large amount on property, owned by one of his own responsible and deceived directors, and if at that time that honest individual had looked over the books of the company, he would have unearthed an immense swindle, and have learned some of the secrets of "wild cat" insurance companies and their methods, which would have been a profitable revelation to him.

The examination, however, was successfully passed, the commissioner was fully satisfied as to the assets of "The Security," and Holton was given a certificate accordingly. Thus far everything had prospered with Holton and his schemes, but, not satisfied with his present success, he became ambitious for further efforts, and more daring exploits.

He conceived a gigantic plan to flood the Philadelphia money market with forged stocks and bonds and he carefully made his preparations for that event. He extended his acquaintance among professional forgers and middle men, and he soon was hand and glove with a coterie of professional criminals, who under the guise of assisting him in his unlawful ventures were simply making him the tool of their work and profit. He engaged the services of several experts in this particular line, among whom was the notorious Jacob Canter, who was the most skillful penman in the United States, and whose forgeries were almost miraculous for their close and uniform imitations. About this time another insurance company in the same city, and in a similar condition, was ordered by the insurance commissioner to make an exhibition of their assets. The officers of this company were not so ingenious as Mr. Holton, and were in a great dilemma. Being on friendly terms with the officers of this company, however, Mr. Holton was appealed to for help in this dire difficulty. Holton readily agreed to help this sister bogus company, provided he were well paid for his trouble. His proposition was readily accepted, and he received some seventy-five hundred dollars in advance, for his services. In return for this he furnished the other company with the altered Southern bonds, and some of the forged railroad stock, which had served him so well. This time, however, the commissioner was more particular, and the securities offered were at once rejected as insufficient and valueless, and as a consequence the "Community Fire Insurance Co." incontinently collapsed. As soon as this company had dissolved, Holton, knowing full well that the secretary of the defunct institution was fully aware of his tricky methods, and might prove dangerous to him, began to circulate damaging reports about him, which compelled him to leave the country, much to the relief of the ingenious and unscrupulous Holton. Holton, at this time, was living in a most luxurious manner with a lady, presumably his wife, in one of the first hotels of the city. He had plenty of money at his command, drove a span of spirited horses, and his diamonds were the envy of all beholders. Meanwhile he was preparing the way for his grand issue of forged securities. He had opened accounts with several banks both in New York and Philadelphia, in order to facilitate his operations when he was ready to make his grand movement. His plan was to deposit these worthless securities with the several banks where he was acquainted, as collateral for loans, which he could readily effect, and the fraudulent nature of the security would not be discovered until either the principal or interest should become due, and he should fail to make proper and prompt payments.

From an unsuspecting banking house in Philadelphia he obtained a loan of forty-five thousand dollars, and deposited, as security, forged and stolen United States registered bonds, and from a prominent merchant of his acquaintance he obtained five thousand dollars upon another spurious United States bond, for the same amount. Upon this latter debt becoming due Holton failed to pay it, and the bond he had given was sold. It passed through several hands without suspicion, and finally reached the United States Treasury Department, where it was at once discovered to have been originally stolen and altered. It was therefore returned through its various channels to the gentleman who had made the loan to Holton, and Holton immediately redeemed it and thus escaped, for the time being, exposure and arrest.

As soon as this accident to his plan occurred, Holton, fearing that the banking institution from which he had obtained the forty-five thousand dollars would learn of it, and would discover that the securities they held were also valueless, determined upon a bold stroke in order to save himself. He therefore went boldly to the bank and announced that he had serious doubts as to the validity of the bonds he had deposited with them, and requested the privilege of replacing them with others. He was just in time, for that very day, a messenger from the gentleman from whom Holton had borrowed the five thousand dollars, arrived at the bank with the story of that gentleman's experience. The bank, however, permitted Holton to replace the United States bonds, with forged railroad bonds, some bank stock which he persuaded a friend to hypothecate, and a judgment note which he also procured from the same obliging and deceived friend. By these means he was enabled to escape detection for a time, but failing to pay his interest promptly, the bank threatened to offer the railroad bonds for sale in order to recover their money. This must be avoided at all hazards, as a sale would have revealed their fraudulent character at once. Thus pressed, the young man took the desperate chance of openly disposing of some other stolen and forged securities which he held, and being successful in this; he redeemed his note with the bank, and recovered possession of the questionable bonds, which he had deposited with them. While all this was going on, and while these desperate make-shifts were destroying his reputation as a respectable business man, and effectually preventing the operation of his great scheme, Holton was diligently employed in another direction with his professional forger friends. He had opened an office in New York City, in close proximity to the exchange, where he was transacting business under the firm of Benedict and Co. with Mr. Holton passing under the name of Benedict. Here he disposed of bonds to a large amount, and delivered four of them of the value of one thousand dollars each. These bonds were immediately discovered to be forgeries, and the next day Holton was peremptorily requested to return the money he had received for them. This he did, and shortly afterward fifteen thousand dollars worth of Chicago and Northwestern Railroad bonds, which Holton had sold in Philadelphia, were discovered to be forgeries, and decisive measures were taken to apprehend him. After many fruitless efforts to escape, he was finally captured, and an examination was made of the premises he had occupied in New York. Desks were broken open, and carpets torn up, resulting in the discovery of a number of forged United States bonds, and other securities, and also a counterfeit plate for printing United States currency. It was evident that Holton or Benedict had been preparing himself for operations on a large scale, and that he was exposed in the nick of time. These fraudulent documents were eventually destroyed, and Holton, in order to save himself, turned state's evidence, and revealed the whole transaction, thus leading to the arrest of the principals, and the breaking up of the entire organization.

A Forger of Many Experiences.

AMONG the notable characters who have prominently figured in criminal circles, is a man whose name is well-known in banking circles throughout the land. He is probably the greatest and most successful thief and forger of modern times, and his final arrest and imprisonment was a relief to the entire community. His name is Walter Sheridan, but during his career he has adopted a number of aliases, and among the number were those of Walter Stewart and Charles Ralston. It will be remembered that in 1873, a famous gang of forgers among whom were Walter Sheridan, George Wilkes, Andrew J. Roberts, and Frank Gleason, nearly disrupted the Wall Street markets by their gigantic issue of fraudulent stocks, and these men were also connected with that wonderful attempt at forgery on the Bank of England in which several millions of dollars were attempted to be obtained from "the old lady of Threadneedle Street." As to the conception of this scheme, the plans were all laid in New York City, and the capital necessary to carry on the operation, was subscribed by the men I have named, and by George MacDonnell, Austin and Biron Bidwell, and Samuel Perry. The former of these, finding that MacDonnell, and the Bidwells, were leading a fast life in England, and were associating with notorious and disreputable women in London, in such a manner as to seriously affect the success of their scheme, they at once withdrew from the operation, and allowed these latter gentlemen to pursue their way alone. When Sheridan deserted this party, his place was supplied by one George or Gottlieb Engels, another famous forger, and he in turn withdrew from them, and they were thus left to accomplish the forgeries alone. It is unnecessary to say that they failed, and fleeing to America they were arrested by me, and are now serving out life-sentences in Great Britain.

To retrieve the losses occasioned by the failure of these Bank of England forgeries, a gigantic combination was formed among the remaining members of the party in this country. Plates were prepared, and false bonds printed and openly sold on the market, of the New York Central Railroad, the Buffalo and Erie Railroad, the Chicago and Northwestern Railroad, the New Jersey Central Railroad, the California and Oregon Railroad, the Union Pacific Railroad, the Tebo and Neosho Railroad, Allentown School Fund bonds and Erie Water bonds. As nearly as can be estimated the total amount of the bonds thus forged, reached the amount of two and a half million dollars. The forged writing on them is claimed to have been done by George Engels, who was undoubtedly the most accomplished forger in the country in his particular line. All of the parties were eventually arrested and brought to justice, but not until many hundreds of thousands of these worthless securities had been floated upon the market.

The career of Walter Sheridan is a most wonderful one, considering the life of an ordinary criminal as a comparison. He is now about forty-five years old. He was born in New Orleans, of respectable parents, and received a fine education. He is about five feet seven inches in height, a decided blonde, and of very handsome person and gentlemanly address.

When a mere boy he drifted into crime, and made his first appearance in the character of a criminal in Western Missouri as a horse thief. Then he became an accomplished general thief and confidence man, but was especially distinguished as a bank sneak. In 1858 he was arrested in company with Joseph Moran, a noted western robber, for a bank robbery in Chicago, and was sentenced to five years imprisonment in the Alton Penitentiary, which term he faithfully served. The next operation of any magnitude in which he was concerned, was the robbery of the First National Bank of Springfield, Ill., in company with Charles Hicks and Philip Pearson. Sheridan engaged the teller of the bank in conversation, while Hicks and Pearson crawled through a window and stole thirty-five thousand dollars from the vaults. Pearson escaped to Europe, Hicks was arrested and sentenced to eight years imprisonment in Joliet Prison, and Sheridan was subsequently arrested in Toledo, Ohio, by my son, William A. Pinkerton, with twenty-two thousand dollars in his possession. He was placed on trial, but strange to say, the jury acquitted him. He was next concerned in the sneak robbery of the Maryland Fire Insurance Company of Baltimore, by which the thieves secured one hundred twenty thousand dollars in bonds, and after this came the successful robbery of the Merchants and Mechanics Bank of Scranton, Penn., by which thirty-seven thousand dollars in bonds were secured by Sheridan. Then came the robbery of a bank in Cleveland, Ohio, by which forty thousand dollars was carried off by Jesse Allen, James Griffin, Joseph Butts and Sheridan. Allen and Griffin were convicted and sentenced to prison, Butts was discharged and Sheridan managed to escape capture. Possibly the neatest robbery in which Sheridan was ever engaged, was that of Mr. Blatchford, the father of United States Judge Blatchford, who was plundered of seventy-five thousand dollars in bonds while buying an apple at Nassau and Liberty Streets, in New York City, some few years ago. Mr. Blatchford was pleasantly accosted by Sheridan, who engaged him in conversation, and so interested him that he unthinkingly laid down his wallet containing the bonds, upon the apple stand, from which it was removed at once by a confederate. A portion of these bonds were subsequently found in the possession of Horace C. Corp, a brother-in-law of Gleason, who was arrested at the time, but discharged for want of evidence.

When the forgery scheme was laid, after the failure of the Bank of England forgeries, Sheridan became a member of the New York Produce Exchange, under the name of Charles Ralston, and under this same name he carried on business as a dealer in fancy marbles, under the title of "The Belgian Stone Company." The forged bonds being placed on the market, he obtained a loan of seventy thousand dollars from The New York Guaranty and Indemnity Company, giving as collateral security one hundred two thousand dollars in forged bonds of the Buffalo & Erie Railroad, and on the following day obtained a loan of thirty thousand dollars on forty thousand dollars of the same forged securities. When later, the forgeries became known, Sheridan escaped to Europe, and remained in Belgium for a long time, after which he returned again to America. He was finally arrested by my son Robert, who had been on his trail for a long time, and was arraigned in New York City in the Court of General Sessions on eighty-four indictments for forgery. While in the prisoners box he ascertained that he would be confronted by a number of his victims for identification, and fearing this trying ordeal, he exchanged clothes with one of the meanest looking criminals, by whom he was surrounded, giving his fashionable clothes and hat for the worst garments he could find. As may be imagined, his appearance underwent a thorough change, and those who had seen him an hour before in his usual costume, found it extremely difficult, if not impossible, to recognize him. He was finally pursued to conviction, and now after long years of crime, he is a prisoner in an Eastern Penitentiary.

The Bank of England Forgers.

ON the 26th day of August, 1873, in the Old Bailey Court, in London, the most remarkable story of daring forgery and fraud that the world has known, was brought to a conclusion by the sentence of George MacDonnell, two brothers, whose names were Austin and Biron Bidwell, and an individual calling himself Edwin Noyes, to penal servitude for life, for forgery on the Bank of England.

The amount of these forgeries aggregated nearly to the sum of one million dollars, but even this gigantic amount was not the only feature which gave particular importance to the case. The history of this crime shows that four men of very marked intelligence, and of considerable education, had been working for years in concert, with the deliberate intention of defrauding the world, and with a certain degree of pride in their dishonest undertakings. For nearly ten years they had defied the efforts of the authorities to detect them, and emboldened by their success, they determined to attack the institution in England, which more than any other, represents caution, security and unlimited capital; fully believing that by careful combination they could swindle, to an enormous amount, the shrewd and experienced men who controlled it.

They laid their plans carefully, and performed their work coolly and deliberately. They established an office in the business portion of the city, and invested a large amount of capital in the enterprise, just as men of honesty would put out their money in a legitimate under-taking, entertaining no doubt that in due time they would amply reap the reward of their labor and foresight. The capital that "Messrs. MacDonnell & Co." depended upon to give them access to the vaults of the Bank of England, was English gold deposited in strict accordance with commercial usage, in the vaults of the bank itself.

Nor were they hasty or imprudent in carrying out their designs. For months they conducted their operations with a most business-like caution, and they might have eventually succeeded in gaining the coveted millions, had not the first flush of success so unnerved them that they grew careless, and made a most foolish and unnecessary error. This at once exposed them, and resulted in bringing their finely arranged plots to naught, and themselves to a life of servitude among felons less intelligent and refined, and, it may be said, less crafty and hardened than themselves.

The manner in which these men worked was as simple as it was ingenious. George MacDonnell began by opening a deposit account of an ordinary character with the western branch of the bank. For this purpose he needed only an introduction by some regular and known customer of the bank, and the sole evidence of solvency which the institution required of him, was the deposit of a sufficient cash balance to warrant their carrying the account. This amount was forthcoming from the results of previous depreciations, and constituted part of the capital with which the fraud was carried on. The manager of the scheme was patient and conducted himself for a time as an ordinary customer of good resources. He was apparently cautious in all his operations, and aimed at acquiring the reputation of a person engaged in legitimate and profitable business affairs.

At length the time came for which they had been long waiting. Their name was established, their credit was good, and then came the presentation of the forged bills. So excellently were they executed, that they were discounted without hesitation, and the authors of the fraud had to all appearances succeeded in pocketing about five hundred thousand dollars. In order to avoid arousing the suspicions of the bank authorities a part of this money was invested in United States bonds.

The manufacture of these forged bills required the greatest amount of ingenuity and labor. Many of the large firms, upon whom the bills purported to be drawn, use a particular kind of paper, with certain water marks and printed symbols. As the bills were drawn on more than one firm there were several of such imitations required, and yet, in all cases, these forgeries were so nearly perfect, that not one of them was questioned on the ground of a doubt of the acceptor's signatures or of their genuine appearance. The bills were all drawn at three months date, and the money was regularly obtained. No further inquiry was likely to be made about them, until they fell due, and the forgers would have ample time to place themselves beyond all risk of capture. Yet notwithstanding all this, and strange as it may seem, these men, who had exerted a skill, foresight and perseverance, sufficient to insure the unhesitating acceptance of these numerous forged bills, did not escape the commission of one trivial blunder which led to the immediate discovery of the whole dishonest transaction.

They omitted to put the date of acceptance upon two of the bills which they had presented, and in order to rectify this, the bills were taken to the firms, who were alleged to have signed them, for the purpose of having the dates filled up by the proper parties. Upon their being presented to these firms, they were at once pronounced to be forgeries.

The forgers were well-known, and an attempt was immediately made to arrest them before they had an opportunity to make their escape, but their movements were too late, the criminals had taken the alarm and fled, and after dividing their money, had separated. It was soon discovered that George MacDonnell had started for New York, but by what vessel, could not then be learned. The news was telegraphed to America, and a full description of the man was given. The police authorities of this country were aroused, and they resolved that if the forger attempted to land he would be arrested at once.

Accordingly the police-boat was ordered out, and cruised about the harbor of New York for several days without success. Several vessels were boarded, but no trace of the absconding MacDonnell could be found. Late on the following day the "Thuringia" arrived at Quarantine, and a detective went on board. The passengers were called up for examination by the health officer, and the detective accompanied him. Their search was crowned with gratifying success, and a passenger who answered the description of George MacDonnell, was found among the number. He was immediately placed under arrest, and his trunks were taken in charge by the officers. A careful examination of his effects disclosed about forty thousand dollars in gold coin, valuable diamonds, and a variety of watches, jewelry and fancy goods, that was quite astonishing. The prisoner affected to be highly indignant at the outrage which he claimed had been committed upon his person and his liberty, and threatened loudly that the officers should be made to pay dearly for what they were now doing.

His angry demonstrations, however, had no effect upon the officers, and as quickly as possible, Mr. MacDonnell was conveyed to the jail in New York City, and locked in a cell to await an examination. After a diligent search, in which nearly all of the prominent detectives of the country were engaged, the entire number of the suspected criminals were captured and conveyed to London, where, after a protracted trial George MacDonnell, the two Bidwells, and Edward Noyes were convicted and sentenced to hard labor for life. Nearly all of the stolen property was recovered, and the discomfited prisoners may now reflect in bitterness of spirit upon the fearful punishment which their crimes have brought upon them. This was by no means the first crime with which George MacDonnell had been connected. For years prior to this time he had been associated with criminals of the lighter order, and by his rascality had amassed a considerable sum of money.

The first knowledge which I gained of him was in connection with a gang of adroit swindlers who operated around Wall Street in New York City, in 1867, and among the number were the two Bidwells, who shared his fate in this Bank of England forgery. The headquarters of this gang were on Broad Street, in the very center of the financial circles of the great metropolis, and where they were within easy reach of all the large banking institutions of the city. Their mode of operation was to procure checks of some well-known firms for small amounts, and then to forge the signatures of those who gave them, for large sums which they succeeded without difficulty in passing upon the large banking houses and business firms. So ingeniously were their schemes planned and so cleverly was their work executed, that for a long time, they escaped detection. At length, so closely were they watched, that they were compelled to change the scene of their operations, and MacDonnell and his two friends separated from the others and went into partnership upon their own account.

Shortly after this, James W. Barnard, a well-known physician on Fifth Avenue advertised the front parlor of his house to let. MacDonnell went there on the morning of October 30, 1867, and finding the wife of the physician at home, he pretended that he was a rich Englishman traveling for pleasure, and that being disgusted with American hotel life; he had resolved to locate himself in comfortable private apartments. He presented his card on which appeared the name of Henry B. Livingston, which he stated was his name. He was accompanied by one of the Bidwells, who took the part of his valet, and whom he frequently addressed as Clarence. After some conversation MacDonnell engaged the parlor and two rooms adjoining for a large sum, and at once paid an installment in advance.

Two hours afterwards, he in company with his servant went to a prominent jewelry establishment on Broadway, and requested to be shown some expensive diamonds. A tray was placed before him, and after a careful and critical inspection of the gems, he selected a solitaire ring, a brooch with seven stones, two diamond ear-drops and two large unset diamonds, the total value of the precious stones amounting to nearly two thousand five hundred dollars. He informed the salesman that his name was W. H. Barnard; that his residence was on Fifth Avenue, and that he would go down town to see his father, and would return in two hours with the money for the jewels. He afterwards returned to the jewelers, and stated that he had missed seeing his father, but had left word at his place of business for the money to be left at the house. He requested to have the diamonds sent there and invited the salesman to accompany him in a carriage, which was waiting for him at the door. A coachman in all the glory of new livery sat upon the box, and MacDonnell addressed him as "Charles." The salesman accepted the invitation, entered the carriage, and was driven to the reputed residence on Fifth Avenue.

The name of Barnard was upon the door, and as the carriage drew up, MacDonnell alighted, and with the salesman entered the front-parlor, where they found Bidwell busily engaged in reading at one of the windows. As they entered the room MacDonnell addressed him:

"Clarence, where is father?"

"He has just stepped out," answered Clarence.

"Do you know where he has gone?"

"Yes, I think he has gone around to the building."

"Clarence," then said MacDonnell, "the carriage is at the door, and I wish you would go around and see father. This gentleman is from Tiffany's, and he desires the money for the goods I have purchased of them."

Without demurring in the least, Clarence entered the carriage, and was driven away, and MacDonnell entertained his guest while waiting.

In a short time Clarence returned with a check, which he handed to MacDonnell who in turn handed it to the salesman. It was drawn upon a prominent city bank, and for the exact amount of the purchases that had been made. The check was also signed by James W. Barnard, and purported to be duly certified by the bank on which it was drawn. Everything appearing to be satisfactory, the salesman left the jewelry and departed from the house with the worthless check in his possession. Ten minutes afterwards, MacDonnell and Bidwell were on their way to the Eastern States.

In their hurry to get away, or controlled by a desire to avoid dividing with their other accomplice, Charles, the coachman, they left that individual in the lurch. This omission was fatal to them, for the indignant dupe at once repaired to police headquarters, and related the whole story to the detectives. Steps were immediately taken to effect their arrest, and MacDonnell was tracked to Portland, Maine, where he was found in jail in the month of December, he having been committed for some trifling offense. He was brought to New York where he was tried for the forgery and robbery, and being fully identified by the victimized salesman, was convicted and sentenced to three years imprisonment. Bidwell was not found.

While serving out his imprisonment MacDonnell was employed as a waiter in the shoe manufacturing department, but he only served two years and two months when his fine was remitted, and he was released.

After leaving the prison he started for the West, and a few months afterward he entered the cars at Louisville, Ky., with a ticket for Liverpool. He sat in the seat with a jolly-looking, good-natured drover, whom he soon fascinated with his entertaining conversation. MacDonnell carried with him a flask of very excellent brandy, and in the course of their journey, the two men drank quite frequently. The cattle dealer soon succumbed to the effects of the liquor, and while he was asleep MacDonnell abstracted two thousand six hundred dollars from his pocket-book.

He had with him several newspapers and wrappers, and folding the stolen bills in with these publications, he enclosed them in the wrappers, and addressed them to a fictitious name in New York City. He posted them at the next station, and then quietly resumed his seat beside the sleeping drover. When the latter recovered from his stupor the train reached a junction, where a change of cars was necessary, and he proposed that they should take lunch together. MacDonnell consenting, they entered the dining room, and ordered their repast. After finishing their meal, the drover opened his pocket-book to pay for the meal, when he discovered, to his dismay that his money had disappeared. He turned to MacDonnell, and presenting the empty wallet, exclaimed:

"I had twenty-six hundred dollars when you took a seat beside me, and now I haven't a cent!"

MacDonnell drew back in well affected amazement.

"Do you think I would take your money? If you do, I insist upon being arrested and searched at once! Here are my checks, get my baggage, and let the officers make such an examination as will satisfy them and you."

He was accordingly searched, but nothing being found upon him, he was fully exonerated, and the drover humbly apologized for his suspicions. MacDonnell paid the fare of the drover to Buffalo, and upon arriving there the two men parted with mutual expressions of esteem. MacDonnell then came on to New York, where he obtained the newspapers, with their valuable enclosures from the post-office, which he quickly dissipated in extravagant and riotous living.

Some time after this, MacDonnell was suspected of a large diamond robbery that had been effected in a very scientific manner and I was engaged to ascertain if the suspicions were correctly founded. MacDonnell was then living with a beautiful young lady whom he represented as his wife, in a commodious residence in Brooklyn. I immediately arranged that one of my female operatives should make the acquaintance of the reputed Mrs. MacDonnell, which she did so successfully that before many days, my operative and her husband, who was also engaged on my force, were domiciled beneath the roof of the suspected man.

MacDonnell, it was soon learned, was in arrears for two months rent, and just before the day for payment arrived, he suggested a trip to Boston with my operative, and accompanied by their respective wives, they departed. When the owner went to the house to demand his rent, he found no one there but the servant, who informed him of the departure of his tenant. An examination of the house was made, which revealed the fact that nearly all of the rooms were unfurnished. Upon the return of MacDonnell and his friend from Boston, they engaged rooms at one of the hotels in the city, and here they were found by the owner of the house who had procured an order for his arrest, as an absconding debtor. As the officer entered his room, and informed him that he was a prisoner, MacDonnell turned deathly pale, and inquired nervously, the charge for which he was to answer.

On being informed that it was to answer the suit of his landlord, he instantly recovered himself, and requested the officer to accompany him to the room of my operative, who guaranteed the payment, which was subsequently made, and the man was released. This act of kindness led to a close confidence between MacDonnell and the detective, and the result was the disclosure that he had stolen the diamonds, and still had them in his possession. He was accused of the crime and made a full confession, and upon returning the diamonds, the parties who were robbed, refused to prosecute him, and he was released.

From that time, while in America he was constantly under the surveillance of the detectives, and police authorities. His handiwork could be traced in numerous swindles which were perpetrated upon dry-goods houses and banking firms, but the officers were always baffled in their attempts to catch him in the actual commission of any offense. He seemed to be perfectly informed of all the technicalities of criminal law, and so adroitly did he manage his affairs, that it was impossible to legally convict him. At one time he was arrested for passing a spurious fifty dollar check for payment of a hotel bill, but the proprietors refused to prosecute, and he escaped. On another occasion, he went to a wholesale liquor store, and purchased sixty-three dollars worth of brandy, representing that it was for Congressman S. S. Cox. He presented in payment a one hundred dollar note, and requested a check for thirty-seven dollars in change. He received the check and made an exact imitation of it, except that the new production called for twenty-five hundred dollars. By some means, the bank officials were apprised of the fraud, and when the check was presented MacDonnell's messenger was arrested. MacDonnell himself was subsequently arrested, but his tracks were two well covered, to prove him to be the forger, and he again escaped the penalties of the law.

At one time he attempted to swindle the banking firm of Jay Cooke & Co., out of one hundred thirty thousand dollars in United States bonds. The banking house was visited by an elegantly dressed gentleman, who gave the name as J. W. Kenney, who stated that he was a lawyer whose office was in close proximity to the banker's, and that he was the executor of a large estate in New Jersey. He expressed his desire to invest one hundred thirty thousand dollars in government bonds for the benefit of the minor heirs of the estate. He ordered the bonds sent to his office, saying that they would be paid for there with a certified check on the National Park Bank.

He was in negotiation with the banking house for several days, but the detectives had received intelligence that the intended purchase was a swindle, and made arrangements to secure Kenney's capture. Kenney, however, took alarm from some cause and did not wait for the bonds to be delivered to him, but suddenly disappeared. His plan, as afterwards discovered, was to have two checks—one of them a forgery for the full amount of the purchase money, and the other a genuine one for a small amount. When the messenger from Jay Cooke & Co. arrived at his office with the bonds, he had intended to get him to accompany him to the bank to have the check certified. At the bank he would have the good check certified before the messenger, and then get the latter to return with him to his office under the pretense that he was afraid to carry the bonds himself. On the way he was to substitute the forged check for the one that had been certified and so pass it off in payment for the bonds. This was discovered after MacDonnell had been arrested for the Bank of England forgery, when he was identified as the man who had attempted to personate the J. W. Kenney in the above case. As he had not committed any overt act, Jay Cooke & Co. were unable to prosecute him.

In the fall of 1871, MacDonnell purchased twenty-three hundred dollars worth of goods from Arnold, Constable & Co. under the name of Edward Johnson. He represented to them that he owned a large store in the west, and that he would send a check for the goods if he was not able to call himself. On the day following, a carman called at the store of Arnold, Constable & Co., and presented a letter which was written on the bill head paper of a respectable firm, and which purported to be signed by them, stating that Mr. Johnson had left the city, and that they had been requested to forward the goods to him, together with some others which they had sold. Enclosed in the letter was a check for the amount of the bill. The goods were then delivered, and the swindled firm learned, when too late, that the check was utterly worthless and a forgery. MacDonnell was arrested for this attempt at swindling, but as there was no one to swear that he was the forger, he was released.

A large lace importing firm were the last victims of MacDonnell, prior to his departure for Europe. He succeeded in this case, in obtaining laces to the amount of two thousand dollars, by the same tactics which he pursued in the case of Arnold, Constable & Co. He was arrested however, for this offense, with the laces still in his possession, but again evaded punishment by some ingenious legal technicality.

Soon after this he went to Europe and remained for a time in Germany, where he managed to success-fully swindle a number of merchants, and by that means obtained the large sum of money which enabled him to so completely win the confidence of the exceedingly cautious officers of the Bank of England, and eventually to carry out the gigantic forgeries upon that institution.

After his arrest for this forgery, which took place in New York, he was placed in the custody of the United States authorities, and he was taken to Fort Columbus in the harbor of New York, for safe-keeping until the following day. That night was one of the most beautiful of the season—the moon shone brilliantly, lighting up the harbor for miles, and enabling one to view the broad expanse of glistening water that surrounded them.

About nine o'clock a small boat containing two men was observed by the sentry, seemingly drifting toward Governor's Island. It stopped just under the walls of the fort, and the occupants waited there for an hour conversing in low tones with the soldiers on guard. MacDonnell stepped outside to the closet several times, in company with the officers, and each time he gazed anxiously in the direction of the boat. Whatever may have been his intentions that night, they were not carried out, for the vigilance of his guard was never relaxed for a moment, and at a late hour the boat was rowed away and MacDonnell was compelled to retire within the fort. A few days afterward, however, a person who had been very solicitous about MacDonnell while he was in confinement, inquired of the officer if he had noticed anything strange about the fort on the night that MacDonnell was there. The marshal mentioned the circumstance of the boat, and he was then informed that the vessel had been sent there for the purpose of attempting to effect the rescue of the imprisoned forger. The sentinels, it was asserted, had been paid fifty dollars each not to fire at him so as to hit him, in case he should jump into the water and attempt to swim to the boat; but MacDonnell was afraid that the marshal, who was directly responsible for him, might aim more accurately than the soldiers, and hence the attempt was not made.

George MacDonnell was never married, although in his long and varied career, several women have taken his name. He was possessed of great natural advantages, and could be very winning when he chose. He was tall, and well-proportioned, and was a remarkably handsome man. He wore a long, waving dark brown beard and his complexion was as fair as a woman's. His voice was soft and rich and his powers of conversation were remarkably attractive. He was a brilliant linguist, and while he was imprisoned in Ludlow Street Jail, he acted as an interpreter for a Chinaman and for the famous Carl Vogt, the Belgian valet who was charged with the murder of the Count Du Bois de Bianco.

At last, however, justice overtook him, and now under the life-sentence of a criminal, he is suffering the stings of anguished conscience and the hard physical drudgery of the branded convict.

Family, education, personal appearance, and great business qualifications were all sacrificed at the bidding of crime, and the malefactor is now suffering the severe penalties of the outraged law.

A Forger of Two Continents.

IN the criminal history of the present day no man attained a more widespread reputation as an accomplished, daring and expert criminal than William Ringgold Cooper who attained a wide celebrity both in America and England for his wonderful deeds of forgery. Certainly no man has ever sustained the dual character of a gentleman and a forger with equal success. Young, accomplished, of elegant personal appearance, and of the most fascinating address, William R. Cooper might have adorned any station in society, and yet for years, under various and almost undetectable disguises, he preyed upon his best friends, and the world at large, until in the fullness of his success, he imagined failure or detection impossible. This young man was born in Smyrna, Del., of respectable family, his father having been a county judge for five years, and regarded with the highest esteem by all of his friends and associates. Owing to a scandal with which the name of a young lady of his native city was connected, young Cooper resigned his position in the Smyrna National Bank, and disappeared. The breaking out of the rebellion, found him an enlisted member of the United States Navy, and after two years service, he became an ensign on the staff of Admiral Lee, of the North Atlantic Squadron. By his engaging manners and strict attention to his duties, he became a great favorite among his superior officers, and through their influence he was appointed an assistant paymaster in the Navy.

While in Washington, he formed the acquaintance of a number of gamblers and accomplished forgers, who soon instructed him into the methods and mysteries of aristocratic crime. As a consequence of this course of study, he forged a warrant for one hundred seventy-five thousand dollars purporting to have been signed by United States Paymaster Spaulding. At the time of this forgery he was engaged to be married to a beautiful and accomplished young lady, the daughter of Mr. Defrees, the government printer, and the forgery of the paymaster's warrant was not discovered until the day after the wedding ceremony had been performed. Cooper was immediately arrested and sentenced to five years imprisonment in the Eastern Penitentiary of Pennsylvania, which time he faithfully served. It was generally supposed that he died in prison, but upon his release he went to

New Orleans, where, undismayed by his first experience, he perpetrated another successful forgery for forty-five thousand dollars, and then fled to San Francisco, Cal., where he became a mining, stock, and gold broker.

While in San Francisco, his own wife having married again, supposing him to be dead, he formed the acquaintance of a handsome and clever woman to whom he was married and who clung steadfastly to her erring husband, through all the varying fortunes of his future career.

For a brief season Cooper maintained an enviable reputation in the San Francisco Exchange, but the crash soon came, and he absconded after having forged a check for sixty thousand dollars upon his business partner. In this transaction, singular as it may seem, as well as in all his other criminal transactions, he employed the services of a boy to cash the forged check and to hand him the proceeds. An investigation followed immediately after this forgery was discovered, but no information was ever gained of William Cooper, his wife Kate, or the boy Fred Caul and their disappearance was as effectual as it had been mysterious.

Nothing was heard of Cooper until his arrest in London, under the name of Neville Hunter, in the summer of 1879, notwithstanding the fact that he had taken no pains to live in seclusion, or to avert curiosity.

On leaving California he went to London, arriving there in the fall of 1877, and instead of registering at the Langham Hotel, he engaged apartments for himself and wife in a private hotel near the Strand. Here he gave the name of Henry C. Neville, an American iron merchant and a manufacturer of mowing machines. After remaining a short time in this hotel, he negotiated with a firm of solicitors for the lease of East Lodge, a beautiful country seat, with spacious grounds, at Hemel-Hempstead, in Herefordshire. He obtained possession of this estate at a heavy yearly rental, and set up his carriage and horses, maintaining a half dozen servants in his establishment. He owned his stud of hunters, rode to hounds with the country squires, and by various processes he secured the friendship and acquaintance of the surrounding gentry and their families, with whom he and his wife became speedily very intimate, and general favorites.

This intimacy he turned to good account, and by inviting them to dinners and receptions, and receiving their replies, he familiarized himself with the character of their handwriting, and forged checks on their bankers in London. On June 28th, 1878, he sent a boy to the Bank of England with a forged check for four hundred pounds, purporting to have been made by Hugh Cheever Goodwin, of Hemel-Hempstead. The clerk of the bank, however, suspected the forgery, and hurried out with the boy, only to find that Cooper was being driven rapidly away in his carriage, having changed his reversible coat, and removed the false whiskers he wore when he hired the messenger. In all his crimes of this nature he stood above the other Anglo-American forgers, from the fact that he never appeared in any public place in London except at the opera, and that, unlike MacDonnell and the Bidwells, the Bank of England forgers, he never associated with abandoned women, or conducted himself in any other manner than that of a thorough gentleman and man of the world.

Too much success, however, made Cooper over confident, and he began to evince signs of carelessness in his work. At last, he presented to Glynn, Mills & Co., Bankers, a check for nearly four thousand pounds, which was duly honored, and he would have escaped without detection, but, hearing that he was suspected, he returned to the bank, and, with supreme audacity, demanded of the bankers to know why they presumed to doubt his honesty. He was at once arrested, and was identified by the boy he had employed, and by the cabman, and the barber who had made his false wig and whiskers.

He was arraigned for trial, and his neighbors and friends from Hemel-Hempstead, testified with tears in their eyes, that they could not believe him to be dishonest, but finding that the evidence against him was overwhelming, Cooper pleaded guilty to both of the charges of forgery.

While in England he made, but one fatal mistake, and that was to have his photograph taken, and a copy of this speaking portrait was sent to my Agency for identification; should therefore his trial in London have proved a failure, I was prepared with extradition-papers to bring him to America to answer for his crimes here, but having pleaded guilty there, his punishment was meted out to him by the English court.

Perhaps the saddest commentary upon the life of this unfortunate young man and a fit illustration of his hypocrisy are the words which came from his own lips when he was called up for sentence:

"I am by birth and education a gentleman," said he. "When I took the house at Hemel-Hempstead, I thought I could honestly maintain it, I furnished it for the sake of my wife. We garnished that house with hopeful anticipation. Every article it contained, every flower in its windows, was arranged by my wife's loving hands, and we cherished the fond expectation that there we should happily spend the remainder of our days. I met with reverses, however, and was ashamed to look my wife in the face. I was tempted and I fell." And here the prisoner's head sunk on his breast, and he wept aloud. "My crime is the greater," he continued after a pause, "because my wife would have followed me to the end of the earth, and would have shared my last crust of bread in poverty. I have now lost hope, future, honor, everything, but a sense of shame which will follow me forever."

This was very dramatic, very pathetic and exceedingly effective, but every word was known to be false, and the court sentenced him to five years penal servitude.

Conclusion.

THE incidents I have above related, which are but a few of the many, that have come under my notice during the thirty years of my detective life, comprise some of the more important operations of the expert forgers, who have from time to time plied their vocation in the United States. In addition to these, however, there is a numerous class of forgeries in which no attempt is made upon the banks, or the moneyed institutions of the country and which are, in the main, perpetrated by skillful and unscrupulous amateurs who have sought to realize at one bold stroke the benefit of years of toil and economy.

One of the prominent illustrations of this species of crime, was the celebrated Whitaker will case, in which an attempt was made to defraud the heirs of an aged and miserly millionaire in Philadelphia a few years ago.

In this case the parties to the forgery were an aged and hitherto respectable lawyer, who had for years been the confidential adviser and counselor of the deceased, and three other men whom he had selected for his purposes, to forge the seals and to sign fictitious names of witnesses. This was one of the best planned and carefully executed forgeries with which the courts have had to deal, and many months were spent in the investigation and trial which finally ended in conviction. The attorney, by reason of his intimate knowledge of the business habits and characteristics of Mr. Robert Whitaker, the testator, and from the fact that he had actually drawn the genuine will, and had it confided to his keeping, was enabled to work with every advantage in his favor. The forged will which was offered for probate was written upon the same paper as that of the original, and the signature of Robert Whitaker, the testator, was so perfectly imitated, that many intimate friends of the deceased testified to its genuineness. The signatures of the subscribing witnesses were perfect, and upon its face the will appeared to be thoroughly genuine and worthy of acceptance. But the attorney had been too grasping; under the terms of this forged will he had sought to obtain the lion's share of the miser's wealth, while his family were left with scarcely the legal allowance as their part and share in the estate. This fact led to suspicion, and suspicion led to inquiry. My investigations in this case extended over a long period of time; more than twenty operatives were engaged at various times, and a large sum of money was expended, but in the end, the base designs of the forgers were fully exposed, and their schemes utterly defeated, while the principals found themselves behind iron bars as a penalty for their evil-doing. By an ingenious and scientific course of investigation we were able to determine, beyond a doubt, that the paper on which this forged will was written, was not really manufactured for some months after the date on which the will purported to be executed. It is true it was manufactured by the same firm, from the same materials, bore the same trade-mark, and was intended to be the same paper in every respect, but it was ascertained that by some little derangement in the setting of the machine which ruled the lines upon the paper, there had been caused a scarcely noticeable difference in the two papers. This once proved, it became necessary to more fully establish the question of a conspiracy to defraud, and finally, one of the parties to the forgery was induced to disclose the whole affair, and the entire scheme of these unscrupulous men was fully divulged. In the end the fraudulent will was set aside, the heirs came legally into their estate, and the guilty forgers were condemned to imprisonment.

Several instances have occurred in which designing women have forged or caused to be forged marriage certificates, through which they endeavored to lay claim to the property of wealthy men who died, by attempting to prove that they were the widows of the decedents, and thus entitled to their legal dower in the estates of their deceased husbands. Deeds of title to real estate, bills of sale, orders for the payment of money, and receipts of payment, have all been forged by dishonest persons, who have attempted to defraud the community and enrich themselves by their nefarious actions.

Altogether forgery is one of the most dangerous of crimes, and the amount of money thus unlawfully obtained, if it could be correctly computed, would startle the community with its enormity. I am happy to state, however, that in every case of this character, in which I have been engaged, I have invariably succeeded in discovering the perpetrators of the fraud, and in a large majority of instances, I have recovered the major portion of the amounts thus illegally obtained.

Counterfeiting
and Counterfeiters

EVER since the existence of man, human ingenuity has been taxed to devise means of exchange between individuals and communities. Barter and sale, trade and exchange, are as old as humanity itself, and it is a matter of interest to note the various materials and commodities, which have in former times, in all portions of the globe, served as a medium of communication. The purposes which money is serving have been served in different countries and in different ages, by a variety of products, according to the tastes and the circumstances of the people. Cattle have been employed as money among pastoral people in almost all periods of the world, and are still employed for this purpose in Africa. Slaves served the same uses among the Anglo-Saxon, and wampum among the American Indians. Nails in Scotland, stamped leather among the Carthaginians, salt in Abyssinia, and cod-fish in Massachusetts, have all done duty as money in the absence of a general standard. Bark stamped with the sovereign in China, platina in Russia, copper, simple or compounded with other metals, among the ancient Romans, and most other nations, and iron among the Spartans, have at various times been received as the equivalent of values which were regularly determined upon the basis of the nature of the return.

Thus it is written that Hiram, King of Tyre, furnished to King Solomon a certain quantity of cedars from Lebanon, and Solomon, in return, furnished to the Tyrians a certain quantity of wheat and oil.

Abraham, in the olden time, purchased the famous cave and field of Macpelah, for which he weighed out four hundred shekels of silver, current money, with the merchant, and this is the first record we have of a monetary transaction of any kind whatever. The shekel in those days was about half an ounce in English avoirdupois weight, and the value of the coin was two shillings seven pence. There were two standards of the shekel— namely, the shekel of the sanctuary, which was used in calculating the offerings of the temple, and all sums connected with the sacred law, and the royal or profane shekel, used for all civil payments and are still using gold and silver as the medium of commercial exchange and as the proper standard of value.

At length, civilized nations sooner or later adopted and are still using gold and silver as the medium of commercial exchange and as the proper standard of value.

It must be acknowledged, that of all the products mentioned above the last two have shown themselves to be the best adopted for the purposes of money, and consequently have come into universal use in the commercial world.

Experience has not only demonstrated the superiority of these metals over all other forms of money, as is shown by the fact of their universal adoption, but reason also is able to tell us why gold and silver are the best money. On account of their comparatively unchangeable value, the uniform cost of production and their fluency, they become the standard of value, and when in cases of wars and other emergencies nations are compelled to issue a paper currency, or certificates of indebtedness, the value of this currency and these certificates is predicated upon the standard value of the gold and the silver dollar. A dollar is a tangible commodity; a dollar bill is a promise to give this commodity to bearer. Paper money, then, always has in it the element of credit, while the golden money has in it only the element of present and actual value.

However these facts may be, it is equally true that for the purposes of convenience in trade, and to enable governments and individuals to meet financial obligations, the paper dollar, and the certificate of indebtedness, become for the time being and for all practical business purposes, a good, marketable and exchangeable medium of commerce, at the value of one hundred cents, when relative values have determined its proper standard. For centuries and in all countries the issuing, both of the metal money and the paper currency, has been indorsed and accepted by the people, and from the time that money was invented there have existed men who sought to pervert its use and to imitate its worth. With the advent of money the counterfeiter made his appearance, and as both have artistically advanced, the dangers and difficulties of spurious currencies must be apparent to every thinking mind. Counterfeiting at the present day is literally one of the advanced arts. From the earliest age the art and practice of counterfeiting has always demanded skill and audacity, and it naturally partakes of the general progress of the age. It therefore of necessity becomes more and more able and artful, as the multiplication of checks and the sharpness of discrimination increase. It is no longer the common "shover of the queer," as he is called in police circles, who is the worst and most dangerous pirate upon the monetary seas, for behind these vulgar fellows, who are merely brazen and dexterous, and who are daily being apprehended, there stands an organization composed of men of actual genius and of unbounded resources. These men take the lead and utilize the skill of unscrupulous artists and engravers of the highest order of merit, and when fully prepared make their assaults upon the commonwealth with all the combined subtlety of a Gortchakoff and concentrated energy of a Bismarck.

The trained and faithful detective, who is called upon, in the performance of duty, to match his skill against the educated rogue, just as he must face the bullet and the knife of the degraded and ignorant ruffian, is often most painfully reminded how little mere education, or the restraints of high social position, with correct moral discipline, and the true development of high personal integrity, can do for the public safety. In the game of sharps, the advantage, at the outset, is with the depredator, and although the officer pursues the lawbreaker to a prison or the grave at last, it is often a stern chase in which it is the moral stamina of the detective alone that gives the superlative pluck and endurance that wins the desperate race. It is literally, a battle of life or death in almost every case, and yet it is the universal price that must be paid for even comparative public safety. It is not too much to say, that to a certain extent, the general public lend material aid to the counterfeiters by too great ignorance, and an almost criminal carelessness. They do not, as a rule, take the pains necessary to become good judges of current money, and if they happen to receive a bill or note which afterwards excites their doubts, they make haste to dispose of the suspicious exchange, rather than bear the burden of the loss which would be entailed upon them by determining the question of its genuineness. There are too many persons who are like the ingenious store-keeper, who received in the course of his business a note, about which he was not altogether satisfied. As he explained the situation—"One day I thought it was good and the next day I would think it was bad, and so on one of the days when I thought it was good, I just passed it out in change, and that relieved me from any further trouble." As long therefore as people who would indignantly repudiate the imputation of fraud, and who claim to be highly respectable, are willing to connive at felonious crime, to take and pass bad bills, there can be but little improvement expected in the general condition of the body politic with reference to the subject of counterfeiters. Of course this is not generally the case, but instances are sufficiently numerous to warrant the expressions I have used.

The government deals with an iron hand when counterfeiters are detected, and the strictest and most unrelenting justice is meted out to those who manufacture and deal in spurious money of all kinds, and it is to the almost superhuman efforts of the detective, that the public are now in the enjoyment of the comparative safety which has been thus secured.

As early as the year 1721, the government of Great Britain pronounced itself against counterfeiting and in that year the first execution for counterfeiting occurred. According to the nature of the times, this punishment was cruel in the extreme, but the law prescribed the penalty and it was carried into force and effect. On that occasion the victim was a woman named Barbara Spencer, and after a due and formal trial, she was convicted of "high treason, in counterfeiting the King's current coin of the realm."

The law which existed at that time was that women convicted of high or petit treason, should be publicly burned, but in this case the wisdom and humanity of the authorities provided a more easy death for the unfortunate culprit, and they directed that the malefactor should be strangled while tied to the stake, and that the body should be afterwards consumed by fire. The decree of the court was duly earned out at Tyburn on the 5th of July, 1721.

England, with two hundred years of ecclesiastical barbarism for example, believing there could be no higher crime than counterfeiting the coin of the realm, adopted this mode of execution, and until the thirteenth year of the reign of George III, this punishment was also inflicted on women who were convicted of murdering their husbands, which crime was denominated petit treason.

The Newgate Calendar, in chronicling this first execution for counterfeiting in England, states that: "This is the first case on record in which any person appears to have been executed for counterfeiting the coin of the realm. The punishment for this offense, if at first, of necessity, severe, to check the alarming prevalence of crime, has long since been mitigated; and although the evil still exists to a great degree, it has been diminished very considerably in consequence of the judicious steps taken by the officers of the mint."

On the 9th day of June, 1731, ten years later, another public display was made in Great Britain, in the punishment of one Japhet Crook, alias St. Peter Stronger. This malefactor was brought to the pillory at Charing Cross, to answer for his crimes of forging and counterfeiting. The prisoner was compelled to stand for one hour on the pillory, in the presence of a jeering multitude, and after that a chair was brought for him, and he was placed therein. The hangman then approached him and clipped off both his ears, after which a surgeon immediately clapped a styptic over the bleeding stumps. The executioner with a pair of scissors then cut his left nostril twice before it was quite through, and afterward cut through the right nostril at once. The prisoner exhibited great patience and fortitude, but when in pursuance of his sentence his right nostril was severed with a red-hot iron, he was in such violent pain that his left nostril was let alone, and he was then taken from the pillory. After this barbarous performance, the victim was conveyed in this bleeding and mangled condition, back to the King's Bench prison there to remain for life. He died in confinement about three years afterward.

These are only two instances, which even in those early days marked the determination of the government to put a stop to the nefarious practice of counterfeiting and forging, and although the treatment of both victims was barbarous in the extreme, yet even these executions fail to have the effect desired. From 1797 to 1817 eight hundred and five persons were convicted of either forging notes of the Governor and Company of the Bank of England or for knowingly uttering or possessing such forged notes, knowing them to be forgeries, and nearly two hundred fifty thousand pounds were expended by the crown in conducting the prosecutions of these criminals. From this it will be seen that counterfeiting is no new science, although the present modes of operation are far different from those practiced in the early days. Despite the prosecutions and the punishments of centuries, the counterfeiter still exists, and his presence in the community at this time is, if anything, far more dangerous and pernicious than when burning and maiming were the punishments meted out to the offenders.

In our own country, counterfeiting was practiced in the colonies at a comparatively early day. Turning to the records of the olden time, we find that in January, 1773, the amount of counterfeit money in circulation was estimated at eight thousand pounds, and a bill was presented to the colonial legislature to remedy the evils which this fraud inflicted on the community. The currency thus forged was colonial, and the task of counterfeiting it was not difficult, as the genuine itself was but poorly engraved.

Philip Schuyler, afterwards famed in the Revolution, proposed to meet the difficulty with an improvement in art. His idea was to have a plate made so perfect, that it would successfully defy imitation. He did not seem to consider for a moment that fraud generally enlists the services of the best workmen. Among other things suggested by this gentleman, was the idea of having engraved upon the notes, peculiar devices, which should awaken terror in the minds of the people. Every genuine note was to bear the imprint of an eye looking out of a cloud; also a cart, a coffin and a gallows. On the gallows were to be hung three counter-feiters, surrounded by weeping mothers and children. Underneath this agonizing scene was to be inscribed the legend: "Let the name of the money maker rot."

As an additional security, it was required that the government printer should make oath that the plates had never been out of his hands, and when his task was done the plates were to be sealed up and placed in the treasurer's hands. A reward was also to be offered for the detection of counterfeiters, whose punishment was death.

Notwithstanding Philip Schuyler's precautions, however, counterfeiting both in currency and specie has continued to be a prominent feature in crime, and every improvement in the art of engraving or coinage is met by a corresponding advance in this branch of fraud.

The question is frequently asked how can it be that such perfect counterfeits are made, but when it is remembered that the principal agent in producing this perfection is some first-class engraver who may have lost his regular employment through dissipation, and who being reduced to poverty by his evil courses is easily reached by the designing men who desire to control him, the artistic correctness of the work can readily be understood.

In imitating the coin of the country the ambition of the counterfeiter is limited by the issue of the government. Our largest coin is the double-eagle or twenty dollar piece, but in the counterfeiting of government and National Bank notes, and in the bonds issued by the government a larger and more remunerative field is opened for the dishonest imitator. From one dollar up to one thousand dollars the counterfeiters have succeeded in imitating the

Treasury notes of the government and many of these have been so well executed as almost to defy detection except from experienced eyes. In the National Bank notes counterfeits have not been attempted above the one hundred dollar bills, and with very few exceptions the work upon these spurious notes has been in all respects excellent. Government bonds of all issues have been counterfeited in the denominations of fifty, one hundred and one thousand dollars, and in the case of the one thousand dollar, 7.30 United States bonds the government receivers themselves redeemed ninety thousand dollars worth of these counterfeits before their true character was discovered. As these bonds have matured and the interest upon them stopped, the authorities issued a general warning to the public to decline to receive all bonds of this character and denomination. When such a warning is considered necessary the counterfeiter is without question a person to be feared. Railroad and telegraph bonds, steamship companies and even municipal corporations that have issued certificates of bonded indebtedness have been the victims of these artistic rascals, and counterfeit bonds of all classes have been sold and negotiated in all the principal cities of the country. An important use, to which these counterfeit bonds have been put, is to swell the assets of doubtful corporations whose capital and assets ostensibly of hundreds of thousands of dollars have been entirely represented by the forged and counterfeited bonds of the government and the railroad companies throughout the country. An investigation not long since developed the fact that an insurance company in one of the prominent cities of the East was transacting a legitimate business, and insuring houses, stores and other properties for unlimited amounts with no other financial standing or responsibility than a presumed capital and assets of two hundred fifty thousand dollars, which was composed entirely of forged and counterfeit securities which had been purchased from well-known criminals for the purpose of imposing upon the general public. A remarkable feature in this case was the fact that in one instance the company had actually effected a loan of a large amount of money from one of the principal banks of the city and had deposited some of these worthless bonds as collateral security for the money advanced. These are not mere idle stories but actual occurrences, and the fraud in this latter case was not discovered until default was made in the payment of the loan of the bank, and that institution attempted to realize upon their valueless hypothecations. A public expose then occurred, and in the investigation which followed the insurance company was wiped out of existence and the perpetrators of the fraud were remanded to prison. It is a gratifying fact therefore that punishment usually follows the commission of such crimes, but before discoveries are made, thousands of innocent persons are compelled to suffer and many of them are financially ruined.

In the counterfeiting of coin every denomination from the paltry three cent piece to the double-eagle has been successfully imitated, and all of them have an attractive exterior well calculated to deceive even good judges. This is all the more reasonable, since in the larger gold pieces it is really a good shell formed by splitting a genuine coin, of which two-thirds of the interior is removed. The space is then filled in with platinum and the sides are joined together in a very finished manner, the milling upon the edges being neatly renewed. The weight is precisely that of the genuine, and upon the whole it is a remarkable success. These counterfeits contain therefore, about six dollars worth of gold, the balance of fourteen dollars going into the pockets of the scoundrels who have doctored them.

Eagles and half-eagles are also frequently counterfeited, and the latter of 1872 are so finished and perfect an imitation that they may really be termed "dangerous." They were really worth sixty percent, of their expressed value, and this left too small a margin for ordinary circulation, for to pay in a satisfactory manner they ought not to cost more than thirty percent.

Gold coin is tampered with in a variety of ways, each of which is very ingenious. One operation consists in "sweating" or jingling the coin together in a buckskin bag, by which five percent can be made, without injury to the coin itself. Twice as much, however, can be made by filing the edges of the coins, but this requires a master hand, since the appearance must not be marred in the slightest degree.

Trade dollars are extensively imitated, and there is also a large business done in half dollars, quarters and dimes. One of the best is the half dollar of 1876, the metal being composed of antimony, lead and tin. There are many issues of the quarters exhibiting a great variety of skill and merit. The denomination of the quarter of 1854 has frequently deceived the best judges in the country. Of the dimes, and even the nickels, it may be said that the false issue is very inferior to the genuine, and yet, they are in general circulation. It is a comparatively easy matter to pass such pieces, and hence the public is easily imposed upon.

In the matter of counterfeiting the National Bank notes of the country, several precautions have been adopted by the government to secure the innocent public.

The United States government prints all the paper money of the nation from plates, which are made four in a set, and lettered in order respectively A, B, C, D, though of late, in a few exceptional cases, certain banks have been supplied with bills lettered respectively E, F, G, H. These four plates being in one piece and perfectly alike except the single different letter on each one, are used together and printed at one time upon one large sheet, a series or set of four bills. By this means each bill is always marked with the same one letter of its own plate. The counterfeiter, owing to the trouble and expense involved, makes but one plate, copying but one bill of one letter of the genuine set.

Whenever, therefore, any counterfeit National Bank bill appears, the United States Redemption Agency quickly gathers up and retires from circulation all genuine bills of the same denomination, National Bank and letter, and thus leaves the field to the counterfeit. Consequently, as a matter of safety, all National Bank bills of the same denomination, letter and date as the counterfeit should be refused by every person who desires to avoid great risk. All bills of the same denomination and National Bank of the other and different check letters are not counterfeited and still continue in circulation. Counterfeiters seldom use the same plate on two or more check letters of the same denomination of any National Bank; but when the counterfeit has become notorious they change the issue by inserting with the aid of skeleton plates, the name of another and unsuspected National Bank on which no counterfeit of that particular denomination has yet appeared. The principle, thus explained, is quite plain, and the method of discrimination most concise and certain.

Whenever a note is presented at any of the Sub-Treasury Departments, and it is ascertained to be counterfeit, the officer in charge immediately stamps across the face of it in large letters the word "COUNTERFEIT," and thus the career of that particular piece of dishonesty is at once brought to a sudden and untimely end, and its power of deception forever taken away.

In describing the methods resorted to by the counterfeiters it will be necessary to introduce some of the most famous of the men who have figured in this particular line of dishonesty, in order that the reader may fully appreciate the nature and extent of their peculiar operations.

A Counterfeiter of Millions.

AMONG the most successful of these dangerous counterfeiters were E.W. Spencer, better known by his alias of "Bill Brockway," and Charles H. Smith, whose imitations of the six percent one thousand dollar bonds bonds and the six varieties of one hundred dollar National Bank notes were the most perfect of their kind. No words can be found, or sentences framed to fitly express our astonishment at and admiration for the wonderful exploits of these two men, or to properly estimate the genius of the former or the skill of the latter. On the other hand, when it is remembered to what base uses they applied their gifts, natural and acquired, the mind becomes confused in its efforts in seeking fitting terms to denounce the turpitude of their acts. And therefore, though their work and their methods of accomplishing it, surpass everything in the counterfeiting line which has yet been developed, and demonstrate how weak and insufficient are the mechanical barriers that have been interposed for the protection of the people by the government against this class of criminals, yet for want of proper phrase, we descend to the positive degree of comparison, and simply designate them as counterfeiters.

A pertinent inquiry at this point may be, "Does it pay to pursue this unlawful business of counterfeiting?" In reply, I dismiss the mere moral aspect of the question, with the oft-repeated axiom, that "It never pays to commit a wrong." But in a pecuniary sense, has it paid these men to follow their nefarious calling? Brockway is probably the most gigantic, and has been, so far as keeping out of the clutches of the law is concerned, the most successful counterfeiter known to modern times. He owned the following counterfeit plates: The one thousand dollar bond, the five hundred and one hundred dollar Treasury notes, the one thousand dollar six percent United States bond, and six varieties of the one hundred dollar National Bank notes, all of which, in their execution and design, were acknowledged by the most expert judges in the country to be equal to and scarcely detected from the genuine, and yet to-day he is homeless and penniless, and a felon. He was convinced that the counterfeits which he held were so identical with the genuine that the spurious could not be readily detected, and yet, after all his labor and expense, his toil and his anxiety, his hopes were dashed to the ground by reading in the newspapers of the discovery of his counterfeits almost on the very day of their issue. Undismayed by these defeats, he would instantly withdraw that note, and prepare a plate for another imitation on a different bank, in which the defects which had led to the detection of the first were sought to be remedied in every particular. This process he repeated until he had issued the six counterfeits now so widely known. It is perfectly safe to state that the detection of four of these notes followed so quickly upon their issue, that the amount put into circulation did not compensate him for the labor bestowed upon them. A short description of the tools and materials used by this redoubtable counterfeiter, may give an approximate idea of the nature of counterfeiting as a fine art.

The plates for printing the back border tint of the counterfeit one hundred dollar National Bank notes are four in number, and all on copper plates. One of these was carefully and artistically engraved by hand, and the other three electrotyped; the former by Charles H. Smith, the latter the work of Brockway himself. Each plate is the counterpart of the other, except the panel which contains the coat of arms seen at the left end on the back of the note. As the counterfeits had thus far been confined to three states, Massachusetts, Pennsylvania and Maryland, so three of these plates showed on their respective panels the arms of these several states, while in the fourth the panel was left blank, until they had decided upon which state they would renew their depredations.

The vignette entitled "Signing the Declaration of Independence," also common to all notes of this denomination, is a plate of polished steel and engraved with the most faultless precision. It has since been the object of admiration of all men who are skilled in the higher branches of that delicate handicraft.

There are also three copper plates, one engraved and two electrotyped. These represent all the character and designs on the face of the note, excepting the name and location of the bank, and the signatures of the officers.

These omissions are called by the counterfeiters, "titles." The plates which supply these omissions are called skeletons, and in addition to these, other plates are required for printing the little red seal, and the numbers by which all national notes are registered.

In the production of the facsimiles of the highly figured United States bonds, those monetary evidences of a nation's trouble, and the holder's happiness, the work of the counterfeiters is fully equal to, if not superior to the genuine article itself.

The government had been at work for a long time endeavoring to discover the counterfeiters of a National Bank note of the Revere Bank of Boston, Mass. Brockway, or Spencer as he was called, whose skillful counterfeits had for years harassed the officers of the law, was at once suspected. As they proceeded in their investigations in this case, they found other counterfeits of the same denomination in existence upon the Pittsfield National Bank of Mass., the Second National Bank of Wilkes-Barre, Pa., and the National Exchange Bank of Baltimore, Md., and shortly afterwards a new one hundred dollar counterfeit from the same plate, appeared on the Pittsburgh National Bank, of Pa. These notes were at first readily accepted by the New York banks. They were almost faultless in engraving, and several of them were worn as though they had passed through many hands, and the signatures of the bank officers were forged in different colored inks.

The number of these counterfeits that were discovered to be afloat, alarmed the authorities exceedingly, and their efforts, strenuous as they were, were fruitless in obtaining any clue to the whereabouts of this master-plate. As Brockway was suspected, the officers were obliged to proceed very cautiously for fear of alarming either him or his associates, and at the same time keep him under close surveillance. It was soon noticed that one by one the most skillful counterfeiters of the country were visitors at Brockway's house. He supported his wife at one place, while he boarded in an obscure locality in Brooklyn, where he was known as Mr. Edward Spencer. It was soon discovered that he and J. B. Doyle were more frequently together than any of the others. Doyle was a prominent member of the old gang of counterfeiters at Bradford, Ill., to which Nat. B. Foster, his brother-in-law, and Tom King alias Thomas Shotwell, another relative, belonged. Doyle first took up his residence in Brooklyn, where he could be near to Brockway, and he rented a post-office box under his own name. Brockway was repeatedly seen to enter Doyle's room, and these two men were found to be intimate also with one Jasper Owens, who was once arrested in this city on suspicion, and a press and materials for counterfeiting were found in his possession. William H. Smythe, an elderly man, who was well-known as one of the best engravers in America, was also noticed visiting Doyle on frequent occasions. Among engravers it is stated that any particular man's work can be identified as readily as handwriting, and an examination of these counterfeits revealed the handiwork of Charles Smith. At that time no suspicion was entertained that these men were engaged in a bond forgery of gigantic dimensions.

It was noticed shortly after this that all these men had keys to Doyle's room, which they entered at will, and without knocking. Doyle and Owens were observed to make frequent excursions to East New York, as though upon fishing jaunts. After watching Brockway for a long time he was at last seen buying a notary public's seal, and a valise which he carried straight way to Doyle's room. A few minutes afterwards it was noticed that they took down the shades from the windows of the room, and after a short interval both made their appearance on the street carrying the newly purchased valise. From this point they wended their way to a fashionable restaurant where they procured supper, and there they separated, Brockway returning to his own quarter, and Doyle proceeding to Jersey City where he took a train for Chicago. The detectives were keenly alert to all these movements, and boarded the same train with Doyle. When they reached Chicago Doyle was arrested as he was about to step from the cars. To the intense surprise of the officers when the valise was examined, instead of containing one hundred dollar counterfeit bills as they had every reason to suspect, they discovered two hundred four thousand dollars in government coupon six percent bonds wrapped up in the identical window curtains, which had been taken down from Doyle's room before his departure. There were also twenty-five one hundred dollar notes of genuine money and two doubtful one hundred dollar notes, found in the satchel. When this arrest and discovery were made known the bankers and brokers of Chicago, to whom they were exhibited, expressed themselves perfectly willing to indorse their genuineness, and to purchase the entire lot at market value, so perfect was their imitation. For a long time public opinion was unanimous in pronouncing the arrest of Doyle a mistake, and an act of cruelty and persecution which ought not to be persisted in or countenanced.

Immediately after the information of the arrest of Doyle was received in New York, steps were taken to capture his confederates. Brockway was found at his residence, and Owens and Smythe were arrested in the street. Smythe was completely broken down by the sudden discovery of his crime, and turned state's evidence against his companions. He fully admitted engraving the one hundred dollar counterfeit and the one thousand dollar bonds. The printing was done by Owens. Brockway supplied the signatures and Doyle was to manage the sale of these worthless securities.

The differences which existed between these counterfeits and the genuine bonds were readily detected when the discrepancies were pointed out, by comparing them with the assistance of the magnifying glass.

The first things that are noticeable under this searching investigation of mechanical ingenuity and patient labor are two small engrossed dies in copper. They will measure one and a quarter by three-quarters of an inch, and are completed figures of cycloid engraving of the most perfect character.

It was from these small dies that matrixes were made by Brockway, by which he was enabled, one by one, to produce two hundred and seven faultless and perfect imitations of the border to the six percent bonds of 1881. This was the denomination of which Doyle had hypothecated three to secure him a sum of money to bear his current expenses, and at the time of his arrest he was going to take them up, only to float the whole two hundred seven thousand dollars before the interest became due. But for his arrest, in one week's time the whole of that vast amount would have been placed on the Chicago and Illinois bankers generally. As it was, fortunately only three thousand dollars were lost, and that was by the Peoria Bank.

In like manner did Brockway take the engraved plate and electrotype a genuine "counter," which is the circle that encloses the one hundred and the large C in the National Bank notes.

These bond plates are of copper, the larger one having the border of the bond and five coupons from which four were cut off when the loan was made. The other plates contained a medallion portrait of the Secretary of the Treasury, Salmon P. Chase, and the other designs incident to the bond. In all their printed stipulations, signatures, seals, etc., they were precisely the same as the genuine, or as near perfect imitations as it was possible to make them by hand. Two extra plates were also made for printing the coupons; and the two seals representing respectively the Loan Division and the Treasury Department, were as perfect as could possibly be produced by the hands of man.

All of these articles were captured by the detectives, together with their machinery, which consisted of a rotary hand-press, and two first-class ruling machines, all registered and prepared for the most minute work, and they were such as are found only in first-class bank note printing establishments.

These various counterfeits were considered by every one to be the most perfect specimens of their kind ever prepared, and the entire financial community breathed a sigh of relief when they were finally captured and destroyed.

William Brockway is about fifty-five years old, and has gray hair, whiskers and mustache. His form is spare and tall, and his presence is impressive and commanding. The number of similar counterfeiting and forging experiences in which he has taken part is legion. He is an expert in scientific knowledge, having been a pupil under Prof. Lilliman of Yale College. By means of the special talents which he possessed, he was able, twenty-five years ago, to make a counterfeit of the plate then used by the New Haven Bank in printing their circulating notes.

He was concerned, while still a lad, in counterfeiting a five dollar note on the North River Bank, and a two dollar note on the New York State Bank. For this last mentioned crime he was sentenced to five years imprisonment in the State Prison of New York. In 1867 he was connected with a forgery of over ninety thousand dollars of government 7.30 bonds, a number of which were accepted by the famous banker Jay Cooke, before the counterfeit was discovered. Brockway was convicted of this crime, but received a pardon after serving a few months, on condition of his surrendering the plates from which these bonds were printed.

The story of Brockway's counterfeiting in New Haven is interesting. In 1850, he was engaged as an apprentice in a printing establishment in that city, where the New Haven Bank notes were printed. The plates were kept in the strong vault of the bank, and when used by the printer, were taken to his establishment by two bank directors who carefully watched the operation of printing, and who then returned with the plates to the bank. Young Brockway was a skillful workman, and his employer sent him to Yale College to study electro-chemistry, in which he soon became proficient. The newly acquired knowledge he communicated to his employer, and between them a scheme was devised to obtain a facsimile of one of the New Haven Bank plates. The next printing for the bank that was required was for five dollar bills, and the directors brought the plate with them for that purpose. While the notes were being rapidly run from the press, the proprietor of the establishment attracted the attention of the watchful directors to another part of the room, and taking advantage of their temporary absence, young Brockway quickly obtained an impression of the plate upon a sheet of soft metal, which he had kept concealed beneath his apron. This copy was electrotyped and then transferred to a copper-faced plate. Paper was procured and one hundred thousand dollars in bogus money was printed, Brockway forging the signatures of the president and the cashier. These false notes were speedily put on the market, and in a few weeks thereafter many of them had safely passed over the counter of the New Haven Bank itself. The officers, however, at last detected the fraudulent signatures, but they redeemed this worthless paper, because they believed that the notes had been printed from the genuine plate, which had been obtained for that purpose by some surreptitious means. In return for his share of the work the printer swindled Brockway out of his portion of the profits, but gave him, instead, the forged plate, of which he made excellent use without being detected.

For the printing and counterfeiting of this last government one thousand dollar bond, the parties were all punished, and most of them made restitution by surrendering the inimitable plates and the various materials with which their work was so successfully accomplished.

During the present year William Brockway again made his appearance in the role of a gigantic forger, notwithstanding the fact that a sentence of thirty years imprisonment had been suspended, conditional upon his entirely refraining from the practice of his dishonest calling.

The particulars of this last forgery are as follows. During the month of March, 1883, Chief Drummond, who is the New York agent of the Secret Service Department of the government, was informed of the suspicious actions of an individual, in reference to some plate printing. It appeared that a stranger had visited one of the prominent printing establishments in New York City, and had displayed a piece of steel plate which was about six inches long, two inches wide and about a quarter of an inch in thickness. Upon this plate—which is known in the trade as a "bed-piece" there was engraved in a highly artistic manner, the figures "$1,000," and a small but elaborately ornamental corner of scroll work. Inquiries were at once instituted, and it was learned that this plate had been left at the printing office for the avowed purpose of having several proofs, or impressions, taken from it, and was to be called for in a few days. This seemed upon the surface to be a very innocent proceeding, and savored very little of dishonesty, but a suspicion was engendered in the mind of the astute officer, that there were indications that some person was preparing to issue a security of some kind, but whether it was genuine or a forgery was a question which he resolved to settle for himself.

As a valuable piece of evidence in case of need, a proof of this plate was procured, and not content with this, it was resolved to discover the identity of the party who had brought this steel plate to the office, and by that means perhaps, at the outset, ascertain all that was necessary in the matter. Accordingly a man was detailed to watch the premises of the printer, and at the same time a particular signal was arranged to be given by that gentleman, to the watching detective, whenever the suspected party should make his appearance. The officer's vigil was not of long duration, and he soon noticed a well-known figure alighting from a car opposite to the establishment, and after a hurried but searching glance in all directions, the figure disappeared through the printer's door. Five minutes elapsed when the same man left the building, and hurriedly walked up the street, carefully scrutinizing every person whom he met or passed. As the man emerged from the building, the signal was given, and the officer started in pursuit, muttering as he did so—"It's Bill Brockway, and he's at it again." He had little difficulty in following Brockway—for such the man proved to be—to his dwelling-place, and having made sure of his location, he reported his discoveries to the Chief.

The matter was at once communicated to the Treasury authorities at Washington, and the proof of the engraved border was also submitted to them for inspection. An examination failed to disclose any imitation between the engraving and the work upon any government security. From this it was evident that no attempt upon the government was contemplated, and under these circumstances, the Secret Service would not be justified in expending the government funds in the pursuit. It was resolved, however to notify the New York police authorities of this discovery, and to place the matter in their hands. Having in the meantime discovered Brockway's address, and the location of the places which be frequented, the matter was left with the Police Department, and nothing further was heard of it for some time. On the 15th of August, Chief Drummond received information from Washington that rumors were rife that Brockway was engaged in preparing a new counterfeit note on some National Bank, and he was ordered to look carefully after the movements of that gentleman. This order was implicitly obeyed, and Brockway was soon found, residing in a respectable quarter of the city, under the name of E. W. Spencer, his well-known alias of other days. Brockway was always one of the most difficult men to shadow, and his past experience had made him more careful and watchful than before, and consequently the detectives were constantly at their wits ends to keep track of him, without exciting his suspicion. His movements were spasmodical in the extreme. He would jump from a railroad car in the middle of a block, retrace his steps, turn the corners of the streets suddenly, and then stop, waiting for some one to hurry around after him. He would leave the elevated train at the very last moment, or would wait on the platform, until the gate was about to close before entering a train. He seemed to be constantly on the alert, and ever practicing some dodge in order to outwit anyone who might be following him. As may be imagined, this mode of procedure rendered the task of the detective a decidedly difficult one; but they worked hard, and kept him in sight as long as they could, and when compelled to drop him from fear of detection, they bore their defeat as patiently as possible. At length, however, they succeeded in tracking him to a house on Lexington Avenue, and this property being watched, it was found that Brockway made frequent visits to this place, and remained there a long time. This was deemed of importance, and it was soon learned that the house was occupied by a small-sized man, who spent nearly all his time indoors, going out only for a few minutes each day, as if for the purpose of stretching his limbs, and taking the air. Brockway's visits continued for some time, and finally the two men were seen to leave the house in company, and take the elevated train. A description of Brockway's companion was forwarded to Mr. James J. Brooks, the Chief of the Secret Service at Washington, and that officer at once forwarded a photograph of Nathan R. Foster, a noted counterfeiter of the town of Bradford, Illinois, who was also a brother-in-law of James B. Doyle, a former associate of Brockway's. This photograph was instantly recognized as that of the small gentleman whom the officers were now shadowing, and Brockway's companion was thoroughly identified. Brockway was also tracked to the St. James Hotel, where he made frequent visits of long duration, and after many efforts he was found to be in communication with a tall, fine-looking gentleman who wore iron-gray whiskers and mustache, and who was apparently about sixty years of age.

A detective was now located in the hotel, to watch this stranger, and shortly afterwards he was found engaged in writing a letter in the reading room. He was noticed deliberately tearing up a letter which he carelessly threw away, and in a few minutes after his departure, the pieces were carefully collected by the watchful detective. These pieces were put together, and from their connection, the officers had no difficulty in identifying the third man as Lewis R. Martin. Martin was known as a printer and engraver of skill and ingenuity, and with Brockway, both printer, engraver, and one of the ablest electrotypers ever known, and Nathan Foster, a noted shover of counterfeits, negotiator of counterfeit bonds, and a manufacturer of gold coin, this was one of the most skillful and formidable bands of forgers and counterfeiters which were known in detective annals, and the detectives were stimulated to renewed exertions, in order to effect their capture, under such circumstances as would unquestionably ensure their conviction.

From the movements of these parties, it was evident that their work was nearing completion. Brockway visited Wall Street on two occasions and purchased two bonds of railroad companies, and paid mysterious visits to two or more steel plate engravers in the lower part of the city. Shortly after this, he and Foster were seen to walk out to the end of the long pier at Thirty-Second Street, and to critically examine what seemed to be an embossed seal of some kind. Again becoming convinced that these forgers were not at work upon any government counterfeiting, the matter was turned over to the police authorities, as the Secret Service had no power to act in the premises.

At last, on the 10th day of November, more than eight months after the investigation had been commenced; it was decided to make the descent upon this gang, as, by this time, it was believed that everything was in readiness for the issue of the counterfeit and forged bonds, of whatever nature they might be. Warrants were duly procured, and the men were in convenient places to be of service, in case of resistance or miscalculation. At one o'clock on the day above mentioned, one of the detectives reported to the Inspector, that Brockway, Foster and Martin, were all together at the house of Foster. He was directed to repair to the premises, and after a delay of fifteen minutes, in order to allow a sufficient time for the orders to be communicated to the detectives stationed at Brockway's residence, and the St. James Hotel, he was to enter the house and arrest the three men. When the officer returned to Foster's residence, he found that Brockway had left almost at the same time that he did, and that he had boarded an elevated railway train near by.

One of the detectives had followed him, and when the train reached Houston Street, arrested him and conveyed him to the police central office. The remaining detectives ascended the steps of Foster's residence and pulled the bell twice in quick succession, just as they had seen the forgers do when they wished to gain admission. All ordinary rings, they had noticed, were disregarded, and peddlers and tramps had learned long before to consider the place unapproachable. In this case, however, the door that was invariably closed to a single summons was opened to the waiting officers, who immediately crowded in and arrested Foster and Martin in the midst of their counterfeits and counterfeiting implements. The capture was an immense one and the men were soon strongly secured. The counterfeiting apparatus seized, consisted of plates, stamps, dies, and every kind of material necessary for forging. The work the men had been engaged upon, were of one thousand dollar Morris & Essex Railroad construction bonds payable in 1901, and Central Pacific Railroad Company one thousand dollar six percent, gold-bearing bonds, series B. Stamps intended for both bonds, including the London stamp of the last-named bonds, were also found. A large number of bonds already printed, were seized, and an examination disclosed the fact that they were the most perfect imitations that had ever been brought to the notice of detectives or experts.

Types which were set up and used to print the certificates on the back of the Central Pacific bonds were captured, reading as follows:

According to a resolution of the Board of Directors of the Central Pacific Railroad Company, dated Oct. 28, 1872, said company, for value received, hereby agree with holder at the time being that the within bond and accompanying coupons, or any of the same, shall be payable at or after maturing, at the option of the holder at the time being, at the banking house of Speyer & Brother in the city of London, at the rate of forty nine pence sterling per dollar; and, resolved further, that the president or vice-president of this company shall be, and hereby is, authorized to sign the above endorsement on behalf of this company on each bond, and shall affix its corporate seal.

(Signed),
HUNTINGTON.

Other type arranged for printing read:

We hereby certify that this bond is one of the seventy-two hundred bonds of like date, secured by mortgage executed and delivered to us. Daniel S. Dodge, one of the trustees within named, being dead, Philip C. Calhoun has been duly nominated and appointed in his place and stead, in accordance with the provisions of said mortgage.

There were also seized eighteen sets of type for each of the eighteen coupons, reading as follows:

This coupon is also payable at the option of the holder at the banking house of Speyer & Brother, London, at the rate of forty nine pence sterling per dollar, in accordance with the endorsement on the bond.

Types set up for other parts of the bonds, together with the figures used for printing the scrolls were also seized, and in fact everything pertaining to a first-class establishment for printing, engraving and lithographing in the finest style of the art.

So much for Foster's apartments. At Brockway's house the detectives found but comparatively little to prove that forgery had been attempted, but in Martin's room at the St. James Hotel, there were discovered twenty one counterfeit Morris & Essex Railroad one thousand dollar seven percent mortgage construction bonds, all duly numbered and wanting but the signatures of the president and treasurer to put them upon the market. These signatures would evidently soon have been added. Mr. Samuel Sloan, the president of the company, usually writes with a quill pen, and a bundle of quills, cut and ready for use, were found wrapped up in this bundle of bonds. Thirty-three more bonds, not yet numbered, and also unsigned, were found in a bureau drawer in Martin's room, together with four counterfeit dies, several seals, including two electrotype, high embossed seals, to be used on the Morris & Essex bonds, and a quantity of tracing paper upon which could be plainly discerned, tracings of the signatures of the various officers of the companies, whose bonds were about to be so successfully imitated.

On Brockway's person there were found a genuine one thousand dollar seven percent construction bond of the Morris & Essex Railroad, a one thousand dollar six percent gold-bearing Central Pacific bond, about one hundred sixty dollars in money, and a number of criminating stamps, drawings, and letters. The drawings were counterfeits of different bonds, and the stamps were imitations of those necessary to the completion of the spurious certificates. One of the drawings was identified as that of a counterfeit United States revenue stamp for a one thousand dollar bond, and part of a genuine bond, the back of which was cut out where the stamp fitted.

From all that can be learned, it is not believed that any of these counterfeits have been put upon the market, either in this country or abroad, and the arrest was made in the very nick of time, as from the completeness of everything found, it was but a question of a few days when these daring forgers would have realized probably hundreds of thousands of dollars from their fraudulent issue of the certificates they had so ingeniously and so laboriously prepared. Nothing superior to this work has ever been discovered by those who have examined these bonds. It was absolutely necessary to submit them under a strong glass, in order to even doubt their genuineness, so marvelously perfect are they in every minute particular and detail.

Of the three men who performed this work, a few words may be required. Of Brockway and his career, however, the reader has already been fully informed, but of the other two, I desire to say a few words.

Lewis R. Martin is believed to be the capitalist of the gang. He is sixty years old, and is a fine looking man, whose face is familiar to all frequenters of the racing tracks throughout the country. In 1875, this fine old gentleman was indicted in the United States Court of the Western District of Pennsylvania, as an accomplice, of Henry Maxie alias Sweet, in passing counterfeit five hundred dollar treasury notes; but by some means he escaped being tried for this offense. Previous to that time, the records of the Secret Service show that he was known as an engraver and printer of counterfeits under the name of Luther R. Martin. He owned the plate from which the counterfeit five hundred dollar notes were printed, and was intimately acquainted with Brockway, Tom Ballard and Hank Hall, in producing this remarkable bill. He was the principal in the counterfeit one hundred dollar compound-interest note job, and was an important member of the gang that floated the fifty dollar legal-tender frauds, but during the preparation of these last forgeries, he was well-known in commercial circles, as being extensively engaged in the transportation of cattle between Australia, New York, and England, in which he was doing a legitimate and thriving business. Nathan R. Foster, the third prisoner, is about forty-three years old, and a native of Bradford, Ill. It is apparent that he was brought on to New York to perform an important part of the work on this big job, for he is comparatively a stranger in the east, and had been in the city only from the time when the preparations of these forgeries were first discovered.

He was the occupant of the Lexington Avenue house, and kept to his work there very closely. He rarely left the premises, and was not easy to follow when he did venture out. Even in the morning when he would walk out to procure a drink of liquor, he used elaborate precautions to prevent his being observed, without his knowledge. Foster's father, his sister and his brother-in-law James Doyle, are all counterfeiters. In 1868 he was arrested in Quincy, Ill., but gave bail for his appearance and was never tried. He was an intimate associate of Theodore Shotwell alias Tom King, the counterfeiter and bank-burglar, who died recently in Greenland, California. Since the latter's death, Foster has been passing as the husband of Shotwell's sister, a Mrs. Blakely, altogether, these three men are considered as the most finished and daring artisans in their particular profession, and now that they have been at last secured, the whole financial circle of the country breathes a sigh of relief, and experiences a sense of security and safety.

A Genius Among Counterfeiters.

AMONG the most prominent of the counterfeiting fraternity, and one who used his fine talents to improve the devices of his art, was Thomas Ballard, who was almost a phenomenon in criminal annals. Handsome in person and captivating in manner, his appearance was genteel and refined to a remarkable degree. His personal habits also were unexceptionable. He never smoked a cigar or drank a glass of liquor, and all his associations were among the respectable people and the upper classes of New York. He was at one time the master of a Masonic lodge, and was everywhere regarded as above reproach, and yet this man was one of the most expert and successful counterfeiters which the country has ever produced.

A short description of his career and his remarkable achievements cannot fail to prove of interest, in the study of this wonderful science of counterfeiting.

The father of Thomas Ballard was a carriage-painter, and to this business the young man was brought up. So carefully did he apply himself that he soon became one of the most proficient experts in his line, particularly in the fancy or more artistic branches of the work. As he grew older he became anxious to make money more rapidly, and he was seized with an ambition to occupy a vastly higher social position. His uneasiness, his talent, his enterprise or his destiny, if we may call it so, led him to New York City, where in 1858, at eighteen years of age, he engaged himself with one of the most celebrated carriage builders of the metropolis, whose name was Henry Hinman. This gentleman, unfortunately for Thomas Ballard, was related by marriage to the noted Joshua D. Miner, a noted politician, a city contractor and the autocrat of the Coney men, and it was an evil day for the young man when he made his acquaintance. Miner carefully observed young Ballard's genius and ambition, and he conceived the idea that he had found the very person to serve his purposes in the grand criminal schemes of counterfeiting which occupied his mind. The young man proved a pliant tool in the hands of the more experienced tempter, and Ballard was induced to acquire the art of bank note engraving, which he did by serving four years in one of the New York bank note companies. While thus engaged, and through Miner's political influence, the young engraver was enabled to obtain by actual observation, a full knowledge of the operations of the Treasury Department. As early as 1862 Thomas Ballard, under the direction of Miner, and Henry C. Cole, one of the most successful counterfeiters of his day, produced a plate for printing counterfeits of the one dollar United States Treasury notes of the old issue. Though extensively and variously used, this first plate was a poor thing in comparison to subsequent work from the same hands, but it must be remembered that the standard of discrimination was not as high as at the present time. The next plate prepared was a two dollar counterfeit on the National Shoe & Leather Bank of New York. Following this came a ten dollar counterfeit on the same bank, and then emboldened by their success they produced imitations of the one hundred and five hundred dollar old issue United States Treasury note, and an immense amount more of the same general description, just as the supposed emergencies of a vast scheme for counterfeiting the United States currency required.

A more dangerous criminal combination than that of which Thomas Ballard became an employee and partner it would be difficult to imagine, and no more favorable circumstances for the success of their fraudulent operations could have been found in the history of a thousand years. The principal members of this gang were Henry Hinman, Joshua D. Miner and Thomas Ballard. Hinman and Miner were the capitalists and managers, and Thomas Ballard was at once an engraver, a chemist, an inventor, a mechanic of rare skill and an expert in the manufacture of paper. The financial resources of these men were great to begin with, and they occupied respectable positions in society and the world of business. The necessities of the war compelled the government to a hasty issue of hundreds of millions of new and different kinds of legal-tenders, securities and paper money. All was excitement, change, bustle and confusion, and the counterfeiters pushing their felonious purposes with coolness and industry, found themselves the masters of a business which was a virtual open sesame to the riches of the nation. As the government multiplied its issues and enlarged its indebtedness, these men with the use of Ballard's perfectly prepared plates, ran a race with the Treasury Department in the inflation of the currency. Vastly as this was increased, the percentage of counterfeits made, was for a long time as great as ever. Thomas Ballard was compelled to be very industrious, as he not only made the plates for the counterfeits, but he was also the only man in existence, outside of the Glen Mills, at West Chester Pa., who could make the famous government fiber paper, which was supposed to be proof against imitation. These mills were run exclusively for the Treasury Department, under the supervision of official watchmen, and the counterfeiters being unable to purchase any of this paper at any price, were compelled to manufacture every ounce of the stock used in the counterfeiting of United States Treasury notes and the fractional currency. For the National Bank bills, however, they were enabled to buy white bond paper, such as is used by railroad companies and other corporations, and to treat it chemically so as to tinge it properly to imitate the Treasury Department material. At his obscure quarters, which were occupied by his aunt and his brother, Thomas Ballard worked almost daily as an engraver, paper maker, colorist and ink manufacturer, universal genius and practically jack-of-all-trades as long as daylight lasted. Leaving this house at nightfall, and giving his neighbors there to understand that he was a night watchman in the custom house, he would proceed to his comfortable and well furnished home in upper New York, where his unsuspicious wife awaited his coming. Thus the people about his home, supposed him to be successfully employed all day in a carriage factory down town, while those near the building which he used as a work-shop supposed him to be a single young man who was employed all night in the custom house, and who remained at home all day in bed. By these means the counterfeiter lived without suspicion, respected, in the double life he pretended, by two sets of people upon whom he imposed, and certainly with reason, highly prized by those who were associated with him in his true character.

The Treasury Department and the money experts of the United States felt satisfied that the fiber paper was a complete protection against counterfeiting. When, at last, the discovery was made that their vaunted safeguard had been successfully imitated, the Department was literally dumbfounded over Ballard's work. The best engravers owned him to be their superior, and declared, with no little truth, that he must have acquired his art in the Treasury building. As year after year went on, and still no issues appeared from the presses of Ballard & Co., the country became infested with all kinds of spurious paper money. Losses were frequent, the lawful currency was disparaged and the capture of the unknown producers of all this vast amount of fraud became an imperative necessity. But through the adroit management of Miner, the watchfulness of Henry C. Cole as a dealer, and the temperate prudence of Ballard, the arrest and conviction of this gang was made as difficult, as it was for any ordinary person to detect the artistic imitations of money they were engaged for so long a time in throwing into circulation.

Joshua D. Miner was known to the police; but his craft, his unbounded command of money, and his influence in this city and in organized societies, all combined, under his resolute will and perfect coolness to save him from arrest, though probably not a man upon the government detective force, and aware of his existence, but was as confident of his guilt as conviction in court would have made them. A detective is justly allowed some latitude at times, but he must work within the law, and rigidly respect the rights of citizens even in mere technicalities, or otherwise his case is lost. To arrest Miner, therefore, without full proof and due process was worse than useless, and to show cause against him seemed almost impossible. Whether continued immunity made him over-bold at last, or whether he grew weary of seemingly needless precautions does not appear; but, at all events, he soon became well-known to an inconvenient number of criminals in his own line, and in consequence of this multiplicity of acquaintances, he at last found himself, through the imprudence of some of his agents, in the grasp of the officers of the law.

The arrest of Miner led to serious complications, and to purchase his own freedom he surrendered some of the plates in his possession, and being pressed for others, he made disclosures and false statements, which eventually led to the disruption of the gang, and the arrest of all the parties connected with their gigantic schemes of fraud.

The manner of Miner's arrest was as follows—from the nature of their business great care was necessary in order to cover their transactions as much as possible, and so these counterfeits passed through a number of hands before they reached the person who was to place them in circulation. Henry C. Cole was what is known as the "first hand man," or wholesale dealer. Cole, after receiving the counterfeits in large quantities, would distribute them to perhaps half a dozen dealers in quantities ranging from one hundred to five thousand dollars, and these men in turn would sell to probably twenty still smaller dealers, and thus by the time the counterfeit notes reached the market the number of hands through which they had passed, and the secret and careful manner in which these transactions were conducted made it exceedingly difficult to trace these fraudulent imitations to their original source.

Notwithstanding the fact that these operations were continuously conducted for more than four years, Thomas Ballard, and his brother, never saw Cole, and Cole in turn was in perfect ignorance of the existence of the Ballards. The parties to whom Cole sold his goods did not know either Miner or the Ballard Bros., and, in fact, the only man known to and by Ballard was Miner himself.

Among the number, however, connected with this gigantic combination, was one Bill Gurney, one of the heaviest dealers in counterfeit money in the United States. After a time, Gurney discovered that Miner was the fountain head of supply, and he began to deal direct with that individual. Gurney, however, was not as temperate as Tom Ballard, as wary as Cole, or as sagacious as Miner, and in consequence of his want of care, he in time came to grief himself, and, as a natural consequence, involved the others in his fall.

The Ballard counterfeit of the twenty dollar National Shoe and Leather Bank of N. Y., made its appearance in 1870, and was soon traced to Gurney, as a wholesale dealer. A watch was placed upon this gentleman, and he was arrested in the act of selling his unlawful wares to a detective, who had personated successfully the character of a buyer. Gurney, to save himself, informed on Miner, and Miner in turn made the revelations I have mentioned above.

These revelations secured Miner his freedom, but they excited the other members of the gang to a spirit of revenge, and they resolved to amply repay him for his contemptible actions. During all this time, and amid all this ill-feeling, Thomas Ballard was entirely unknown, and perfectly ignorant of the tempest that was in motion around him. Miner had not included him in his revelations and he was therefore untouched.

Cole having been arrested by Miner's acting and placed under heavy bonds, entered into an arrangement to secure the capture of Miner, upon important grounds, and to save himself. Nursing his wrath, therefore, and preserving an outward friendliness, he began to negotiate with Miner, for some of his goods and plates. An agreement was made to meet at a certain obscure locality in New York City, and the detectives were on hand, disguised as laborers, with picks and shovels, as though returning from some job of night work.

The night was extremely dark, a heavy mist hung in the air, and the rain descended in torrents, as Cole took up his position of waiting. Shortly afterward, a man came into view through the darkness and in the middle of the street, and was soon joined by another. They then walked together out to the intersection of the streets, and stood in the open space unmindful of the drenching storm to which they were exposed. The officers crept out as near to the two men in the street as possible, without being noticed, and then lay down flat in the mud. One of the counterfeiters had a large umbrella, and when his companion reached his side, he closed it down over the two, so that neither of them could be distinctly seen, nor could it be detected what they were doing. The detectives strained their ears, but they could not distinguish a word of the conversation that was going on so near them. Presently, however, the two men separated and started off in different directions. The critical moment had now arrived, and one of the detectives instantly caught hold of the man nearest him. A desperate struggle ensued, in which the detective's fingers were badly bitten, while the counterfeiter had four teeth knocked out, and in the melee, the plates and the marked money which Cole had been furnished with to hand over to his victim, were hurled away into the darkness; the money package broken, and the bills scattered in the mud of the street. This man proved to be Joshua D. Miner, and he soon found himself powerless for further resistance. The second officer had immediately followed the rapidly retreating second party. Laying his hand suddenly upon the broad breast of the stranger, he flashed his revolver in dangerous proximity to his head. A few energetic words convinced the escaping man of the folly of resistance, and he yielded without a struggle.

This man gave his name as Thomas Avery, and declared his business to be that of a painter.

Inquiries soon developed the fact that the captured individual was none other than the famous and long sought counterfeiter, Thomas Ballard. Ballard broke down under the humiliating circumstances, and believing that Miner had selfishly made him the victim of his own acts, ultimately revealed the full particulars of the whole business, and informed the officers where the tools, implements and materials could be found.

This arrest occurred on the 25th day of October, 1871, and on the 15th day of November Ballard and two other criminals succeeded in escaping from Ludlow Street Jail, which has frequently been the scene of miraculous and inexplicable escapes, both before and since this event. There is little doubt that Miner's money opened the prison doors for his skillful employee, and thus removed the principal witness against him at his coming trial.

From Ballard's revelations, the detectives succeeded in securing a vast number of counterfeiting material, among which were a one thousand dollar unfinished plate of United States Treasury note, five unfinished plates of National Bank notes of two dollars, ten dollars and twenty dollars; a large number of miscellaneous plates of various descriptions and denominations; forty-five thousand dollars in counterfeit money, one hundred and fifty pounds of counterfeit fiber paper and all the complete appliances for making the same.

After Ballard's escape a reward of five thousand dollars was offered for his apprehension, but he remained successfully hidden until the 12th day of October, 1874. When a sharp criminal escapes he does not go off on a long crazy flight, but disappears, as near his prison as convenient, for a time. Ballard remained in the city of New York, or its vicinity, week after week, before he finally departed for the country. At the date above mentioned, however, the detectives had finally located Thomas Ballard in a small frame cottage in the outskirts of the city of Buffalo, N. Y., where he was again engaged in this nefarious occupation of counterfeiting.

When the officers made their appearance and demanded admission, a man was seen to emerge from a window in the attic and climb out upon the roof with the agility of a cat. He was at once recognized as Thomas Ballard, and ordered to come down. This he declined to do, and began to run on the roof as if to get away in some manner, but a shot from a revolver being sent over the house after him, the would-be fugitive showed his good sense by surrendering at once. He was immediately secured and put in irons.

The interior of this house was found to be a miniature Treasury Department on its own account, fitted up with every modern convenience for counterfeiting. A complete chemical laboratory was found in one of the rooms, presses and paper occupied another, and the plates used in printing counterfeits were discovered in a third. Among the paper taken was a large roll of the imitation fiber paper, equal in every respect to that manufactured by the secret printing service of the United States; steel and electrotype plates, printing-presses, engravers tools, and in fact the full paraphernalia of a first-class establishment, including one hundred and fifteen thousand dollars worth of excellently executed counterfeit money. At the time of his arrest Ballard was engaged upon a steel counterfeit plate of the Bank of British North America of Montreal, Canada. One of the experts, who examined this plate under a magnifying glass, declared that Thomas Ballard had the ability, as he boasted, "to bankrupt all Canada." For, in appearance, the other counterfeits which had been successfully circulated were no more to be compared to this one in fineness of execution and perfection of detail, than an ordinary wood-cut was to a fine steel engraving.

If the workshop would have been a curiosity to the skilled mechanic, the sitting-room in this little frame building, which was used by Ballard as a study, would have been none the less so to the ripe and progressive scholar in chemistry. Files of the Scientific American and other scientific periodicals were there, the tables were covered with rare books, and treatises on practical chemistry and metallurgy, electricity, paper-making and photography. In fact, everything gave indication of the perfect scientist and the advanced scholar.

Notwithstanding his wonderful abilities, Thomas Ballard was a criminal. He had prostituted his great talents to base uses—and his sins had found him out. He was conducted to the Auburn jail, and after remaining quietly there for three days, he opened the doors of the prison and walked out upon the streets of Auburn. He might again have escaped the penalty of his crimes, but he was penniless and destitute, and in a moment of weakness he telegraphed to his friends in New York for money. This was furnished him, but the detectives had learned of his application, and when he appeared in disguise to claim the money he was rearrested and conveyed back to jail. Again he made an attempt to escape, and although he succeeded in breaking out of his prison, he was recaptured within two days. He was finally brought to trial at Albany in January, 1875, and, being convicted of the charges preferred against him, was sentenced to undergo an imprisonment in the Albany Penitentiary of thirty years. Upon the announcement of this dreadful doom, the crushed and broken prisoner fell down in a dead swoon in the open court.

During his imprisonment Thomas Ballard has made two unsuccessful attempts at self-destruction, the last one being on the 16th day of April, 1879. He was standing quietly at his work, when suddenly, without any previous intimation of what he was about to do, he drew a sharp knife across his throat, making a wound about five inches long, severing the muscles and blood-vessels, and cutting the windpipe almost asunder. For many days after this rash act, he did not speak, and his death was looked upon as almost certain. But it seems that after all fate, which to him had assuredly been severe, had not finally doomed him to a horrible death by suicide. Since his recovery he has been a patient, resigned man, submitting in silence to the dreadful punishment which his own unlawful actions havc brought upon him.

A Hero of Balaklava as a Counterfeiter.

HENRY C. COLE, who has been mentioned incidentally in connection with Thomas Ballard and Joshua D. Miner, is one of the oldest and most thorough counterfeiters known in criminal annals. He is at this date about sixty-three years of age, and as early as 1854 he was arrested and convicted for passing counterfeit money. At that time he was working on a canal-boat in New York, the captain of which was a regular dealer in the "queer." For this offense he was sentenced to an imprisonment of five years, which he faithfully served. Immediately after his release, he resumed his calling of dealing in counterfeit money, and from that date until February, 1879, he was actively engaged in the fraudulent occupation which he had deliberately chosen, undergoing various terms of imprisonment during that period. Up to the time of the arrest of Miner and Ballard, Cole had simply acted as a dealer in furnishing to the smaller fraternity such amounts as they desired, he receiving his counterfeits from the hands of Miner, direct. When this gang was disorganized and broken up, however, and after Cole had managed to escape the machinations of his enemies, a process that was costly in the extreme, he commenced the business of manufacturing counterfeits on his own account. For this purpose he sought out Charles Ulrich, a skillful and painstaking engraver, who had been previously engaged in counterfeiting, and Jacob Ott, a thorough, practical lithographer, who also had some experience in that line of work. This combination of genius, artistic skill and phenomenal audacity perfected several of the most dangerous imitations that were ever imposed upon the financial world.

As my intention is to disclose fully, the means and devices used by these counterfeiters in producing their deceptive imitations, I will devote a few words to the two experts who joined with Henry C. Cole in his assaults upon the public.

For practical industrial skill, artistic genius, intellectual capacity and general education, the criminal world has produced no one superior to Charles Frederick Ulrich. This man was born near Berlin, in Prussia, in 1836. When about fourteen years old he was apprenticed to an engraver, under whom he worked and studied for nearly five years, when he emigrated to England. As to the particular causes which compelled him to leave his native land at so early an age, there are different statements advanced. Ulrich himself under oath in the United States courts, declared that he went to England with the full knowledge and consent of his father, in order to escape the conscription which requires military service of all the young men of Prussia when about twenty years of age. There is another story afloat, however, which if true, shows that Ulrich was engaged in criminal transactions even in his early youth. From this account it appears that the city of Berlin was thrown into a fever of excitement, by the victimizing of five large banking houses in that place through a number of forged acceptances, which had been negotiated. Five different and totally dissimilar descriptions were furnished the police, of the person who passed the fraudulent paper, by as many bank clerks. The police, however, fastened their suspicions on young Ulrich, and he becoming aware of the fact fled to England. He is also said to have engaged in crooked work while there, and to be the only person who ever successfully engraved an imitation of the Bank of England paper. In consequence of his efforts in this direction, Ulrich is alleged to have attracted the attention of the English authorities, and was obliged in turn to leave that country, from which he fled to America. Whichever statement is true, it is certain that the young man left a comfortable home in Prussia, and arrived in the United States without either money or definite prospects.

This occurred in 1853, and after wandering about the city in the unsuccessful search for work, for about ten days, Ulrich fell in with a party of Englishmen, who were privately recruiting in New York for the British army, then preparing for war with Russia. From his own account of himself, Ulrich became a member of that renowned organization, known as "The Light Brigade," and was present at that famous charge at Balaklava which has immortalized every member of that daring band. Our purpose is not, however, to detail the life of the subject of our sketch, but to describe his career and operations as a counterfeiter. Charles Ulrich was severely wounded at Balaklava, and for thirty-six hours he lay upon the field of battle, his skull crushed by a Russian musket, and the blood welling up from a bayonet wound in his side. He was finally found, and being carefully nursed, recovered, and was transported to England, discharged, and paid off. The choice was offered him of lands at Cape of Good Hope, and seven years in the militia, or extra pay to the amount of over eighteen pounds in money. Ulrich accepted the money, and returned to the United States.

This was in 1854, and for a young man hardly of age, who expatriated himself to keep out of the army, Ulrich had obtained a pretty thorough knowledge of war. In the light of his subsequent career, it would have been far better for himself and those who were associated with him, if his bones had whitened on the bloody field of Balaklava, and he had then died a hero's death.

More fortunate than when he first came to New York, Ulrich soon found remunerative employment at his trade, and for a long time after his second arrival in America, he was one of the greatest mysteries that ever befogged the minds of American detectives. It soon became evident that a master hand was at work in the country, but who and where he was became an aggravating conundrum. Ten dollar notes raised to hundreds were discovered to be in circulation, and these were the product of the most consummate art. A long and fruitless investigation followed, and all that could be learned was that it was the work of a certain unknown "Dutch Charlie," but this was all.

After a time, however, he became entangled in the meshes of the law as all criminals of his class are sure to do, and he was arrested and imprisoned. The first charge that was brought against him was for engraving a vignette on a copper card plate, and he claimed that he was not aware what it was to be used for. He was tried and sentenced to five years imprisonment at Sing Sing prison, but in 1861 he was set at liberty. Within a year from this time he began counterfeiting in practical earnest, as a regular profession. He had made the acquaintance in prison of two well-known counterfeiters, and after their release they searched out Ulrich and introduced him to Jimmy Colbert, who was intimately connected with a large gang of counter-feiters, among whom Henry C. Cole was the most prominent figure. This unlawful combination sealed the fate of the young Prussian engraver, and from that time he was identified with most of the ambitious and successful counterfeits that have been imposed upon the community. Ulrich confined himself to engraving the plates for these fraudulent issues, and had nothing to do with the printing or with getting them upon the market. From the fifty-cent currency note to the five hundred dollar note he was equally perfect and painstaking, and his work was held in high repute among the leading "Koniackers" of the country. Among the number of plates which he engraved was a one hundred dollar bill of Central National Bank of N. Y. City, with a number of skeleton plates as already described, which would enable the counterfeiters to produce similar bills upon the Ohio National Bank of Cincinnati, and the First National Bank of Boston, Mass. Two hundred thousand dollars of the first counterfeit were printed and disposed of in two days. By shadowing a package of money directed to Charles Ulrich at Cincinnati, the detectives arrested that gentleman at the Express Office, where he had called to receive it. In order to secure the clemency of the law, Ulrich obtained and surrendered the plates above described and all the presses and appliances used in printing them. In addition to these he also surrendered the back plate and a nearly finished front plate of a five hundred dollar counterfeit National

Bank note. This last note was pronounced by the experts of the Treasury Department to be, in all respects, equal to the genuine. Notwithstanding these overtures on the part of Ulrich he was finally sentenced to an imprisonment of twelve years in the state prison at Columbus, Ohio. He remained in confinement eight years, and was pardoned in June, 1876.

The spirit of counterfeiting seemed now to have taken possession of him, and before the year of his liberation from prison expired, he had formed the partnership with Henry C. Cole and Jacob Ott, as mentioned previously. They established their headquarters in the vicinity of Philadelphia and domiciled themselves with the family of Jacob Ott at a place called Oak Lane, about six miles north of the city. Ulrich was soon at work upon new plates for printing counterfeit fifty dollar notes of the various National Banks of the state of New York. The general work on the genuine plates of the National Bank issues is produced by regular transfers from the same original dies, and of course should be precisely alike. This general work Ulrich imitated with great exactness, but instead of engraving the name of any particular bank upon his plate, he left that part of the surface untouched, where the name of the bank and its location generally appears, so that when his bills were struck off through the process used by plate printers, there should be a blank space left for the name of some bank and that of the town or city where it was located. Bills thus printed, it is evident, might afterward be issued in the name of any bank, the title of which could be printed in the blank space upon them, that is to say upon any number of banks in the state of New York, having titles of about the same length or number of letters. To print these several titles, "skeleton plates" bearing requisite inscriptions, were all that was needed, and the counterfeit fifties could be issued whenever desired in exact imitation of the bills of the banks which they had selected for their purpose.

Every thing now being prepared for work, Henry C. Cole, who was the capitalist and manager of the business, secured all the materials and implements for printing, among which was a plate press of excellent design. This machine was set up in the attic of Ott's house, and the printing was duly commenced. Though a first-class lithographer, Ott was not a plate printer by trade, and the work he did at first was evidence of his want of experience. But whatever their defects, the bills were readily sold by Cole, and within ten days over forty thousand dollars of these bills were thrown into circulation. The first bill was passed in Baltimore on the 10th of May, 1877, and went through one of the banks without suspicion. On the 11th, a similar bill was passed in New York, and in a few hours, the metropolitan press was teeming with the news of a new, excellent and exceedingly dangerous counterfeit fifty dollar bill on the Central National Bank of that city.

The counterfeiters, however, were fully prepared for the exposure, and before the public had recovered from the first scare, they issued another lot of fifties upon an entirely different bank, by the simple process of using their skeleton title plate to fill in the blank spaces of their original note. Over one hundred thousand dollars of this counterfeit plate were used and placed in circulation.

Henry C. Cole, though one of the "smartest" men in the criminal calendar of any country, was curiously deficient in some very important respects. Accustomed for years to imitations of the currency, he not only failed to understand the charter number of a genuine bill, but was so wanting in discrimination, that the paper he selected for the counterfeit on the Third National Bank of Buffalo was entirely too thick for the purpose, and resembled pasteboard more than bank note paper. As a matter of course this second fraud was far less dangerous, and was detected almost instantly.

In the meantime, Charles Ulrich had finished a new plate for printing five dollar bills on the First National Bank of Tamaqua, Pa. From this plate eight thousand bills, forty thousand dollars were printed and soon placed in circulation. This issue was universally pronounced as "very dangerous," and the extensive circulation of that bill since, even among so called "good judges," justifies the claims for excellence which were originally made for it. Shortly after this, they printed one hundred thousand dollars of fifty dollar notes on the Tradesmen's and Broadway National Banks of New York City, and these were sold in bulk, unsigned, and carried to Germany, by J. E. Conkling and John Baker, and by them passed off upon the German bankers and people. None of these notes were circulated in the United States at the time, and it was not until a large sum of them were brought back to New York all at once, by emigrants on the German steamer *Herder*, which arrived on the 22nd day of May, 1878, that their existence was discovered. Subsequently, many were circulated in this country and some of them are still afloat.

Encouraged by the grand success of their previous efforts and emboldened by the immunity they seemed to enjoy, Cole and Ulrich now planned a new and most stupendous fraud, which, if successful, would forever eclipse all others of the kind that had been done in the past, and raise at one swoop the bold and daring operators to luxurious independence for life.

Up to this time, the new issue of the Treasury notes had not been counterfeited at all, and it was supposed by those in authority that it was impossible to imitate them on account of the intricacy of the geometric scroll-work upon them. Charles Ulrich, however, knew much better than this, and with Cole as his manager, had agreed to produce a counterfeit plate of the one hundred dollar new issue, from which a million dollars were to be struck as fast as possible, and the whole amount put into circulation in America and in Europe.

In order to obscure himself more thoroughly from the detectives who had already become suspicious of this combination, Ulrich removed to Scotch Plains, near Plainfield, in New Jersey. Here he assumed the name of James Winell, and with a woman, presumed to be his wife, represented himself as a gentleman of leisure.

Ott, by this time, had separated from his former companions, and having sold out his presses and material, went to New York City, where he opened a liquor saloon. For his share in the work of counterfeiting, he had received some eight thousand dollars, besides an excellent living for his family for the last two years. He was, however, not qualified for business, and together with his bad management he became excessively intemperate, and as a consequence, in a very short time he had dissipated all his money and was finally sold out under distress for rent. During all the time that Ott was connected with Cole and

Ulrich, he had serious trouble with his wife. This lady was seriously opposed to her husband's business of counterfeiting, and had repeatedly threatened to inform the officers of the law of the whole affair. At last the trio of criminals resolved that their only safety lay in getting rid of this fractious woman for a time at least, and by various arguments and large monetary considerations, they at last induced her to return to Germany with the understanding that her husband would follow her in a short time.

After his failure in the liquor business, Ott turned his attention to his regular business of lithography, and being an excellent workman, soon secured lucrative employment. Up to this time he had remained entirely unknown, and was not suspected of any collusion with his dishonest partners.

It was at this time that Cole and Ulrich had resolved upon their stupendous fraud with the one hundred dollar treasury note and they sought out Ott to again assist them in the printing. They paid frequent visits to New York, where they visited different establishments and made several suspicious purchases of steel plates and engravers tools of fine quality. At this time the parties were all under the surveillance of detectives, and it was not until now that they were able to connect Ott with the gang at all. "James Winell" now became an object of very especial attention in his new residence, and it was soon discovered that his movements and those of Henry C. Cole, who made frequent visits to Scotch Plains, were remarkably suspicious. At last the detectives resolved to make a raid upon the premises, and by a well-timed movement they were able to capture Mr. Charles Ulrich, alias Mr. James Winell, hard at work upon a new counterfeit plate of the one hundred dollar new issue of legal-tender notes. This plate was confiscated, and upon being exhibited to the Treasury experts of the United States it was found to be a master-piece of imitative engraving, in which the boasted inimitable geometric lathe-work was reproduced to a microscopic nicety, almost impossible to detect.

Ulrich to save himself, made a full confession, in which he implicated his partner and manager, Henry C. Cole. Ulrich was arrested on the 30th day of November, 1878, and was allowed to remain in the premises he occupied, in the company of one of the detectives, in order to effect the capture of Cole at a time when he would furnish convincing proofs of his own guilt. Affairs remained in this condition for over six weeks, and during that period Cole visited the house several times, entirely unsuspicious and undisturbed, and it was not until the 17th day of January, 1879, that matters shaped themselves so as to perfectly suit the full purposes of the patiently waiting officers.

On that day, Cole, who had purchased all the materials for plate printing at various establishments in Philadelphia, slyly left that city for Scotch Plains. A telegram from a watchful officer flashed ahead of him the news of his departure, and his arrival, was eagerly awaited at the residence of Mr. Winell. Meanwhile Cole, in blissful ignorance of the fate in store for him, sped on his way, and was soon in the company of his able engraver and partner, who was now also his betrayer. All unconscious of the hidden eyes and ears which were drinking in every move and sound, Cole eagerly discussed the plans of the future with Ulrich, and chuckled with satisfaction over the excellence of the workmanship of the unfinished plate.

He brought the materials purchased in Philadelphia to be used by Ulrich in printing the notes, and spent an hour in pleasant conversation upon their wonderful and grandly promising scheme. He finally rose to depart, and, as had been his custom on previous occasions, he handed fifty dollars to his partner as an earnest of his good will and kindly intentions. While Ulrich was counting the money thus given to him, the detectives suddenly stepped out in front of Cole, and he found himself in irons before he could realize what had occurred. By these means a clear case was established against both parties, and this most dangerous criminal combination of the age was completely broken up, their entire outfit captured, and, by one grand move, justice was triumphant over crime.

Ott was soon after arrested, and Ulrich appeared as a witness against his two partners in crime. They were both convicted, and on February 11, 1879, Cole was sentenced to an imprisonment of twelve years, while on the 11th of March succeeding, Ott received a sentence of ten years. Charles Ulrich, for his share in the capture of his companion, his testimony against them at the trial, and his valuable assistance in unearthing the plates and materials of the counterfeiters, was released upon his own recognizance, with the injunction from the court that any further attempt on his part to again engage in his illegal calling would be swiftly followed by severe and lasting punishment.

Thus one of the most successful criminal combinations that ever existed was at last broken up, the principals duly punished, and the outraged law fully sustained.

A Prince Among Counterfeiters.
A Thrilling Existence.

AS a sample of the remarkable ingenuity which men devoted to criminal purposes, may be mentioned a wonderful production of a twenty dollar counterfeit of the new greenback issue, which was detected a short time ago, at the United States Sub-Treasury at New Orleans. This phenomenal piece of imitation was entirely executed with pen and ink. Figures, corners, vignettes, seal, fine scroll-work, and even the fibers of the paper, were carefully reproduced by no other means than an ordinary steel pen and inks of the various colors required for the work. The signatures of Register Allison and United States Treasurer John C. New were also excellently counterfeited. This note is calculated to deceive almost any person who is not thoroughly able to judge, and who is accustomed to handling such bills. Two United States bonds have also been discovered, both of which have been produced by the same process. Of course these specimens are few and scarce, as the amount of skilled and pains-taking labor involved prevent their being manufactured for very extensive circulation. Any man could, at any honest, menial labor, earn more money in the time that would be consumed in perfecting one of these imitations, and it seems a lamentable waste of artistic talent to devote them to such unproductive employment.

In the United States the crime of making and passing counterfeit money has been stimulated by peculiar and national conditions, tolerated by a lax public sentiment, and even facilitated by the institutions of a speculative and a defective and corrupt financial system. A new and free country, sparsely settled, filled with the spirit of exciting enterprises, among a reckless and extremely inventive population, intensely inspired by the aspiration for great and sudden wealth, presented the most favorable circumstances and opportunities for speculative financiering, which, through public carelessness, and an apparent ingredient of dishonesty, not only degraded the popular conscience, but, by debauching the currency, gave rise to abuses, of which counterfeiting was not altogether the worst.

A community which could endure and endorse the old-style currency of this country and allow itself to be swindled year after year by shyster banking for decades, may be said to have offered a premium for imposture and paved the way for crime. When compared with the genuine issues of fraudulent banks of that time, the handsome counterfeits of the currency put forth by the old-time "Coney men," were not only equal in artistic appearance, but in point of fact based upon an almost equivalent in value. It was a popular remark among men of business at that time, that they preferred a good counterfeit on a solid bank to any genuine bill upon the "shyster" institutions. All this, of course, favored the counterfeiter to the greatest possible extent, and gave him reason to believe, that, however dangerous his course of action, he could be but little worse than some of his neighbors, who as pretentious "bankers," claimed respectable positions in society. During the war, circumstances which I have already noted again encouraged the production of counterfeit money, and the skill and activity of such men as Joshua Miner, Thomas Ballard, Henry C. Cole, Charles Ulrich, Miles Ogle, Ben Boyd, Peter

McCartney, and others, have been caused and fostered by the demoralizations due to long-continued civil strife.

The suppression of the great Southern Rebellion not only decided the question of slavery and nationality, but gave us incidentally a national currency and first-class national credit, and this, leading to the insurance of national bonds and current money, again offered a wide and profitable field to the forger and the counterfeiter. In this connection my work of revelation would be entirely incomplete without an account of John Peter McCartney, the man in every sense, the master of the art and for a long time the veritable "King of the Koniackers." This bad preeminence may be claimed for others, but for none can the claim so successfully be made as for this man who, in conjunction with his imitative abilities, was deservedly known as the great American briber, magician of arts and Master of Arts.

John Peter McCartney, unlike the large majority of his associates in the profession of counterfeiting, was possessed of little or no education, and his artificial abilities were meager in the extreme. He was born in the state of Illinois, and when a boy was engaged by a farmer at Mattoon, in that state. The conditions of a new country, and his own narrow circumstances deprived him of the benefits of an education, even such as the common schools give the youth of older communities. Though able to read and write his proficiency in those arts was nothing more than rudimental; his written letters were rough, uncouth-looking documents and his spelling a perfect wonder of crooked orthography. If the studious habits of Thomas Ballard were the preludes of a career of crime, that fact can offer no disparagement of popular education, for the unlettered ignorance of McCartney was no security against a precisely similar course of life. The natural talents and abilities of young McCartney were, however, in every way excellent, and at all times he manifested a quickness and versatility of action and acquirement so significant of the quick-witted Irish race from which he had his origin.

While engaged at Mattoon, McCartney made the acquaintance of a family by the name of Johnson, some of whom were printers and engravers, and, becoming interested in that profession he rapidly learned much of the art of engraving from them. One of the female members of this family was married to the famous Coney man Miles Ogle, and the entire family had at various times been engaged in counterfeiting. Indeed, the grandfather, the father, and the brother of the man who instructed McCartney in his art, had all been convicted of that crime in times past.

When young McCartney had arrived at the age of eighteen years, he became desirous of visiting his relatives in the northern part of Illinois, and he obtained the consent of his employer for this purpose. The honest old farmer not only approved of the intended journey, but in his good will and friendship for the boy, he furnished McCartney with a team and a small supply of goods, which he might sell and barter along the route, and account for his proceeds on his return, when he was to receive half of the profits. This venture proved successful and the result was satisfactory to both parties; McCartney kept perfect faith with the man who had trusted him, and rendered a full account of his trading operations.

According to McCartney's own statement, it was while on the above mentioned trip that he first conceived the idea of making and passing fraudulent, bogus and counterfeit money. At that time the whole West was flooded with paper money; broken banks were numerous, and small bills were abundant. One day, while alone on the prairie looking over his large stock of one dollar bills, the thought occurred to him—"Why should anybody make one dollar bills, when it was just as easy to make fives or tens?" Thinking how easy it would have been to make more money by simply changing the figures, the temptation came upon him to try the experiment himself, and by changing the figures of his own money to thus materially increase his own property. At this time the question of right or wrong did not occur to him, although he had frequent causes to remember it afterwards. Looking upon the paper as money in itself, his simple line of reasoning was that it would be a very good thing to make more of it by increasing the denominations of the bills. He accordingly put these criminal theories into practice, and carefully scraped off the "ones" and pasted "fives" and "tens" over them. These "fives" and "tens" were readily obtained from the bills of broken banks, of which he had a number, and he thus found his materials ready to his hand. A few trials satisfied him that this work could be done successfully, and from that time his career as a counterfeiter was begun.

The easy road to wealth thus opened to his vision was too attractive to allow him to willingly settle down to common and poorly paid labor again; and so, after settling with his employer on his return, he started out on his own account. After visiting some friends about

Covington, he made his way to Indianapolis, Ind., where he first attempted to practice his new vocation. Sauntering about the town, he entered a grocery store, made some purchases and tendered in payment one of his raised notes. On taking it up the grocer observed—"I don't know about that," and the young man's heart stood still, as he feared that detection had overtaken him at the outset. But it proved to be only a question of the grocer's ability to make the change for so large a note, for the money drawer was opened, a favorable answer given, and the change counted out to him without a word.

It is officially stated, that of all the adult criminals found in London, England, not two in a hundred have entered upon their course of crime, who have led an honest life up to the age of twenty years. In fact, it has been shown that nearly all grown-up criminals began their career of evil-doing at from ten to sixteen years of age. To this general rule, it will be seen McCartney was no exception, and further, that when once started on his crooked road, he made counterfeiting his business, following it with diligence, pertinacity and success.

In order to perfect himself in engraving, he early made the acquaintance of that famous plate cutter, Ben Boyd, and McCartney improved exceedingly under the instruction of Boyd, in the skill in engraving which he had but vaguely acquired under the Johnsons. McCartney served no regular apprenticeship to the trade of an engraver, but having observed the operations of the Johnsons and Boyd, he set himself to work, and although he had at the time never been inside of the office of a regular engraver, or had proper instruction in the art, he executed a plate which sold readily at a good price.

Before the breaking out of the war of the rebellion, McCartney was extensively engaged in the manufacture and circulation of false or bogus coins, his first acquaintance with that branch of crime having been made at Cincinnati, where the work was carried on at a factory out in Walnut Hills, the principal of the concern being a prominent citizen of Cincinnati, a church member and one of the leading members of the school board, named Thomas Taylor. In 1852, McCartney was a resident of Indianapolis, and was married to a young girl named Martha Ackerman, who was the daughter of an old German counterfeiter, and who, when but a girl of eleven, being very bright and skillful, had been engaged in printing counterfeits in her father's house, under his paternal directions. McCartney made this city his principal headquarters for several years, and here he acquired a large amount of real estate. His ostensible business was that of a dealer in horses, but in whatever vocation he labored, he made all else subservient to his grand purpose of passing counterfeit money. Here he was known as Joseph Woods, and he lived in the style of a fortunate trader and speculator.

He did not, however, achieve all this without trouble, nor without some notoriety. He had been in tight places more than once, but had always managed to escape by paving the way to freedom with bribes, or by taking the most desperate chances of physical danger, when such a course was rendered necessary.

In 1862, he was arrested at a military camp in West Virginia, for passing counterfeit money, and started under a guard of soldiers over the Baltimore and Ohio Railroad for Washington, where he was to be confined in the Old Capital Prison, of which I was then in charge, in my official capacity as Chief of the Secret Service of the United States. It was at this time that McCartney literally jumped into public notice. He had been arrested in a manner that left no doubt of his guilt, and he moreover realized the difference between military usage and that of the civil authorities, and as a consequence, the prospect before him seemed to be the most discouraging of any in his experience. The soldiers who guarded him were exceedingly watchful, and they had taken the precaution to doubly iron their prisoner. Both his arms and legs were shackled, but the stout-hearted counterfeiter made the best of the situation, kept perfectly quiet and silently calculated the chances of escape. "I didn't want to go to Washington," he said afterwards. "Old Pinkerton had charge of the prison, and I didn't like the look of that arrangement. I could manage the boys out West. I had managed them frequently, but in Washington, I knew it would be different. So I made up my mind I had rather not go to Washington, and I didn't."

The train was a fast one, and when it was under full headway, the guards, trusting to the manacles upon the prisoner, and thinking no sane man would attempt to jump off at such flying speed, even if unfettered, relaxed their vigilance. McCartney did not fail to notice this, but it did not imbue him with very sanguine hopes. He had however come to consider his case as one of life or death; he had determined not to go to Washington alive and yet when he felt his irons and noted the speed at which the train was going it seemed as though an attempt at escape was almost equivalent to that of suicide. He was a desperate man, however, and having decided upon his mode of action, he seized a favorable moment, and quietly stealing to the rear of the car, he sprang out and was gone.

The train swept on, and as there was a slight curve in the road just beyond, the cars were out of sight of the spot in a moment. The prisoner was quickly missed, the alarm cord was pulled, and the train was stopped as speedily as possible. Filled with rage and excitement, the soldiers rushed back in search of the man who had so daringly eluded them. The train had been running at the rate of thirty-five miles an hour, and the officers fully expected to find the reckless fugitive dead beside the track, or thoroughly mangled, even if alive. Their search, however, was unavailing, the bold counterfeiter could not be found in any condition, and that party never saw the face of McCartney again.

Fettered as he was when he made this reckless leap for liberty, McCartney sustained an ugly fall, but fortunately for himself, he alighted upon a bed of loose gravel, beside the roadway. He did not escape serious injury, however, for he came to earth in such a forcible and awkward manner that two of his ribs were broken, and he was almost stunned by the tremendous shock.

"I was hurt, of course," said McCartney, as he afterward detailed his escape; "but I at once crawled off the track, and hid among the weeds until I got my breath. Then I made my way slowly into the woods as best I could, where I hid again, and kept quiet until all was still, and the train had gone on again. After this, I painfully struggled on for hours, until comparatively safe, and then I secreted myself once more. With a stone I finally broke the clumsy and not very strongly made irons from my limbs. I suffered very much from hunger and from the bruises I had got; but daylight came at last, and after a journey of two long, painful days I reached friends where I rested in safety."

This terrible shaking up, together with the excitement caused in detective circles by his miraculous escape, compelled McCartney to seek seclusion for some time. He had brought nothing home but broken bones from his West Virginia campaign, and his bad luck turned his mind to acts of peace and deeds of love. He became an operating dentist with a prominent gentleman at Springfield, Illinois, and devoted himself to his congenial and accomplished wife.

This young woman was very handsome and much devoted to her husband, and having been born and bred in the midst of counterfeiters, she had become a critic and an expert in relation to all kinds of crooked operations. With such a helpmate, it may be imagined that the cares of regular vocation soon grew tiresome and he shortly afterward gave diligent attention to what he had come to consider as his regular business. He managed his affairs as adroitly as usual, but he could not escape, what he regarded as the annoying and persecuting attentions of the officers of the law.

In 1864 he located at Nauvoo, Ill., and while there he engraved the plates from which he printed the successful counterfeits of the ten dollar United States Treasury note, of the greenback variety, of the issue of March 10, 1862. He had laid his plans carefully, and had made extensive arrangements for circulating large quantities of these notes, in all of which he was remarkably successful, more than a hundred thousand dollars worth of them having been disposed of. These plates passed into several hands, and were largely used, until they were finally surrendered by Mrs. Missouri Rittenhouse of Osgood, Indiana, in November, 1868, when her husband, Jefferson Rittenhouse, and Lyle Levi were arrested with a number of other counterfeiters at that place.

During the year 1866, McCartney was arrested in St. Louis, where he had been industrious and successful, and where he had in his possession over eight thousand dollars in good money. But he managed to escape, and, to use his own words, he found it "as easy as falling off a log." He openly declared that he found no difficulty in buying his way out of danger. "I was flush," he remarked, "they had made a pretty sure thing on me, and I was well-known, but I managed to leave the jail, the city, and over eight thousand dollars behind me, there in one night. I haven't been there since," he remarked, with a sly twinkle in his eyes, "to make any inquiries as to what they thought of my taking 'French leave' of the hospitality of the municipal officials."

During the years 1866, 1867, and 1868 McCartney conceived and carried out a new and bold scheme. He assumed the name of Professor Joseph Woods, and, traveling through all the principal cities of the West, he delivered his lectures on "Counterfeit money and how to detect it." At this branch of education, Professor Woods thrived amazingly. To the detectives who knew him he professed a great deal of penitence for his past career and solemnly stated that he had abandoned counterfeiting forever. He gave wise and sagacious hints and advice to Treasury officials and to bankers, and was altogether regarded as quite a rosebud of moral and virtuous promise. While he was thus appearing before the public, Miles Ogle with James Lyons as his "boodle carrier and right bower" were engaged in the constant manufacture and sale of counterfeit five dollar United States Treasury notes of the issue of March 10, 1863, and of the twenty dollar note of March 10, 1862, both of which plates had been just finished by the deft hands of Professor Joseph Woods, in his true character of John Peter McCartney.

An ordinarily skillful engraver can, it is stated, cut a counterfeit of the greenback plate in from six to twelve months. Incredible stories have been told of the rapidity with which McCartney engraved the five dollar plate above described, the time of his entire work upon it having been positively stated to be less than two weeks. He was a fast man in more respects than one, but such a performance in the time given, would certainly have been little less than a miracle. The "fives" from the above plate, though handsome when well printed, bear unmistakable evidences of haste in the engraving, but the "twenties" were excellent; and, although McCartney improved this plate, retouching and altering it from time to time to the end of his career, from the very first it produced the most dangerous imitations of the genuine, and placed him at the head of the "Coney" business as a cutter or engraver. It is suggestive of the character and value of the public teachings of "Professor Joseph Woods," that these counterfeits along with others were regularly passed as change from the ticket offices of the various halls and lecture rooms, where that expert and public benefactor so frequently and powerfully held forth.

During the summer of 1866, McCartney was arrested in Illinois, and taken to the county jail, at Springfield, for confinement. On his person, among other things, was found two thousand dollars in good money, which was deposited by the officers having him in charge in a bank at Springfield, for safe keeping. On the 11th of October, McCartney having been in jail but a short time, his wife, who arrived in town some time before, received this money. One week after this, when the officers of the jail made their earliest morning rounds, they found the doors of McCartney's cell and that of a companion open. A further examination developed the fact that the doors of the corridor and that of the outside wall of the jail were also open, and that these two men were nowhere to be found. Mrs. McCartney, strange to relate, had also disappeared with her husband. Considering the notorious character of the escaping prisoner, it was most positively assumed that some one had been bribed to allow him to thus get away. The sheriff was indicted for this offense, but no proof being produced, he was acquitted.

This daring counterfeiter was now but a little over forty years of age, and in the perfection of his power and faculties. He was of large stature, strongly framed and stout limbed, of a generally prepossessing appearance, wearing a full natural black beard, and in a crowd, wearing a common dress, he would have been readily taken for an ordinary, good-looking farmer or drover. A closer inspections however, led to a different conclusion. Under his bushy eye-brows were to be found a pair of cold, piercing grayish-blue eyes, so changeable and quick that they have been frequently described as darker. Above the eyes there rose a broad and high forehead, giving an indication of mental capacity, to which a clear-cut, regular aquiline nose added a suggestion of sharpness and decision. His face wore habitually a keen, watchful expression, as of a man continually upon his guard, and his whole appearance indicated to the trained observer a subtle, cunning and powerful personage. Despite his regular features, the face of McCartney seemed to be narrow; he had a cynical, crafty look, calculated to excite distrust, yet, his manner was that of quiet gentleman-liness, which would divert suspicion, while his whole form and bearing were the embodiment of activity, resolution and imperious will.

He would have been an object of interest to any intelligent person under any circumstances. He had become one of the very best and most rapid engravers of counterfeit plates. An excellent plate printer, he was a good practical manufacturing chemist, and was capable of skillful mechanical work in almost anything he undertook. Although he had literally "picked up" his art, owing but little to text-books and instruction, McCartney had become exceedingly skillful; he had invented a machine for copying the geometrical scroll work on the government Treasury notes; he had mastered the art of chemically discharging all color from the Treasury notes of small value, in order to get the paper to print counter-feits of those of a larger denomination, instead of making the fiber paper after the manner of Thomas Ballard. Thus he made a fine art of counterfeiting, and as one safeguard after another was adopted by the government, he enlarged the scope of his own processes, and was at all times able to meet the most delicate tests the Treasury Department had devised.

As a counterfeiter, McCartney was above prejudice, exceedingly versatile and perfectly able to play every part in the great game. Beginning as he did by what is called "bugging," and raising small notes, he became a shover and a false coiner of gold and silver; he acquired the art of engraving, made his own plates and sold them: made others and printed from them; sold his own bills at wholesale or at retail; bought plates and bills to sell, and worked in every imaginable disguise in putting his own or others make of "queer" into circulation. He had an exceedingly low estimate of men generally, believing that every one could be bought, and by this means he always calculated to escape difficulty. He had the faculty to appreciate the ability of others, and made his selections of special agents with great discretion. He always treated them liberally, worked through them and with them, standing squarely by his partners when they became involved in trouble. When arrested himself, he kept his own counsel, never betrayed others, and exercised the utmost liberality, cunning and bravery in his struggles for freedom. In this way, at different times, he practiced medicine, extracted teeth, served as a peddler, as a drummer or commercial traveler, delivered public lectures, acted as an agent of the Secret Service and a Treasury expert, represented a gentleman of elegant leisure, an artist, a cattle or mule drover, a stableman, or, in fact, any character that might serve to give success to his undertakings or to elude the watchfulness of the detective authorities. He has been known, when hard pressed by the officers of the law, to locate in the city of Washington, D.C., and to lie safely concealed almost within the very shadows of the Treasury buildings. It may be truthfully said that no man in his particular line has passed through as many varied and romantic experiences, or has success-fully assumed so many and difficult characters.

After his escape from the Springfield County Jail, McCartney engaged in business as a daguerreotype artist, under the name of Warren, at Cairo, Ill. There he spent some time, and probably gave full satisfaction to the blooming beauties of that low-lying section of the country, for he remained there some time, while he made good use of his spare moments in studying chemistry, experimenting in inks, colors, etc., and materially improved himself in the art of counterfeiting, even while laboring in an honest calling.

From Cairo, McCartney went to Rolla, Mo., where, still adhering to the name of Warren, he changed his business to that of a livery stable, purchasing the entire outfit of a gentleman already in that location. It must not be supposed, however, that his entire time was absorbed in the contemplation of his horses, or in following the occupation he had chosen. He still continued his counter-feiting operations, and on more than one occasion was obliged to liberally remunerate the so-called detectives, who threatened him with exposure and punishment. Soon, however, he was obliged to leave this place of retreat, and decamping suddenly, he left his wife to settle up his business, while he went flying over the country with the officers at his heels. McCartney's tracks were always diligently followed up from time to time, and he was arrested again and again, but always managed to effect a release. When unable to escape by bribery or audacity, and being fairly cornered, he on several occasions surren-dered counterfeit plates and money, which he had or could, procure, and making fervent promises of future good behavior, he would get off in consideration of his efforts in furtherance of the purposes of the government. But in all these trials it was impossible to induce him to betray his confederates. Some of them were known counterfeiters and all were marked men, but they were too vigilant to expose themselves to conviction, and McCartney kept their secrets with fidelity worthy of the noblest brotherhood in some holy cause.

He was arrested shortly after this at Mattoon, Ill., by the City Marshal of that place. Among the effects taken upon his person, was a check for his baggage, and upon presenting this at the railroad baggage room, the officers received a peculiarly constructed red chest. Upon opening this they discovered a printing-press, a quantity of printing material, a roll of note-paper, and twenty-three thousand four hundred dollars in counterfeits of the compound interest United States Treasury notes of the denomination of fifty dollars. By making some revelations concerning himself, and surrendering other material then in his possession, he was enabled to again secure his liberty, and was once more a free man.

In August, 1870, McCartney was again arrested, this time in Cincinnati, Ohio, in company with one Charley Johnson. No counterfeit money was found on McCartney, but he had three thousand five hundred dollars in genuine money in his possession. Johnson, however, had over four hundred dollars in counterfeits in twenty dollar and five dollar greenbacks and in fractional currency; together with a set of twenty dollar counterfeit United States Treasury note plates.

The government detectives hastened to Cincinnati to obtain an interview with this "King of the Koniackers," but before they arrived McCartney had departed. He had broken jail as usual and left for parts unknown. This little escape, it is said, cost the renowned counterfeiter two thousand dollars in government money.

In November of the same year, he was again arrested by the police of Cincinnati, but he soon escaped, leaving behind him three one thousand dollar genuine United States bonds and five hundred dollars in genuine bills, which with a well executed counterfeit plate was found on his person when arrested. What disposition was made of this money was never known, but McCartney had effectually disposed of it so far as his own uses were concerned.

He enjoyed his dearly bought liberty but a short time, and he was soon after located at a small town in Illinois known as Venice, situated opposite an island, in the Mississippi River, where he was in hiding with one Fred Beibush, a warm friend and active counterfeiter. McCartney, who had left Cincinnati very quietly, was not expecting an official call of any sort, and the officers dropped upon him so unceremoniously, that he was made a fast prisoner, before there was even time to think of making an effort to escape.

It is a difficult thing to capture a man like McCartney, and a still more difficult undertaking to hold him and convict him. When such a man is arrested, but little can be done unless the plates, tools and facilities of the counterfeiter are captured along with him. If there is counterfeit money in existence, it will get into circulation even if the maker of it be in a state prison. If there are counterfeit plates not captured, they will be printed from, no matter how many engravers suffer the penalty of the law. Consequently, all vigilant officers have a keen appetite for large sums of counterfeit money, and for anything from which such stuff can be manufactured or printed. Astute and powerful "Coney" men know full well the advantage of this, and when brought fairly to terms, surrender false bills, plates, tools, presses and materials in consideration of effecting their release. McCartney knew this also, and he now offered a large amount of counterfeit plates, dies and materials, among which were complete sets of plates for making all denominations of the national currency from fifty cents to fifty dollars, and also sixty thousand dollars in counterfeit money, all ready to be thrown into circulation, and afterwards offered an additional fifty, sixty and even eighty-five thousand dollars in counterfeits for his release. These offers, however, were all declined, and he was conveyed to Springfield, Ill., and committed to the very jail from which he had escaped in 1866.

This time, however, he was left in charge of the United States Marshal, who took the precaution of providing an extra guard of such strength that another flight from the old prison seemed to the official mind absolutely impossible.

A story is related in connection with this imprisonment of McCartney which is worth relating. McCartney had been safely placed in his cell, and Col. Whitley, of the Secret Service of the United States, having finished his interview with the prisoner, turned to leave the apartment. McCartney, his face beaming with good humor, exclaimed:

"You won't leave me here, I suppose, Colonel?"

"Yes, for the present you are safe here now," was the answer of the Colonel.

"Oh, I can get out of here easy enough," said McCartney; "I have done so before, and I know I can do it again."

"I don't think so," said the Chief.

"What hotel are you stopping at, and what is the number of your room?"

Col. Whitley informed him.

"Well," said McCartney, "I will call upon you there at ten o'clock this evening."

The Chief smiled at the jest, and laughingly took his leave. He returned to his hotel, and engaged in writing, entirely forgot the amusing incident.

Ten o'clock came, and the busy Colonel wrote on. Just a few moments later, a courteous rap was heard upon the door.

"Come in," called the Chief, when to his intense astonishment in walked John Peter McCartney, with a bland smile and a quiet salutation: "Good evening, Colonel!"

Whitley was completely nonplussed, but he sprang to his feet and drew his revolver.

"McCartney, how are you here?" he exclaimed, as he caught him by the arm.

"Oh, put up your shootin-iron, Colonel," replied the strange visitor. "I only called to pay my respects. I am going back, of course."

The two men then left the hotel, and McCartney returned to his cell, in which he afterward remained quietly enough.

He never explained how he obtained his liberty so miraculously, but always spoke of it as one of his "little jokes," just to show that some things could be done as well as others.

Thus it will be seen, that McCartney was a man of nerve, cool, daring and even desperate courage, but he was also a person of intelligence and cool calculation as well. He felt perfectly competent to deal in one way or another with the local western police, but, as has been shown, he recklessly risked life and limb to escape from what he rightly considered the more formidable authority of the federal courts at Washington, in time of war. He was not averse to taking risks, but he was unwilling to do so unless there was a strong chance of success.

He early tried to make terms with the Secret Service, and he does not give a very favorable account of the officers with whom he came in contact about this time. To quote his own language again, "I really wanted to get out of the Coney business, but I couldn't see my way clear to do it. Everybody was down on me—government officers, police, lawyers and all hands; I could have no peace anywhere, no matter what I was about; some of the government detectives didn't want me to quit the Coney. They were on the make and had a soft thing of it. They put up jobs on me continually, and cheated me with false promises. They said if there were no counterfeiters there would be no work to detect, and consequently, they couldn't and wouldn't afford to let me quit."

McCartney was completely nonplussed by the refusal of his offers at compromise. He seemed panic-stricken, and at last, believing that the proper time had arrived for obtaining the most from his fears, it was resolved to test his sincerity still further. The idea of the officers was to strike, through McCartney, a deadly blow at the whole counterfeiting business of which he was so prominent a leader, and so important a part. A few visits satisfied them that their prisoner was sincere and worthy of confidence, and McCartney gave them much valuable information. He even practically illustrated his method of working, and on one occasion he went through the process of taking the name of a bank out of a bill, and filling in the name of another bank, in the presence of the officers.

In order to further show his sincerity, McCartney, accompanied by the officers, journeyed to Decatur,

Illinois, where, in a corn-field, he dug up and turned over to them several tin cans containing sixty thousand dollars in well-made counterfeits, and a set of five dollar counterfeit plates on Western National banks. Soon after this they journeyed to St. Louis, and walking out into the country some distance, they reached an old frame house, apparently long deserted. McCartney, creeping under this, brought out several sets of well-executed dies for gold and silver coins, which were hidden there. And again they went to Cincinnati, where McCartney unearthed a large amount of counterfeit bills and several parts of unfinished plates for counterfeits. These acts of restitution secured for him a release upon his furnishing security to the amount of five thousand dollars, and the great counterfeiter was once more free.

McCartney's chief desire now was to avoid presenting himself for trial, and he sought to effect some arrangement by which his services to the government would be accepted by the authorities as an expiation of the crimes of his past. Through his wife, therefore, the proposition was made to this effect, and McCartney offered to meet an officer of the government in some retired place, where he would place in his hands a large amount of counterfeits and finished plates. One stipulation, however, McCartney insisted on, and that was that he should be exempt from arrest or any personal molestation for the time. After considerable diplomacy, it was agreed that the meeting should take place in an isolated corn-field at midnight. To this meeting the officer was to come unarmed, and accompanied only by Mrs. McCartney. McCartney was to meet them in the darkness fully armed; but promised to do no injury unless imposed upon by some attempt at treachery. The meeting took place according to the agreement made. Unarmed, but alert, the officer accompanied the handsome and discreet wife of the counterfeiter to the place appointed for their nocturnal meeting. McCartney was first upon the ground, and as the officer approached, he was met by two men with arms in their hands, who escorted him to where McCartney was, upon the further side of a fence. The men with loaded weapons covering the detective, stood by him during this interview, and McCartney himself presented a musket across the dividing fence at the breast of the officer. In this manner they discussed their business. McCartney offered, upon the conditions already mentioned, to place in the hands of the government a large number of very valuable and desirable counterfeit plates of different denomination; and many thousands of dollars of counterfeit bills. The officer listened patiently to the offer thus made, and then informed those around him that he was not authorized to any promises, but that he would make his report fully at headquarters, and await results. This was deemed satisfactory, and the meeting broke up, the officer being escorted back in safety from this somewhat romantic adventure.

These negotiations were a regular case of "diamond cut diamond," the officers were looking to the suppression of counterfeiting, and McCartney, as a matter of course, to his own safety. McCartney absolutely controlled, and could surrender the immense amount of crooked property he offered for his ransom, and the authorities were extremely anxious to recover all that was possible. Circumstances soon after offered the wished-for opportunity for the unconditional arrest of McCartney, who could not resist the inducements to ply his vocation; as a consequence, instead of the general exemption he had so arrogantly demanded, he was glad to surrender all of the counterfeits and materials of which he had confessed the control of. These plates, dies, presses, materials, etc., were many and valuable, and the counterfeit money amounted to over sixty-five thousand dollars nominal value. The midnight negotiation resulted in the surrender of the crooked property proposed, but upon very different terms from that set forth by their unscrupulous possessor.

McCartney now took refuge in Canada, and made Windsor his hiding place. While under cover at this place he executed several pieces of work, which are proof of his dexterity and artistic patience. Procuring a bank note detector, wherein the vignettes, numbers, and other portions of notes were neatly printed, on thick paper, for the instruction of bankers and others, he carefully cut them out, and by the use of a fine piece of silk, placed these various pieces together so perfectly as to form the body of a whole well-executed note. Filling in and connecting these various parts and details through extra devices, and deft touches, of marvelous accuracy and finish, then by cutting the paper away from the back of his work to half the thickness of a bank note, he joined the back and front together, and thus produced a handsome bill which might have deceived many. This is stated, simply to show the patient and artistic genius of the man.

Limited space prevents me from minutely tracing the exciting and romantic career of this wonderful man. His numerous arrests and miraculous escapes have already been partly related, but his subsequent experience, was perhaps more exciting than that which had transpired.

His next arrest took place in 1874, at St. Louis, and was the result of a betrayal by a friend. Information was lodged with the authorities, that a man by the name of Captain Judd, was at that time in the city, and the informer could secure his arrest if desired. The plans were soon agreed upon, and when the informer kept his appointment with Captain Judd for the purchase of some counterfeit bills, the detectives suddenly appeared and attempted to arrest him and a companion, who was also a well-known counterfeiter. This Captain Judd was none other than our old friend McCartney, and on the appearance of the officers, he at once suspected treachery, and prepared to defend himself. A general fight ensued, in which one Bloomfield, a United States officer, distinguished himself, by jumping squarely through the door of the room in which the encounter took place, breaking out two of the panels as he went. The informer, strange to say, was a brave man and placing himself before the broken door, completely blocking the passage out, he fired repeatedly at Captain Judd, the balls each time finding a lodgment in his arms and legs. Captain Judd, or McCartney, fought desperately for his liberty, and with a long murderous knife endeavored to carve his way to freedom, through the body of the obstinate informer. The police, however, were attracted by the noise of the conflict, and soon made their appearance, when the entire party all badly wounded, were arrested and carried off.

McCartney's wounds were dressed, and his recovery speedy, and after remaining in confinement but a few months, he again managed to escape, with a number of the most desperate inmates of the jail.

But an end must come at last. McCartney fled to Texas, where he distinguished himself in various ways, and finally made a tour through the Eastern and Southern cities in company with several old time companions. They visited New York City, Richmond, Washington Philadelphia, Parkersburg, besides many places of lesser note, in all of which they zealously, but discreetly labored to promote prosperity, by adding in their own way, to the volume of the national currency.

On the 23rd day of November, two men named Charles Lang and Henry Boland were arrested in Richmond, Indiana, for passing counterfeit money in that city by the marshal of the place. The United States officers were notified, and upon arriving at Richmond they were rejoiced to discover in the person of Charles Lang, no less an individual then their old enemy Peter McCartney. This discovery was hailed with delight, and an examination of their persons revealed the presence of two thousand seven hundred thirteen dollars, of which eighteen hundred fifty-three were genuine, and the balance, eight hundred sixty dollars, were counterfeit. Among the latter were several good imitations of the fifty dollar United States Treasury note of 1869, with thirty-three twenty dollar bills United States Treasury notes, while the remainder were five dollar counterfeits of the Traders Bank of Chicago.

Their trial took place at Indianapolis, and on the 29th day of November 1876, McCartney was sentenced to undergo an imprisonment of fifteen years at hard labor, and he was conveyed at once to Michigan City where he now is.

When ordinary men are immured in prison to serve long terms of years, it is as if the grave had closed over them, the felon is dead in law, even his wife is released from her duty as such, just as if he were buried. McCartney was not an ordinary man, and when he disappeared suddenly, it was as if some great wreck had gone down at sea. The waters were tossed and troubled, while ruin engulfed the smaller craft around him, and many of the less ambitious Coney men, who depended for their protection and security upon this bold and daring prisoner, were soon after detected and brought to punishment.

But the reckless spirit could not be content within the limited walls of a prison, and McCartney again essayed to escape. One night about six months after he had passed within the gloomy portals, the guards, who were watchful and alert, detected him in the act. He had sawed off three of the bars of his cell door, and after the guard had passed along his tier of cells and to the second floor above, he quietly slipped through the opening he had thus made, and walked down to the outer door of the cell house. While opening this door the guard saw him, and hastening to him, he found him standing between the wooden door and iron grating. When he was angrily asked what he was doing there he simply and quietly replied: "I am going out." He had made for himself a pair of pants out of one of his blankets, and had a knitted shirt over his striped prison garment. Finding that his efforts were fruitless and his designs frustrated he quietly submitted to be returned to a cell, and his watchers were ever afterwards more rigid and severe than before.

John Peter McCartney was one of the most daring and successful counterfeiters of his time. He had made as many as fifty different counterfeit-plates in his life, and more than a million dollars of counterfeit money had passed through his hands. He had defied the power of the government and the laws of the nation, but at last the arm of outraged justice had been reached out, and this genius of unlawful talents, this miracle of self-taught skill, this governor of evil-minded men, found himself in the end, a felon—an outcast, and despised of all honest people. There in his prison he still remains, shorn of his power for evil, and growing rapidly old—and there we will leave him.

Lesser Lights.

IT is impossible in the limits of the present article to give full particulars of the careers of the many notable men who have figured so prominently in the manufacture and sale of counterfeits. The Secret Service of the United States, which is now under the control of Chief Joseph J. Brooks, to whom I am indebted for many facts here presented, have performed Herculean labor, in ferreting out and bringing to just punishment, hundreds of men who have devoted their talents and energies to the corruption of the currency, and to counterfeiting the various kinds of money current in the country. The exploits of this branch of the government service, would require several volumes such as this, in which to fully depict the many daring episodes and courageous captures which they have made. For my purpose, however, I have been compelled to select some of the most prominent and successful of this fraternity of counterfeiters, and by relating their experiences afford the reader some idea of their manner of working, the extent of their operations and of the vast amount of spurious money they have been able to foist upon the honest and unsuspicious community. The government has taken every precaution to preserve the purity of the currency which it issues both of the Treasury notes and those of the National Banks throughout the country, but in spite of their unremitting and watchful efforts for the suppression of counterfeiting and the arrest of the counterfeiters, this dishonest calling is still being pursued, and the toiling masses are made the victims of these daring imitators.

As one means of safety and precaution, as soon as a note or bill of a particular class or denomination is found to have been counterfeited, the government takes immediate steps to retire from circulation all the genuine notes of that particular class or series, and thus leave the field entirely to the counterfeits, which may thus be readily detected and uniformly refused by the tradesmen and others to whom they may be offered. The banks are thus kept fully posted by the government of all the counterfeits in existence as soon as they are discovered, and the tellers of these institutions are at all times prepared to detect the imitations, and by the authority of the nation, they stamp the word "Counterfeit" across the face of every spurious note which comes before them. This process effectually prevents the further circulation of that particular piece of deceitful paper, and to that extent is a protection to the people, in whose name these notes are issued.

Among the vast number of those who have practiced the art of counterfeiting, with varying fortunes and with distinguished success may be mentioned Irvine White, who under numerous aliases for more than fifty years was identified with many of the boldest and most unscrupulous counterfeiters of the times in which he lived. A half century ago White was engaged in engraving plates for printing counterfeits of the currency, and from that time until the year 1876 he was identified with the actions of his dishonest associates. During that time, however, he had undergone one or more terms of imprisonment, but these produced no repentant inclinations in his mind and immediately upon gaining his liberty, he resumed his occupation of counterfeiting until in 1876 he was sentenced to an imprisonment of ten years in Kings County prison, which he is still serving. It is estimated that during these fifty years White has prepared the plates from which several millions of counterfeits were printed and put into circulation. Among other notables may be mentioned the redoubtable forger and counterfeiter "Col." J. B. Cross, who upon one occasion while undergoing a term of imprisonment, actually forged a pardon from the Governor of Pennsylvania, and would undoubtedly have obtained his liberty, had there not of necessity been some defect in the manner of its transmission to the prison authorities.

William Cregar, too, was a famous man in his time, who worked with Henry T. Condron and his brother, Charles. On one occasion, when a raid was made upon the premises occupied by these men, they were found busily engaged at their respective occupation of counterfeiting. In the room were found a printing-press, upon which were three separate piles of counterfeit money, the top notes of which were still fresh and green with the ink that had been used in printing them. On the floor were several bundles of these counterfeit notes wrapped in damp cloths, and stretched in wires across the room, hung a large quantity of five dollar National Bank notes, in an unfinished state.

In the room there was a box with a stone cover, under which was a lighted gas jet, and on the top of which lay a steel plate recently inked with the words, "The Castleton"—"Castleton, New York," engraved upon it. In the premises there were also found a small hand press, and on it a steel plate for the red ink seal of the Treasury of the United States, and engraved on this same plate was the coat of arms of the state of Rhode Island. On a table near at hand were two piles of counterfeit National Bank notes on the National Bank of Castleton, New York, together with a large number of miscellaneous plates for printing the various portions of the National and currency notes. These plates were all identified as the handiwork of Irvine White, who, at that time, must have been over sixty years of age. The parties thus taken were all sentenced to long terms of imprisonment and their materials utterly destroyed.

A Trio of Criminal Artists.

I CANNOT better close this article, in which I have attempted to give some idea of the nature and extent of the counterfeiting business in the United States, than by devoting a short space to the operations of three dangerous and daring men, who, for a time, figured prominently in the ranks of the successful imitators of the nation's currency. These men were Miles Ogle, Ben Boyd and William Rhodes Johnson, and their careers were marked with many wonderful and daring experiences which fully justify relation.

When John Peter McCartney was captured and incarcerated at last within the walls of a prison at Michigan City, the ablest and most competent counterfeiter then at liberty was Miles Ogle, whose desperate life and crafty adventures, with those of his partners and relatives, furnished rare and dangerous work for the officers of the law.

Miles Ogle was of German parentage, and was born in 1841. When but twenty years of age, he was connected with a gang of robbers who infested the western country. They made their headquarters upon a flat-boat, and the towns and cities along the Ohio River were the scenes of their numerous depredations. At last they were traced by the officers, and their boat was boarded near Rockport, Indiana. As the officers came on board the boat, Miles Ogle, then a mere stripling, deliberately pointed a gun at their leader and killed him instantly. For this offense he was, strange to say, sentenced to only five years imprisonment, which he faithfully served.

Upon his release from prison, he soon proved himself a worthy follower of the teachings he had received. He almost immediately joined the "Reno gang," a combination of bandits and scoundrels, which for years was the terror of all southern Indiana, and actually subjected and tyrannized over whole counties in the most lawless and audacious manner. The recital of their daring and desperate deeds has already been given, and it is sufficient to say that at last the ring leaders of this band were captured and punished, the two Reno brothers being summarily lynched by long-suffering people, who, driven to desperation, finally took the law into their own hands, and made short work of their just execution. Ogle had left this gang before the final catastrophe overtook them, and locating at Fort Wayne, Indiana, worked in connection with McCartney, where he was constantly engaged in the manufacture of counterfeits of the five dollar United States Treasury notes, and of the twenty dollar greenback note of 1862, the plates for which were furnished by McCartney.

There was a great difference, however, between McCartney and Miles Ogle. The first, although exceedingly shrewd and quick-witted, was often reckless to a remarkable degree, seeming in some cases to almost enjoy being involved in danger, because of the opportunities it afforded for the exercise of his genius for trickery, bribery and sharp practice in evading punishment. Ogle, however, as became his German origin, was more plegmatic, careful and secretive, and rarely exposed himself to the danger of detection.

After numerous experiences, in which he distinguished himself, it is supposed, in disbursing more than a quarter of a million of counterfeit money, Ogle was at length traced to Cincinnati, Ohio, where he was found in company with his brother-in-law, William Rhodes Johnson, who had also been known to deal extensively in the unlawful imitations of the governmental issues.

The officers had been carefully watching these men for a long time, and at last their vigilance was rewarded. On Saturday evening, the 6th day of January, 1876, Ogle left his home in Cincinnati, and proceeding to the railroad, set off at a rapid pace toward a place called Brighton Flats, which had long been suspected as being a rendezvous for counterfeiters. After journeying a short distance he was joined by Johnson, who stepped out from between two freight cars that stood upon the track. It now became evident to the detectives that something important was about to occur, and their hitherto careful observation was quickened by absorbing interest. Ogle, always exceedingly cautious, and ever alert, was evidently more watchful than usual, and apparently in a dangerous mood, while his companion, keen as a weasel, observed with sharp-eyed attention every sign which might indicate danger.

After traveling some distance in this manner, Ogle and Johnson left the railroad track, and turned toward a point on the common, where stood a large elm tree. Daylight was fast fading into darkness, and the forms of the two counterfeiters soon became lost to distinct view, amid the rapidly gathering shadows of the uncertain landscape. Obscurity, while it favors concealment, also lends its assistance to skilled observation as well, and adopting their own methods of approach, the detectives became convinced that the men before them, were engaged in the important occupation of "raising a plant," a species of labor, which regardless of the adaptiveness of the phrase, has naught to do with agricultural pursuits, but consisted in digging out of the ground a deposit of some peculiar nature. In this case, there was but little doubt that the "plant" they "raised" contained counterfeit money, or the means of making the same, and very probably both of them together.

When the two men prepared to return, one of them carried a rough-looking and heavy valise, and he was discovered to be Johnson, while Ogle strode beside him, with a look upon his face which gave serious warning to all who attempted to interfere with them.

Had Miles Ogle been an ordinary man, he would have been arrested then and there, for the officers were among the cars upon the track when the counterfeiters reached it, but the man who had shot an officer dead on sight, when a mere boy, and who kept a band of cut-throats at his call, was not the character to provoke a duel with, man to man, particularly in a locality where he had more friends by far than the officers could hope to rally, before some one lost his life.

As manslaughter was not their mission, it is no reflection upon the courage of the officers, but rather a compliment to their discretion, that they allowed these men to pass for the time, and laid their plans to capture them both alive, and to secure their booty without butchery.

The first move of the detectives was to soil their faces and hands, and then as the men passed them, to pretend to be actively engaged in work upon the cars, thus appearing to be a most faithful and industrious pair of brakemen.

On came the two counterfeiters, and as Ogle passed close to the detectives, his hand was upon his hip ready for action; but his scrutiny seemed to be satisfactory, and without a word they proceeded on their way. The two men went to the railroad station, where they procured their tickets, and entered an Eastern bound train, immediately followed by the detectives who had now made themselves presentable and were prepared to accompany the counterfeiters to the end of their journey if necessary. Ogle and Johnson occupied different positions in the car, and it was an easy matter to capture them both. Stepping up to Ogle, one of the detectives extended his hand as if to an old acquaintance, and said, in a friendly manner:

"How do you do, Mr. Hall?"

Ogle extended his hand to answer the salutation, when, quick as a flash, the detective grasped the proffered palm with his right hand, and the other hand with his left. A struggle ensued, Ogle tried to reach his revolver, but the officer was muscular and in the end the counterfeiter found himself fitted with a pair of handcuffs, which prevented further violence on his part.

While this had been going on, Johnson had been secured by the second officer, and an examination of the persons of the prisoners, was then made. Ogle was found to be literally stuffed full of counterfeit money, having a bundle of spurious note in each pocket, amounting in all to several thousand dollars, and Johnson attempted to throw away a package of nearly an equal amount.

On their arrival at their destination, which was Pittsburgh, Penn., the valise which they had dug up was examined, and it was found to contain sets of plates for printing ten dollar National Bank notes, on about forty banks of Indiana. The original Richmond counterfeit engraved plate, with the border and center back, and forty-three electrotype plates from the ten dollar bills. Also a set of plates for the printing of counterfeit fifty-cent notes, with fifty-two electrotypes of the same, and about twenty-five thousand dollars in counterfeit money.

By this capture, the government was placed in possession of all the plates for printing the ten dollar counterfeits of the Treasury and National Bank notes, then known to be in existence. A further examination of the ground around the old elm-tree at Brighton Flats, revealed another buried treasure, which was found to be about fifty thousand dollars in counterfeit money of the same denomination as those found on the persons of the arrested counterfeiters.

Ogle and Johnson were speedily brought to trial, and being duly convicted were sentenced to long terms of imprisonment in the Western Penitentiary at Allegheny, Penn., and for a time the government breathed freer and more safely.

Conclusion

OF Ben Boyd, volumes might be written before the story was duly told, but for our purpose a few extracts may not prove uninteresting. Ben Boyd and Nelson Driggs were the giants of the western counterfeiters, and through those two men a large portion of the counterfeit money was placed upon the market, and a large majority of the dealers in spurious money were under contribution to these men. Ben Boyd, however, after running his course more or less successfully, was finally captured. His trial took place in Chicago, Ill., and in February, 1875, he was sentenced to an imprisonment of ten years.

The conviction and imprisonment of Ben Boyd, and the breaking up of his business with Nelson Driggs, was a heavy blow to the trade of a host of dealers in counterfeit money in the South and West. They could of course obtain the counterfeits, but they were now so far removed from the manufacturers, that their profits were too small for the risks they were obliged to take. Every means was used to prevent the conviction of Ben Boyd, and when he was at last imprisoned for ten years, all sorts of devices were employed to effect his release, or to secure for him a pardon.

Among these enterprises, was one which from its ghostly character and the particulars of its purpose occasioned a national excitement and a world of speculative controversy, so that its mention here seems requisite and proper.

During the winter of 1875-76, there was organized at Lincoln, Ill., under the lead of a St. Louis counterfeiter of distinction in this nefarious line, a gang of desperadoes and ghouls for the purpose of stealing the remains of President Lincoln from their resting place, beneath the monument erected to his memory, with the intention of concealing them and holding them for ransom. The body of the noble President was only to be restored in consideration of immunity for the robbers, the payment of two hundred thousand dollars in money, and the pardon of Ben Boyd. The date fixed for this outrage to be consummated was carefully considered by these conspirators, and the Fourth of July, 1876, was agreed upon. Fortunately for the nation the scheme was divulged to the Police of Springfield, by an abandoned woman, who gained her intelligence from a drunken companion, and it was in consequence of this, abandoned for the time being.

This attempt was, however, made upon the night of November 7, 1876, but having obtained information regarding it in advance, both the government officers and several picked men of my force were present to receive these sacrilegious fiends. Three men approached the monument by filing off the staple of the lock, and two men entered for the purposes of the robbery. They had lifted the lid from the sarcophagus, and were in the act of raising the coffin from its resting place, when the officers advanced upon them. They attempted to escape, but all were finally captured, and sentenced to imprisonment.

This closes my reference to counterfeiting and counterfeiters. The long list of imitators that once seemed to successfully defy the law, and to practice this criminal calling with apparent safety has been sadly depleted, the giants have fallen to a man, and to-day no really expert counterfeiter breathes the air of liberty. Some of them are dead, many of them are in prison, and the practitioners of this crime are now composed of a number of ignorant and unskillful men who after a short questionable success find themselves in the hands of justice. The country to-day is comparatively safe from those marauders. The engraver of perfect counterfeits no longer exists and the false coiners are few and easy of detection. Absolute safety, however, has not been assured, nor will it be until humanity shall be so purified and exalted that dishonesty is no longer possible, and law-breaking becomes a thing of the past.

The Express Robber

DURING the thirty years of my experience as a detective, I have performed many services for the various Express Companies throughout the country. During the earlier years of their existence robberies were very numerous, and the companies suffered to an alarming extent. Money packages of large amounts were appropriated by dishonest employees and safes with valuable contents in transit, were seized by daring robbers, who broke open the iron chests and appropriated all that was of value within them.

In works previously published by me, I have detailed some of the most important operations of this character, giving in full the process of detecting of the moneys taken. These robberies are now of rare occurrence, and, in my opinion, the present safety of the Express Companies may be mainly attributed to the vigorous measures which they adopted in the past, to bring these robbers to justice and to punishment.

The two following significant acknowledgments will show what part I bore in this work of detection and recovery, which were elaborately engrossed, and forwarded to me by the officers of the Adams Express Company. They speak for themselves.

These are but two of the many operations in which I have succeeded in apprehending the robbers and recovering the money taken, and in the following pages, I shall relate a few instances in which some new features of express robbing are developed, although the events related took place some years ago.

La Pierre House,
Philadelphia, Pa., August 3, 1859.

Received, this date, from Allan Pinkerton, of Chicago, Ills., $39,515.00, being the amount recovered of $40,000.00 stolen from the Adams Express Co. at Montgomery, Ala., on the 28th day of the previous January, and delivered to the undersigned, in the original sealed package, in which it had been buried in the cellar of a dwelling-house in Jenkintown, Montgomery Co., Pennsylvania.

(Signed)   E. S. Sanford, Vice-Prest.
and Genl. Supt. Adams Ex. Co.

The Adams Express Company, Baltimore, Md.

Received April 10, 1865, from Allan Pinkerton, of Chicago, Ills., the sum of $84,594.50, being the amount recovered by him in his professional capacity from Levi Hoffman, John Dix, William Isaacs, Joseph P. Kane, Harry Laughlin, W. & N. Davis and F. Lancaster, who robbed the Messenger Safe of the Adams Express Co. of nearly $100,000.00 in money and checks, after throwing it from the train near Parkton, while in motion, on the Northern Central R. R. on the night of the 18th March, 1865.

(Signed)   Henry Sanford,
Ass't Gen'l Supt. of the Adams Express Company.

A BOLD EXPRESS ROBBERY.
CLEVER DETECTIVE WORK.
THE ROBBERS BROUGHT TO JUSTICE.

In 186-, the village of Grafton, in West Virginia, was the scene of a carefully planned and skillfully executed express robbery, by which the attempt was made to defraud the Adams Express Company of the amount of twenty-seven thousand dollars.

Grafton, at that time, was a post village in Taylor County, and contained but a small population. It was located on the Baltimore and Ohio Railroad, and was also the junction of the Parkersburg branch road. The village was built upon the banks of Tygarts Valley River, which flows through the Northwestern part of the state, and here the Adams Express Company, with their usual energy and thrift, had established an office for the transmission of freight and valuables.

The war with its bloody scenes had ended; the North and the South were at peace; the Union soldiers had laid aside the blue uniforms and the musket, and had returned to pursue the peaceful avocations of trade and agriculture. The Southern veteran had doffed the tattered butternut, and had surrendered to the conquering hosts of the North. The country was at peace, and the merchant, the mechanic and the husbandman turned again to those pursuits which they had followed, before the dark cloud of war had overshadowed this fair land. The dead had been buried, the wounded had been nursed back to life, and the survivors were again toiling in the marts of trade, in the workshop, or at the plow. From the desolation and the ravages of war the country was emerging into the sunshine of an enduring peace.

During the continuance of the conflict which had raged so persistently and so disastrously for four long years, many men had accumulated riches, who were now seeking for legitimate investment. It is needless to say that these were not the men who fought in the ranks, and bore the brunt of battle. But the fact remains that men grew wealthy from the needs of the country, and that opportunities were needed by which this wealth could be invested. The rebellion had also given birth to a horde of adventurers, who for years afterward infested the country, and preyed with systematic rigor and success upon honest industry and frugal enterprise.

The demoralizing influences of the war upon humanity has long been felt, and will not be entirely eradicated for years to come, and the crimes that have been engendered by its influence would appall the casual reader or the indifferent observer.

The country surrounding the village of Grafton was soon found, by inquiring minds, to be rich with internal products. Coal and petroleum were found in abundance beneath the surface of the ground, and mining operations and oil-boring became fruitful sources of investments to the capitalist.

It was no rare thing, therefore, for the Express Company to have consigned to them at this place money packages aggregating to thousands of dollars, which would enable the adventurous to purchase lands, the speculative to develop hidden stores of wealth, and the industrious to remunerate labor and to construct manufactories.

The Express Office was located in the building used as the railroad station, and was in charge of men who had been proven to be thoroughly honest, energetic, and capable. For several years their labor had been performed carefully, and no event had occurred to occasion complaint or to entail loss upon the company they represented, and Grafton bade fair to rival in a short time towns which were much older and enterprises of larger experience and greater renown.

One Monday morning, however, in the early spring, the agent and the messenger of the Express Company repaired to their office for the purpose of transacting their daily routine of business. On the Saturday previous, two money packages, one of them containing twelve thousand dollars, and the other purporting to enclose the amount of fifteen thousand dollars, had been received, and had been safely locked in the safe by the agent, awaiting the demand of the consignees. Upon going to the safe on the morning in question, for the purpose of removing such papers as were necessary for their daily business, the agent at once discovered, to his amazement, that the safe was unlocked, and that these two valuable packages were missing.

The safe, he was confident, had been securely locked on the Saturday evening previous, the key had never left his possession from that time to the present moment, and yet the safe was now open, the lock intact, and the packages had been abstracted in the interim.

The agent immediately communicated the astonishing news to the messenger, but neither of them could, in any manner, account for the mysterious disappearance of the two packages of money. The fact alone remained that they were gone.

Mr. Henry Adams, the agent, was nearly distracted with amazement, and with the fear that he would be charged with the crime. But he lost no time in informing the chief officers of the company of the loss that had been sustained, and requesting an examination into the affair.

The president of the company immediately engaged the services of my Agency, and Mr. George H. Bangs, my General Superintendent, was at once dispatched to Grafton, authorized to make a full and thorough investigation into the seeming mystery.

Upon the arrival of Mr. Bangs, he at once proceeded to the Express Office, and had an interview with Mr. Adams, the agent. That gentleman had scarcely recovered from the excitement with which the robbery had affected him, but he gave a comprehensive account of all that had transpired in connection with the matter.

According to his statement and that of his assistant, the messenger, the packages had arrived and had been placed in the safe, on the Saturday previous to the robbery. The safe had been securely locked, and the two men left the office together and proceeded to their homes. On Monday morning, upon repairing to the safe, which was unlocked, but gave no indications of being tampered with, the packages were missed, and no clue to them had as yet been discovered.

One of these packages had been addressed to John Risley, a resident of the village, and was reported to contain fifteen thousand dollars. Mr. Risley, it was ascertained, had gone to Wheeling a few days previous, in order to dispose of some lands which he owned in the state of Wisconsin, and the money contained in the package, was the proceeds of that sale, which he had expressed in his own name to Grafton, believing that process would be safer than carrying the money upon his person, during his journey homeward.

Mr. Risley had arrived in Grafton on the afternoon prior to the robbery, upon the train which brought his money, and had inquired of Mr. Adams whether his package had been safely delivered. Upon being answered in the affirmative he requested Mr. Adams to hold the package for him as he did not care to assume the risk himself, and was not yet prepared to make an investment which he contemplated.

The other package was addressed to an individual who resided some distance in the country, who was operating some oil wells, and contained the sum of twelve thousand dollars, and the notes were alleged to be all of the issue of one particular bank. This party was unknown to Mr. Adams, except by name and general reputation.

It was further learned, that the railroad station and Express Office was the general resort of the unoccupied villagers. They would assemble there at all hours of the day, and indulge in the exchange of news items, in arguments upon the various topics of the times, and, in fact, made it a regular place of rendezvous.

A brother of Mr. Risley was the proprietor of the railroad hotel and both men were reported to be respectable and wealthy. They had been contemplating for some time the idea of investing in land in the vicinity of Grafton, and of developing the petroleum deposits which were contained beneath it, but as yet no land had been purchased and no operations begun.

Mr. Bangs closely questioned the two expressmen, and was fully convinced that both of them were honest and trustworthy, and as a rule were exceedingly careful and attentive to their business. Therefore no suspicion could reasonably attach to them, and he was required to look further for the parties who had perpetrated the crime.

Two theories were presented to his mind upon the conclusion of his investigation. One was that the safe had been left open inadvertently, by the officer in charge, or else that one of the many frequenters of the office had been enabled to obtain duplicate keys, and by that means effect an entrance into the office and open the safe undisturbed. The latter theory seemed to be the more reasonable, and he determined to follow that up, before leaving the place.

By a rigid examination of all the parties concerned, he ascertained that during the day and while the villagers were lounging about the office the officers of the Express Company would frequently go outside to attend to their business, leaving the key in the safe where it might be used by anyone so inclined, for the purpose of obtaining an impression, and by that means a perfect duplicate.

John Risley was also interviewed by Mr. Bangs. He was a tall venerable looking man of about fifty-five years of age, of quiet manners and steady habits. He had lately come from the state of Wisconsin, where he had resided for a number of years. His general reputation was unimpeachable, and at one time he had served a term as a member of the Legislature of Wisconsin. At one time he was quite wealthy, but at present his resources were rather meager, and except for the lands which he was reported to own in Wisconsin, he was comparatively poor. This state of affairs had been produced by yielding to the spirit of reckless speculation which prevailed throughout the

West, and which had resulted unfortunately to him, and stripped him of his fortune.

Mr. Risley gave his statement in an apparently straight-forward manner, but Mr. Bangs noticed that he carefully avoided looking him in the face, a fact at all times of a suspicious nature. He further stated that he had gone to Wheeling, and had disposed of the lands which he owned, for the sum of fifteen thousand dollars, and that it was this money that had been taken from the Express Company's safe. He had arrived home on Saturday, when he learned of the receipt of his package and also of the other, and that the person to whom the latter was addressed, would not be likely to call for it until the following Monday.

Mr. Risley at once began suit against the company for the recovery of his money, and expressed his determination to press the matter as speedily as possible.

An investigation proved that Mr. Risley's associates were two men of the name of Joseph Marks and William Meredith. Marks was a man who had previously borne a good reputation and was formerly a contractor for the building of bridges. Meredith was what is known as an "Oil Sharper," who had been identified with several fraudulent oil companies. Marks was a resident of Wheeling, living in the suburbs of that city, but made frequent visits to Grafton where he was contemplating an investment, while Meredith was a resident of Grafton, and boarded in the Hotel owned by Henry Risley, the brother of the man whose money had been stolen. These three men met frequently at the hotel, and would engage in gambling for small sums of money, when the opportunity was afforded.

Mr. Bangs visited Wheeling and sought out the parties to whom Risley was alleged to have sold his property, but could obtain no definite information concerning that transaction, and he became convinced that Risley was in some way implicated in the robbery. He was, however, requested to furnish proof of the money having been sent, and that the package which he delivered to the Express Company contained the amount which was claimed. Mr. Risley at once came to Wheeling, and introduced Mr. Bangs to a very estimable young man, who stated under oath that he had been called into the hotel by Marks and Risley, to witness the arrangement of the money for expressing, and that he had seen Mr. Risley put up the money for that purpose.

Upon a rigid cross-examination the young man explained that he had not seen the money counted, but that he saw a roll, or pile of what represented money, and on the top of this was a fifty dollar bill.

So many cases had arisen previously that had come under my notice in which "dummy" packages had been entrusted to the care of the Express Company, the safe afterwards robbed and suits brought to recover the stated value of the money sent, that Mr. Bangs was firmly convinced of the fact that this was but another effort of the same nature. Directing the Express Company to withhold payment until satisfactory proof could be adduced, Mr. Bangs at once commenced a systematic course of inquiry, which would solve the mystery beyond all doubt.

Having ascertained that William Meredith had made frequent visits to Wheeling recently, and that he was in the company of Marks and Risley upon the occasion of these visits, the idea occurred to Mr. Bangs that the duplicate key to the safe at Grafton might have been procured here.

He immediately telegraphed to my Agency at New York, for an operative to assist him in the investigation. Upon his arrival he was directed to visit every locksmith in the city, taking with him the keys of the plundered safe, and to endeavor to ascertain if anyone of them had furnished to any parties a key at all resembling the one to be exhibited, and if so to obtain a description of the party, if the memory of the smith was sufficiently retentive upon the subject.

The operative at once began his inquiries, and by nightfall had succeeded in finding one man, who remembered having furnished a blank key of the same size as the one shown to him, and which with little labor could have been made into a perfect facsimile. He described the man to whom he sold the key, in such a manner as to leave no doubt in the mind of Mr. Bangs that it could be no other than William Meredith.

Mr. Bangs had communicated his suspicion of the trio, Risley, Mark, and Meredith, to Mr. Adams, the agent of the Express Company, and requested him to inform him of the movements of these gentlemen, during his absence from Grafton. As he was about to enter the dining-hall of the hotel at which he was stopping for his evening repast, a telegram was handed to him, which upon opening hastily, he found to be from Mr. Adams. Its contents were as follows:

"MR. GEORGE H. BANGS.

Meredith left this afternoon for Wheeling.

(Signed)

HENRY ADAMS."

As the train was not due for some time, the two detectives partook of their supper, and upon its conclusion Mr. Bangs directed the operative to repair to the railroad station, and await the arrival of Mr. Meredith. He was furnished with a minute description of that gentleman, and thus armed he would be able to single him out from among a hundred others. He was also directed to watch the individual until he had entered some building of the nature of a hotel, and then to inform him (Mr. Bangs) of the fact at once.

The operative departed upon his mission, and Mr. Bangs at once repaired to the store of the locksmith, whom he was fortunate enough to find still engaged at his work. The man expressed himself as being fully able to identify the person to whom he had sold the key, if he should ever see him again, and at Mr. Bangs's request, and for a pecuniary consideration, he at once closed his store, and accompanied him to his hotel.

They did not have long to wait, for soon the operative returned with the information that Mr. Meredith had arrived safely at Wheeling, and that he had been met at the train by another man who fully answered the description of Joseph Marks. The two men had proceeded together to a hotel, where they registered themselves, and had gone into supper, after which the detective left and made his report as above stated.

The operative was then instructed to accompany the locksmith to the hotel and Mr. Bangs would follow afterward, in order to fully assure himself that the parties were those he was in search of, and to test the memory of the locksmith for identification.

As they approached the hotel, two men came out smoking their cigars, and stood in the doorway apparently engaged in earnest conversation, when the operative and the locksmith drew near enough to distinguish the faces of these men. The maker of keys turned suddenly to the operative and exclaimed:

"The tallest of those two men, is the one I sold the blank key to!"

The man designated by him was William Meredith, and upon the arrival of Mr. Bangs, who had also noticed the two men, the fact was at once reported to him.

This identification was a matter of profound gratification to Mr. Bangs, and at once removed all doubts as to one of the parties, whom he had originally suspected. He now felt confident that his first theories had been correctly founded, and determined to follow the clue until it led him to decisive results. He at once telegraphed for additional men to assist him in the operations, and after directing the operative present, to keep watch upon the two men while together, and if they separated to pay strict attention to Mr. Meredith, he, in company with the locksmith, returned to the hotel.

There was another feature in the case which had not been overlooked. The other package which had been taken had no doubt contained the money which it was represented to enclose, and the identical bank which had issued these notes, was fully known to us. The party, to whom they had been addressed, was a respectable operator in oil, whose reputation and business standing were unquestioned. The thieves, therefore, had not only succeeded in abstracting the evidently spurious package directed to John Risley, but they had possessed themselves also of the twelve thousand dollars belonging to the responsible party in Grafton to whom it had been consigned.

It was necessary therefore, not only to expose the intended fraud upon the Express Company, but to discover the thieves and endeavor to recover the stolen property. Great care must therefore be exercised, in order to avoid the possibility of the three men suspecting that they were believed to have been connected with the matter at all.

At this stage of the inquiry, I was fully informed of the results thus far attained, and from the reports furnished me I was fully convinced of the correctness of the views entertained by my General Superintendent. After a mutual consultation, and having received ample authority from the officers of the Express Company, we began the work of detecting the thieves and the attempt to recover the money stolen.

A week passed by, and the matter of the robbery of the Express Company had ceased to be the absorbing topic of public interest.

The opening of a new well in the vicinity, whose daily yield was surprisingly large, a railroad accident and many other events, had transpired in the meantime, to divert the attention of the citizens from the abstraction of the two packages of money in the safe at Grafton.

On the evening of a beautiful day in April, a stranger arrived at the village and secured quarters at the Railroad Hotel. The new-comer was an elderly man about fifty years of age, whose gray hair surmounted a face, the features of which beamed with benevolence and good nature, of a tall and commanding figure, dressed in the quiet garb of a retired gentleman, and with an ease of manner that showed an intimate knowledge of the world, and of association with gentlemen. He became at once the subject of considerable curiosity and speculation among the guests at the hotel, and the residents of the village who congregated there during the evening.

Apparently unconscious of the scrutiny to which he was generally subjected, the stranger conducted himself with the utmost unconcern for those about him. He went into supper, and after finishing his repast, lighted a cigar, and seating himself in the reading-room, he drew from his pocket a newspaper and soon became absorbed in its contents. Meanwhile the people around him had engaged in subdued conversation, of which his appearance was evidently the leading topic. One by one they had inspected the register of the hotel in order to ascertain the name of this apparently well-to-do stranger, and numerous speculations were indulged in as to the probable cause of his visit to Grafton.

The register afforded them but little information. The man had simply entered himself as David Fowler, Cleveland, Ohio, and he had not as yet indulged in conversation with anyone except the clerk of the hotel, and that only in relation to the room he was to occupy, and to state that he would probably remain in Grafton several days.

Among those who were seated about the hotel this evening, were John Risley and William Meredith, and their conversation, which was carried on in low tones, was principally concerning the gentlemanly looking stranger, whom they finally concluded was a man of wealth from Ohio, who had come to Grafton with the intention of speculating in coal or oil.

Meredith, with his eye always to the main chance, and having several schemes at present on hand, imagined that in this Mr. Fowler he would find an opportunity to enrich himself, by inducing him to invest his money, if such was his object, through Mr. Meredith's agency.

As the evening wore on and Mr. Fowler evinced no disposition to be communicative or inquisitive, Mr. Risley walked over to where he sat with his paper before him, and sat down beside him.

As he took his seat, Mr. Fowler looked up and a mutual salutation passed between them, and the genial face of the stranger lighted up with a cheery smile as he made room for Risley to sit down.

With the natural curiosity of an old resident, Risley plied Mr. Fowler with numerous questions, all of which were intended to glean from the stranger the object of his visit and the possibility of his intention to invest in the undeveloped lands round about.

To all of these interrogations Mr. Fowler answered in an easy, good-natured manner, which soon put Risley at his ease, and tended to render their conversation familiar and communicative. In a short time Mr. Fowler had informed Mr. Risley that he had been engaged in the business of a cattle drover in the west, where he had accumulated quite a snug sum of money. Hearing of the resources of Grafton, he had paid a visit to the locality in order to ascertain the correctness of his information, and if he found a good opportunity, the probabilities were that he would engage in some enterprise that promised a profitable return.

They got along swimmingly together, these two men. The good-nature of Mr. Fowler imparted itself to his companion, and soon the two old gentlemen were laughing heartily at each other's sallies, and their pleasant acquaintance was an assured fact.

They conversed for a long time together, and at last Mr. Fowler during a lull in their conversation, drew his watch from his pocket, and apparently surprised at the lateness of the hour, excused himself and retired to his room.

Bidding his new acquaintance good night, Mr. Risley immediately sought out Meredith, who was in the bar-room of the hotel, and these two worthies were soon engaged in earnest conference. After a while, selecting two others, they ascended to a room in one of the upper floors, where they engaged in a friendly game of poker with small moneyed hazards, until the early hours of morning warned them to desist, when they separated and retired to their several couches.

In the morning Mr. Fowler and Mr. Risley again met, and the friendliness, commenced on the previous evening manifested itself in their friendly greetings of each other.

After breakfast, Mr. Risley invited Mr. Fowler to ride with him through the oil country, and that gentleman cordially accepting the invitation; they were soon on their way to the productive fields beyond the town.

During their drive, Mr. Fowler evinced the liveliest interest in all that related to the development of the oil lands, and the mining of coal which was said to be found in large quantities in this locality. His open friendliness soon won the friendship and confidence of the other, and he began to feel as though they were old friends, instead of recent acquaintances.

Upon reaching the locality which Mr. Risley desired particularly to call to the notice of his friend, they were both somewhat surprised to find Mr. Meredith already there. Mr. Risley introduced his companion to Meredith, and the three men walked over the grounds, both Risley and Meredith expatiating with a great deal of enthusiasm upon the rare opportunities that were offered for the accumulation of a fortune in a very short space of time. Nothing could exceed the attention and interest displayed by Mr. Fowler as this information was received, and as they drove back to town, he spoke most favorably of the proposed enterprise.

"I expect a remittance in a few days," said Mr. Fowler, "but it will not be sufficient for the expenses that will be necessary to develop the land in order to make it profitable."

"I will have some money of my own shortly," said Risley, "as soon as my suit against the Adams Express Company is settled."

"Have you a suit against that company?" inquired Mr. Fowler.

"Yes," replied the other, "a suit for fifteen thousand dollars," and he related to Mr. Fowler the facts as far as known in relation to the robbery of the safe and the abstraction of the two packages of money. He then added, "When I receive that, I intend to invest it in this way, and if you have no objections, we can join together in the matter."

"'That is perfectly satisfactory to me" said Mr. Fowler, "and I hope you will have no trouble in recovering your money."

Mr. Fowler did not seem to display any curiosity about the robbery of the Express Company, but contented himself with casual inquiries about the circumstances connected with it, and whether anyone was suspected of committing the crime.

On arriving at the hotel the two men went into the bar-room and indulged in a drink, and while there Mr.

Fowler's attention was attracted by a poster which hung upon the wall.

Immediately upon the facts of the robbery being fully made known to me, I had caused posters to be printed which contained a full account of the affair, and which also stated the name of the bank which had issued the notes which were contained in the twelve thousand dollar package. A reward was offered for the apprehension of the thieves, or for such information as would lead to their arrest, and it was this poster which attracted the notice of Mr. Fowler.

Mr. Risley and Mr. Fowler walked over to where the poster was displayed and silently perused its wording—Mr. Fowler, with the undisturbed air of a disinterested observer, while Mr. Risley displayed a nervousness which did not escape his companion, and which would ordinarily have excited suspicion. Mr. Fowler paid no attention to this however, and after a careless remark about the robbery, they left the bar-room and went into dinner.

Several days passed on, and at the end of that time the new-comer and Mr. Risley had become inseparable friends, they rode out together, they smoked their after-dinner cigars in company, and in the evening they would join with the others in their card-playing for small stakes, in which it almost invariably happened that Mr. Fowler and Mr. Risley were winners. Mr. Fowler had extended his circle of acquaintances, and had become quite popular with the villagers and the guests at the hotel. He also visited the Express Office, and made the acquaintance of Mr. Adams, agent of the company, with whom he conversed about the robbery, in the presence of others, and in a careless good-natured manner offered his opinion, that the thieves, whoever they were, must have been pretty smart fellows.

This was said with a quiet smile, and with a sly wink at Mr. Risley, which greatly confused that gentleman and prevented him from replying.

It was the general impression that the detectives had given up the task, and that no further investigations were being made into the affair. That the only thing to be done was for the gentlemen who had lost their money, to await the opening of the spring term of the court, and to substantiate their claim when the money would be promptly refunded to them.

Meanwhile Mr. Fowler had interested himself to a very great extent, in the oil speculations which he had announced was the occasion of his visit to Grafton.

He had repeated conversations with Risley, Meredith and Marks, who often came to Grafton, upon the subject. He deeply deplored the delay to which Risley was subjected in receiving his money, and at length suggested a scheme that would probably obviate all difficulty.

He would visit a number of his friends in the West, who were cattle-drovers with means, and in company with Risley they would endeavor to interest them in the speculation, and if they succeeded in that, all further trouble about money would be successfully overcome.

Risley eagerly consented to the proposition, and, after making full preparations for their journey, the two men departed. They went together to Cincinnati and to Chicago, and saw various western cities, Fowler having a large acquaintance among men who were engaged in the droving business, introducing his friend to them, and wherever they went they were hospitably entertained. It was arranged that Fowler should invariably broach the subject of the proposed investment, and that at a time when Risley would be absent. That Risley should be introduced to these men as being largely interested in oil and coal lands, which gave promise of large yields, but that he should not be understood as advertising his possessions, or as seeking for assistance in working them.

Fowler would, therefore, report to his friend Risley, the result of his conversations with his friends, all of which was of a character to inspire the hopes of Risley in the success of the schemes in which they were engaged.

It soon became apparent that Risley was one of those happy-go-lucky fellows, who was fond of a "good time," and who would drink more than was good for him when in the company of congenial spirits. Mr. Fowler, too, laid aside much of his dignity and frequently indulged in these little irregularities which both of the old fellows seemed to enjoy very much.

By this time they had become bosom friends, and had reposed in each other mutual confidences which drew them nearer together. One day, Fowler returned to the hotel where they were stopping in Chicago, and found Risley in rather a mellow mood, impatiently awaiting his coming. He was not intoxicated, but rather in that peculiarly gracious and communicative mood which is produced by imbibing a trifle too much of "strong water." "Well, old man, what luck?" was his first salutation, as Fowler entered the room.

"Pretty good to-day," answered Fowler, in an easy manner.

"Did you find anybody that wanted to invest?" was the next inquiry.

"Yes, I found two, and if you only had your money now we would be all right," said Mr. Fowler.

"Well, maybe I have got some that will do just as well," said Risley, as he drew a large wallet from his pocket, and threw it down upon the table.

He opened the wallet and displayed to the gaze of his companion a bundle of bills, new and crisp, of the denomination of a hundred dollars.

"How will that do old fellow, for a first installment?" he asked with a chuckle.

"Well, that will do all right, I guess," answered Fowler as he drew near to the table, and took up the bundle of notes. As he did so, he noticed with a start, that the notes were all issued by the bank whose name had been mentioned in my poster, and he felt certain that these could be none others than the notes stolen from the express safe at Grafton. The amount of them which Risley had amounted to five thousand dollars.

"You are a sly old coon," said Fowler, slapping him upon the back. "You did a pretty good job with the safe, and I congratulate you."

Risley looked up into his companion's face, but seeing there only a sly twinkle in the eye and a good-natured smile upon the lips, he burst into a loud and hearty laugh.

"Yes, yes," he said after his laugh was over, "we managed that pretty well, didn't we?"

"I should think you did," said Fowler, "but we must get rid of these notes, they are well-known and might compromise us, you know."

"I know that," said Risley, "but how are we going to do it?"

"Oh, I'll fix that," said Fowler, with a confident air. "I used to deal in counterfeit money a little, some time ago, and I can fix this all right. I will give you other money for this, and then dispose of it in safety."

"You're a pretty good sort of a fellow," said Risley, "and just the kind of a friend a man ought to have," and he reached over and warmly clasped the hand of Mr. Fowler.

"Where is the rest of the money?" said Mr. Fowler, "we might as well dispose of the whole of it, while we are about it."

"Why Marks and Meredith divided the balance, but they have been afraid to dispose of it ever since."

"Well, you write to them, tell them it will be all right, and they can either bring it on themselves or send it by express. I have friends here who will manage it to a dot."

"All right," said Risley, "I'll write to them to-night."

"Let me see," said Fowler, "I guess we had better have this done out of the United States. Suppose you write to them to meet you in Windsor, Canada, and then we will be perfectly safe."

"That's a good idea," said Risley, "I'll fix it that way, and then we will be sure to be all right."

That night he wrote to both of his friends, detailed the circumstances fully to them, and advised them to come to Detroit, when they would all go over to Windsor, and Mr. Fowler would give them other money for what they had.

Risley was overjoyed at the prospect before him, and the friendliness he manifested towards Fowler became so demonstrative, that it almost grew wearisome. However, in a few days they received a telegram from Marks and Meredith, signifying their acceptance of Fowler's offer, and stating that they would be in Detroit upon a day which they named.

During the absence of Risley and Fowler, my operatives had kept close watch upon the movements of the two men who remained at home, Messrs. Meredith and Marks, but their carefulness was not rewarded by anything which appeared at all suspicious. Both of them attended to their affairs in a business-like manner, and seemed to be entirely occupied by matters of a purely legitimate character.

Upon the day, however, when Meredith sent the telegram to Risley, the detective was on hand, and after Meredith had left the office, the operative entered hurriedly and approaching the clerk said:

"Mr. Meredith has just sent a dispatch, but he thinks he has made a mistake in it, will you allow me to correct it?"

"Certainly, sir," said the unsuspecting clerk, handing over the blank which Meredith had filled up.

The detective carefully read the words, and having fixed them in his mind handed it back saying:

"No, there is no mistake; Mr. Meredith thought he had named the wrong day," and then thanking the clerk for his courtesy, he withdrew.

He had very little time, to spare, for the train was due in a half hour, and Meredith would no doubt take passage upon it. He was not disappointed, for soon Meredith appeared with a satchel and purchasing a ticket for Wheeling, he entered the car. The detective followed him, and after reaching Wheeling he telegraphed to Mr. Bangs the discovery, he had made.

Meredith soon met Marks, and the two operatives were thrown together, and that evening the quartette started upon their journey to Detroit. Messrs. Fowler and Risley had also left Chicago for the same destination, and the transfer of the money would soon no doubt be made.

Each of the three men were congratulating themselves upon the happy chance which brought Mr. Fowler to Grafton, in time to do them so great a service, and the detectives were active and alert for any developments that might be made.

The two men, Joseph Marks and William Meredith, accompanied by their unknown and unnoticed attendants, arrived in Detroit just as the gathering twilight was throwing its darkening shadows over the city. They were met at the station by John Risley and Mr. Fowler, and the greetings exchanged were the most cordial.

The two detectives were standing at a convenient distance, keeping the parties in full view, when they were accosted by another operative from my New York office. Without unnecessary delay he directed them to repair at once to a hotel, which he named, and that he would take care of the gentlemen who were now conversing so good-naturedly together. Having been trained to obey instructions without asking unnecessary questions, the two men did as they were directed, and to their surprise they found the portly and imposing figure of Mr. Bangs standing in the doorway of the hotel. They could not account for his presence there, in advance of them, and he did not enlighten them upon the subject.

He requested them to come up to his room, and then, after hearing a full report of what had transpired, he gave them full and explicit orders as to their course of action. After all the arrangements had been duly made, Mr. Bangs, in company with the two men, left the hotel, and proceeded in the direction which the persons they had been watching, would naturally take, in reaching the same house. They had not walked far, when they espied the four men walking leisurely along, and apparently in great good humor. Risley was relating some of his experiences in Chicago, which were evidently of an amusing nature, for his friends laughed heartily at the recital.

The detectives approached them, and at a sign from Mr. Bangs, the two men with him, and the one on the rear, advanced toward Risley, Marks and Meredith, while Mr. Bangs himself took care of Mr. Fowler.

Before the four gentlemen could realize their position, a heavy hand was laid on each their shoulders, and the stern voice of Mr. Bangs fell upon their ears:

"Gentlemen, I demand your surrender for the robbery of the Express Company at Grafton, and an attempt to escape will be fatal to the man who makes the effort."

There was no mistaking the resolute tone of that voice, and no evading the strong grip which each man felt upon his arm. Escape would be impossible, and they realized it at once. Besides that, their surprise was almost overpowering, their laugh was still ringing in the air when they were thus accosted, and they had not yet recovered from the shock which the notice of their arrest had occasioned.

Each looked at the other in hopeless dismay, and not a word was spoken until they reached the hotel. Four rooms had previously been engaged by Mr. Bangs, and as they ascended the stairs the curious eyes of the guests who were lounging about the hotel, followed them on their way.

One man was assigned to each room, a detective being delegated to guard each prisoner, and in a short space of time the lock of each door clicked behind them, and they found themselves shut in, with an officer of the law for a companion. Mr. Bangs had secured two communicating rooms in which to place Mr. Fowler and John Risley, as it was his intention that Risley should hear all that transpired between himself and Mr. Fowler.

By a systematic course of questioning, which proved that he was fully posted as to the movements of the men who had been arrested, Mr. Bangs gradually induced Mr. Fowler to become communicative.

Meanwhile John Risley had crouched upon his knees beside the door, his ears strained to catch every word uttered by the two men in the room adjoining; with eyes glaring and with his hands clenched, he listened to what was transpiring, and when at length Mr. Fowler broke completely down and handed over the money which he had received, John Risley uttered a cry of agony accompanied by terrible oaths, and threw himself upon the bed. Presently a knock was heard at the door, and as the detective opened it, Mr. Bangs and Mr. Fowler stood in the doorway. Silently they entered, and Fowler going up to Risley, laid his hand upon his shoulder and said:

"It's of no use, Risley, Mr. Bangs knows all about it, and we may as well give up."

Risley started to his feet and gazed fiercely at Fowler, but as his eye encountered the steady genial look of the other, his fierceness was gone and he was plastic in our hands. He realized that subterfuge and untruthfulness could avail him no further, and he made a full and thorough confession of all the facts in relation to the robbery.

From his statement it appeared that Meredith first suggested and planned the robbery, and by his arguments and solicitations, Risley was finally induced to join in the attempt, Meredith furnished Risley with a lump of wax and explained to him the use of it, and one day while both the agent and messenger of the company were outside, he quietly removed the key from the safe, and in a few moments had a perfect impression of it in wax.

Meredith then procured the blank key at Wheeling, and assisted by Marks, the instrument was made which so successfully opened the way to their robbery. The work was performed by Meredith and Marks after Mr. Risley had sent his "dummy" package from Wheeling, and the fact of the second package being there had not entered into their original calculations at all. When they learned of it, however, their cupidity was not proof against the temptation, and they secured both packages. One of them contained what it represented to do: twelve thousand dollars, and the other a bundle of brown paper with a fifty dollar National Bank note upon the top—for which fifteen thousand dollars was to be claimed through the courts of law.

The confession of John Risley was most complete and full, and at its conclusion he with tearful eyes besought Mr. Bangs to deal as leniently with him as was possible. His gay demeanor had disappeared and he whined piteously and begged for mercy. Mr. Bangs informed him that he would do all that he could for him, but that the matter would rest entirely with the court before which he would have to be tried, and that he could promise nothing.

After leaving Risley Mr. Bangs proceeded to the rooms occupied by Meredith and Marks. Meredith was morose and silent, he seemed to have given up all hope and had resigned himself to his fate, but he declined peremptorily to make any statement that might criminate himself. He was searched and upon his person was found his share of the robbery, four thousand dollars, all in the original notes which had been taken and which he had hitherto been afraid to dispose of.

In the meantime Marks had been chafing like a caged tiger; of an excitable disposition, he stormed and raved at the detective, and with terrible oaths threatened vengeance upon his captors. He walked his room impatiently and his eyes flashed with anger and hate. He was no doubt a dangerous man when aroused and the detective watched him carefully lest he should make an attack upon him, and attempt to effect his escape.

When Mr. Bangs entered the room he was received with curses and denunciations from the baffled thief, but his quiet, stern manner soon convinced the desperado that fuming would avail him but little, and that his threats were but idle breathings when launched at the fearless man who stood before him. The handcuffs were placed upon his wrists and although he evinced a disposition to resist their application, a word of stern command from Mr. Bangs convinced him of the folly of such a proceeding, and he submitted with a dogged silence to the humiliating operation.

His person was also searched and his share of the transaction was found in the lining of his coat, three thousand dollars—and thus the entire amount of the stolen property had been successfully recovered.

Mr. Bangs returned to his room where he found Mr. Fowler awaiting him. Grasping his hand cordially Mr. Bangs exclaimed:

"Fowler, you have managed this case admirably, and the success we have accomplished is mainly owing to your tact, energy and intelligence."

As the reader has no doubt already divined, Mr. Fowler, the elderly and gentlemanly cattle drover, was an operative upon my force, who had been selected by me for this investigation, and through whose agency, acting under my instructions, the matter had been brought to a successful issue.

The stolen money was now all in my hands, and the thieves were all under the watchful charge of my men. Risley's confession had been fully made and would be sufficient for the conviction of the prisoners. Thus far all had been successfully accomplished, and nothing further remained to be done, but to transport the discomfited gentlemen back to Virginia.

As a train left that evening Mr. Bangs determined to lose no time in transferring his prisoners to the state in which the crime had been committed. Other matters were requiring his attention, and he was desirous of rendering up his charges to the proper authorities when his task would be ended, and he would be at liberty to devote himself to pressing affairs that required his individual services and presence.

The prisoners were therefore handcuffed to their captors, the shackles being placed upon the right wrist of the prisoners, and upon the left arm of their escort, and thus in couples, led by Mr. Bangs, the party proceeded to the depot, where entering the cars, they were soon speeding upon their way to the scene of their burglarious exploit. Mr. Fowler having performed all the duties required of him, returned to Chicago, where he was soon engaged upon an operation of an entirely different character.

Without accident, the prisoners and their escorts arrived at Wheeling. Mr. Bangs secured rooms at a hotel for the party, and they retired to bed; each operative taking the precaution to lock the door of his room and to wheel the bedstead directly across the doorway to prevent any attempt at escape.

For three days and nights these men had scarcely slept an hour, and entering their rooms they handcuffed their prisoners, and then throwing themselves on the bed without disrobing, they soon fell asleep.

An hour afterwards, there were strange indications of wakefulness in one of the rooms. Joseph Marks, who had been strangely sullen and quiet during their journey, slowly raised himself upon his elbow and listened attentively to the labored breathing of his detective companion. Silently and breathlessly he listened, and at last becoming satisfied, that slumber had firmly bound the fatigued operative, he noiselessly slipped from the bed and stood upon the floor.

Handcuffed as he was he began quietly and by slow degrees to push the bedstead from its position across the door, pausing at frequent intervals, to note its effect upon the sleeping man, but the deep sonorous breathing of the sleeper gave undoubted proof that no danger was to be apprehended from him. After he had succeeded in moving the bed a sufficient distance to admit of the passage of his body, he searched the pockets of the detective and found the key. Without a sound the bolt shot back in the lock and freedom was before the criminal. Snatching up his hat and throwing his coat over his shoulders, buttoning it around his neck he started for the door.

As he did so, a movement of the sleeper aroused his fears, and hastening to the side of the bed, he assured himself that he was safe. Again he turned toward the door, and then opening it noiselessly, he passed out, closing it behind him. Stealthily he glided along the corridors, and with cat-like steps descended the stairs. In safety he reached the street door, and in another moment he stood in the open air a free man.

Raising his shackled hands, he shook them savagely in the direction of the building, and then as he strode away, he chuckled to himself at the success which had attended him. Reaching the railroad track, near the station, he found a freight train loaded with hay, and he climbed upon one of the open cars and hid himself between two bundles of hay. In a few moments he was rattling away from the scene of his captivity, and from the company of his companions and their guards.

When the exhausted detective arose on the following morning, and found that the place beside him was empty, and that his bed had been moved away from the door, he sat and gazed in a state of dazed stupor, unable to utter a word. Finally as he recovered his scattered senses, he started quickly from the bed, and rushing directly to the room occupied by Mr. Bangs, he astonished that gentleman by his revelations. A hasty search proved conclusively that the bird had flown, and that expedition was necessary if his recapture was to be accomplished.

Of course this action on the part of my operative merited, and afterwards received, a just degree of censure, but I did not feel disposed to be very harsh with him, because of the fatigue and exhaustion which he had suffered previous to his retiring upon that night. There are limits to the powers of endurance of human nature, and while regretting the temporary escape of the prisoner, I was disposed to be more lenient than under any other circumstances would have been the case.

In order to be entirely untrammeled in the pursuit of Joseph Marks, Mr. Bangs at once surrendered his two remaining prisoners to the care of the city officials of Wheeling, and placed the fifteen thousand dollars, stolen money that had been recovered, in the custody of a bank in that city. This being done, he began to lay his plans for the recovery of the fugitive.

Obtaining the assistance of two men from the Chief of Police of the city, a vigorous search was at once commenced. It was soon learned that a freight train, the only one that had departed since the evening before, had passed through Wheeling shortly after midnight, and that it had stopped at the depot for a long time. It was a local freight train and made stoppages at all the stations along the road. From this Mr. Bangs was induced to believe that Marks had availed himself of the mode of travel thus afforded him, and he thought it might be possible that he had left the train at the next station and had gone to his residence but a short distance away.

One of the city officials who was unknown to Marks was deputed to repair to the vicinity of the residence of that individual and endeavor to ascertain if such was the case.

Late in the afternoon, Mr. Bangs received a dispatch from this official to the effect that Marks was at home, and that preparations were being made for a hasty departure.

Mr. Bangs lost no time in getting his men together, and taking one of the city force with him, he took the train for Marks's house. It was nine o'clock when the party started, and the clock of the village church struck ten as they halted near their place of destination. The night was dark, heavy clouds had been gathering during the day and a slight shower began to fall as the party of detectives came in view of the house. The residence occupied by Marks was a pretty frame structure of the style of a Swiss cottage, surrounded by a beautiful lawn and numerous shade-trees, and at the rear of the house was a large strip of woods.

A low light was burning in one of the rooms of the house. Quietly the men approached, and after reaching a convenient distance Mr. Bangs directed them to surround the building so as to prevent the exit of anyone from either side. When this had been done, he ascended the steps and knocked loudly upon the front door. Instantly the light was extinguished within, and all was darkness and silence. Failing to receive any response to his first summons, Mr. Bangs knocked again, and presently he heard hurried footsteps within the dwelling, and a female inquired in a trembling voice, who it was that knocked.

"Open the door!" cried Mr. Bangs, unheeding the inquiry, "or I will force it from its hinges."

A stifled cry came from the lady, whoever she was, and the sound of her swiftly retreating feet could be plainly heard.

Again Mr. Bangs knocked at the door, this time louder than previously, and another female voice cried from within:

"Wait a moment, and I will let you in."

"Make haste," again cried Mr. Bangs. "I cannot be kept waiting any longer."

As he spoke, the lock was turned, and the door was slowly opened. Throwing it forcibly back, he strode into the passage-way, which was dark as Erebus. Drawing his dark lantern from his pocket, he threw its penetrating rays over the scene presented before him. The hall in which he stood was wide and capacious, extending the entire length of the building, from front to rear, the door of the various rooms opening into it. Before him stood two pale-faced women, their eyes heavy with weeping, and their hands clasped piteously before them. He had no time to notice them particularly, and as he walked to the rear of the hall he saw that one of the doors was open. Turning his lamp in that direction, he saw that the window in the rear was raised, and that a man whose body half protruded through the opening thus made, was about to escape from the building.

"Stop or I fire!" cried Mr. Bangs.

But at that instant, two stalwart arms from without grasped the shoulders of the man he addressed, and the cheery confident voice of my operative replied:

"All right, Captain, I've got him, and I guess I can take care of him," and with these words the form of the man disappeared through the window.

Rushing to the spot, my General Superintendent saw with gratification that the discomfited Mr. Marks was in the strong arms of Henry Wilson, a brawny and careful detective. The prisoner made a desperate effort to resist, but a sturdy blow from the detective soon convinced him that such an attempt would be useless, and he sullenly resigned himself to his fate.

The other men were called together; the prisoner was safely secured, and the successful and elated party returned to the station, where they took the train, and soon after had placed their prisoner within the enclosing embraces of a prison cell, while a ponderous lock held him secure.

On the following day the prisoners were handed over to the authorities, and were held to await their trial. Risley appeared to have broken down completely, his nerves were terribly shaken, and he seemed to feel deeply the disgrace which he had brought upon himself and his family. Meredith displayed the utmost unconcern and chatted with his keeper, and such of his friends who visited him, with great good humor. Marks, on the contrary, evinced a most belligerent disposition, he became almost savage under his long confinement, he swore loudly at every one who approached his cell, and threatened a desperate vengeance upon those who had been instrumental in his arrest.

During certain hours of the day, the prisoners were allowed the liberty of walking in the corridor, and during these times Risley and Meredith would converse in low tones upon their situation, while Marks held himself aloof from them and consorted with the other prisoners, with whom he soon became a great favorite. His dauntless spirit and fiery temper seemed to excite their admiration, and his threats of vengeance found a ready echo in the breasts of many more hardened, though less determined than himself. His influence soon communicated itself to the more reckless of the prisoners, and he became the center of a band of ruffians of all grades of crime.

One day, after they had enjoyed the relaxation generally allowed them, and as they were about to be returned to their cells, the prisoners were alarmed by loud voices as if in fierce altercation, and the powerful form of Marks was seen grappling fiercely with one of the keepers.

This was intended to be the signal for a general mutiny among those with whom Marks had associated, but when the moment for action arrived, their hearts failed them, and they dared not perform their part of the compact.

Marks was soon overpowered, but not until he had seriously injured the keeper, whom he had attacked, and he was conducted again to his cell.

That night he made another attempt to escape, and in the desperate encounter which ensued, he was shot and killed. Thus ended, in a prison, a life which had been begun in honor and respectability, and a career that had hitherto won for him the confidence and regard of friends and of the community in which he moved. It was his first criminal offense, and the fierce nature brooking no control was chafed into madness by his disgrace and confinement.

The trial of the two others, Risley and Meredith, was held, and the evidence against them proving indisputable, they were convicted. Risley, on account of his confession, was sentenced to only three and a half years, while Meredith was sentenced to fifteen years.

Thus was the law finally vindicated, and the wrongdoers were compelled to expiate their crimes. From all that could be learned, Meredith had been remotely connected with several other incidents of a criminal nature, although he had thus far escaped punishment. Risley, on the contrary had always prior to this lived an honest and respectable life. His family were all honorable and respected, he himself had once been a man of prominence and wealth; his voice had once been heard in the council of the state, and but for this blot upon his fair name, the few remaining years of his life would have passed peacefully away, and he would have gone to his grave honored and revered. But temptation came, and the weak brain and speculative mind were not secure against the siren voice of the tempter; the possibility of suddenly and without danger, accumulating riches, was too powerful for his weak nature, and he yielded to the influences that had wrought his ruin.

Our task was done, the stolen money had been recovered, the criminals had been punished, and leaving the prisoners to their better reflections, the detective enters again into other scenes which, while the world rolls on and humanity continues frail, will ever engross his mind and exercise his abilities.

The End

The epitaph of Allan Pinkerton
1819-1884

A friend to honesty and a foe to crime.

Devoting himself for a generation to the prevention and detection of crime in many countries.

He was the founder in America of a noble profession. In the hour of the nation's peril he conducted Abraham Lincoln safely through the ranks of treason to the scene of his first inauguration is President.

He sympathized with, protected and defended the slaves and labored earnestly for their freedom.

Hating wrong and loving good he was strong, brave, tender and true.

About the Author

Allan Pinkerton was born in 1819 in Scotland and immigrated to the United States at the age of twenty-three. After starting the Pinkerton Detective Agency he pioneered many crime-fighting techniques including mug shots, rap sheets, code books, instruction for detectives, and infiltration, to name but a few. During the Civil War Pinkerton was the head of the Union Intelligence Service and foiled an assassination plot against Abraham Lincoln. He also organized and directed an espionage system behind Confederate lines. Pinkerton wrote several books detailing the exploits of his detectives, but no other book captures the criminal mindset and the efforts to thwart it as does *Thirty Years A Detective*. Allan Pinkerton died, peacefully, in 1884.

HISTORICAL MEMOIRS
FROM 1500 BOOKS

The Private Life of Marie Antoinette by Madame Campan – An intimate account of the intrigue and drama of the royal court from the Queen's trusted Lady-in-Waiting.

A Minstrel In France by Harry Lauder – A world famous performer's life is forever changed by the loss of his beloved son in World War I. With a piano lashed to his jeep Lauder tours the battlefront in France paying tribute to the troops.

A Year With A Whaler by Walter Noble Burns – The stories of the able-bodied seamen, the great mammals, and the ever changing sea are the central figures in this narrative of a carefree boy shipping out and a wise man returning.

A New Voyage Round the World by William Dampier – A fascinating travelogue, a scientific journey, and a buccaneering adventure from Dampier – gentleman sailor and pirate.

To Cuba and Back by Richard Henry Dana – The bestselling author's account of his 1859 trip to the tropical island where colonial expansionism and slavery meet head on.

Excerpt from

A MINSTREL IN FRANCE

by

HARRY LAUDER

At the foot of the ridge I saw men fighting for the first time – actually fighting, seeking to hurt an enemy. It was a Canadian battery we saw, and it was firing, steadily and methodically, at the Huns. Up to now I had seen only the vast industrial side of war, its business and its labor. Now I was, for the first time, in touch with actual fighting. I saw the guns belching death and destruction, destined for men miles away. It was high angle fire, of course, directed by observers in the air.

But even that seemed part of the sheer, factory-like industry of war. There was no passion, no coming to grips in hot blood, here. Orders were given by the battery commander and the other officers as the foreman in a machine shop might give them. And the busy artillerymen worked like laborers, too, clearing their guns after a salvo, loading them, bringing up fresh supplies of ammunition. It was all methodical, all a matter of routine.

"Good artillery work is like that," said Captain Godfrey, when I spoke to him about it. "It's a science. It's all a matter of the higher mathematics. Everything is worked out to half a dozen places of decimals. We've eliminated chance and guesswork just as far as possible from modern artillery actions."

But there was something about it all that was disappointing, at first sight. It let you down a bit. Only the guns themselves kept up the tradition. Only they were acting as they should, and showing a proper passion and excitement. I could hear them growling ominously, like dogs locked in their kennel when they would be loose and about, and hunting. And then they would spit, angrily. They inflamed my imagination, did those guns; they satisfied me and my old-fashioned conception of war and fighting, more than anything else that I had seen had done. And it seemed to me that after they had spit out their deadly charge they wiped their muzzles with red tongues of flame, satisfied beyond all words or measure with what they had done.

We were rising now, as we walked, and getting a better view of the country that lay beyond. And so I came to understand a little better the value of a height even so low and insignificant as Vimy Ridge in that flat country. While the Germans held it they could overlook all our positions, and all the advantage of natural placing had been to them. Now, thanks to the Canadians, it was our turn, and we were looking down.

Weel, I was under fire. There was no doubt about it. There was a droning over us now, like the noise bees make, or many flies in a small room on a hot summer's day. That was the drone of the German shells. There was a little freshening of the artillery activity on both sides, Captain Godfrey said, as if in my honor. When one side increased its fire the other always answered – played copy cat. There was no telling, ye ken, when such an increase of fire might not be the first sign of an attack. And neither side took more chances than it must.

I had known, before I left Britain, that I would come under fire. And I had wondered what it would be like: I had expected to be afraid, nervous. Brave men had told me, one after another, that every man is afraid when he first comes under fire. And so I had wondered how I would be, and I had expected to be badly scared and extremely nervous. Now I could hear that constant droning of shells, and, in the distance, I could see, very often, powdery squirts of smoke and dirt along the ground, where our shells were striking, so that I knew I had the Hun lines in sight.

And I can truthfully say that, that day, at least, I felt no great fear or nervousness. Later I did, as I shall tell you, but that day one overpowering emotion mastered every other. It was a desire for vengeance! You were the Huns – the men who had killed my boy. They were almost within my reach. And as I looked at them there in their lines a savage desire possessed me, almost overwhelmed me, indeed, that made me want to rush to those guns and turn them to my own mad purpose of vengeance.

It was all I could do, I tell you, to restrain myself – to check that wild, almost ungovernable impulse to rush to the guns and grapple with them myself – myself fire them at the men who had killed my boy. I wanted to fight! I wanted to fight with my two hands – to tear and rend, and have the consciousness that I flash back, like a telegraph message from my satiated hands to my eager brain that was spurring me on.

But that was not to be. I knew it, and I grew calmer, presently. The roughness of the going helped me to do that, for it took all a man's wits and faculties to grope his way along the path we were following now. Indeed, it was no path at all that led us to the Pimple – the topmost point of Vimy Ridge, which changed hands half a dozen times in the few minutes of bloody fighting that had gone on here during the great attack.

The ground was absolutely riddled with shell holes here. There must have been a mine of metal underneath us. What path there was zigzagged around. It had been worn to such smoothness as it possessed since the battle, and it evaded the worst craters by going around them. My madness was passed now, and a great sadness had taken its place. For here, where I was walking, men had stumbled up with bullets and shells raining about them. At every step I trod ground that must have been the last resting-place of some Canadian soldier, who had died that I might climb this ridge in a safety so immeasurably greater than his had been.

If it was hard for us to make this climb, if we stumbled as we walked, what had it been for them? Our breath came hard and fast – how had it been with them? Yet they had done it! They had stormed the ridge the Huns had proudly called impregnable. They had taken, in a swift rush, that nothing could stay, a position the Kaiser's generals had assured him would never be lost – could never be reached by mortal troops.

The Pimple, for which we were heading now, was an observation post at that time. There there was a detachment of soldiers, for it was an important post, covering much of the Hun territory beyond. A major of infantry was in command; his headquarters were a large hole in the ground, dug for him by a German shell – fired by German gunners who had no thought further from their minds than to do a favor for a British officer. And he was sitting calmly in front of his headquarters, smoking a pipe, when we reached the crest and came to the Pimple.

He was a very calm man, that major, given, I should say, to the greatest repression. I think nothing would have moved him from that phlegmatic calm of his! He watched us coming, climbing and making hard going of it. If he was amused he gave no sign, as he puffed at his pipe. I, for one, was puffing, too – I was panting like a grampus. I had thought myself in good condition, but I found out at Vimy Ridge that I was soft and flabby.

Not a sign did that major give until we reached him. And then, as we stood looking at him, and beyond him at the panorama of the trenches, he took his pipe from his mouth.

"Welcome to Vimy Ridge!" he said, in the manner of a host greeting a party bidden for the weekend. I was determined that that major should not outdo me. I had precious little wind left to breathe with, much less to talk, but I called for the last of it.

"Thank you, major," I said. "May I join you in a smoke?"

"Of course you can!" he said, unsmiling. "That is, if you've brought your pipe with you."

"Aye, I've my pipe," I told him. "I may forget to pay my debt, but I'll never forget my pipe." And no more I will.

So I sat down beside him, and drew out my pipe, and made a long business of filling it, and pushing the tobacco down just so, since that gave me a chance to get my wind. And when I was ready to light up I felt better, and I was breathing right, so that I could talk as I pleased without fighting for breath.

My friend the major proved an entertaining chap, and a talkative one, too, for all his seeming brusqueness. He pointed out the spots that had been made famous in the battle, and explained to me what it was the Canadians had done. And I saw and understood better than ever before what a great feat that had been, and how heavily it had counted. He lent me his binoculars, too, and with them I swept the whole valley toward Lens, where the great French coal mines are, and where the Germans have been under steady fire so long, and have been hanging on by their eyelashes.

It was not the place I should choose, ordinarily, to do a bit of sight-seeing. The German shells were still humming through the air above us, though not quite so often as they had. But there were enough of them, and they seemed to me close enough for me to feel the wind they raised as they passed. I thought for sure one of them would come along, presently, and clip my ears right off. And sometimes I felt myself ducking my head – as if that would do me any good! But I did not think about it; I would feel myself doing it, without having intended to do anything of the sort. I was a bit nervous, I suppose, but no one could be really scared or alarmed in the unplumbable depths of calm in which that British major was plunged!

It was a grand view I had of the valley, but it was not the sort of thing I had expected to see. I knew there were thousands of men there, and I think I had expected to see men really fighting. But there was nothing of the sort. Not a man could I see in all the valley. They were under cover, of course. When I stopped to think about it, that was what I should have expected, of course. If I could have seen our laddies there below, why, the Huns could have seen them too. And that would never have done.

I could hear our guns, too, now, very well. They were giving voice all around me, but never a gun could I see, for all my peering and searching around. Even the battery we had passed below was out of sight now. And it was a weird thing, and an uncanny thing to think of all that riot of sound around, and not a sight to be had of the batteries that were making it!

Hogge came up while I was talking to the major. "Hello!" he said. "What have you done to your knee, Lauder?" I looked down and saw a trickle of blood running down, below my knee. It was bare, of course, because I wore my kilt.

"Oh, that's nothing," I said.

I knew at once what it was. I remembered that, as I stumbled up the hill, I had tripped over a bit of barbed wire and scratched my leg. And so I explained. "And I fell into a shell-hole, too," I said. "A wee one, as they go around here." But I laughed. "Still, I'll be able to say I was wounded on Vimy Ridge."

I glanced at the major as I said that, and was half sorry I had made the poor jest. And I saw him smile, in one corner of his mouth, as I said I had been "wounded." It was the corner furthest from me, but I saw it. And it was a dry smile, a withered smile. I could guess his thought.

"Wounded!" he must have said to himself, scornfully. And he must have remembered the real wounds the Canadians had received on that hillside. Aye, I could guess his thought. And I shared it, although I did not tell him so. But I think he understood.

He was still sitting there, puffing away at his old pipe, as quiet and calm and imperturbable as ever, when Captain Godfrey gathered us together to go on. He gazed out over the valley.

He was a man to be remembered for a long time, that major. I can see him now, in my mind's eye, sitting there, brooding, staring out toward Lens and the German lines. And I think that if I were choosing a figure for some great sculptor to immortalize, to typify and represent the superb, the majestic imperturbability of the British Empire in time of stress and storm, his would be the one. I could think of no finer figure than his for such a statue. You would see him, if the sculptor followed my thought, sitting in front of his shell-hole on Vimy Ridge, calm, dispassionate, devoted to his duty and the day's work, quietly giving the directions that guided the British guns in their work of blasting the Hun out of the refuge he had chosen when the Canadians had driven him from the spot where the major sat.

"The best memoirs in any language…
a supreme masterpiece"
The Sunday Times (UK)

MEMOIRS OF
DUC DE
SAINT-SIMON

Available Fall 2007

Edited and translated from the French by
Lucy Norton

"Miss Norton has caught Saint-Simon alive…an English
classic."
Nancy Mitford

"Written with wit, poignancy and total frankness…."
Auberon Waugh

Warwick, NY

We hope you enjoyed Allen Pinkerton's Thirty Years A Detective. This edition was entirely redesigned from the text of the original book, published in 1884, although spelling, punctuation and vernacular were maintained. For additional information and other interesting memoirs from 1500 Books visit our website at www.1500Books.com.